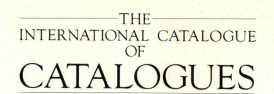

THE
INTERNATIONAL CATALOGUE
OF
CATALOGUES

THE
INTERNATIONAL CATALOGUE
OF
CATALOGUES

MARIA ELENA DE LA IGLESIA

1817

HARPER & ROW, PUBLISHERS, New York

Cambridge, Philadelphia, San Francisco, London, Mexico City, São Paulo, Sydney

Books by Maria Elena de La Iglesia

The Catalogue of Catalogues
The New Catalogue of Catalogues
The Catalogue of American Catalogues
The Cat and the Mouse
The Oak That Would Not Pay

Portions of this work originally appeared in *Woman's Day*.

THE INTERNATIONAL CATALOGUE OF CATALOGUES. Copyright ©
1982 by Maria Elena de La Iglesia. All rights reserved. Printed in
the United States of America. No part of this book may be used or
reproduced in any manner whatsoever without written permission
except in the case of brief quotations embodied in critical articles
and reviews. For information address Harper & Row, Publishers,
Inc., 10 East 53rd Street, New York, N.Y. 10022. Published
simultaneously in Canada by Fitzhenry & Whiteside Limited,
Toronto; in Great Britain by Harper & Row Limited, 28 Tavistock
Street, London WC2E 7PN; and in Australia and New Zealand by
Harper & Row (Australasia) Pty. Limited, P.O. Box 226, Artarmon,
New South Wales 2064.

FIRST EDITION

Designer: Abigail Sturges

Library of Congress Cataloging in Publication Data

De La Iglesia, Maria Elena.
    The international catalogue of catalogues.

    Rev. ed. of: The new catalogue of catalogues. 1975.
    Includes index.
    1. Mail-order business—Directories. I. Title.
HF5466.D45   1982   380.1'025   81-48041
                          AACR2

ISBN 0-06-014985-X
(cloth)   82 83 84 85 10 9 8 7 6 5 4 3 2 1
ISBN 0-06-090942-0
(pbk U.S.A. and Canada)   82 83 84 85 10 9 8 7 6 5 4 3 2 1
ISBN 0-06-337029-8
(pbk except U.S.A. and Canada)   82 83 84 85 10 9 8 7 6 5 4 3 2 1

CONTENTS

ACKNOWLEDGMENTS

Of the many people who helped with this book, my warmest thanks go to Hugh and Geraldine Van Dusen, who gave me the chance of writing it, and to Carol Campion, Jack Dohany, George and Sheila Green, Charles E. Flynn, Jerry Hoffnagel, Clement Meadmore, Jack Stephenson, Deirdre Wulf and Stephan Wilkinson, all of whom were extraordinarily generous with their time and their help.

FOREWORD

American mail order is an amazing phenomenon. Although in England the better London stores have long had shipping departments to send provisions to stately homes and colonial outposts, it was an American, Montgomery Ward, who ran the first really successful firm that was exclusively mail-order. On his journeys around the country, Ward, a traveling salesman, noticed that the general stores, the only sources of supply for settlers and ranchers, were often ill stocked, overpriced and far from home. Ward decided that there was "a great opening for a house to sell directly to consumers and save them the profit of a middle man." In 1872 he issued his first price list, which soon became a fat catalogue that brought wider choice, lower prices and the latest inventions to the largely rural yet comparatively literate American people.

Since then, mail order has flourished in America as in no other country. More than $30 billion worth of goods and services are sold through the mail each year, and sales are estimated to be increasing by 15 percent annually. Catalogues are generally highly sophisticated, often fully illustrated with color photographs, and deliver far more information than the average salesclerk can give.

Although buying by mail does require more patience than shopping in person, there are several advantages. People who live deep in the countryside not only can choose by mail from the wealth of goods otherwise only available in the largest cities, but through mail order small manufacturers and crafts people can work in out-of-the-way places, and still reach customers around the world. It is often these small manufacturers and distributors that, whether they exist in town or country, provide the carefully made, high-quality goods for specialized interests. By mail you can find better tools than at most hardware stores, more advanced sports equipment than at most sports outfitters, more varied and exotic plants and seeds than at most garden stores, more interesting furniture and household goods than in most housewares stores, and far better professional equipment and supplies for work and hobbies than in most neighborhood retail outlets.

In earlier times, a lack of American manufacturers forced the well-to-do to order constantly from Europe. (Thomas Jefferson and George Washington did it all the time.) Nowadays American travelers buy from abroad by writing to favorite shops discovered on vacations. Where brand-name goods are concerned it is easy to save about a third of the price even after paying postage and duty. (Notably on knitwear from Scotland, china from England, glass from Ireland and Sweden, toys from Germany and perfumes from France.) With many other foreign-made goods, such as fabrics and crafts, there is a wider choice in buying from abroad, and prices are often lower than they are for similar imported things sold in the United States.

However, I am afraid that shops change addresses and policy annoyingly often. If you would like to know if/when I update the information in this book, send me a self-addressed envelope with stamp or International Reply Coupon to International Catalogue of Catalogues, 250 West 94th Street, New York, NY 10025. I will *not* reply until I have some sort of update to announce. Suggestions for future listings are most welcome, whether from customers or from shops.

Please remember that this is a guide to the shops listed, not an endorsement of them, and my descriptions are intended to give just an idea of the prices and goods. Alas, both change, so it is important to write for an up-to-date catalogue and compare prices for yourself before ordering.
M.E.I.
January 1982

HOW TO BUY

Note

U.S. telephone numbers that start with 800 are toll free, there is no charge to the caller, but the number can't be dialed within the state or out of the country.

Letters given after catalogue listings represent the charge and credit cards accepted: AE = American Express, DC = Diners Club, MC = MasterCard (Access in Britain), V = Visa (outside of the U.S., often known by the name of the issuing bank, e.g., BarclayCard).

In the listings, shops marked with crowns are royal warrant holders. Each crown means that the shop has supplied a member of the royal family with goods for at least two years and is allowed to boast about it—a handy indication that the shop is very reputable but possibly expensive.

General Information

CATALOGUES

Many catalogues are seasonal and go out of print while the next one is being prepared. If you write just as a catalogue has run out, you may have to wait a couple of months before receiving an up-to-date one. This is especially likely to happen from July to September, just before Christmas catalogues are published.

Where listings say the price of a catalogue is refundable, it means that it is credited towards a purchase.

OVERSEAS CATALOGUES

If there is a charge for a foreign catalogue, the best way to pay is to send currency (notes not coins). Although it is riskier than a check, banks charge the recipient about $3 for converting foreign checks.

Most of the catalogues listed as free will come by surface mail and take at least four weeks to arrive. Do remember to send your request by air mail if you are in a hurry. Airmail letters to and from foreign countries take between seven and fourteen days each way. Sea-mail letters take between one and two months each way. Air-mail parcels take roughly two to three weeks, and sea-mail parcels roughly one to two months. And, as you know, everything takes longer before Christmas.

ORDERING

There are conversion tables at the back of this book to give you a very rough guide to prices in foreign currencies. If you want to know an exact price in your own currency, get the official exchange rate from a newspaper or a bank. Then multiply the price of the goods by the dollar equivalent to one unit of the foreign currency. Or, in other countries, multiply the price by the equivalent in your currency (say pounds) of one unit of the currency the price is in. A calculator is invaluable for math phobics.

When you buy from outside your own state and outside your own country, you do not pay the other state or country's sales tax. This is sometimes quite a saving.

PAYING

When buying within your own country, personal checks are the easiest, if slowest, way of paying. For greater speed use bank money orders, certified checks or credit cards.

When buying from other countries, an international check (called a bank draft outside the United States) bought at the bank is the best method. Charge and credit cards are quick, easy and increasingly popular. In some countries, sending actual currency by registered mail is allowed. But do this only if you are a gambler; sending money through the mail is extremely risky, and you have no proof whatever that money has been sent or received. More information on all these methods of paying can be found in the appendix.

DUTY

Duty isn't as high as you may think. In the United States it is usually charged on the wholesale value of the goods (about 33 percent less than the retail value). Also gifts worth less than $25 are exempt from duty altogether but only when bought by someone who is outside the country, so the very common practice of asking shops to mark parcels "Gift" is in fact illegal. However, I have found customs officers to be rather lenient with small parcels—only one out of about ten toy or record parcels seems to be charged.

There is a guide to various rates of duty at the end of this book, but the rules for applying them are sometimes complicated, so you can't be sure what the exact charge will be until you receive the goods. If you ever think you have been overcharged, either refuse the parcel and write a protest to your postmaster or accept the parcel, pay the duty, but send copies of the receipt for the duty and the shop's bill to the address given on the receipt. You may be able to get a refund, though not of the $2.50 post office handling charge called "postage due." If you ever want to return goods you have bought from abroad, write to the address on the receipt for duty to see whether and how you can get a refund.

AVOIDING PROBLEMS

Before ordering, check the guarantee. Many firms now give a no-questions-asked, money-back guarantee if for any reason you don't like what you ordered.

Make sure you order from an up-to-date catalogue. Write clearly, be specific and keep a detailed and exact record of each order.

Firms must send ordered goods within thirty days. If they do not, they must let you know so you can cancel the order and get a full refund. If you don't ask for a refund within seven days of notification, the firm is allowed another thirty days to deliver.

These rules are enforced by the Federal Trade Commission, so if they are broken, write to the Bureau of Consumer Protection, Federal Trade Commission, Washington, DC 20508. The FTC will forward your letter to the offending firm, but beyond that does not deal with individual cases. It gathers records of, investigates and sometimes takes to court firms about which there are many complaints.

PROBLEMS

If you buy by mail and run into trouble, write directly to the offending firm (*keeping copies of your letter*). If that does not achieve the results you want, write to the Chief Postal Inspector, United States Postal Service, Washington, DC 20260. Give the name and address of the firm you are complaining about with a brief description of your problem and what you would like done about it (new merchandise or money back). Also send a copy (never the original) of your check, money order or credit-card slip. The postal service says that it is very successful at settling complaints, because it can withhold mail from misbehaving firms.

The Mail Order Action Line, Direct Mail Marketing Association, 6 East 43rd Street, New York, NY 10017, also says that it will complain on your behalf to the problem firm. DMMA needs exactly the same information as the post office.

Canadian and FPO and APO Readers

In the listings you count as United States customers, not "overseas." The catalogues cost you whatever they cost United States customers; and most shops, except for some in the gardening and the food sections, can sell to you.

Overseas Readers

America produces an abundance of manufactured goods, and almost all of them are available through catalogues. [A copy of the American *Consumer Reports Buying Guide* will be a great help in choosing.] I believe that these American goods will be of special interest overseas: electric and electronic appliances, of which there are many brands and many models, generally sold at much lower prices than in other countries; work and outdoor clothes and shoes, such as jeans, overalls, insulated coats, etc., traditionally made well in the United States and now popular the world over; tools and equipment for work and hobbies. Although some of the finest tools are made outside the country, American catalogues have such a wealth of goods and information that they are invaluable to hobbyists and professionals in other countries. America has quality merchandise and advanced designs for most sporting goods and outdoor equipment, and when better equipment is produced by other countries, you may find it more easily in American catalogues than in your own area. Phonograph records have always been less expensive in America. Good looks have not been always a strong point of American products, but American museum shops sell beautiful things not available in other countries. Colorful sheets and thick towels are less expensive here than in many countries.

CATALOGUES

I have put whether a catalogue is free or given its price in the listing of all the American firms that are able to send goods overseas. If there is no mention of whether or not there is a charge for sending the catalogue of an American shop overseas, the firm has told me they cannot sell to customers outside the United States and Canada. The catalogues that are free and many of the others will come by sea; as you know, this means a delay of several weeks.

The most sensible way of paying for catalogues is with bank notes, because even though there is a chance of loss, you do avoid the charges involved in paying through a bank, which are high for small sums. I'm afraid that American firms insist on being paid in dollars for their catalogues, so serious mail-order shoppers should stock up on dollar bills ordered through your bank or the nearest bank that deals in foreign currencies. Another possible, though unpopular with shops, way of paying for catalogues is with International Reply Coupons bought at the post office.

PAYING

Shops in other countries generally don't mind which currency they are paid in, so you can pay with a personal check (adding $2 for bank charges). American firms, I'm sorry to say, usually insist on being paid in dollars. The easiest way to do this is with a credit card (information on credit cards at the back of the book). Your country may allow you to make out an ordinary personal check in American dollars, in which case you mail the check with your order exactly as though you were ordering within your own country. A personal check will delay the arrival of your goods, as most firms will wait for the check to clear (roughly three weeks) before filling the order.

If your country does not allow you to write out a personal check in dollars, go to your bank for a transfer or draft in dollars.

DUTY

If duty is charged by your customs department, it must be paid when you receive whatever you bought. It cannot be included in the sum you send the shop. Information on customs in Australia, Canada and Britain is included in the back of the book.

How to Buy at a Discount

Remembering that a penny saved is a penny and a tenth to almost two pennies earned (depending on income-tax bracket), I have become an enthusiastic discount shopper in recent years. I wouldn't dream of buying the brand-name goods that are available at a discount at department stores where I used to buy them. But I'm too lazy to make a detour to the out-of-my-way districts where most of the discount stores are, so I do it by telephone and mail.

People who haven't been initiated into the joys of discount shopping worry, quite reasonably, about the trustworthiness of discount stores—Are the discounts real? Are the goods damaged? Are there hidden charges? Although there are *undoubtedly* shops that indulge in knavish tricks, there is also a perfectly respectable type of store that as a matter of policy takes a smaller mark-up on all the goods it sells as a way of attracting customers. If you buy there, you get the usual manufacturer's guarantee just as you would at a nondiscount store, plus prices that are usually 15 to 30 percent below prices charged by nondiscount firms.

What's the hitch? The hitch is that you must know exactly what you want to buy. Discount stores offer no-frills service, do not publish catalogues and do not give information apart from price information, so you must know exactly what you want including brand and model number where applicable.

I have worked very hard indeed spot-checking and comparing prices, and trying to choose from many discount

firms those shops which seem to have a policy of consistently giving discounts on brand-name goods, and answer mail or telephone inquiries with a price quote. I have also tried to give a realistic idea of the actual discounts I found, and not just vaguely quote an optimistic "up to 60 percent." However, I would hate *anyone* to buy from a discount store and then see the very same object at a lower price locally, so *please* always check your own prices and include delivery prices in your calculations.

INSTRUCTIONS FOR BUYING AT A DISCOUNT

For the discount sections of this book, I have chosen (with one or two exceptions) firms that sell not their own "equivalent" brands, but exactly the same brand-name goods that are sold in other shops. These are firms which, instead of attracting customers by advertising; attentive service; and large, pleasant, easy-to-reach stores with goods on display, save money by ignoring these amenities. Their method is to attract customers by taking a smaller mark-up on the goods they sell and offering their goods at a discount. If you want to buy from them with a minimum of annoyance, expect the following:

- To buy from a discount store without a catalogue, get details of brand, size, color, etc. (and model number if applicable) from the manufacturers, *Consumer Reports* or another store. Write or telephone the discount stores for a price quote including shipping.
- Discount stores offer no-frills service; they will probably growl or not answer if you ask for too many prices, too much information or for something they don't stock.
- If you pay with a personal check, the discount store will hold your goods until the check has cleared. If you are in a hurry, get your check certified at the bank (the bank guarantees to hold money to clear the check). Also, make sure the shop has what you want in stock.

1
ANTIQUES

Whether you are looking for what the shops call "important pieces" ("significant examples of important styles in good condition") or just attractive-looking antiques to furnish a house, you will have a wider choice if you try these shops. But except for one or two of the mail-order specialists, don't expect the same service from antique shops that you get from stores in other sections. They can only answer requests for specific items, and if you don't get an answer, you must assume that the store doesn't have what you want.

No duty is charged for anything that is over a hundred years old.

Clocks

Strike One, 51 Camden Passage, London N1 8EA, England. Telephone (01) 226 9709
Annual subscription to catalogues, $5. AE, DC.
"Clocks for decoration, interest and investment," Strike One says enticingly. Their specialty is an ongoing responsibility for their clocks even after the clocks are ticking away in the new owners' homes. Everything is thoroughly overhauled and sold in perfect working order with a one-year guarantee (you can mail them back to be fixed).

Some of the clocks are quite old: A seventeenth-century, one-handed lantern clock has a square brass dial decorated and signed "Thomas Parker" in beautiful copperplate writing. A Black Forest cuckoo clock in the earliest style has roses painted around the face, and the cuckoo pops out from a bouquet of flowers. All sorts of clocks are sold—wall, shelf and long-case—and prices are usually over $2000.

Keith Harding Antiques (Music Boxes) also sells antique clocks.

Curios

Goss and Crested China, 62 Murray Road, Horndean, Hampshire, England. Telephone 0705 597 440
Subscription to twelve monthly catalogues, $12; air mail $20. MC, V.
Nicholas Pine writes that the shelves of Victorian and Edwardian souvenir shops were crammed with Goss china—miniature crested shoes, urns, figures, cottages and the like. The "ivory porcelain" was created in the nineteenth century by William Goss, who realized there would be a demand for souvenirs from the newly developing "tripper class." The china was an instant success, and later, when it was no longer popular with trippers, it became popular with collectors. Nicholas Pine is one of the few specialists. Most pieces cost between $15 and $25.

A. Goto, 1–23–9 Higashi, Shibuya-Ku, Tokyo, Japan
Price lists, free. Prices in $.
An intriguing list of small Japanese things, most of which are just under one hundred years old. The list I looked at had netsukes (small hanging ornaments) made of all sorts of different materials, from incised yak horn (from Tibet) starting at $15 up to hornbill starting at $70. There were small antique figurines, gunpowder holders and snuff bottles. Minimum order, $30.

Ingram Warick, 20A High Street, Amersham, Old Town, Buckinghamshire MP7 ODJ, England. Telephone 024 03 21033
Price list, free. V.

1

2

1 *Strike One* Tavern or Act of Parliament clock, circa 1760. Gold-leaf dial and typical chinoiserie decoration on unusual green lacquer ground (most Tavern clocks are black). Price about $6120.

2 *Strike One* An early repeating carriage clock by Jacot, in a gilded corniche case. Price about $1500.

3

4

5

Jewels, silver, maps and oddities are sold by this family business, which was established in South Molton Street, London, in 1912, and moved to Amersham in 1975. On the list I saw there was a carved ivory magnifying glass, a silver plate sweetmeat trough, and a late Victorian posy vase, all for under $35, and most other things cost under $100.

Dolls

The Magnificent Doll, P.O. Box 1981, Centerville, MA 02632.
Send self-addressed stamped envelope for information.
Helen Nolan offers a brokerage service for antique dolls; she asks me to stress that the emphasis is on *antique* dolls as an investment (sixty years or older). She stresses that she only buys dolls of high quality: "We don't buy dolls with 'hairlines'; We don't buy 'repaired dolls.'" You can either tell her what you want, and she'll let you know when she finds it and will charge what she sees fit; or you can commission her to find the doll (through auctions, doll shows), pay a deposit and then pay her exactly what she paid, plus a 25-percent commission.

Fine Arts

W. & F. C. Bonham and Sons, Montpellier Galleries, Montpellier Street, Knightsbridge, London SW7 1HH, England. Telephone (01) 584 9161
Catalogue subscription price list, free.
Bonham's, established in 1793, boasts of two distinctions: It is the only firm of London auctioneers to remain a family business, and the sister of the present chairman was the first English lady auctioneer. Auctions are held in all the usual main categories and, judging by the catalogue Bonham's sent me, their wares are much more affordable than those auctioned at the international houses.

Phillips, 867 Madison Avenue, New York, NY 10021. Telephone (212) 570 4830
Catalogue subscription price list, free U.S. and overseas.
Phillips, an English auctioneer established in 1796, is not as large or well known as Christie's and Sotheby's, but nevertheless has started a New York branch, and sends its catalogues to subscribers around the world. Like the other firms, they hold regular auctions in furniture, art and many other specialties such as lead soldiers, scientific instruments, postage stamps, collectors' china. Ask them for addresses of other branches with catalogue subscriptions.

C. G. Sloane and Company, 715 13th Street, N.W., Washington, DC 20005. Telephone (202) 628 1468
Announcements of future auctions, free.
These auctioneers hold auctions that last for several days with art and antiques from different collections. The catalogue I looked at had a wonderful variety: a collection of six hundred shaving mugs. Another of Victorian circus posters, paintings, American furniture, rugs and carousel animals. In the next auction a "magnificent" Picasso crayon drawing and "lovely" watercolors by Berthe Morisot were the stars. Estimated bids are given in the catalogue, you may telephone to consult with the staff, and there is a form in each catalogue for absentee bidders.

3 *W. & F. C. Bonham and Sons* German tinplate reversing engine by Hess in original box with rails and key, circa 1895. Auctioned for $720.

4 *Phillips* One of three drawings from "Mickey's Circus," 1936. Auctioned in 1981 for $275.

5 *The Magnificent Doll* Fifteen-inch French doll made by Jumeau, Paris, in the late 1880s. Blue paperweight eyes, wood and papier-mâché body, antique clothes. Head stamped, body signed. Similar dolls available for prices between $2000 and $3000.

Christie's, Subscription Department, 141 East 25th Street, New York, NY 10010. Telephone (212) 546 1000

Sotheby Park Bernet, Subscription Department, 411 East 76th Street, New York, NY 10021. Telephone (212) 472 3413
Subscription information for catalogues for all branches, free U.S. and overseas.
These grand international auction houses almost daily auction off "the things most worth living with," as one of them put it, frequently achieving world-record prices. (I read in *The New York Times* that Christie's got a world-record price for an undrinkable old bottle of wine; the next week that Sotheby's got one for a Stradivarius.) Comes the revolution, all this will be done away with, but meanwhile, in spite of the phenomenal record sales that get international publicity, there are plenty of things that people who are merely moderately well off can afford. You can subscribe to semi-illustrated catalogues throughout the season, more or less the academic year, for prices between $16 for something like pewter and $100 for Old Master painting. Auctions are held of furniture, clocks, works of art, ceramics and glass, silver, jewelry, coins and medals, arms and armor, art nouveau, art deco posters.

You receive catalogues about two weeks before auctions, and if you want to bid you can write the house for an estimate of what the bids will be, and then send in your own. At the actual auction a member of the staff will bid for you. If you win, you are notified within two weeks and must inform the house where you want your prize shipped or stored. You can also subscribe to price lists that will arrive later, telling you what each item finally went for.

Spink and Son, 5–7 King Street, St. James's, London SW1, England. Telephone (01) 930 7888
Octagon, free. Numismatic circular (ten per year), $20 per year.
The omnipresent Spink's main enterprises are the fine arts sections, which contain only the most rare and important pieces. They send their old customers *Octagon*, a quarterly journal with articles and illustrations of new acquisitions (without prices). If you are serious and wealthy enough to want to become an old customer, write and inquire about your interests. Their Oriental Art is perhaps their best-known department, but they also have English silver and English paintings and now a small gallery of furniture.

Furniture and General Antiques

F. G. and C. Collins, Church Street, Wheathampstead, Herts AL4 8AP, England. Telephone 058 283 3111
Brochure, free. V.
If you are ready for the adventurous undertaking of buying antique furniture from abroad, F. G. and C. Collins, appropriately housed in two buildings of historical and architectural interest, is a good place to start. This family firm was established in 1907, stocks seventeenth-, eighteenth-, nineteenth-century furniture, and sends out photocopies of photographs of furniture currently in stock. The brochure I looked at had an attractive assortment of English furniture. Prices were mainly between $500 and $2000.

6

7

8

9

6 *F. G. and C. Collins* Mahogany D-shaped card table with a swing leg, circa 1790, $1170.

7 *F. G. and C. Collins* Rosewood davenport, circa 1840, $1440.

8 *F. G. and C. Collins* Walnut chest on stand with marquetry inlay, circa 1690, $3250.

9 *F. G. and C. Collins* Mahogany social table, circa 1840, $2520.

10

11

10 *Christopher Sykes* Miniature grandfather clock watch holders, circa 1840, from $120. Bracket clock in walnut case, circa 1850, $650. Wedgwood blue and white candlesticks, circa 1840, $400. Oil paintings are always in stock, at prices starting at $200.

11 *Christopher Sykes* Staffordshire ceramic figures, circa 1810. Prices $70 to $200.

Margery Dean Antiques, The Galleries, Wivenhoe, Colchester, Essex, England. Telephone 0206 222 523
Information in reply to specific request, 5 International Reply Coupons.
Margery Dean, author of *English Antique Furniture,* has been selling reasonably priced English period furniture since 1947. Because of inflation she has stopped putting out a price list, but instead answers specific inquiries. Besides telling her what piece of furniture you need, don't forget to mention which period and which wood you want. If the information she sends you "proves acceptable," she will send a Polaroid photograph of the piece she has.

Furniture is stocked dating from 1600 on, including Victorian furniture and economical country furniture, so this is a very good place for people who want antiques that aren't too expensive.

Christopher Sykes Antiques,
The Old Parsonage, Woburn, Milton Keynes,
Bedfordshire MK17 9QL, England.
Telephone 052 525 259
P. Pottery and Porcelain Catalogue (English, Continental and Oriental): Staffordshire figures, Wedgwood, Worcester, Spode, Blue and White, Transfer pottery.
M. Metalware Catalogue (pewter, wrought iron, brass and copper), specializing in early Lighting, Cooking Utensils, Trade Tools, Apothecary Mortars, Locks and Keys, Corkscrews.
S. Scientific Catalogue (microscopes, sundials, telescopes, sextants, levels, measuring instruments, clocks, medical instruments).
C. Collectibles Catalogue (toys, games, needlework, samplers, music boxes, mechanical, ship and horse models, musical instruments, ormolu, glass, etc.).
O. Oil Paintings and Watercolors Catalogue (seascapes, sporting, genre, landscapes, portraits, miniatures).
Each catalogue, $5 (air mail).
Christopher Sykes, who has often appeared on British television and radio programs, has a large antique shop in Woburn village filled with antique pottery, porcelain, pewter, brass, copper, scientific instruments, tea caddies, etc., ranging in price from $80 to $1000 each. He is wonderfully well organized to sell by mail, and since more than half his sales go to America, this is probably the best antique shop for you.

Edward G. Wilson, 1802 Chestnut Street,
Philadelphia, PA 19103. Telephone (215) 563 7369
Price lists: (1) Souvenir and Unusual Spoons, $1; (2) Children's Books, $1; (3) Antique Silver, $1; (4) Sewing Items and Thimbles, $1.
The firm has been in business for over fifty years and sells antique jewelry, antique and estate silver, fine china, glass and miscellaneous collector's items. Goods are described only on the lists, but may be returned for a full refund if you aren't pleased with them.

Gambling

East Coast Casino Antiques, 98 Main Street,
Fishkill, NY 12524. Telephone (914) 896 9492
80-page catalogue, $4; overseas, $6. MC, V.
Rare and early gambling antiquities—from a $5 pair of miniature dice, through cards and gaming kits, to slot machines and one-armed bandits, going for hundreds of dollars.
Recommended by reader Carol Campion.

Instruments

Historical Technology, 6 Mugford Street, Marblehead, MA 01945.
58-page catalogue, $4 introductory subscription to two issues; overseas, $8 for introductory subscription to two issues.
Antique instruments for astrology, marine navigation, microscopy, photography and much more; charts, maps and related books are all sold by catalogue to private collectors and museums around the world. In the catalogue I looked at, most instruments cost between $100 and $1000.

Harriet Wynter, Arts & Sciences, 50 Redcliffe Road, London SW10 9NJ, England. Telephone (01) 352 6494
Brochure, free; air mail $1.25. MC, V.
Molly Freeman, the real Harriet Wynter, collects and deals in old scientific instruments.

She supplies museums and exhibitions and stocks sextants, lodestones, astrolabs, telescopes, sundials, microscopes, and all sorts of other curiosities such as quizzing glasses and thumb bleeders. Prices for the instruments are available on request only, but the list of books on instruments gives book prices.

12

Jewelry

N. Bloom & Son, 40 Conduit Street, London WI, England.
Color brochure, $2.
Bloom stocks ornate and interesting antique silver and jewelry; the brochure illustrates nineteenth- and early-twentieth-century jewelry. Try them for a seventeenth-century Cupid with skull stick pin, an art nouveau pen knife, a George III silver bosun's whistle. The director, Ian Harris, says wistfully, "We sell quite a fair amount from this catalogue to customers of ours in the U.S.A., and will be very pleased to sell more, especially in these hard times." Prices start at about $400 and are usually in the thousands.

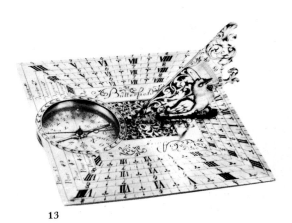

13

Military and Nautical

N. Flayderman and Company, Squash Hollow, R.F.D. 2, New Milford, CT 06776
Catalogue, $2.50.
Mr. Flayderman has an impressive list of official positions as adviser to various institutions. His firm has been publishing catalogues longer than any other firm in the antique-arms, military and nautical business; and the stock of firearms, edged weapons and arms literature is well known to people in the field. But what would be of interest to less dedicated people, who are simply trying to decorate their homes, is that amid the scrimshaws and muskets are some fascinating pieces of Americana.

John F. Rinaldi, Nautical Antiques, Box 765 CC, Dock Square, Kennebunkport, ME 04046
26-page catalogue, $2; overseas $5.
Nautical antiques that range in price from "Advertising pamphlet from Hudson river steamer *Mary Powell*" at $19.50, through "Sailor-made carved and inlaid sewing box" at $695 to "Two historically important scrimshaw carved whale's teeth with subject matter affiliated with the Wilkes expedition" at $5850. Many instruments, much scrimshaw

14

12 *Historical Technology* Henry Bryant's "Celestial Indicator." American, circa 1870.

13 *Historical Technology* Large pocket sundial by Butterfield. Paris, circa 1700.

14 *Historical Technology* Table tripod reflecting Gregorian telescope. English, circa 1750. Once owned by William Emerson.

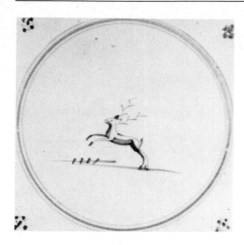

15

and interesting oddities such as captain's walking sticks and mechanical pirates.

Music Boxes

Keith Harding Antiques, 93 Hornsey Road, London N7 6DJ, England. Telephone (01) 607 6181
Lists of cylinder and disc music boxes, list of spare parts for antique boxes, list of books on music boxes, list of clocks, $2; air mail $5.
The last lines on the Keith Harding music box price list are: "You might think we go to a great deal of trouble to give you exactly what you want. We do." And this does look like a place where music boxes and music box lovers will be equally cared for and cosseted. There are twelve craftsmen working and four floors of showrooms, museum, workshop and storage, plus a main workshop in another building.
Customers' own music boxes and clocks are repaired and cylinders repinned.

Silver

Denise Poole, Timberland House, Horncastle Road, Woodhall Spa, Lincolnshire, LN10 6UZ, England
Catalogue, free.
Denise Poole sells choice eighteenth- and nineteenth-century English silver almost exclusively by mail and she is well set up for it. Mugs, jugs, spoons, salt dishes, wine labels, sugar baskets, teapots, trays and more are photographed and described in detail in the catalogue, and she has a mailing list to keep customers up to date on recent acquisitions.

Tiles

Helen Williams, Antique Delft Tiles, 12643 Hortense Street, North Hollywood, CA 91604
Leaflet, self-addressed stamped envelope; overseas 1 International Reply Coupon.
Delft tiles were bought by American colonists for use around the chimneys in "finer" homes from 1650 until 1800 when English "transfer" tiles replaced the hand-painted Dutch ones. Subjects included Dutch scenes, Bible stories, flowers and animals. Helen Williams sells mainly the seventeenth- and eighteenth-century Delft tiles, but also has English transfer, and antique Spanish and Portuguese tiles.

Tools

Iron Horse Antiques, R.D. 2, Poultney, VT 05764. Telephone (802) 287 4050
74-page catalogue, $7.50 a year U.S. and overseas. MC, V.
Iron Horse specializes in old and antique tools, a fascinating area which is, as far as I know, still virgin soil for antique dealers. A particular expertise is needed, and the catalogue itself notes the difficulties in dating axes, for instance. The catalogue is divided into various kinds of tools—metalworking, agricultural, woodworking, etc.—and includes pages of such specialized trades as coopers' tools, coachmakers' instruments, etc. The catalogue is fully, though rather primitively, illustrated and contains a list of the still relatively few books that are available on this subject.

15 *Helen Williams* Eighteenth-century Delft tiles sell for between $25 and $35, depending on design.

ART

Buying art by mail might sound a very odd thing to do, but collectors do it, and with color transparencies and liberal return policies, it isn't really such a gamble.

The big auction galleries listed in the Antiques sections are a main source of original works of art. In the Graphics section, I have listed shops that sell original prints made from a block, plate or stone on which the artist himself worked and from which a high-quality, small edition was produced. The Maps and Prints section lists original prints made by the same methods, but some of these prints have been produced for magazines and other mass media.

There is no duty on art.

Drawings and Paintings

Amadeus Gallery, 16 Oxford Street, Woodstock, Oxfordshire, England
Catalogue, $1 bill. Prices in $.
John and Sara Tyndall sell "paintings of quality, saleable at a reasonable price" to customers around the world. When choosing a painting, John Tyndall says, "We don't mind what period or country it originated from, although we tend to prefer eighteenth-century English paintings; and we like pictures of people doing things—such as hunting scenes, or fishermen, or family groups, so long as they are natural and unpretentious." Price range of paintings is $600 to $10,000, which includes delivery to customers' nearest international airport.

G. Cramer, Javastraat 38, 2585AP The Hague, Holland. Telephone 011 31 70 630 758
Catalogue and supplement, $30 including air-mail postage.
"Oude Kunst" says the stately Cramer letterhead, but "paintings by Old Masters" is a closer description than "old art." The Cramer catalogues, with one illustration per page, are clearly aimed at museums and very wealthy collectors. Cramer writes that the listing is "for a very specialized public [and therefore] there is no printed price list, but every serious inquiry will be replied separately." A fascinating look at the caliber of work still available for sale, but not for the casual browser.

Judy and Alan Goffman Fine Art, P.O. Box 350A, Blue Bell, PA 19422. Telephone (215) 643 6310
Color catalogue, $7.50.
This gallery sells nineteenth- and twentieth-century American painting specializing in American illustrators. Their current catalogue ranges from Remington to Rockwell (the original oils of some of his famous magazine covers), Pyle, Parrish and other popular names, bound to arouse nostalgic interest. Prices not listed.

Hauswedell und Nolte, D-2000 Hamburg 13, Poseldorfer Weg, 1, Germany. Telephone 040 44 83 66
Auction catalogues at varying mailing costs, from $5 to $15.
This German auction house looks like their version of Christie's, publishing very extensive and impressive catalogues of books, manuscripts and works of art. The 460-page modern art catalogue, for instance, is practically a history of the subject, strongest of course in the Germans but offering a very wide range. Primarily for serious collectors, but well worth getting for its own sake.

Hirschl and Adler Galleries, 21 East 70th Street, New York, NY 10021. Telephone (212) 535 8810
Extensive color catalogues. Price depends on differing costs.
This is one of New York's better-known galleries, offering

1

1 *Amadeus Gallery English Hunting Scene,* circa 1800. Oil on board, 19″ by 23¾″. About $2500, including delivery to customer's nearest international airport.

2

3

4

2 *Alister Mathews* Guisseppe Zocchi of Florence, 1711–1767. "Colosseum" pen and ink and brown wash with touches of pale green, 8¼" by 11⅓". About $1050.

3 *Alister Mathews* Valentine Gross, wife of Jean Hugo, 1890–1968. Nijinsky dancing *Le Spectre de la Rose*, pastel and chalk drawing, 13¼" by 9¾". About $2258.

4 *Collectors Treasures* Canadian Bartlett steel engraving, circa 1840. Similar engravings, hand-colored and mounted, $18 to $22.

some very fine works of art. Their current American catalogue includes paintings by Cassatt, Sargent, Hopper and Prendergast but also some drawings and sketches that might be affordable to nonmillionaires. Prices are not listed.

Alister Mathews, Fremington, 58 West Overcliff Drive, Bournemouth BH4 8AB, England.
Telephone 0202 761 547
Catalogue, $3.
I got a very emphatic letter (with important points typed or underlined in red) from Alister Mathews, who since 1937 has been selling original antiquarian drawings (not prints) from the sixteenth to twentieth centuries; drawings by book illustrators (not books, not prints); and some manuscripts. The catalogue I looked at described over one hundred works (and had about sixteen illustrations).

Old Hall Gallery, Crown Lodge, Crown Road, Morden, Surrey SM4 5BY, England.
Telephone (01) 540 9918
6-page catalogue, $2.
The Old Hall Gallery is a small family firm that sells seventeenth-, eighteenth-, and nineteenth-century paintings, but specializes in the "rising field" (though all the art fields seem to be "rising fields") of Victoriana. They supply museums and galleries; in England they have supplied institutions such as the Victoria and Albert, London; and the Ashmolean, Oxford; and in America, the Capitol Museum, Washington State; the Princeton Museum; and others. Everything is efficiently organized: Catalogues with black-and-white photographs of framed paintings are published several times a year, prices mainly between $300 and $1500.

Frank S. Schwarz and Son, 1806 Chestnut Street, Philadelphia, PA 19103. Telephone (215) 563 4887
Black-and-white catalogue, $5.
Specialists in American drawings and paintings, this firm offers traditional American art, much of it by less well known artists whose work is therefore still relatively affordable. That is to say, many of the watercolors listed are in the $500-to-$1000 range, some dearer.

Graphics

Associated American Artists, 663 Fifth Avenue, New York, NY 10022. Telephone (212) 755 4211
Catalogue, $1; overseas $2.
The AAA was founded in 1934 to provide people with original prints for very low prices, and it offered the works of such popular artists as Thomas Hart Benton and Grant Wood for as little as $5 each. AAA now possesses America's largest collection of original prints and commissions many of its prints directly from the artists, which means that some, though not all, of its offerings are reasonably priced. The artists represented tend to be realistic in style. There are few abstractions.

Christie's Print Collection, 799 Madison Avenue, New York, NY 10021. Telephone (212) 535 4422
Catalogues, free. AE, DC, MC, V.
The famous art auctioneers have gone into the business of printing original graphics by contemporary artists and have been very successful. Their editions are usually limited to one hundred and fifty to two hundred prints and prices are

usually in the $100-to-$300 range. Some are by well-known artists, but most aren't and are clearly in the category of work that you should buy if it appeals to your own taste, and not as an investment.

Galerie des Peintres Graveurs,
159bis Boulevard du Montparnasse, Paris 75006, France.
Telephone 326 62 29
16-page price list, free.
Leading specialists in original prints and lithographs, this Paris firm offers the work of many of the great French printmakers. Bonnard, Rouault, Maillol and Utrillo are all listed, many with work originally available in printings of twenty-five to one hundred. Not much more expensive than some contemporary offerings and in many instances far better value for the money.

Marilyn Pink, Master Prints and Drawings,
817 North LaCienega Boulevard, Los Angeles, CA 90069.
Telephone (213) 657 5810
Two catalogues annually, $12 for subscription or $6.50 each; overseas air mail $3 extra.
"Significant works on paper, woodcuts, etchings, engravings, watercolors—fifteenth-century through twentieth-century" is the gallery's austere description of its wares, ranging in the recent catalogue from a Stuart Davis drawing to a Piranesi print. A wide choice.

Orangerie Veriag, Helenestrasse 2, 5 Cologne 1,
Germany
Catalogue with some color, $6; air mail $8. In German.
This German publishing house and art gallery sells a vast number of prints both of its own making and printed by others. The catalogue is so extensive that collectors may be interested in it simply to see what the going prices are for their favorite artists. Such prices can be very high indeed, with a number of lithograph listings in the thousands rather than hundreds of dollars. It would be wise to check with Orangerie about the details of any print you may wish to buy.

The Red Lantern Shop, 236 Shimmonzen Street,
Higashiya-Ku, Kyoto 605, Japan
Color brochure, free.
Red Lantern specializes in modern Japanese prints, all the works being carved and printed by the artists in signed and numbered editions. The styles range widely, and while a few are clearly modern versions of traditional wood blocks, others seem much more Western, while others are much more old-fashioned. Prices, in any case, are very reasonable.

David Tunick, 12 East 81st Street, New York, NY 10028.
Telephone (212) 570 0090
Extensive color catalogues, $8; air mail $10 U.S. and overseas.
One of the best sources in New York for prints and engravings, Tunick publishes very handsome catalogues that are practically worth having for their own sake. Whether a Toulouse-Lautrec color lithograph or a complete set of the eighty Goya *Caprichos*, the offerings are important works and expensive ones. Prices not listed.

William Weston Gallery,
7 Royal Arcade, Albemarle Street, London WI, England.
Telephone (01) 493 0722
A year's subscription to six brochures, $15. AE, DC.
Perfectly set up for mail order, the William Weston Gallery issues black-and-white brochures of recent acquisitions.

They stock original etchings, engravings, lithographs, etc., by nineteenth- and twentieth-century masters and hold occasional special exhibitions for which they also send out brochures. I was sent a current brochure which illustrated sixty-five works by artists such as Albers, Feininger, Manet, Munch, Palmer, Rouault, Vuillard, and a few others not so well known. Prices started at about $440 for a signed-in-pencil lithograph *Au Café* by Henry Gabrielibels, but were mainly between $1000 and $2000.

The Yoseido Gallery, 5–15 Ginza 5 Chome, Chuo-Ku,
Tokyo, Japan
100-page catalogue with some color, $8; air mail $12. Prices in $.
A first-rate catalogue of limited-edition, signed wood-block prints by modern Japanese artists. The wood block is still highly valued and much used in Japan, and the Yoseido Gallery handles the works of all the best-known Japanese artists using this medium. Most modern styles are represented, and many pictures show overwhelmingly Western influences.

Maps and Prints

Collectors Treasures, Hogarth House, High Street,
Wendover, Bucks HP22 6DU, England.
Telephone Wendover 624402
Price lists, annual subscription $9; airmail $18.
Specialists in Old English prints and maps, this firm offers maps of just about every part of England as well as prints and views of traditional England. A wide choice as well of prints of such popular subjects as the Holy Land, Picturesque America and other nineteenth-century favorites. Prices range from $10 for a small flower engraving, with most prints averaging $40.

Richard Nicholson of Chester, 25 Watergate Street,
Chester, CH3 7AG, England. Telephone 0244 26818
24-page black-and-white catalogue, $1; air mail $3.
Antique maps and prints. This shop also runs postal auctions which they say give their overseas customers an equal chance at their choicer items.

The Parker Gallery, 2 Albemarle Street,
London W1X 3HR, England
Catalogue, free; air mail $2. October. AE.
The oldest established firm of picture and print dealers in London has an enormous collection of prints and publishes a semi-illustrated catalogue each October. The catalogue I looked at listed the kinds of prints in stock at the shop: marine, military, topography, sporting, transport, trades, caricatures, weapons, family portraits and decorative. The Parker Gallery is willing to send prints "on approval," and will look for anything special you want that is not in stock.

The Print Mint Gallery, 1147 Greenleaf Avenue,
Wilmette, IL 60091. Telephone (312) 256 4140
Price list, free; overseas $1. AE, CB, MC, V.
Specialists in relatively inexpensive nineteenth- and twentieth-century American prints as well as in illustrations from old books. Old ads, Currier and Ives prints, Indian portraits from the eleventh United States census, etc. The store also runs a finding service for old prints, for which there is a $10 fee.

5

6

7

5 *P. J. Radford* A map of Virginia by Henry Hondius, 1633. About $800.

6 *P. J. Radford* Lithographs printed in color, by the Reverend W. Houghton, 1879. Mounted, 12½" by 9". About $36.

7 *P. J. Radford* Print with original hand coloring, circa 1851, 7¾" by 5⅛". Similar prints $15 to $20.

Paul Prouté, S.A., 74 Rue de Seine, Paris 75006, France. Telephone 362 8980
Catalogue $14. Available March–May only.
Paul Prouté is well known for its immense stock of half a million prints, which are sold to private individuals and American dealers. Stock ranges from the fifteenth century to contemporary artists, and includes Old-Master prints, views of cities, portraits, old maps.

P. J. Radford, Sheffield Park, Uckfield, Sussex, England. Telephone 0825 720531
50-page map catalogue: Americana, free.
50-page map catalogue: British Isles, free.
50-page prints catalogue, free.
General catalogue, free. Any catalogue, air mail $5.
P. J. Radford, author of *Antique Maps*, published in England, has a magnificent stock of prints and rare maps, especially Americana, described and displayed in his temptingly well-designed catalogues. Even non–map collectors might be seduced by some of these: Indigenous inhabitants, ships in full sail, sea monsters, mythological figures, the seasons and the elements crowd the map with decorative activity.

 If you want to pay much less, ask for the prints catalogue and look at the nineteenth-century prints of Europe and America. Taken from engravings, they were often used as tourists' mementos, and show a blissfully unspoiled, pastoral world.

Sifton, Praed and Company, 54 Beauchamp Place, Knightsbridge, London SW3 1NY, England. Telephone (01) 589 4325
No catalogue. AE, V.
Sifton, Praed and Company writes: "We have one of the best collections of antique maps in Britain, and although we do not do a catalogue as our stock turns over too fast, we are always willing to send our lists on any particular area or cartographer."

Turtle Bay Galleries, Box 115, Darien, CT 06820 0115
Color leaflet, $1; overseas $2. MC, V.
Colorful, naive lithographs of plump cats and nostalgic wedding, village and schoolhouse scenes. Prices around $16 and $35.

Posters

Art Poster Company, 22255 Greenfield Road, Southfield, MI 48075. Telephone (800) 521 8634
32-page color catalogue, $2 (refundable). MC, V.
A popular selection of contemporary posters, some by famous names such as Hockney and Steinberg but mostly by illustrators and chosen more for the appeal of the subject than the fame of the artist. Some lovely floral prints; a number of announcements of concerts and museum shows.

Fiesta Arts, Greenvale, NY 11548. Telephone (516) 671 6888
Color brochure, $2.50; overseas $3.50.
This firm has United States distribution rights for the Ricordi posters, lovely turn-of-the-century Italian posters now reprinted from the original stone matrixes. The charming, lively full-color posters are of the traditional fin de siècle subjects, from cars and bicycles to opera posters and femmes fatales advertising diverse goods. These are, however, among the most attractive of the genre, perfect for fans of the period or even of the items advertised.

8

9

10

.TURANDOT.
MUSICA DI **G. PUCCINI**   LIBRETTO DI
G. ADAMI e R. SIMONI

11

12

8 *P. J. Radford* Flower print by Jane Loudon, with original hand coloring, 7½″ by 10½″. This series from $27.

9 *P. J. Radford* Fashion print, with original hand coloring, circa 1825–1829. This series from $18.

10 *Turtle Bay Galleries The Schoolhouse*, lithograph, about $35.

11 *Fiesta Arts* One of a series of Italian turn-of-the-century posters published by Ricordi and now reprinted in full color from the original stone matrix, $8.

12 *Gemini Studio* Suzanne Farrell and Peter Martins in *Chaconne*. Available as a poster for $6; as postcards, ten for $6. (*Photograph by Max Waldman*.)

13

14

**Gemini Studio, 21 West 17th Street,
New York, NY 10011**
Brochure, free; overseas $2.
Posters and postcards (from photos) of contemporary ballet
dancers. From Panov to Makarova, here are excellent photos
of the great names in action. Perfect for ballet fans of all
ages, $6 per poster, 60 cents per card.

**Icart Vendor Gallery, 7956 Beverly Boulevard,
Los Angeles, CA 90048. Telephone (213) 653 3190**
*Art Deco/Icart Catalogue, $3. Original Poster Catalogue,
$7.50.*
This firm specializes in art nouveau/art deco posters and
particularly in the period eroticism of Louis Icart, whose
women tend to recline naked on fur rugs or against butterfly
wings and other period backgrounds. More modern pin-ups
are available as well as posters by Erte, Parish, Mucha. A
very wide choice of original posters, less erotic but marvelously varied.

**London Transport, Publishing and Souvenirs Division,
Griffith House, 280 Old Marylebone Road,
London NW1 5RJ, England. Telephone (01) 262 3444**
Leaflet, free.
For years London Transport has been responsible for the
best public-information service that I have ever seen. They
have published books, guidebooks, and famous subway posters, some of which were commissioned in the twenties from
leading graphic artists. Now an appealing batch of souvenirs
has been added, likely to amuse anyone with fond memories
of London.

Miscellaneous Man, Box 1776, New Freedom, PA 17349
Occasional catalogues, $2 each. MC, V.
George Theofilos is one of the best-known dealers in posters
and other graphic ephemera, and his Miscellaneous Man is
a wonderful source of decorative pieces. George hates "the
preppy view of life"—people who won't allow anything
tacky into their lives. Instead he relishes the posters, baggage
stickers, movie flyers, sheet music and any other oddments,
sober, quirky or outrageous, that give a sense of their period.

The Miscellaneous Man stocks posters by the famous
poster artists in categories such as prohibition and antivice,
war, motion pictures, travel of all sorts, sports, automobile,
food, drink, etc.

Besides the posters, labels, lobby cards, leaflets, flyers and
sheet music, out-of-print books on poster art are also sold.

If you are selling, not buying, you may be interested in
the long list of things that the Miscellaneous Man wants,
which includes—besides, of course, posters, etc.—categories
such as common or uncommon cause material, bizarrely
designed everyday items and "Dimwitiana: statuary, objects,
graphics, etc., where a nonreligious personality is somehow
extremely elevated to deity status (one of the latest examples
would be Elvis Dimwitiana). Any period."

**Pomegranate Publication, P.O. Box 713,
Corte Madera, CA 94925. Telephone (415) 924 8141**
Poster, print and card catalogues, free. U.S. and overseas.
This firm offers a fascinating range of posters, prints, cards,
etc., which I suppose you have to describe as Californian.
The major emphasis is on fantasy, of the kind favored by
record albums and science-fiction books. However, Pomegranate pays homage to its ancestors and offers lovely reproductions of the pre-Raphaelites, Frederic Church and Howard Pyle. Lots of Escher, naturally, and contemporary
concert posters. Many contemporary artists on posters and
on hundreds of notecards.

13 *Miscellaneous Man* "To Have and to Hold," 1943 government
war-bonds poster in full color, $35.

14 *Poster Originals* Paul Davis poster, mainly in white, brown,
blue and green, for $15.

Poster Originals, 924 Madison Avenue, New York, NY 10021
124-page color catalogue, $7.50; overseas $13. AE, MC, V.
Poster Originals is a gallery devoted entirely to posters, printed here or abroad, by artists for their own shows. Posters may include the work of living artists for current shows or feature pictures chosen by a museum or gallery for an exhibit by an artist from an earlier time. Some are in their second printing. In addition to contemporary artists, there are a number of very striking posters recently printed for exhibits of the classics. A handsome, extensive offering.

Poster Pals, 1003 Crest Circle, Cincinnati, OH 45208. Telephone (513) 871 5057
Color catalogue, $1 (refundable); overseas $2. MC, V.
Specialists in original, wood-cut circus posters and billboards, this firm has been printing traditional American posters for decades. These are the same images you doubtless remember as a child (whatever your age), available in poster or billboard size, at very reasonable prices (from $6 for the smallest to $60 for the billboard size to cover a wall or ceiling).

Triton Gallery, 323 West 45th Street, New York, NY 10036. Telephone (212) 765 2472
Annual color brochure, 50 cents; overseas $1. MC, V.
Current and past theater posters, some original, most under $10 each, though some originals can cost much more. Dance, TV, Broadway shows; small cards and big posters.

Reproductions

Bernardo, Avalon Square, 108 West, 2400 Westheimer Road, Houston, TX 77098. Telephone (713) 526 2686
24-page black-and-white catalogue, $2 (refundable); overseas air mail $3.
United States distributor for Mexican rubbings and serigraphs based on Mayan temple ruins. These rubbings capture traditional figures and motifs and cost from $7.50 up, most of them in the $20-to-$30 range. This, however, includes the cost of registered air mail from Mexico.

Buck Hill Associates, Garnet Lake Road, Johnsburg, NY 12843
Price list, $1; overseas $2.
A humorous collection of reproductions of old American posters, handbills, broadsides, documents and prints, including Revolutionary and Civil War posters, reward posters, political cartoons, antique fashion posters, playbills and a curious lot of old advertisements—a fill-your-teeth-yourself ad for a home dental outfit; a noiseless-vacuum-toothpick ad, "a boon to well-bred people"; and an 1877 telephone handbill, "Prof. Bell Speaks and Sings." Unfortunately the price list is unillustrated, but fortunately the posters cost about $1 each.

Cambridge Brass Rubbing Centre, The Wesley Church Library, King Street, Cambridge, England. Telephone 0223 61318
Leaflet, free.
Brass rubbings and facsimiles of the original brasses. These handsome rubbings are not made from the original brasses, but from the facsimiles, but the Centre claims that the final result is indistinguishable. The rubbings themselves are

Cinera cum flore.

Hortus Eystettensis, Eichstatt, 1613

15

16

15 *Poster Originals* New York Botanical Garden poster, "Cinera," in white, green, purple, ochre and orange, for $15.

16 *Triton Gallery* Charlie Chaplin Gold Rush poster, $4. Out-of-print theatrical posters can be photographically reproduced to order.

17

18

17 *Buck Hill Associates* Reproduction of 1916 Coca-Cola advertisement. Black on pink paper, 65 cents. A set of three in this series, $1.60.

18 *Cambridge Brass Rubbing Centre* Rubbings in gold on black paper based on medieval brass memorials. Prices mainly between $3 and $15.

hung on simple wooden rods, and made with gold wax on black paper.

EHG, 4201 North Marshall Way, Scottsdale, AZ 85251. Telephone (602) 941 9348
Color brochure, $2.50 U.S. and overseas. AE, BA, MC, V.
Posters and reproductions by artists from the American Southwest, mostly with a regional theme. O'Keeffe and Scholder are featured, as well as some Pueblo and Kiowa Indian paintings. Prices range from $10 to $30, mostly in the $15-to-$20 range.

EROS Data Center, Sioux Falls, SD 57198. Telephone (605) 594 6151
Brochure, free U.S. and overseas.
EROS, The Earth Resources Observation Systems Program of the Department of the Interior, was established in 1966 to apply "remote sensing" techniques to the monitoring and managing of natural resources. At its data center in South Dakota its own imagery and aerial photography along with imagery collected by NASA from research aircrafts and from Skylab, Apollo, and Gemini spacecraft are stored. EROS provides "the remotely sensed data at nominal cost to scientists, resource planners, managers and the public." Which means that dramatic images of the world from space can be bought here, providing new views of familiar areas and striking decorations.

Greater London Council Map and Print Collection, Greater London Record Office, 40 Northampton Road, London EC1, England. Telephone (01) 633 7193
Price list, free.
The Greater London Council sells fine-line black-and-white lithographic and color reproductions from the collection in the Council's library at *very* low prices. There are sixteenth-, seventeenth-, and eighteenth-century maps of London, old views of London, and various London scenes by Hogarth—all for about $2.50 in black-and-white; color prints are $6 each. Also of interest is *Buck's Long View,* a set of five panoramic views of the Thames published in 1749 by the brothers Buck.

Historic Urban Plans, Box 276, Ithaca, NY 14850
Fully illustrated Historic City Plans and Views catalogue, $1. Historic American Maps and Urban Views, free.
Historical Urban Plans has bird's-eye views of American cities. These are nice reproductions of rare and expensive urban plans and prints. Most American cities are included and many European capitals too. Prices are $10 to $15 for each reproduction; some are colored, others black-and-white.

Postaprint, Taidswood, Sevenhills Road, Iver Heath, Bucks, SLO OPQ, England. Telephone 0895 833720
Catalogue, $3; air mail $5.
Reproductions of antique and mostly British engravings and maps. These are largely inexpensive (under $5) modern copies of classic English subjects—hunting scenes, views of town, ships and ports.

Vignari Art Enterprises, Box 355, 2 Main Street, Ogunquit, ME 03907. Telephone (207) 646 4450
40-page catalogue, $3 U.S. and overseas. MC, V.
People who are looking for pictures of the sea or ships are almost certain to find what they want in this catalogue compiled by marine artist John T. Vignari. There are reproductions of paintings by famous painters from Canaletto on, many of whom were not primarily marine artists but happened to paint a picture or two involving ships or sea.

3
BOOKS

1

2

3

1–3 Dover Publications

Blackwell's, Broad Street, Oxford OX1 3BQ, England
Specialized catalogues, free.
Blackwell's must be the world's most famous academic bookstore. Their stock allows them to fill almost any order on receipt; if not, the book is ordered from the publisher or the order is kept until the title shows up.

Books on Tape, P.O. Box 7900,
Newport Beach, CA 92660. Telephone 800 854 6758
Catalogue, free. MC, V.
Friends of mine enthusiastically recommend Books on Tape. She is a sculptress, he commutes by car, and now they are happily listening to Charles Dickens and William Shakespeare while they work and drive. Even if you eschew the classics, you can still enjoy the works of Irma Bombeck, Ellery Queen and other popular writers. Books last about eight to fourteen hours each, and rent for about $11 or $12 postpaid for thirty days.

CoEvolution Quarterly, P. O. Box 428,
Sausalito, CA 94966
608-page The Next Whole Earth Catalogue, $16 U.S. and overseas sea mail.
The updated version of the famous *Whole Earth Catalogue* is a fascinating and invaluable source of books and supplies. The *Catalogue* has information on almost six hundred different subjects, under general groupings such as "land use," "soft technology," "crafts," "community" and "politics." The entries, usually written by people who know a great deal about the subject, include practical advice, and a listing of the best sources of supply and books in that area. I find that whenever I develop a new interest (such as printing) or need (such as cheap airplane tickets) the *Whole Earth Catalogue* has amazingly useful information that no one else has. Almost all the recommended books can be bought by mail from The Whole Earth Household Store.

Dillon's University Bookshop, 1 Malet Street,
London WC1E 7JB, England. Telephone (01) 636 1577
Specialized catalogues, free. AE, MC, V.
Because of its location in the heart of London, near Russell Square, Dillon's is the one academic bookstore that most visitors may have happened to come across. There is a sense of excitement for any book lover in discovering Dillon's and finding that what looked like one store goes on and on, to cover several buildings, each housing departments that are complete stores in themselves. Here, one finds not just a complete stock of books but pamphlets, little magazines, teaching aids, etc. Dillon's stocks 75,000 new titles, besides maintaining a substantial second-hand department, and they too cover most academic fields with special strength in areas such as psychology, languages, education, history and the sciences.

Dover Publications, 180 Varick Street,
New York, NY 10014. Telephone (212) 255 3755
Catalogues: general, pictorial, archive, needlecraft, chess, children, music, nature, all free.
Dover, a publisher not a bookshop, began by reprinting as quality paperbacks important books in specialized fields. Their range has broadened, and as quality is still high and prices low (all their books are paperbacks), there is plenty to please every reader—arts, antiques, hobbies, travel, history, social protest, philosophy and religion, plus classic children's books and classic ghost and mystery stories.

Dover publishes novelties such as *Old Fashioned Christmas Cards for Hand Tinting, Decorative Labels for Home Canning, Preserving and Other Uses,* and *Cut and Assemble a Western Frontier Town,* and the world's largest collection of copyright-free art. Marvelous catalogues.

The Folio Society, 202 Great Suffolk Street, London SE1 1PR, England
MC, V.
The Folio Society specializes in illustrated and deluxe editions of previously published books, but it puts out a large number of titles itself. The society says it has a growing number of American subscribers and offers an American catalogue of its books, which cover a wide variety of areas. Most of the titles are classics just right for those seeking the kind of book that used to be available, for instance, in the illustrated Modern Library, but now much, much dearer.

The Good Book Guide, P.O. Box 400, Havelock Terrace, London SW8 4AU, England. Telephone (01) 622 1262
Subscription to five catalogues, $10 (refundable). AE, DC, MC, V.
Most of the Good Book Guide subscribers live in the Outer Hebrides, remote parts of Ireland and Wales, or even further from good English-language bookshops. The Good Book Guide is an exclusively mail-order bookstore started by two men who have lived in Africa and know how hard it is to find out about books, never mind buy them, in certain parts of the world. About a thousand general adult and children's books are in stock, and new additions are described in color catalogues published five times a year. What makes the catalogues useful is that the books sold are thoughtfully chosen, and fairly well described (often by an expert in the field), so that you can not only buy, but also keep informed, through the catalogue.

If you are a general reader and are not satisfied with the books and information about books now available to you, you should most certainly subscribe to the Good Book Guide. It does cost $10, but that is immediately returned to you in the form of a book token.

♣ ♣ Hatchard's, 187 Piccadilly, London W1V 9DA, England. ♣ Telephone (01) 439 9921
Catalogue, free. October. List of large-print books, free. AE, V.
If you want the latest British novel, mystery or gift book, they are most likely to have the book you want in stock. Their letter to me refers to hundreds of parcels that go to America each week, and their catalogue (illustrated) gives you a fair sample of the new and popular. Hatchard's also has an out-of-print department and a special stock of leather bindings; you can order any book to be bound in full or half leather. Hatchard's stocks and also special orders large-print books for the visually handicapped.

W. Heffer and Sons, 20 Trinity Street, Cambridge CB2 3NG, England. Telephone (0223) 358 351
Specialized price lists, free.
The major bookseller in Cambridge and also a leading international supplier. Heffer's issues a large list of specialized catalogues, covering just about any field, such as archaeology, management, chemistry, linguistics, etc.

The Scribner Bookstore, 597 Fifth Avenue, New York, NY 10017. Telephone (212) 486 4070
Catalogue, free. Available September to December only. AE, V.
Scribner's, one of New York's oldest and most invitingly bookish bookstores, publishes a catalogue for Christmas and will order any hardback book and the more expensive paperbacks. They will also search for out-of-print books.

Books in Special Fields

ALTERNATIVE TECHNOLOGY

Conservation Books, 228 London Road, Reading, Berkshire, RG6 1AH, England. Telephone 0734 663 281
Book list, free. MC, V.
The best source I've seen for books on conservation, ecology, resources, etc. listing many books and reports not available in the U.S. Practical as well as philosophical books, along with food and self-sufficiency titles. Recycled stationery, nature greeting cards and jigsaw puzzles also available.

ANTIQUES AND COLLECTIBLES

Collector's Shelf of Books, P.O. Box 6, Westfield, NY 14787. Telephone (716) 326 3676
Book list, free.
Specialists in new books on antiques and collectibles, this store offers a very complete choice, from netsuke to kitchen antiques.

Hotchkiss House, 18 Hearthstone Road, Pittsford, NY 14534. Telephone (716) 381 4735
8-page catalogue, free U.S. and overseas.
The Hotchkiss House catalogue is by far the most thorough compilation of books on antiques and other collectibles that I have seen. "Divided and Indexed into recognized categories of Antiques, Arts, Hobbies and Collecting."

ART

Art Catalogues, 8227 Santa Monica Boulevard, Los Angeles, CA 90046
Price list, $1; overseas $2. MC, V.
An excellent idea, now that catalogues are such an essential part of art publishing. This California store sells only museum, gallery and exhibition catalogues from the world over; more than twelve hundred listed in its current catalogue.

Hacker Art Books, 54 West 57th Street, New York, NY 10019. Telephone (212) 757 1450
Reprint and sale catalogues, semiannually, free. Rare-book and fine-binding catalogues, free.
Hacker's is one of New York's best art-book shops with an excellent stock not only of current titles but of old and rare books as well. If you know specifically what you want, Hacker's will try to find an unlisted title for you.

**Harmer Johnson Books, 667 Madison Avenue,
New York, NY 10021. Telephone (212) 752 1189**
Price list, free.
In- and out-of-print books on tribal and ancient art. Catalogues are available of books on ancient, African, Oceanic, pre-Columbian and American Indian art.

**Wittenborn and Company, 1018 Madison Avenue,
New York, NY 10021. Telephone (212) 288 1558**
Price list, free U.S. and overseas. MC, V.
Wittenborn is one of the country's best art-book shops; a marvelously crowded and endlessly tempting storehouse of art books from the world over. Wittenborn not only stocks books and periodicals from most publishers but also sells a number of special catalogues, many of which are unavailable elsewhere.

**A. Zwemmer, 76–80 Charing Cross Road,
London WC2H OBH, England. Telephone (01) 836 4710**
Price list, free.
Zwemmer's is probably London's best-known art-book store; it sells primarily new books and has an excellent stock of art books from all nations.

ASIA

**China Books and Periodicals, 2929–24 Street,
San Francisco, CA 94110. Telephone (415) 282 2994**
24-page catalogue, $1 U.S. and overseas.
For several years now, China Books and Periodicals has been a major source of materials from and about the People's Republic and the countries and movements associated with it. With interest in China taking a great leap forward, they have expanded their imports to include records, posters, wood-block prints, etc.

This exceptionally useful catalogue lists pages of titles on China today, over two pages of the writings of Chairman Mao (many of these published in English in China), as well as a very full selection of books on Chinese art, literature, philosophy, crafts, and practical books on learning the language and travel to China. The books imported from China are very inexpensive and include current novels, plays and children's books.

**The Dawn Horse Depot, P.O. Box 3680,
Clearlake, CA 95422. Telephone (707) 994 8281**
Catalogue, free. MC, V.
Dawn Horse specializes in "spiritual literature" and Asian religions, but nonetheless seems to practice Western efficiency with a monthly catalogue and a promise to fill all orders within three days of receipt. In addition to various books on spiritual literature from the world over, they have listings of traditional writings (Assisi, Theresa), Indian Classics, books for women and children, healing and health, yoga and exercise, a good selection of cookbooks, and even a selection of incense and religious articles (temple bells, altar cloths, conch shell trumpets and even Holy Cat oil, which is not what you might think but oil to be applied to sandalwood).

BELLES LETTRES

**The Gotham Book Mart, 41 West 47th Street,
New York, NY 10036. Telephone (212) 757 0367**
Various catalogues and price lists, free.
The Gotham Book Mart has long enjoyed a reputation as the country's leading literary bookstore, a place that not only sells serious fiction and poetry but acts as a gathering place for writers and a disseminator of their work. In the long run, this interest has paid off handsomely, since the store is now one of the few places in the country where one can find the small-press publications, the pamphlets and hand-printed booklets, the rare and out-of-print books where so many of America's major twentieth-century authors first appeared. Gotham also has a huge file of fifty thousand little magazines and periodicals, a thousand of which are listed in a current catalogue.

**The Phoenix Book Shop, 22 Jones Street,
New York, NY 10014. Telephone (212) 675 2794**
20–30-page listings, free; overseas air mail $2.
This very attractive bookstore in the midst of New York's old Greenwich Village specializes, as it should, in the books by the avant-garde writers of the twentieth century that made that area famous. A recent catalogue lists three hundred desirable books by T. S. Eliot and Ezra Pound, and their general catalogue ranges from Auden to Wilson. Prices are reasonable and the holdings extensive, particularly for lesser-known authors.

BUILDING

**The Building Bookshop, 26 Store Street,
London WC1E 7BT, England. Telephone (01) 637 3151**
32-page annual price list, free.
Catalogue, free. September. AE, MC.
The Building Bookshop, located in the Building Centre, is an exceptionally useful source of books for all those interested in the practical aspects of construction. Emphasis is on the technological, with a wide choice of engineering and other texts. There are selections of books on architecture and its history, but here again, the focus is relatively specific.

CHILDREN

**Baker Book Services, Little Mead, Alford Road,
Cranleigh, Surrey, GU6 8NU, England. Telephone (04) 866 5444**
Newsletter three times a year, annual subscription $5 (refundable).
The former owner of London's splendid Children's-Book Centre has set up a mail-order service, selling children's books to libraries and to private customers. They still issue their excellent newsletter on new children's books, which is, in effect, free, if you buy anything from them.

**Children's Book and Music Center,
2500 Santa Monica Boulevard, Santa Monica, CA 90404. Telephone (213) 829 0215**
Catalogue, $1; overseas $2. MC, V.
Books and records for infants to five-year-olds, all intended to teach children to cope with real-life situations (*Divorce Can Happen to the Nicest People, I Am Adopted, Why Did He Die?* and books on sex roles, and even safety and nutrition). Lots of basic skills and multicultural education books, and activity books and records. A useful catalogue of books and records not widely found in bookstores.

**Heffer's Children's Bookshop, 30 Trinity Street,
Cambridge CB2 1TB, England**
56-page annual catalogue, free.
This is now the best source for English-language children's books around. Though the store itself is relatively small, the

catalogue is comprehensive, with an excellent selection of hardcover and paperback books, in fiction and all categories of nonfiction. While English book prices have risen steeply in recent years, their paperbacks are still reasonable; in any case, there is no American competitor to this admirable catalogue.

Nursery Books, 4430 School Way, Castro Valley, CA 94546
Brochure and update flyers, $1 (refundable).
Sita Likuski sells picture books for *very* young children from her home. Books with non-tearing pages that can be wiped clean are suggested for babies of six months and up. A few informative books for parents are also listed. The books are inexpensive, and the adult books are in paperback versions.

Spoken Arts, P.O. Box 289, New Rochelle, NY 10802. Telephone (914) 636 5482
Catalogue, free; sea mail 70 cents; air mail $2.
A creditable collection of classic children's books on cassette, and sometimes on film too. Kate Greenaway, Ralph Caldecott, Rudyard Kipling and Mark Twain are all represented, and so are Richard Scarry, Dr. Seuss and other recent authors. Most sets are intended for schools and libraries, and are expensive (around $100) but there are small sets costing around $12, suitable for home and playgroup.

COMICS

Last Gasp Mail Order, 2180 Bryant Street, San Francisco, CA 94110. Telephone (415) 824 6636
Price list, $1 U.S. and overseas.
Underground comics including Zippy the Pinhead; posters; books on vegetarian cooking, ecology, drugs, etc. No descriptions, just titles.

Rip Off Press, P.O. Box 14158, San Francisco, CA 94114. Telephone (415) 863 5359
Leaflet, self-addressed stamped envelope; overseas air mail $1.
Underground comics and posters beloved of my daughter and others on campuses around the country.

West Side Comics, 107 West 86th Street, New York, NY 10024. Telephone (212) 724 0432
Price list, 50 cents; overseas $1.
New York, and I suspect the country, has seen a proliferation of stores selling old comics; West Side has over 100,000 in stock, which must make them one of the better sources. Here is history from the very first Spiderman at $500 to more recent items at under a dollar.

COOKBOOKS

Corner Cupboard Cookbooks, P.O. Box 171, Zionsville, IN 46077
Price list, free.
Here you can find the cookbooks that aren't in the bookstore, spiral-bound church and community books such as *Our Favorites:* seven hundred recipes from Amish and Mennonite women for $5.95; and *Favorite Recipes First Assembly of God* from Warren, Arkansas, for $6.95.

For more cookbooks, see Antiquarian section.

4 *Heffers Children's Bookshop* A small shop with a long list of available hardback and paperback books for children. Overseas accounts are accepted.

5 *Last Gasp* 1983 "Zippy the Pinhead" calendar, $5.95.

6 *Last Gasp* "Nation of Pinheads" T shirt, white on black, $9.95.

CRAFTS

**Museum Books, 48 East 43rd Street,
New York, NY 10017. Telephone (212) 682 0430**
Price list, free U.S. and overseas. MC, V.
Museum Books is the perfect store for anyone interested in
the applied arts. Though it has a large stock of books on art,
art history, design and graphic arts, its major appeal is the
great thoroughness with which it sells and lists books on the
various handicrafts. Its huge catalogue has entries for batik,
candlemaking, crewel embroidery, knitting, mosaics, rubbings, silkscreen, tatting and lacework, toys and dolls and
woodworking, just to list a few.

**The Unicorn, Box 645, Rockville, MD 20851.
Telephone (301) 881 4770**
Price list, $1 U.S. and overseas. MC, V.
The Unicorn has an extensive list of books for anyone
involved in the fiber crafts—embroiderers, fabric decorators,
lacemakers, weavers, spinners and dyers. Listings contain
good, informative reviews of the books on sale.

ESOTERICA

**Watkins Bookshop, 19–21 Cecil Court,
Charing Cross Road, London WC2N 4HB, England.
Telephone 01 836 2182**
Located just off the major theatrical second-hand-book area
in London, Watkins represents a vast enclave of esoterica
and fascinating expertise. Here is that unique English blend
of magic and religion, of psychology and alchemy, of the
erudite and the exotic, including a variety of titles in various
religions, serious works in psychology, as well as a selection
of their vast stock of books on alchemy, cabala, tarot, occult-
ism, diet and health, and "astrology, palmistry, graphology,
numerology and allied subjects."

FILM

**Cine Books, 692A Yonge Street, Toronto, Canada.
Telephone (416) 964 6476**
Price list, free. AE, MC, V.
This firm specializes in books and related materials on the
film in all its aspects and has already developed a large
American clientele. In addition to books, they stock sound
tracks, posters, magazines and 8-mm films.

FRENCH AND SPANISH

**French and Spanish Book Corporation,
115 Fifth Avenue, New York, NY 10003.
Telephone (212) 673 7400**
*French Books catalogue, $2.95; overseas $5. Spanish Books
catalogue, $2.95; overseas $5. AE, DC, MC, V.*
Many tourists have passed by the windows of this French
bookstore in Rockefeller Center, to see the latest French
bestsellers and fashion magazines displayed there, but the
main business of this store is supplying schools and universities throughout the country. Their catalogues, geared to the
teaching of French and Spanish, are very thorough and
impressive.

GARDENING AND AGRICULTURE

**Brooklyn Botanic Garden, 1000 Washington Avenue,
Brooklyn, NY 11225. Telephone (212) 622 4433**
Book list, free.
Very good gardening handbooks are published by the Bo-
tanic Garden, and cost around $2 each. Subjects range from
general introductions and advice for the complete beginner
(*Home Lawn Handbook:* "How to grow a fine lawn with a
minimum of frustration—and crabgrass") to rarified subjects
such as *Knot and Fragrant Gardens, Community Gardens in
American Cities,* and *Origins of American Horticulture.*

**International Scholarly Book Service, P.O. Box 1632,
Beaverton, OR 97075**
Catalogue, free.
A catalogue (and a bookstore some ten minutes outside of
Portland) specializing in horticultural, botanical, agricultural, landscaping and forestry books. An American entry in a
field largely dominated by the British, this catalogue is
strongest in practical books for both the amateur gardener
and the professional.

**Landsmans Bookshop, Buckenhill, Bromyard,
Herefordshire, England. Telephone Bromyard 3420**
116-page list, $1; air mail $2.
The most comprehensive listing that I've seen on farming,
gardening and forestry. Over one hundred tightly packed
pages of one-line entries, close to a page on orchids, the
same on drainage, etc. No illustrations or color, just the bare
essentials.

**The Royal Horticultural Society, RHS Garden,
Wisley, near Ripley, Woking, Surrey, England.
Telephone Ripley 2163**
Leaflet, free.
England's venerable garden and research society has a renowned horticultural library and a 100-year-old garden.
Those unable to make it to Wisley may find the Society's
booklist a good substitute. It includes its own publications as
well as a broad range of general and specialized gardening
books and handbooks. An excellent source for advanced
books, whether on plant propagation or greenhouse operation.

GENEALOGY

**Heraldry Today, 10 Beauchamp Place,
London SW3, England. Telephone (01) 584 1656**
Catalogues of new and old books sent free; air mail $8.
This store is both a publisher of new books on heraldry and
genealogy and dealer in a wide range of older books on the
subject. "A great many American clients" are particularly
interested in tracing their own ancestors, but the store adds
that "we are not a reference library and our books are
purely for sale."

GERMAN

**Marga Schoeller Bucherstube, Knesebeckstr.
33 (Ecke Mommsenstr.), 1000 Berlin 12,
West Germany. Telephone (030) 881 1112**
This is a bookstore which over the years has come to supply
customers all over the world. While not specializing in mail
orders, as does Van Stockum, they do periodically mail their
customers lists of new titles in such fields as literary criti-
cism, history, education, sociology, psychology, etc.

INTERIOR DECORATION

**The Furniture Library, 1009 North Main Street,
High Point, NC 27262**
Booklist, free.
This four-thousand-volume collection is primarily a research library devoted to the history of furniture. It does, however, issue a list of books on all aspects of furniture, decorating and design, which it sells by mail.

MAPS AND TRAVEL

**Forsyth Travel Library, 9154 West 57th Street,
P.O. Box 2975, Shawnee Mission, KS 66201.
Telephone (913) 384 0496**
Booklist, 25 cents. MC, V.
Travel books, maps and guides, from maps of the major American cities to original editions of all the Baedeker guides published between 1880 and 1939. An invaluable, wide range of books includes guides to cheap guest houses in Canada and New England, sources of free travel information, and guides to buying property and retiring abroad. Books to solve most travel problems, and to suggest interesting new holidays.

**Edward Stanford, 12–14 Long Acre,
London WC2, England. Telephone (01) 836 1321**
List of recommended maps for any one area in the world, free.
International Maps and Atlases in Print (Bowkers), $37.50.
The largest and best-known map retailers in the world can solve any map problem put to them. Modern maps of every kind: road maps for tourists, town plans, geological and thematic maps, maps for sales and educational purposes and maps printed to order. Also magnetic maps, maps mounted on board or cloth to order, maps dissected for the pocket, atlases, globes and guide books.

**Vacation Exchange Club, 350 Broadway,
New York, NY 10013. Telephone (212) 966 2576**
218-page catalogue, February. 60-page catalogue, April, $12 for both; overseas, ask for the address of your nearest affiliate. No catalogue available November-January.
A big catalogue listing people mostly in America, but also in other countries, who want to swap homes for a holiday; if you buy the catalogue, you can be listed too. The listed people all sound reassuringly responsible, professions are mentioned and sound thoroughly respectable, homes sound thoroughly desirable. The Vacation Exchange people say that the happiest subscribers are those who are flexible about places and times they can go. The illustrated catalogue is very well done, mainly by dedicated amateurs, who believe in the idea; it makes exciting reading, and has plenty of sensible advice. Two retired teachers who have been on *forty-eight* exchanges around the world give their impression: "Relax . . . your house is safer with people in it, and think of all the money you are saving." Very tempting.

**Walking News, P.O. Box 352, Canal Street Station,
New York, NY 10013**
Leaflet, self-addressed stamped envelope; overseas 1 International Reply Coupon.
A useful list for walkers and hikers; maps and guides covering the United States and the rest of the world (three different Nepal trail guides, for instance). Mountain craft, canoeing and bicycling books as well.

**Wide World Bookshop, 401 NE 45th Street,
Seattle, WA 98105. Telephone (206) 634 3453**
Price list, free U.S. and overseas.
I really like this short list of travel guides and maps, which mentions the strong points of each guide. It has plenty of books for the impecunious traveler with a genuine interest in the countries he is visiting.

MUSIC

**Martin Brinser, Books on Music, 643 Stuyvesant Avenue,
Irvington, NJ 07111**
Booklist, free. Minimum order, $15.
Over one thousand titles, which Brinser says is the largest selection available in the United States. Includes a large number of British imports.

MYSTERY

**Marjon Books, 16 Mannering Gardens,
Westcliff-on-sea, Essex SSO OBQ, England.
Telephone 0702 47119**
Booklist, free.
This English bookstore specializes in detective fiction, new and second-hand. Books are all hardcover; I could find nothing under $5—mostly recent books, though, many in their first editions. Westcliff is less than an hour from London and visitors are invited for a cup of tea, but asked to call first.

**Murder Ink, 271 West 87th Street, New York, NY 10024.
Telephone (212) 362 8905**
Information, self-addressed stamped envelope; overseas 1 International Reply Coupon.
Carol Brenner has no catalogue but sends her in-print and out-of-print mysteries (and variants on the theme) all over the world. Send her a stamped self-addressed envelope and she'll send you a photocopy letter describing her system of want lists.

**The Mysterious Bookshop, 129 West 56th Street,
New York, NY 10019. Telephone (212) 765 0900**
Booklist, free U.S. and overseas. DC, MC, V.
Another source for new mysteries, hardcover or paperbound. This store issues a short list filled with gift suggestions, but can fill orders for any current titles.

NATURAL HISTORY

**Wheldon & Wesley, Lytton Lodge, Codicote, Hitchin,
Hertfordshire SG4 8TE, England**
Catalogue, free.
This firm specializes in books on natural history, and the catalogue is the most thorough in that field that I have seen. Primarily specialists in old books, theirs is a much more general list with the greatest strength in zoology and botany. They are also agents for the Natural History section of the British Museum and stock a number of the museum's publications now out of print.

PERIODICALS

**European Publishers Representatives,
11–03 46th Avenue, Long Island City, NY 11101.
Telephone (212) 937 4606**
Price lists, free.
Through this firm you can subscribe to most European magazines and newspapers. When writing for lists, specify the language and fields you are interested in. Many areas (literature and the arts, sports, hobbies, business, youth, home, fashion, etc.) are covered, and many papers and magazines not listed can be supplied.

PHOTOGRAPHY

**International Center for Photography,
1130 Fifth Avenue, New York, NY 10028.
Telephone (212) 860 1767**
16-page catalogue, $1; overseas air mail $3.
New York's new photography musuem now offers a useful list of photography books from all publishers, which includes some hard-to-find catalogues and other publications, as well as a selection of posters, some signed by the photographer.

POLITICS

**Freedom Bookshop, 84B Whitechapel High Street
(in Angel Alley), London E1, England**
Price list, 1 International Reply Coupon.
This famous anarchist bookshop is crammed with old books, many of them published earlier in the century. Here is most of what Kropotkin wrote or *Mother Jones' Autobiography* or Shelley's *Mask of Anarchy*. Ironically, many of the books are available in American paperback reissues, but there is still much here that would be difficult to obtain elsewhere.

**Hammersmith Books, Barnes High Street,
London SW13, England. Telephone (01) 876 7254**
Price list, free.
Hammersmith Books' letterhead simply says, "Scarce literature on social economic movements, Afro-Asian-Soviet Affairs, War, Revolution and Peace," and their catalogues live up to that comprehensive heading. Their latest, on the Middle East, includes a wide range of material meticulously annotated and reasonably priced.

RUSSIAN

**Four Continents Book Corporation, 149 Fifth Avenue,
New York, NY 10010. Telephone (212) 533 0250**
Price lists of books in English, sociopolitical books in Russian, Soviet periodicals and reference works, slides, film strips and facsimiles, free. MC, V.
For years Four Continents has been importing books, magazines and other materials from the Soviet Union, and it is the major American source of published works in Russian and the other languages used in the U.S.S.R. Soviet LPs are also available, featuring both contemporary and classical music, as well as a number of readings of plays, verse and prose.

**Imported Publications, 320 West Ohio Street,
Chicago, IL 60610**
68-page catalogue, free. MC, V.
A rival to Four Continents, this is an alternative source for

7

7 *International Center for Photography* The poster "Berlin Dancer" by Lotte Jacobi. Signed, $45; unsigned, $8.

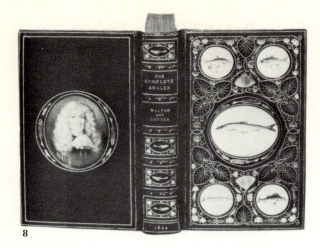

8

9

all publications from the Soviet Union. This catalogue is better but it lists only titles in English (and some in Spanish).

SCIENCE FICTION

The Science Fiction Shop, 56 Eighth Avenue, New York, NY 10014. Telephone (212) 741 0270
Booklist, free U.S. and Canada; elsewhere $1. MC, V.
This bookstore, shaped like a rocket ship, startled even blasé New Yorkers and has taken off very successfully. Their list includes both the latest hardcover and paperback titles, but the store attempts to stock everything in print in its field.

SECOND-HAND BOOKS

Strand Book Store, 828 Broadway, New York, NY 10003. Telephone (212) 473 1452
Price lists in most categories, free.
The Strand is probably New York's best-known used-book store—the largest, I believe, of the old Fourth Avenue stores—which stocks, as its ads proudly proclaim, over a million volumes. The Strand is best known for selling unwanted reviewers' copies, and the tables at the front are filled with brand-new books at half price. These new books are not listed in the Strand's catalogues, but their lists do cover just about every field of interest, and you can write in and ask for what they have, be it literature, Americana, etc.

THEATER

Drama Book Specialists, 821 Broadway, New York, NY 10003. Telephone (212) 228 3400
Catalogue, free.
This firm primarily offers its own publications, of interest to those in the theater world: specialized books on acting, voice, the business of the theater, etc. However, they also list a selection of records, cassettes and vocal scores published by others and a number of full-color toy theaters.

TRANSPORT

Chater & Scott, 8 South Street, Isleworth, Middlesex TW7 7BG, England. Telephone (01) 568 9750
28-page catalogue, 25 cents and self-addressed stamped envelope; air mail $1.
"All new and second-hand books on transport," it says on the letterhead, but the firm's real strength is in books on motor vehicles. Their catalogue, *The World of Motoring*, lists new as well as old books and has helpful sections on remainders and new titles. The firm has a strong line of books on American cars as well as some more out-of-the-way listings on Australian and South African cars.

Motor Books, 33 St. Martins Court, St. Martins Lane, London WC2, England
Railway, automotive, aviation and military lists, 60 cents. MC, V.
Very complete, but very brief, entries for the specialists in the above fields.

8 *J. N. Bartfield Books* A fine exhibition binding, done entirely by hand, of the fishing classic, *The Compleat Angler*.

9 *J. N. Bartfield Books* Old hand-colored color-plate books, including works by John Gould, the British ornithologist.

TRANSPORTATION

**Antheil Booksellers, 2177 Isabelle Court,
No. Bellmore, NY 11710**
32-page catalogue, $2 for four annual catalogues.
Antheil deals exclusively by mail, having a stock of some ten thousand volumes, specializing in books on maritime subjects but also stocking some books on aviation and military subjects. The books are, for the most part, out of print and come from all over the world.

**The Aviation Bookshop, 656 Holloway Road,
London N19 3PD, England**
36-page price list, free; air mail $1. MC, V.
This store thinks it is the only one in the world devoted exclusively to aviation and is obviously a prime source for those interested in airplanes, whether real or model. The shop's list is international and includes magazines, plans, charts, photos, prints, and modeling books and periodicals.

WOMEN

**Womanbooks, 201 West 92nd Street,
New York, NY 10025. Telephone (212) 873 4121**
Price list, self-addressed stamped envelope; overseas 1 International Reply Coupon.
A wide range of books for and about women, from popular biographies, through childrearing, to specialized books on law and history. Many books from small presses.

**Woman's Place Bookstore, 2401 North 32nd Street,
Phoenix, AZ 85008**
20-page booklist twice yearly, 60 cents in stamps; overseas $2.
A long, though not comprehensive, offering of books of interest to feminists and lesbians. Strong on theory and fiction, weaker in the arts and other fields. Also includes children's books, records, buttons and a bimonthly update.

Antiquarian Books

**J. N. Bartfield Books, 45 West 57th Street, New York,
NY 10019. Telephone (212) 753 1830**
104-page catalogue, $1 (refundable).
According to Bartfield's, one of New York's finest dealers in rare books, it has "probably the most select and largest collection of fine bindings in the country, if not the world," and furthermore, its prices are "at least 15-percent lower" than the fine-book departments of the leading bookstores.

**N. V. Boekhandel & Antiquariaat B. M. Israel,
N. Z. Voorburgwal 264, Amsterdam, Holland**
Various price lists, averaging 100 pages each, on different subjects.
B. M. Israel's catalogues are among the most impressive I have seen in the field of rare books. His specialties, to quote him, are "Medicine, Old Sciences, Old Technology, Geography" as well as manuscripts, autographs, illustrated books, etc. The price lists are in English, though the books listed are, of course, in various languages.

**Paul Breman, 1 Rosslyn Hill, London NW3 5UL,
England. Telephone 01 435 7730**
Catalogue, free.
A series of very handsome catalogues specializing in the widest range of illustrated books, not just on art and architecture but technology, gardens, warfare, costumes, advertising and anything else that you can think of that used images and illustrations.

**Janet Clarke Antiquarian Books, 3 Woodside Cottage,
Freshford, Bath BA3 6EJ, England.
Telephone 022 122 3186**
Price list, free.
Fine old cookbooks as well as books on wine and related subjects. Some of the older, eighteenth-century items can cost in the hundreds of pounds, but prices decline noticeably after 1900.

**CooksBooks, 34 Marine Drive, Rottingdean,
Sussex BN2 7HQ, England**
Price list, free.
A very comprehensive and interesting selection of books, reasonably priced. Eliza Acton's 1860 classic, 643 pages including eight engraved plates, and less famous, modern works. A sizable section of foreign books, largely French.

**Francis Edwards, 83 Marylebone High Street,
London W1M 4AL, England**
Catalogues, free. AE, DC, V.
Very satisfactory specialized catalogues in a number of classic fields of interest in which England has always excelled, such as military books, voyages, and travels. Mostly older books, and including such items as autograph letters, etc.

**Arthur H. Minters, 84 University Place,
New York, NY 10003. Telephone (212) 989 0593**
Bimonthly price list, $2; overseas $18 for a year (6 issues). MC, V.
Specialists in the history of art and architecture as well as literature, this New York bookseller has a wide selection of old books, primarily out of print, for collectors. An expensive but thorough catalogue.

**Bernard Quaritch, 5–8 Lower John Street,
Golden Square, London W1V 6AB, England**
This shop specializes in the publications of various learned societies and is an excellent source for the reports of everyone from the British Museum to the Royal Horticultural Society. Some of these items are reprints, others cover the original output of such diverse groups as the Egypt Exploration Society or the Librairie du Liban.

**Justin G. Schiller, 36 East 61st Street,
New York, NY 10021. Telephone (212) 832 8231**
Black-and-white catalogue, $10 U.S. and overseas.
A rich stock of old children's books for collectors and libraries. The current catalogue lists some five hundred items from the world over.

**Henry Sotheran, 2–5 Sackville Street, Piccadilly,
London W1X 2DP, England. Telephone (01) 734 1150**
Catalogue, $1; air mail $2.
One of London's oldest booksellers (established 1761), this shop specializes in early antiquarian books, including colorplate works, especially in natural history. They also stock old bindings of standard authors, letters, maps and old views of British scenery.

**Charles W. Traylen, Castle House, 49–50 Quarry Street,
Guilford, England**
2 catalogues, free; air mail $2.
This store specializes in its own reprints of old prints, maps

10   11

12   13

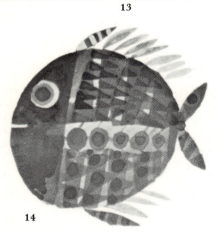

14

10 *The Evergreen Press* Masked dancer appearing at the shrine of the god Pan. Bookplate made for Winifred Knight.

11 *The Evergreen Press* Bookplate made for Stephen Cleveland before 1800.

12 *The Evergreen Press* Bookplate with sixteenth-century engraving.

13 *The Evergreen Press* Kate Greenaway's design for Miss Hannah Jane Locker Lampson's bookplate, circa 1898.

14 *The Evergreen Press* Full-color bookplate.

and scholarly works (such as Ackerman prints) reissued at very reasonable prices, as well as having an extensive stock of out-of-print titles, particularly of the classic English interests in sport, travel, natural history, naval and military history, and theology.

The Wine and Food Library, 1207 West Madison Street, Ann Arbor, MI 48103
32-page price list, $2 U.S. and overseas.
A very full list, ranging from 1500 to the present. From old Fanny Farmer editions to first editions of Escoffier, this famous bookstore stocks some ten thousand volumes. The books are not inexpensive but for the collector, a prime American source.

Charles B. Wood, III, South Woodstock, CT 06267
Large, extensively illustrated catalogues, up to 128 pages, $7.50; overseas $9.
Wood's catalogues are among the most thorough and elaborate; whether on books on the sciences or architecture, or photography, they are careful and well researched and worth having in their own right.

Book Plates

The Evergreen Press, P.O. Box 4971, Walnut Creek, CA 94596. Telephone (415) 825 7850
12-page color catalogue, free; overseas $1.
Evergreen Press publishes a gorgeous collection of bookplates. They have both beautifully colored modern plates designed by artists in various countries and elegant reproductions of old plates designed for or by famous people.

DISCOUNT
Please see information on buying at a discount in the How to Buy section.

Barnes and Noble, 126 Fifth Avenue, New York, NY 10011. Telephone (212) 620 7435
72-page color catalogue, free. AE, MC, V.
The famous discount and remainder book chain issues a very useful catalogue of discounted bestsellers and other books remaindered. Most books these days seem to end up on the remainder table and these selections are certainly comprehensive and catholic, including many scholarly as well as imported titles. Barnes and Noble will order any book, hardback or paperback. There is also a selection of bargain classical records at very low prices.

Edward R. Hamilton, 98 Clapboard Ridge, Danbury, CT 06810
Price list, free.
Edward R. Hamilton has the best quality and selection of the remainder houses. I am on their mailing list and seem to end up, somewhat against my will, buying several books from each catalogue I make the mistake of reading. Knockdown prices.

Publishers Central Bureau, 1 Champion Avenue, Avenel, NJ 07131
66-page catalogue, free.
You probably get this without writing for it; it's one of the most widely mailed lists in the country. Still, this vast listing of remaindered books and cheap records is worth looking at. More downmarket than others, it still has an exceptional choice of bargain records of classical and popular music.

4
CHRISTMAS AND OTHER CELEBRATIONS

1

2

1 *Arabelle Creations* Eight boxed Christmas cards, $5.95.

2 *Library of Congress* (see Museum Section) A lithograph by Currier and Ives, 1895, with color added. Twelve cards, $4.

Cards

Arabelle Creations, Box 5094 Main Station, Westport, CT 06881
Leaflet, free; overseas $1.
An 1880 French doll, Arabelle, and 1910 teddy bears are photographed enacting suitable scenes for greeting cards. On the "get well," Arabelle takes the bear's temperature; on the "Easter," she is surrounded by rabbits; and for birthdays and Christmas there are merry gatherings.

Current, Box 2559, Colorado Springs, CO 80901. Telephone (303) 471 4910
72-page color catalogue, free U.S. and overseas.
Cards, writing papers, wrapping paper, calendars in all sorts of styles, mostly colorful and cheerful featuring flowers and lovable animals. Also good ideas like ornaments to color (in the Christmas catalogue) and organizers for coupons and recipes.

Impress, Slough Farms, Westhall, Halesworth, Suffolk, P19 SRN, England. Telephone 098 681
Price list, $1. V.
Blank cards, gift tags and calendars for people who want to make their own. Also special cards, supplies and wild-flower seeds for flower pressing.

Kokopelli Press, P.O. Box 33666, Phoenix, AZ 85067
Leaflet, free U.S. and overseas.
Kokopelli Press produces note cards and postcards with pictures of American Indians or adapted American Indian designs by modern artists. The cards are of good quality and are quite sophisticated. Hill, owner of the press, says that they are bought by American Indian and Southwest buffs, but they might also appeal to people interested in American life.

Leanin' Tree, Box 9500, Boulder, CO 80301. Telephone (303) 530 1442
24-page color catalogue, free U.S. and overseas. MC, V.
Cards for all occasions, calendars, wrapping paper and even Christmas tree ornaments, with Western and/or wildlife scenes. Wagons, homesteads and buffalo in the snow are most popular, but there are also ski and old Norman Rockwell cards.

The Printery House of Conception Abbey, Conception, MO 64433. Telephone (816) 944 2331
32-page color catalogue, free U.S. and overseas. MC, V.
Bright colors with modern designs and religious, inspirational and sentimental messages such as "Love Is Friendship Set to Music." Cards for just about every occasion, gathered into groups such as "Memories of Friendship," "Gratitude," "Comfort," "Hope" and many more.

UNICEF, 331 East 38th Street, New York, NY 10016. Telephone (212) 686 5522
Holiday cards brochure, free. Fall only. MC, V.
The best-known UNICEF products are the bright Christmas cards, which UNICEF calls "holiday" cards, as they have rather general messages inside like "Peace on Earth" and "Season's Greetings," which will offend the sensibilities of only the most ardent hawks and atheists. But as well as the "holiday" cards there is a small but very pretty collection of cards for gifts, invitations, baby announcements and thank-you notes. There are also some books and games for children and an appointment calendar. The money earned

3

4

5

3 *Puckihuddle Products* (see House Section) Fabric angel ornament decorated with ribbons and lace, $12.

4 *Museum of the City of New York Shop* (see Museum Section) Edwardian gift boxes. A set of four in different sizes, $12.

5 *Oy Stockmann* (see General Section) Wooden bells in red-stained and natural pine.

by these cards and gifts goes to UNICEF programs: emergency relief and rehabilitation, and also long-range programs in child nutrition, disease eradication, and education in developing countries.

Most museum catalogues have cards and calendars; many have wrapping paper and Christmas decorations.

Decorations

Les Ateliers Marcel Corbonel, 84–86 Rue Grignan, 13001 Marseille, France. Telephone 54 26 58
Color leaflet, free.
The famous *santons* of Provence, like other crèches, started with St. Francis of Assisi and developed in the Middle Ages. But it is only to the southern French ones that at the end of the eighteenth century were added all the local village characters who remain traditionally dressed in the clothes of that time. Marcel Carbonel makes *santons* in brightly colored painted but unglazed clay (they are rather fragile). Figures cost $4 to $8 each depending on size, but his minimum order is $250, so you either have to buy buildings and practically a whole village, or buy with friends.

The Christmas Branch, 511 Highland Avenue, Oak Park, IL 60304. Telephone (312) 383 7462
Leaflet, free; overseas, $1. MC, V.
Donna Podmajerski paints wooden Christmas tree ornaments. Most of her ornaments are babies or children engaged in sporting activities, on which she paints a baby's or child's name. She'll even add freckles, or put team colors on sports clothes on request.

Klods Hans, 34 Hans Jensensstraede, DK-5000 Odense, C, Denmark
14-page brochure, $1. Prices in $.
A neat and appealing little brochure showing handmade decorations for Christmas: star, elf and angel tree decorations; choirboy candlesticks, musical angels, pottery elves and snowy cottages; mobiles, wall hangings and calendars (one cotton calendar has twenty-four little girls with pockets in their aprons for small gifts).

For Easter there are hand-painted wooden eggs, chicks, rabbits and candlesticks, and wooden mobiles; and for any other time lots of little things that are bound to please children: face egg cups with hat cozies, tiny ceramic animals and a wall hanging with a removable doll. For adults: brass candlesticks and oil lamps, and Royal Copenhagen figurines.

G. G. Lang sel. Erben, P.O. Box 28, 8103 Oberammergau, Germany. Telephone 0882 508
Nativity brochure, $2. In German.
Main catalogue, $8. In German.
Wood carving has been a traditional craft in the mountain village of Oberammergau ever since the middle of the seventeenth century, and before the days of catalogues, traders would carry a *Kraxen*, a wooden frame, on their backs to foreign trading centers, displaying the carvings for sale as they walked. "The Woodcarving Workshops of G. G. Lang's Heirs" was started in the late eighteenth century and is still producing hand-carved sacred and "profane" (as they put it) works from native German woods. Probably their best-known works are their crèches, where single figures or groups can be bought in plain wood, painted or even dressed in fabric clothes. These are "heirloom" crèches, perhaps to be gradually assembled if you like them but the prices daunt you—a set with figures and crèche in natural wood costs just under $300.

**Annalee's Gift Shop, Box 869, Meredith, NH 03253.
Telephone (603) 279 6543**
20-page color catalogue, 50 cents. MC, V.
Annalee's bashful felt animals are supplanted at Christmas
by gaggles of ho-ho-hoing Father Christmas and mob-
capped wife, doing all sorts of cheery things. Angels with
toothy grins and long eyelashes, and giraffes ridden by elves
will also add to a Christmassy scene. Recommended by Dale
Meyer, owner of Charing Cross Kits (Clothes section).

**Paradise Products, P.O. Box 568, El Cerrito, CA 94530.
Telephone (415) 524 8300**
*72-page color catalogue, $2 U.S. and overseas; air mail $6.
BA, MC.*
"America's party host" sells supplies for parties. There are
kits, and sometimes even food for parties with themes ranging from Easter, Halloween, Thanksgiving and Christmas,
through regional American themes such as Western Chuck
Wagon, Mardi Gras and Night on the Delta Queen, to
Hawaiian (for the Hawaiian you can have fresh flowers
flown in), Mexican, German, Parisienne and Italian, or
miscellaneous (Roaring Twenties, Gay Nineties, etc.). Costumes, makeup, hats (specially printed if you like), masks,
beards, mustaches, wigs, streamers, blowers, etc., are also
sold, and although goods aren't exactly in the best of taste,
there are oddities like gold and silver balloons ($4 a dozen)
which would be very popular at children's parties.

**Schweizer Heimatwerk, Heimethuus,
Rudolf Brun-Bruke, 8023 Zurich, Switzerland**
*Catalogue, free. In German. Available all year, price list
revised each October.*
The official Swiss handicraft center has a catalogue for their
hand-carved wooden Christmas nativity sets. The sets are
expensive but are of high quality. It is extremely hard to
find crèches of similar quality in the United States, and of
course the ornaments will last for many generations.

Twenty-two different sets are illustrated in the catalogue
and include several styles, from graceful modern ones in raw
wood, where features are merely hinted at, and mood is
expressed through shape and posture, to painted traditional
styles. Sets vary in size, with from twelve to fifty-six pieces,
and prices vary from about $24 for Jesus in his crib in one
set, to $118 for Mary with Jesus in painted wood in another
set.

**Shopping International, Department 523,
Norwich, VT 05055. Telpehone 800 451 4371**
*Shopping International, World of Fashion, World of Christ-
mas (October), $1 each U.S. and overseas. AE, MC, V.*
Shopping International publishes several catalogues of imported clothes and gifts throughout the year, but my favorite
is the October *World of Christmas*. In it there are imported
toys and lots of decorations: candle-lit carousels from Germany, crèches from Poland and Spain, glass Christmas trees
from Italy, straw wreaths from Mexico and Christmas tree
decorations from just about everywhere.

**Unicorn Glass Workshops, Tooses Farm, Stoke St.
Michael, Bath BA3 5JJ, England.
Telephone Oakhill 840 654**
Color brochure, free.
Nice, simple and colorful stained-glass Christmas ornaments
to hang in the window: an angel, a bell, a star and a nativity
scene. Prices about $20 to $30 each. Also stylized birds,
flowers and hearts, which can be inscribed with a message
and a beloved's name.

6

7

8

9

6 *Klods Hans* Paper mobile of six angels. About $6.

7 *Klods Hans* Christmas tree star. Straw decorations in several
shapes cost under $1 each. (*Photographs by Gunner Larsen.*)

8 *Klods Hans* Hand-painted wooden elves with knitted caps. About
$6 for both.

9 *Green Tiger Press* (see Toy Section) Decorating the Christmas
tree, by Palmer Cox. From *The Brownies at Home.*

5
CIGARS, PIPES AND TOBACCO

Cigars

Davidoff et Cie, 2 Rue de Rive, 1204 Geneva, Switzerland. Telephone 022 2890 41
List of Cuban cigars, in French, free.
Davidoff et Cie is best known for its Cuban cigars. In fact, one line of Cuban cigars is named after the owner: Davidoff's Nos. 1 and 2, about $50 for twenty-five 6-inch cigars. Owing to U.S. government restrictions, Cuban cigars aren't allowed into the country, so if they are found being imported, they are confiscated. I understand that many Americans ignore these restrictions, which is actually illegal.

Alfred Dunhill of London, 11 East 26th Street, New York, NY 10010. Telephone (212) 481 6900
40-page color catalogue, $4. (Catalogue valid September-December only) AE, MC, V.
The New York branch of Dunhill, posh English tobacconist, produces a glossy catalogue of gifts. Cigars are available on the "diary plan," with correctly aged cigars delivered weekly or monthly; and on the "contract" plan where cigars are kept under "ideal" conditions in a humidor, until the customer wants them delivered.

But the Dunhill catalogue is mostly full of humidors, expensive pens, leather wallets, desk sets, drinking flasks, and other goodies aimed to please their high-living, cigar-smoking customers.

Nat Sherman, 711 Fifth Avenue, New York, NY 10022. Telephone (212) 751 9100
36-page color catalogue, free U.S. and overseas. AE, DC, MC, V.
Sherman is best known for his gimmickry in selling tobacco; cigars and cigarettes with your name imprinted on them or on their box, cigarettes that are extra-long or come in fifteen different colors. But the search for something different has also led Sherman to develop cigarettes without any additives and cigars that are particularly mild. In addition, Sherman has a wide stock of regular cigars.

DISCOUNT
Please see information on buying at a discount in the How to Buy section.

Buying cigars at a discount seems to me an easy and sensible thing to do. I have checked prices of the best brands at these two firms and found that they are about 30 percent below the prices at nondiscount firms. This means Dunhills at a few dollars below Dunhill's own prices and savings of up to $11 per dozen on other cigars.

Famous Smoke Shop, 1450 Broadway, Department CC, New York, NY 10018. Telephone (212) 221 1408
Price list, free.
Famous publishes a thorough list of brand-name cigars with the sizes thoughtfully listed, and they have recently added tobaccos. They sell at really good discount prices, and although they don't accept credit cards ("Just an extra overhead that we would have to build into our prices, as our competition does"), they welcome charge accounts (ask for a credit form). Mr. Zaretsky, president, says that anyone who mentions *The International Catalogue of Catalogues* will get a coupon worth three TE AMO cigars. (Is that all I'm worth?) Established 1936, in mail order since 1978.

J R Tobacco, Tuxedo Square, Tuxedo, NY 10987.
Telephone 800 431 2380
40-page catalogue free, U.S. and abroad. AE, MC, V.
(C.O.D. within the U.S.)
This tobacconist has been widely written up in the press.
Showy Lew Rothman, the president, says, "Why we have
gained notoriety is simple; it is because: One: We sell the
widest variety of cigars in this or any other country. Two:
We ship the same day. Three: We treat our customers like
people. Four: We give everyone their money's worth."
Prices on brand-name cigars are consistently low. J R also
offers their own similar substitutes for well-known cigars.
"Trust us! We'll send you a comparable cigar" at about half
the price of the originals. Established 1972.

Pipes and Tobacco

Astley's, 109 Jermyn Street, London S.W. 1, England.
Telephone (01) 930 1687
18-page catalogue, $1; air mail $2. AE, DC, V.
"You shall avoid all evil company, and all occasions which
may tend to draw you to the same; and make speedy return
when you shall be sent on your master's or mistress's er-
rand," apprentice pipemakers were instructed in the seventeenth century. Astley's pipe shop displays the original document along with famous and not-famous antique pipes, some
of which are for sale. However, their catalogue shows just
their well-known briar pipes and explains the distinctive
characteristics of each one. Prices, including postage, vary
between $30 for their Crusty and Atlantic briars and $100
for Super Straight grained briars. Lots of shapes are shown,
and there is a pageful of unusual designs with a pipe made
out of briar root. Also available are meerschaum pipes,
special tobacco blends, pipe cases, tobacco pouches, smokers'
knives and a repair service by mail for pipes of any make.

Georgetown Tobacco and Pipe Stores,
3144 M Street, Washington DC 20007.
Telephone (202) 338 5100
Catalogue, 50 cents; overseas air mail $2. AE, MC, V.
Georgetown does an international mail-order business, supplying its exclusive pipes and tobaccos as well as stocking a
large choice of other blends, cigars, and various smoker's
accessories. Georgetown also runs a rare mail-order repair
service, replacing stems and bits, reaming shanks and bowls
and carrying out other repairs on the old pipes you can't
bring yourself to throw out.

❦ **W. Larsen, Amagertorv 9, DK 1160 Copenhagen K,**
Denmark. Telephone 01 122050
Brochure, $1.
Besides being purveyors to the Royal Danish Court, this
fifth-generation family firm says it is *the* pipe shop of Europe. The handmade pipes are made from only well-sea-
soned, aged briar in sand-blasted or smooth-grained finish,
hand-polished, and there are many finishes and designs to
choose from in prices starting at about $35.

Andrew Marks, Pipemaker, Frog Hollow Craft Center,
Middlebury, VT 05753
12-page illustrated catalogue, $2 U.S. and abroad.
Andrew Marks makes pipes, either to your design or following his own, using Grecian or Corsican root briar. The
pipes are expensive ($45 and up for standard shapes, $75
and up for made to order) but offer a rare opportunity to
pipe lovers to select exactly the characteristics they would
like to have.

1

2

3

1 *Georgetown Tobacco and Pipe Stores* "McSwine's Sweet Mixture," a combination of Kentucky Burley, black cavendish and rich
red Virginia tobaccos. About $9 a pound.

2 *Georgetown Tobacco and Pipe Stores* "Old Georgetown Blend," a
mixture of string-cut Syrian Latakia, Yenidje and matured Virginia
tobaccos. About $9.75 a pound.

3 *W. Larsen* Straight-grain or Bird's Eye pipes are made in
traditional or fancy shapes, freehand and wax-polished. Prices $35
and up. (*Photograph by Heidi Pohl.*)

4

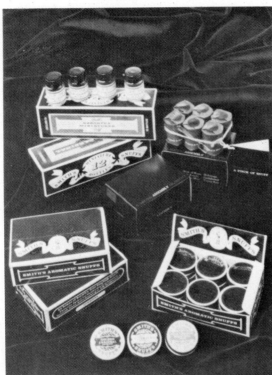

5

4 *Hayim Pinhas* Hand-carved meerschaum pipe, "D'Artagnan," $16.

5 *G. Smith and Sons* Assortments of snuff. Single boxes from $1 to $6 each. Decorated snuff boxes and tobaccos are also sold. (*Photograph by Bob Enever.*)

Hayim Pinhas, P.O.B. 500, Istanbul, Turkey. Telephone 22 9302
36-page brochure, free. Prices in $.
Meerschaum is a stone found only in Turkey. It makes excellent lightweight, porous pipes which smoke turns dark-brown in time. Here you can get hand-carved pipes direct from Turkey and much cheaper than anywhere else. You can buy a sober "English style" or plain with straight or curved stem for $10. But if you would like to be more flamboyant, there are carved creatures—Cleopatra, Abraham Lincoln, Shakespeare, Bacchus—for about $20.

Pipe Dan, Vestergade 13, DK-1456 Copenhagen, Denmark. Telephone (01) 123132
20-page leaflet, free.
Sixty-four pipes are photographed in this clear leaflet. Many of them are of unusual shapes, and they are divided into types: big bowls, verticals, chimneys, lightweight shapes, etc. Prices start at about $15 for a standard mini and, for the handmade pipes, vary between $30 and $55. You can buy Danish pipe tobacco here, and pipes made by other Danish manufacturers if you give the number or sketch the shape of the one you want. And there are several unusual services: You can have a name or initials stamped on the pipe for free; you can have a pipe of your own design made up from your own sketch; or Dan will send you the raw materials and you can make your own pipe.

Irwan Ries and Co., 17 South Wabash Avenue, Chicago, IL 60603. Telephone 800 621 1457
24-page brochure, free. AE, DC, CB, MC, V.
Many different imported pipes, and the firm's own tobaccos and cigars. Not a glamorous catalogue, but Stanley Marcus (of Neiman Marcus) says in his book *Quest for the Best* that Irwan Ries is the best pipe store he has ever come across. It has, he says, the largest selection of pipes from all makers in all qualities, and the most knowledgeable and conscientious staff.

G. Smith and Sons, 74 Charing Cross Road, London WC2H OBG, England. Telephone 01 836 7422
Price list, free. AE, DC, V.
I was once offered some snuff on the New York subway (of all unlikely places) by a man who had given up smoking and was taking snuff instead. Smith the Snuff Blenders produce a price list which not only describes their many blends and various packagings but also includes answers to your queries. To your question "Why is snuff taken?" they answer: "Most snuff takers take snuff because it is refreshing and invigorating and because it counteracts the mental fatigue caused by the stress and strain of modern life. Others take snuff because it keeps them free from colds and gives relief from catarrh and similar complaints. It has also been said that snuff stimulates the mind." To your question "What other advantages are there?" they answer: "Over the years, snuff has been the start of many great friendships. The passing of a snuff-box will 'break the ice' in many a social gathering, serve as an introduction, and create a talking point to the mutual advantage of all snuff takers."

The Tinder Box, P.O. Box 830, Santa Monica, CA 90406. Telephone (213) 829 7948
64-page color catalogue, free U.S. and overseas. AE, MC.
A lavish catalogue shows about 150 pipes, some by the most reputable makers. Also cigars, tobacco, humidors, pipe rests, cuspidors, lighters, ashtrays and a T-shirt emblazoned with the words CIGAR SMOKERS HAVE NICE BUTTS.

6
CLOTHES AND ACCESSORIES

1

2

1 *Eddie Bauer* A new anorak for men in a woven blend of polyester and cotton, treated on the underside to be water-repellent. The hood has a bill to keep goggles dry, there is a large pouch and handwarmer pockets in the front, and velcro-closing cuffs. In tan or navy, sizes small to extra large. About $85.

2 *Eddie Bauer* Parka with two new materials: Thinsulate, a new synthetic insulation for warmth without bulk, and Goretex, a laminate for protection against water. Keeps you warm in temperatures 10 to 30°F. In tan or navy, small to extra-large sizes. About $159.

All sorts of people dislike buying clothes in person. I have a friend in midtown Manhattan who buys her clothes through *New Yorker* ads, and another friend who lives a block from Bloomingdale's, yet buys his trousers from Pennsylvania. For people who hate clothes racks and changing rooms, there is a wide choice of clothes available by mail, and besides the write-ups, I have listed some well-advertised, well-known firms that produce good color catalogues of clothes in certain categories. Buying clothes by mail is also a way of finding things that are not easily available, such as natural fiber clothes, made-to-measure clothes, good outdoor and work clothes, and clothes in unusual sizes.

For Men and Women

Denny Andrews, Clock House Workshop, Colehill, Near Swindon, Wiltshire, England. Telephone 0793 762 476
Leaflet, free.
Denny Andrews sells Welsh shirts at prices about 25 percent under David Morgan's (below) and imports indigenous clothes from India and China. He also has adapted Western designs made up in India. The only problem is that illustrations are sketchy line drawings.

Banana Republic, 410 Townsend, P.O. Box 77133, San Francisco, CA 94107. Telephone (415) 777 5200
30-page brochure, $1; overseas $2. AE, MC, V.
Mel Ziegler and Barbara Gwilliam of Banana Republic say, "We set out to offer the best natural fabric safari and expedition clothing to be found on earth . . . because it was virtually impossible for us to find natural fabric, functional, honest-to-God khakis, whites and jungle greens that were all we ever cared to wear, day or night, evenings or weekends at home or abroad." Khaki, white and jungle green is just about all there is here. Clothes are usually a mixture of some genuine surplus clothing and some copies. A typical catalogue might show bush shirts, Italian army shorts (copies), World War II flight jackets (copy), Women's British Drill Trousers (copies), French Foreign Legion boots (authentic) and Chinese silk long johns (authentic).

Eddie Bauer, P.O. Box 3700, 5th and Union, Seattle, WA 98124. Telephone 800 426 8020
118-page color catalogue, free U.S. and overseas. AE, MC, V.
Eddie Bauer patented America's first quilted, goose-down insulated jacket and went on to specialize in down and warm clothing for the cold. This famous firm is now owned by General Mills, has over thirty stores, a mail-order list of fourteen million, and sells outdoor clothing of all kinds. Although their stock is more expensive than L. L. Bean's, their Eastern competitor's, and excellent down clothing is made by more specialized firms (see Backpacking section), this is still a prime source for good, casual clothing.

L. L. Bean, 9935 Spruce Street, Freeport, ME 04033. Telephone (207) 865 3111
Color catalogue, free U.S. and overseas. AE, MC, V.
You might not guess it when leafing through the plain catalogue, but L. L. Bean is one of the largest and most popular mail-order firms in the country, with a devoted following of rich and poor, famous and unknown customers who dote on the no-nonsense clothing and down-home style.

The firm was started in 1912 by Leon Leonwood Bean, a

3

4

huntsman and fisherman who invented a rubber and leather shoe, more comfortable than the stiff boots then worn, the now famous and widely copied "Maine Hunting Shoe." Sports equipment and outdoor clothes were sold through a shop run in L.L.'s own style—"good merchandise, reasonable prices, and treat your customers like human beings." In L.L.'s day Bean's was thought of more as a curiosity than a business—for its unusual practices of staying open twenty-four hours a day, every day of the year, and attending to every little customer request ("Please unstick my zipper," "Please send another left shoe, the other fell in the river").

In 1967 L.L. died and the firm was later taken over by his grandson, who made the whole thing more businesslike without changing the lovable character. Although Bean prices are no longer the lowest around, they say that their prices are lower for comparable quality, and that they take only a 70-percent mark-up, instead of the more usual retail clothing mark-up of 100 percent. Certainly anyone who wants practical clothing and reliable outdoor equipment at moderate prices should look at the L. L. Bean catalogue.

Brigade Quartermaster, 266 Roswell Street, Marietta, GA 30060. Telephone (404) 428 1234

Catalogue, free U.S. and overseas. MC, V.
Brigade Quartermaster sells clothes and goods for camping, hunting and military needs. It buys from manufacturers, military suppliers, domestic and foreign surplus dealers and sells to United States Marine Corps, West Point, Fish and Wildlife Service and "John Q. Citizen." Tends to have good value—prices on their pure-cotton flannel sheets are 25 percent below Eddie Bauer, and their Genuine United States Army field coat and their New Issue G.I. rain poncho have been independently described as outstanding values.

Camp Beverly Hills, Department COC, 9615 Brighton Way, Suite 210, Beverly Hills, CA 90210. Telephone (213) 202 0069

16-page color catalogue, $1; overseas $2. AE, MC, V.
Camp Beverly Hills looks very California, but was started by New Yorker Jeff Stein, who missed New York's Army-Navy stores. He wanted a store with the comfortable easy-to-care-for surplus/work clothing that he had been used to. His store turns out to stock work clothing with a Hollywood touch: the surgical scrub wear is hot pink and brilliant blue; the union suits are lilac, peach or aqua; the sweat pants are canary yellow—and almost everything has the Camp Beverly Hills fake army logo on it. The store and its *National Enquirer*-spoof catalogue have been a great hit—and the best part is that practically everything costs under $20.

J. C. Cording and Company, 19 Piccadilly, London W1V OPE, England

Catalogue, free.
Top English clothes for the sporty country life—hunting, shooting and fishing, or just walking—both ready-made and made-to-measure (self-measurement charts enclosed). The catalogue explains in admirable detail the various features of each of its classic models: the Yeo coat, "the original waterproof riding coat, often copied but never equalled"; "Grenfell" golfwear, cut from the cloth originally made for Sir Wilfred Grenfell, "heroic doctor/explorer," to wear in the Arctic wastes of Labrador; the "Barlows" Norfolk jacket, based on the original Norfolk jacket; etc.

Deva, P.O. Box C, 303 East Main Street, Burkittsville, MD 21718. Telephone (301) 473 4900

Brochure and fabric samples, free U.S. and overseas.
This friendly cottage industry produces a few separates cut

---

3 *Eddie Bauer* New down-filled fleece-lined ski pullovers with inside pockets for credit cards and valuables. Gray, navy, or tan in men's and women's sizes, $110. Water-resistant down-lined skibibs. Gray, navy, or tan in men's and women's sizes $110.

4 *L. L. Bean* Maine Hunting Shoe. Uppers of leather treated to resist water yet remain supple. Bottoms of strong rubber. Price about $35 to $60 depending on height of the uppers.

generously for "grace . . . and the ultimate comfort in casual wear, yoga, tai-chi, biking, jogging, exercise . . . or whatever." All in pure cotton, as Deva firmly believes that it is better for you, besides not staining as easily and not holding smells. The clothes come in nice solid colors and cost around $20 each.

Dorset Smocks, New House Farm, South Perrott, Beaminster, Dorset DT8 3HU, England
Leaflet, 1 International Reply Coupon.
In the nineteenth century, rural housewives made for their men working smocks of unbleached linen and Sunday-best smocks of cotton twill in white or neutral colors with elaborate and symbolic stitching. Eventually the smocks became associated with simple life and were dropped by rural workers only to be picked up by the upper classes, who dressed their children in exquisitely smocked crepe de chine and shantung garments.

Beverly Marshall makes a traditional smock for men and women, based on one worn by a farmer in her neighborhood until recently. Smocks are made in linen or cotton, can be made in customers' own fabric or varied in detail, and cost just under $100 each.

Filson, 205 Maritime Building, 911 Western Avenue, Seattle, WA 98104. Telephone (206) 624 4437
16-page catalogue, free; overseas $1.
Superlative outdoor clothing has been made by Filson's since 1897. Fabrics, mainly pure wool, made to their own specifications, and the jackets and trousers (originally made for loggers) are long-lasting and hard-wearing.

French Creek Sheep and Wool Company, R.D. 1, Elverson, PA 19520. Telephone (215) 286 5700
40-page color catalogue, free; overseas $2. AE, MC, V.
Several people have recommended French Creek, well known for shearling coats made from its own sheep, and also greasewool sweaters which have been described as some of the finest sweaters made in the United States. The sweaters are undyed ("At French Creek when we want dark color we shear dark sheep") and they and the natural-fiber clothes made by other manufacturers are very handsome.

Fun Wear Brands, P.O. Box 2800, 141 Elkhorn Avenue, Estes Park, CO 80517. Telephone (303) 586 3316
Catalogue, free; overseas $1, overseas air mail $2. AE, MC, V.
Off-putting name and off-putting catalogue (mainly illustrated with fifties-style drawings). Nevertheless, this is a really good place to buy jeans; it stocks a lot of Levi's, including larger sizes, plus boots, hats, and shirts for men, women and children—what they call "rugged Americana Sportswear," generally Western in style.

Gohn Brothers, Box 111, Middlebury, IN 46540. Telephone (219) 825 3400
Price list, free.
Gohn Brothers has sold clothes to the Amish community for eighty-five years, and has plain overalls, socks and shirts, as well as fabric by the yard at very low prices. Colors mainly black, dark blue and natural.

Gokeys, 84 South Wabasha, St. Paul, MN 55107. Telephone (612) 292 3933
Catalogue, free. AE, MC, V.
Gokeys has made "roughing boots" for over a hundred

5

6

5 *L. L. Bean* Chamois cloth shirts, introduced in 1927. Available in six colors for men, women, and children. Prices from about $17 to about $20.

6 *Dorset Smocks* Traditional smock with hand embroidery, in cotton, linen, or customer's own fabric in any length. Price just under $100.

7

8

9   10

7 *Loden Frey* Capes of Loden cloth available in green, brown, or navy blue. Prices about $120 or $150.

8 *Loden Frey* Suits in the style of the Tegernsee region in Bavaria. Man's suit about $200, woman's suit about $216.

9 *Norm Thompson* Reversible navy/silver Apollo jacket made from a fabric developed for spacesuits. Jacket weighs only 10 ounces and can be rolled up. In cold weather, wear with navy side out to absorb warmth from the sun; in warmer weather, wear with silver side out to reflect sunshine. Men's and women's sizes, $55.

10 *Norm Thompson* Pure wool jacket in natural only. About $58.
(*Photographs by Photo Art.*)

years, snakeproof boots, and a whole range of handmade shoes and boots for men and women. Prices range from about $50 for moccasins to about $95 for their famous snakeproof boots (worn daily by the men who work in the Florida snakepits . . .).

Besides their own boots and shoes, Gokeys sells clothes, shoes and sports equipment by other top American and foreign manufacturers.

Good Things Collective, 52 Main Street, Northampton, MA 01060. Telephone (413) 586 5403
16-page catalogue, free.
This cooperative makes pure-cotton clothes (including an inexpensive jogging suit) from a sturdy, textured, American fabric. There are ten solid colors, but unfortunately they aren't shown. Chinese shoes are sold. Prices are low.

Hayashi Kimono, Izui Building, 6–3–6 Ginza, Chuo-Ku, Japan. Telephone (03) 571 1528
Brochure with some color, free.
A top Tokyo shop for antique kimonos which has a mail-order service for Westernized Japanese clothes, marvelous for exotic wear around the house. Full-length, flower-embroidered kimonos in almost any color cost between $28 and $100. Happi coats, which are less spectacular but more practical, since they are knee-length and have narrower sleeves, cost about $45 in silk, $17 in cotton, and in polyester about $5 for children.

Hudson's, 97 Third Avenue, New York, NY 10003. Telephone (212) 473 8869
Catalogue, free U.S. and overseas. AE, MC, V.
Hudson's sells outdoor clothing and name-brand outdoor equipment, plus their own—a sort of smaller-scale L. L. Bean. They include tennis racquets in their summer catalogue and say that a good deal of their business is with customers outside the United States.

Laurence Corner, 62/64 Hampstead Road, London NW1 2NU, England. Telephone (01) 388 6811
80-page catalogue, $1.50 (surface only). AE, DC, MC, V.
Laurence is England's largest dealer in government-surplus clothing and equipment, and also stocks outdoor and camping gear. The catalogue is filled with the familiar British military fashions at reasonable prices.

Loden Frey, Maffeistrasse 7–9, 8000 Munich 2, Germany. Telephone 089 236 930
Color catalogue, free. In German. September. AE, V, CB, DC.
In 1872 the son of the founder of Loden Frey made the first coat of Loden, a brushed woolen fabric which is naturally waterproof. In the intervening years the coat has become extremely popular with hunters and quite popular with Germans in general. The classic model is dark green, with a vent, no lining, a double layer of cloth over the shoulders, holes under the arms and a fly front over the buttons.

In recent years Loden coats have become a status symbol, and although many firms now make them, Loden Frey is still the most highly esteemed source. Each fall the shop publishes a dazzling catalogue in full color showing their variations on the Loden coat in traditional green and in equally authentic dark blue and natural. A typical coat costs $225, and the firm has a worldwide mail-order service.

Moffat Weavers, Ladyknowe Mill, Moffat, Dumfriesshire, Scotland. Telephone 0683 20134
Color catalogue, free. A, AE, CB, DC, MC, V.
Besides making clothes, this small manufacturing and retail

firm sells clothes in tartans and tweeds, sweaters and skirts. Prices are very low: around $20 for pure-wool sweaters and $40 for wool skirts in sizes 10–22.

David Morgan, Box 70190, Seattle, WA 98107. Telephone (206) 282 3300
Catalogue, 25 cents; overseas $1; air mail $2. MC, V.
David Morgan imports from Australia, New Zealand and Wales, mainly traditional tops in natural fibers such as the New Zealand sheepfarmer's "Swanny" jacket, the Welsh steelworker's undershirt and the Cornish sailor's smock. But he also imports Australian cowboy hats, Australian braided belts and toy koala bears, and Welsh jewelry and records.

Partridge Hill Workshop, Box 607, Lyndonville, VT 05851
Leaflet, 25 cents U.S. and overseas. MC, V.
A hand-drawn page shows five natural-fiber tops: a cotton chamois cross-country ski jacket, a reversible musicians vest, a Colonial jacket, a Chinese jacket and a Nepali embroidered velveteen jacket.

La Pelleterie de Fort de Chartres, Fort de Chartres State Historical Site, Prarie du Rocher, IL 62277. Telephone (618) 284 7171
Catalogue, $2 U.S. and overseas; air mail $4. MC, V.
Pat and Karelee Tearney own and operate an eighteenth-century-style French trading post on the grounds of the Fort de Charters which was occupied by the French Marines in 1759. The Tearneys, who dress in the clothes of the time, sell reproduction clothes copied from originals in museums and private collections that are as authentic as they can afford to be. A fascinating catalogue tells the history of the area, throws in some old hints and recipes, and describes the clothes and illustrates them with line drawings. All the clothes are in natural fabrics and hand-finished (but machine-stitched where the stitches don't show). Merchants and trappers shirts cost about $40 each, buckskin trousers $150; coats, Indian dresses, moccasins and bags are also on sale, and can be bought made up or as kits. Also tinware, knives, tinder boxes, fabric and 100-percent-wool Hudson Bay Point blankets. Pat Tearney says, "We have nothing which is cheap. If you desire museum quality at affordable prices I am sure we can serve you."

Royal British Legion, Cambrian Factory, Llanwrtyd Wells, Powys LD5 4SD Wales. Telephone 05913 211
Color leaflet and self-measuring chart, free. MC, V.
At this factory, tweeds are made from Welsh wool by disabled people. The tweeds are of high quality, and colors are fairly earthy: beige, mustards, gray, greens, in herringbone or checks. The tweeds are sold by the yard: the 8/10 ounce tweeds in 29-inch widths cost $13 a yard, including postage. There is also a made-to-measure service: women's skirts cost $60 to $80.

Rugged Wear, P.O. Box 336, Narraganset, RI 02882. Telephone (401) 789 4115
Leaflet, free. MC, V.
Very well made in handsomely colored thick pure cotton, Rugged Wear's rugby jerseys for men and women are on sale around the country or by mail from the manufacturer. Unfortunately, the leaflet only lists the colors and does not show them. Prices around $35 each.

St. Laurie, 84 Fifth Avenue, Department CN, New York, NY 10011. Telephone 800 221 8660
Two catalogues with swatches, $5 (refundable); overseas $7. AE, DC, MC, V.
St. Laurie began as a Brooklyn pants factory, started by the present owner's grandfather in 1913. It now makes and sells by mail classic business suits for men and women (including tall and petite sizes). Emphasis, says the president, is on "old workmanship and finest imported fabrics." He also points out that the women's suits are of exactly the same quality as the men's. A very clear and attractive catalogue shows twelve models and forty swatches. Suits for both men and women generally just over $200.

Flight Suits, 1050-K Pioneer Way, El Cajon, CA 92020. Telephone (714) 440 6976
Color brochure of flight suits, free U.S. and overseas.

Split's Aviation, 1050-K Pioneer Way, El Cajon, CA 92020. Telephone (714) 440 0894
Brochure of flight jackets, helmets and goggles, free U.S. and overseas. AE, MC, V.
These two divisions of one company sell a small selection of aeronautical clothes for men and women. Custom sizes on request.

Strength Company, No. 130B, Deck 1, Cheung Chau Gallery, Ocean Terminal, Kowloon, Hong Kong
Brochure, free. Prices in $.
A good source of inexpensive nylon and polyester/cotton jackets and raincoats for men, women and children. Most of the nylon clothes cost around $20, and polyester/cotton clothes cost around $30. The clothes come lined with nylon or with cotton quilting. Solid colors, mainly bright, but also olive green and navy blue. Your own patterns can be made up.

Norm Thompson, P.O. Box 3999, Portland, OR 97208. Telephone (800) 547 1160
62-page color catalogue, free; overseas $1. AE, DC, MC, V.
This thirty-year-old firm can be relied on for good casual clothing, often imported, in pure natural fibers. Although the firm doesn't boast quite as much nowadays of its tough outdoorsy image (old Norm Thompson copy would proudly say, "This is no city shirt—but a real, rugged, don't-give-a-damn shirt for fishing, camping and boating . . ."), they still occasionally preen themselves on their location: "Here in the Pacific Northwest we've learned various ways to stay comfortable in the wind, rain and cold. . . ." But they are not too chauvinistic about the Northwest to import Irish hats and capes, English dresses and jackets, Scottish sweaters and Italian shoes. Although prices are high, this is one of the few firms that guarantee their goods for the normal life of a product: "If at any time a product fails to satisfy you, return it to us postage prepaid, and we'll either replace the item, or refund your money."

Bill Tosetti, 17632 Chatsworth, Granada Hills, CA 91344. Telephone (213) 363 2192
Catalogue, free. Available only September to January. MC, V.
A good stock of clothes by the old and very reputable Pendleton woolen mills—the most offered through any catalogue, according to Bill Tosetti. Jackets, trousers, skirts, the famous all-wool plaid shirts, and also Park and Indian blankets.

11

12

11 *Nikolaus Exercise* Pure cotton tops and tennis-length cuffed shorts. Man's top about $30; woman's top about $25. Shorts about $30.

12 *Brooks Leather Design* Handmade portfolio briefcase $95. (Photograph by Markatos Photography.)

CLASSIC (PREPPY) CLOTHES

British Isles Collection, Mount Washington Valley, Route 16, Main Street, North Conway, NH 03860
30-page color catalogue, $1 U.S. and overseas. AE, DC, MC, V.

Dunham's of Maine, 64 Main Street, Waterville, ME 04901. Telephone (207) 872 5501
Color catalogue, free U.S. and overseas. AE, DC, MC, V.

Especially Maine, U.S. Route One, Arundel, ME 04046. Telephone (207) 985 3749
Color catalogue, free U.S. and overseas. AE, DC, MC, V.

Carroll Reed, Conway, NH 03818. Telephone (603) 447 2511
64-page color catalogue, free. AE.

OUTDOOR CLOTHES AND EQUIPMENT

Bromley Catalogue, Box 1248, Manchester Center, VT 05255. Telephone (802) 362 3141
32-page color catalogue, free. AE, DC, MC, V.

Kreeger and Sons, 16 West 46th Street, New York, NY 10036. Telephone (212) 575 7825
64-page catalogue, free. AE, MC, V.

Weiss and Mahoney, 142 Fifth Avenue, New York, NY 10011. Telephone (212) 675 1915
Catalogue, $1. AE, MC, V.

SPECIAL SIZES

Top to Toe, 3 Alderney Road, Dewsbury, Yorkshire, England. Telephone 0924 464 304
Swatches and order form, $1.
"Bespoke tailor and complete outfitter," Top to Toe specializes in outsize clothing ("We have made for six feet nine and up to fifty-eight-inch waist—man, of course") and even has an express service for the desperate man or woman. Their styles are not illustrated, so you have to chance it with the swatches and your measurements; pants cost $40 to $50 according to size.

WESTERN CLOTHES

Cutter Bill Western World, 5818 LBJ Freeway, Dallas, Texas 75240. Telephone (214) 980 4244
36-page color catalogue, free U.S. and overseas. AE, DC, MC, V.

Miller Stockman, P.O. Box 5407, Denver, CO 80217
80-page color catalogue, free. AE, MC, V.

Sheplers, 6501 W. Kellog, P.O. Box 7702, Wichita, KS 67277. Telephone (316) 942 8211
80-page color catalogue, free U.S. and overseas.

Dance and Exercise

Capezio Dance Theatre Shop, 755 Seventh Avenue, New York, NY 10019. Telephone (212) 245 2235
48-page color catalogue, $2.50 U.S. and overseas. AE, MC, V.
"Capezio has been dancing since 1887." The firm makes leotards, tights and shoes for men, women and children. Ballet, jazz, cabaret, gymnastics are all glamorously covered. There are even clothes for the less active, such as the silky wraparound skirts currently popular with teenagers.

Nickolaus Exercise, 295 Madison Avenue, New York, NY 10017. Telephone (212) 687 7430
Leaflets, $1; overseas $4. AE, MC, V.
I have found that the least unpleasant way to do exercises is with two friends and the Nickolaus exercise tapes. The exercises consist of deep breathing and stretching, according to instructions given by a nice, soothing, tape-recorded voice. Five tapes, twenty minutes each. Nickolaus is also one of the very few firms selling a full range of pure cotton exercise clothes.

Taffy's, Mail Order Headquarters, 701 Beta Drive, Cleveland, OH 44143. Telephone (216) 461 3360
144-page color dance and exercise catalogue, $3; overseas $6.
80-page Showstoppers Broadway catalogue, $2; overseas $4.
30-page Showstoppers in Concert catalogue, $1; overseas $2.
66-page On Parade catalogue, $2; overseas $4.
112-page Record and Book catalogue, $2; overseas $4. AE, MC, V.
Invaluable and lavish catalogues for anyone involved in any kind of dance. Taffy's sell clothes by manufacturers such as Capezio, Danskin and others; also equipment and music. "Showstoppers" has costumes with lots of razzle-dazzle for Broadway-type shows, circus, fairy tales, rock, etc. "Showstoppers in Concert" is for sober mime and similar performances. "On Parade" has the books, batons, braids, etc., for cheerleaders.

Handbags and Luggage

Brooks Leather Design, Route 1, Box 343, Pittsboro, NC 27312. Telephone (919) 542 4020
Leaflet, free U.S. and overseas. MC, V.
Good-looking chunky bags and briefcases in cowhide with solid brass, made by a craftsman. Prices mainly $65 to $135.

Mark Cross, 645 Fifth Avenue, New York, NY 10022. Telephone (212) 421 3000
28-page color catalogue, $2. AE, CB, DC, MC, V.
Mark Cross—"Here today, here tomorrow"—started in Boston in 1845. They claim to have done all sorts of good things for America, such as introducing cigarette cases, golf clubs, Sheffield cutlery, cocktail sets, the thermos bottle, and they even claim to have designed the wristwatch. Now they make and sell leather goods—address books and photograph albums to luggage. All very expensive, but then they do little things for you like monogram, and help you find your (registered with them) luggage if you lose it on a plane trip.

Jannabags, 19 Samantha Close, Walthamstow, London E17, England. Telephone (01) 556 6607
Leaflet, $1.
These tough canvas bags have had an admiring press in England and have become increasingly popular since the firm was started by Janna Drake in 1970. In fact, with all their pockets, their strong, clear colors, and their flexibility and low price, they are a tempting replacement for stiff, old handbags and suitcases and make great and cheap bookbags. Seven bags are illustrated with line drawings on the leaflet, and prices go from about $10 for a small shoulder bag to about $30 for the biggest bag, intended to replace a small suitcase. It has plenty of outside pockets for tickets, passports, etc. Weekend bags, shopping bags and everyday bags come in oatmeal, denim, black, yellow, red, green or brown.

Leather School, Piazza Santa Croce 16, Florence, Italy
32-page color catalogue, free. Prices in $.
The Leather School in the cloister of the Santa Croce Church was founded by monks to produce a complete line of Florentine leather goods and to technically prepare young boys who wish to specialize in this type of work in a morally sound atmosphere. (The atmosphere isn't so morally sound, however, as to prevent whoever wrapped my parcel from writing *"Niella valore"* on the customs form.)
   There is a wide range of wallets (starting at about $20) and a few cigarette cases, glass cases, photograph frames, etc., in the gold-tooling-on-colored-leather that is typical of Florence. And in calfskin there are attaché cases at about $124 and up, and handbags, both tooled in gold (for about $80) and plain, including some chunky, casual, sport, and shoulder bags. A seven-piece desk set, gilded or plain, costs $198 and comes in all colors.

North Country Leather, 1 Front Street, Box 25, E. Rochester, NH 03867. Telephone (603) 332 0707
Catalogue, $2; overseas $4. MC, V.
Twenty-one leather bags in pleated and tucked garment-weight cowhide are made in this small workshop. Prices are reasonable, under $50.

Saddler Bags, Gladach, Brodick, Isle of Arran, Scotland. Telephone 0770 2311
Brochure, free. MC, V.
Five craftsmen-made bags, including a Gladstone, from best vegetable-tanned bridle leathers. Also several belts. Very appealing; only problem is that colors are not shown. Prices about $50 to $80.

DISCOUNT
Please see discount information in the How to Buy section.

Ace Leather Products, 2211 Avenue U, Brooklyn, NY 11229.
Telephone (212) 891 9713 or 891 0988
U.S. and overseas send stamped self-addressed envelope or telephone with brand name and style number for a specific price. MC, V.
Ace seems to me to be the most efficient of the discount luggage stores. They sell luggage by American Tourister, Diane Von Fürstenberg, Lark, Samsonite, and other widely advertised manufacturers. Leather briefcases by Yves St. Laurent and many others; leather wallets by Bill Blass, Pierre Cardin, Anne Klein, Yves St. Laurent and others; and leather handbags by leading manufacturers. Also, discounts on Cross desk sets, totes umbrellas and Bulova travel clocks. Free gold engraving is available. I checked prices on two pieces of luggage and found Ace prices to be 30 percent below list price. On a Venture garment bag there was a saving of $34 dollars, and on a Samsonite garment bag a saving of $23. However you *must* provide brand name and model number, and will probably get an answer scrawled on your own letter. Established 1959.

Hats

**Virginia Blanc, 71 Aspen Street, Source CC,
Floral Park, NY 11001. Telephone (516) 352 6781**
Leaflet, free; overseas 60 cents.
One winter and five summery crochet hats are hand made
by Virginia Blanc. Prices $22 to $29 postpaid.

**Body and Sole Leather, 22 High Street,
Brattleboro, VT 05301. Telephone (802) 257 4700**
Color leaflet, free U.S. and overseas. MC, V.
A terrific place for warm hats in sheepskin. There are
sixteen shapes, including Western and other brimmed hats,
and one with earmuffs.

**Herbert Johnson, 13 Old Burlington Street,
London W1X 1LA, England. Telephone (01) 439 7397**
*18-page catalogue for men, leaflet for women, free. AE, DC,
MC, V.*
Herbert Johnson opened his hat shop in the nineties at the
suggestion of Edward the Prince of Wales, and now the
shop justifiably prides itself in combining the best of old and
new. There are hats to convince the most adamant hat
haters. Besides every sort of classic hat for men they carry
all-purpose felt, town and formal wear, tweed and leather
hats and caps, sporting headwear, seasonal hats "for warmer
times or cold comfort."

Knitwear

**Alice in Wonderland Creations, Route 1, Box 405,
Millstone, WV 25261. Telephone (304) 354 7531**
Brochure, $1; overseas $2.
Alice and Lee Stough raise sheep, shear them, wash and
card the wool, spin it and knit it. The wool is all from black
(actually brown and gray) sheep carefully fed and shorn, so
the luster, resilience and depth of color is noticeable, say the
Stoughs. The designs are all their own and sweaters cost
from about $52 to about $95, and there are ponchos, shawls,
hats and scarves.

**Castlemoor, Castle Street, Bampton,
Devon, England EX16 9NS. Telephone 31530**
Color leaflet, $1.
Fabric swatches, $1. V.
Castlemoor specializes in goods made from English wool,
and has about eighteen different heavy outdoor sweaters in
wool, many more than you find in any American catalogue.
Also pure-wool blankets, rugs and fabrics by the yard.

**V. Juul Christensen and Son, Strandboulevarden 96,
2100 Copenhagen, Denmark**
Color brochure, $1; air mail $1.50. AE, DC.
Juul Christensen makes lightweight and heavyweight traditional Norwegian hand-knitted sweaters in beautiful and
subtle color combinations, Icelandic hand-knitted sweaters in
natural wool and colors, and hand-knitted Aran sweaters.

**Cushy Numbers, 5 Paul Street, Kingsdown,
Bristol 2, BS2 8HG, England**
Brochure and yarn samples, $1.
This "very *new* very *small* concern" was started by a
"made-redundant" art teacher, who taught herself how to
knit on a machine. Now, with an ex-student, she designs

and makes machine-knitted cushions, dresses and sweaters. I
particularly like the cushions based on Oriental rug designs
in "soft and subtle or rich and jewel-like" color combinations (about $35 each); also the "little bits of fluff and
sparkle" puffy-sleeved evening sweater in black with silver
or gold, for about $50.

**Fairy Dell Knitwear, Department US-CC,
P.O. Box 10, Main Street, Cottingley, Bingley,
West Yorkshire BD16, England. Telephone 274 563 356**
*Brochure, 1 International Reply Coupon; air mail 2 Interna-
tional Reply Coupons.*
The cute name of this firm comes from a local turn-of-the-
century photograph of fairies, not yet proved to be a fake.
The clothes are unusual, simple separates machine knitted,
hand finished in luxurious natural fibers—silk, cashmere,
camel hair and alpaca. Sizes 10 to 18 (with hem lengths to
order); prices mainly around $100.

**Gemini Knitwear, P.O. Box 9, Didcot OX11 8DN,
England. Telephone 0235 813 672**
Brochure planned, free.
A new firm started by Mrs. June Newman makes several
kinds of sweaters—the most unusual being mohair sweaters
for about $60 each, and picture sweaters of cars, planes and
trains, some of which have fourteen different shades, at
about $100 each.

**Guernsey Knitwear, 6 The Bridge, St. Sampson's,
Guernsey, Channel Islands, England**
Leaflet and samples, free. V.
Good-looking traditional heavy sweaters in oiled and wor-
sted yarn are made to measure in any size from 26- to 56-
inch chest. Prices about $30 to $50.

**Handknit Orkney, Old Schoolhouse, Garth,
St. Margaret's Hope, S. Fonaldsay, Orkney,
Great Britain. Telephone 085 683 226**
*Color leaflet, $1 or large self-addressed stamped envelope
with 1 International Reply Coupon.*
In spite of the name, most of the sweaters made by this
small new company on an island off Scotland are hand
framed and finished, but not hand knitted. The attractive
color leaflet shows Fair Isle designs and scenic sweaters in
gentle-colored Shetland wools. Prices only $30 to $70—a
steal for this sort of thing, because the firm cuts out "the
various middlemen." Made-to-measure skirts in matching
wool fabric, about $50 each. Partner Steven Woolham says,
"We look forward . . . to offering an unequaled service to
any future customers from the United States."

**Irish Cottage Industries, 44 Dawson Street,
Dublin 2, Ireland. Telephone 713 039**
Leaflet, free; air mail $1. All major credit cards accepted.
This shop puts out a leaflet of Irish sweaters and woven
goods including several shapes and designs of the colorful,
woven crios belt; the traditional, heavy, off-white Aran
sweaters; lumber jackets; hand-knitted socks for men; string
gloves; and stoles, scarves and ties made out of gossamer-
weight tweed. Tweed is sold by the yard, and samples are
sent on request for specific colors and weights.

**Kennedy's of Ardara, Ardara, County Donegal, Ireland.
Telephone Ardara 6**
Brochure, free; air mail $3. All U.S. credit cards accepted.
Kennedy's of Ardara sells traditional Aran sweaters knitted
by the farmers' and fishermen's wives in their homes. Prices
are slightly lower here than in many stores; at this writing,
sweaters for men and women cost $45 to $60 each.

**Landau, 114 Nassau Street, Box 671,
Princeton, NJ 08540. Telephone (609) 924 3494**
30-page color catalogue, free. AE, MC, V.
Beautiful but expensive sweaters, jackets, hats and scarves,
knitted or woven from the silky wool of the long-haired
Icelandic sheep. Natural colors and Nordic designs.

**Millhaven Knitting Services, Knowstone, South Molton,
Devon, England. Telephone 376**
Details, 3 International Reply Coupons, or $3.
Millhaven will knit or crochet anything to your own measurements. Send them a picture and details of whatever you
want, together with the measurements, and they will tell you
how much it will cost. They buy English yarn and don't
mind using the finer ones.

**Monaghans, 15/17 Grafton Arcade, Dublin 2, Ireland.
Telephone 770 823**
Color brochure, free. AE, V.
A few cashmere, lambswool and Aran sweaters are shown in
the brochure of this popular Dublin shop.

**Muileann Beag a' Chrotail, The Old School House,
Camus Chros, Isle of Skye IV43 8QR, Scotland.
Telephone 047 13 271**
Leaflet and wool shade card, free; air mail $1. MC, V.
Muileann Beag a' Chrotail (the Little Crotal Mill) uses
traditional Hebridean patterns to make sweaters with wool
from island sheep, and has even reproduced the colors that
the crofters used when they did their own spinning and
dyeing.
    Three different wools are used for the sweaters: Shetland;
Harris, rough but strong and warm; and Gotland, a silky
wool from a Swedish sheep now reared on Skye.
    A few of the machine-knitted, hand-sewn styles are shown
in the leaflet at prices between $30 and $40.

**Una O'Neill Designs, 30 Oakley Park, Blackrock,
County Dublin, Ireland. Telephone (01) 886 272**
Leaflet, free. Prices in $. AE, V.
Una O'Neill sells hand-knitted, traditional, off-white Aran
fisherman sweaters and jackets. The complicated symbolic
stitches evolved centuries ago and are so distinctive that in
case of accident a particular design of a sweater could identify the wearer's home village.

**The Peruvian Connection, Canaan Farm, Rural Route 1,
Tonganoxie, KS 66086. Telephone (913) 845 2750**
Catalogue, $1. AE, MC, V.
Anthropologist Annie Hurlbut went to Peru to do research
on women who sell in markets and came across the alpaca
(a relative of the llama). She liked the soft warm wool so
much that, with American taste in mind, she designed a few
fashionable garments and taught some Peruvian women how
to make them. Then she came back to start a business with
her mother on the family farm in Kansas.
    Now The Peruvian Connection sells beautiful alpaca
sweaters, shawls, ponchos and blankets in natural colors
only. Although the sweaters cost around $100 each, Annie
gleefully points out that her pure alpaca throw costs about a
third less than an alpaca and wool throw in the Horchow
catalogue.

**Rammagerdin, Hafnarstraeti 19,
P.O. Box 751, 121 Reykjavik, Iceland**
*Color brochure and yarn samples, free. Prices in $.
AE, MC, V.*
Sweaters, jackets, shawls, hats and rugs of soft Icelandic

13

13 *Muileann Beag a' Chrotail* Hand-finished sweaters in traditional shapes available in three different natural-colored wools, and
reddish brown, moss green, dark blue green, or dusty pink. About
$40 each.

14

15

yarn, in natural colors. Prices about 20- to 30-percent lower, including postage, than similar knitwear bought in the United States (for instance at Landau).

W. S. Robertson, 13/15 High Street, Hawick, Scotland. Telephone 0450 2571
Lyle and Scott and Pringle brochures, $5 per year.
If you like the classic knitwear produced by the famous Scottish firms Lyle and Scott and Pringle, it is still well worth buying directly from Scotland. Robertson carries a far wider range of styles, colors and sizes than most American shops. Even after paying postage, Scottish prices are about a third under American prices.

Romanes and Paterson, The Edinburgh Woollen Mill, Langholm, Dumfriesshire, DG13 OBR, Scotland. Telephone 0541 80092
30-page color catalogue, free. AE, DC, MC, V.
Romanes and Paterson of Princes Street, Edinburgh, was established in 1808. In 1980 they were amalgamated with the Edinburgh Woollen Mill and have now put out a joint catalogue. The catalogue is a terrific one for lovers of classic wool sweaters and skirts. The price range goes from a low of under $20 for Shetland sweaters to a high of around $60 for Pringle and Lyle and Scott (still way below American prices). Inexpensive tweed and tartan skirts and suits in sizes 10 to 18; lambskin jackets, gloves etc., also at excellent prices.

Briar Shepherd, Keepers Cottage, Moor Lane, Halston East, Skipton, North Yorkshire, England. Telephone Bolton Abbey 284
Information and swatch, $1.
Briar Shepherd makes two cobwebby shawls in pure natural-colored mohair, hand crocheted from original Victorian patterns. A smaller one is 40 inches square and has a frilly openwork border; it costs about $30 air mail postpaid. A larger, 45-inch square has a deep lacy frilled border with a shell stitch edging and costs about $35 air mail postpaid.

Sweater Market, 15 Frederkisberggade, DK 1459, Copenhagen, Denmark. Telephone 1 15 27 73
Color leaflet, free. AE, DC, MC, V.
Sweater Market sells hand-knitted pure-wool ski sweaters, inspired by Norwegian designs. Lots of white, with blues and grays in the geometric patterns—really very pleasant looking.

Le Tricoteur, Pirtonnerie Road Estate, St. Peter Port, Guernsey, Channel Islands, England
Leaflet and samples, free. Prices in $.
Loose, long casual sweaters in styles used originally by smugglers and sailors, and knitted on the island of Guernsey, traditionally a great knitting island. Guernsey men have been exporting their hand-knitted stockings since Queen Elizabeth I's day. Mary Queen of Scots wore them. The sweaters are made from partly oiled worsted wool and are still good for sailing, fishing and smuggling. They come in plain colors: red, blue, navy, beige, white, and are priced according to size from $22.50 for a 22-inch chest to $52 to $54 for a 48-inch chest. A good firm.

R. Watson Hogg, Auchterarder, Perthshire, Scotland. Telephone Auchterarder 2151
Ballantyn sweater catalogue, free. AE, MC, V.
Leonard Moss of R. Watson Hogg says that they automatically send the Ballantyn catalogue in response to any inquiries for knitwear. They also deal individually with specific

14 *Icemart* (see Crafts and Local Products section). Sweater of soft Icelandic wool in natural colors. About $70.

15 *Cornelius Furs* Suede lambskin jackets start at about $350.

inquiries "and are quite successful in supplying the customers' needs. . . . We keep what is probably one of the biggest stocks of cashmere knitwear in the United Kingdom, and it is all of the very top quality. We not only keep the classic styles but have very lovely sweaters with Intarsia designs, and we can usually supply cashmere knitted skirts to go with most of our cashmere sweaters and cardigans."

Leather and Fur

Antartex, P.O. Box No. 1, New Lebanon, NY 12125. (Overseas Donald MacDonald [Antartex Ltd.] Lomond Industrial Estate, Alexandria, Dunbartinshire, Scotland.)
Color catalogue, free. AE, MC, V.
The best known of the sheepskin-coat manufacturers, this twenty-five-year-old family firm makes excellent coats and jackets for adults and children from four kinds of skins. The catalogue also has hats and slippers and gloves either made up or in kits to be sewn at home.

Bootleg Leather, P.O. Box 564, Plymouth, WI 53073. Telephone (414) 892 4590
12-page catalogue, $1 U.S. and overseas.
Custom-made old-fashioned deerskin clothes, with lacing, braiding, burning, appliqué and beading to order. Bootleg will make clothes from any skins you provide, so long as they are already tanned. Prices start at about $70 for machine-made vests and $110 for machine-made pants. Clothes can be bought as kits for 35 percent less.

Cornelius Furs, 72 Castlereagh Street, Sydney, Australia 2001
Color leaflet, free. AE, DC, V.
Kangaroo, Australian lamb, Australian fox, sueded sheepskin in coats and jackets—you choose your own fur, color, length and style. A sleek-tailored midilength kangaroo fur coat with leather trimming and buttons costs about $640.

The Deerskin Trading Post, 119 Foster Street, Peabody, MA 01960
84-page color catalogue, free. AE, DC, MC, V.
The Deerskin Trading Post (not a real trading post, despite the man in Indonesia who sent a box of tea in exchange for a hat) is one of the largest retailers in the country of suede and leather. The catalogue shows quantities of leather coats (and a few sheepskin), jackets, shoes, gloves and hats for men and women in most standard styles and colors.

Lewis Leathers, 120 Great Portland Street, London W1A 2DL, England. Telephone (01) 636 4314
Color catalogue, $1; air mail $5. V.
Lewis manufactures leather suits and jackets in black and brilliant primary colors for motorcyclists. They are well known in the field and export their own clothes and other supplies for motorcyclists.

North Beach Leather, P.O. Box 99682, San Francisco, CA 94109 0682. Telephone (415) 922 5452
16-page color catalogue, $2; overseas air mail $3. AE, CB, DC, MC, V.
An exceedingly sophisticated catalogue with some haughty, some fierce models wearing fashionable slinky soft-leather clothes. Khaki jodhpurs, olive blousons, fringed Indian-inspired dresses, fur-trimmed Berber vest. Prices start at around $250.

16

17

16 *North Beach Leather* Leather ski vests sold in recent seasons: left, down-filled, about $225; woman's vest with shearling shawl collar, about $185; right, with zip-up corduroy collar, in men's and women's sizes, about $160.

17 *North Beach Leather* American buffalo coat with sueded hide outside, fur inside. American Indian-inspired cut fringe, silver conchos, beaded rondelles, and hand-painted symbols. Sold in recent seasons for about $1500.

Overland Sheepskin, P.O. Box 588, Taos, NM 87571. Telephone (800) 545 8150
Catalogue, free U.S. and overseas. AE, MC, V.
This is a smallish seven-year-old firm in New Mexico that makes coats in the classic sheepskin and also newer shapes. There are several sporty jackets based on denim, baseball and flight jackets. Also dramatic coats with big, rough-cut collars. Overland make their own hats, boots (with fur on the outside) and gloves. All quite expensive, but designs are pleasing.

The Sheepskin Rug Shop, Mail Order Department, P.O. Box 12175, Penrose, Auckland, New Zealand
Brochure and coat catalogue, free.
The brochure illustrates toys, slippers and rugs, and the loose-leaf catalogue shows coats made of New Zealand sheepskin. Coat styles are unusually varied, from rough-looking, long-wearing "ranchers" through jerkins and leather-trimmed Astra lambskin jackets to rather glamorous, fluffy evening capes.

George M. Trahos and Sons, Corner of 7 Philellinon & Xenophontos Streets, Athens 118, Greece. Telephone 322 8256
Color catalogue, free; air mail $1.
Greece has a thriving industry and specializes in making coats out of fur scraps at very reasonable prices. George M. Trahos's catalogue features somewhat out-of-style girls wearing somewhat out-of-style coats—but prices are very low and a daring shopper might find something he or she likes—a mink hat for $45 or a man's jacket in lynx for $450, with "lower grades" for $225.

Shoes

Caput Magnum Designs, Station Street, Holbeach, Spalding, Lincolnshire PE12 7LF, England. Telephone 0406 24124
Color brochure, free. MC, V.
Simple, good-looking sandals with flat or wedge heels are completely hand made by "a small company of craftsmen" who offer "honestly made" sandals. Prices just over $30 a pair.

Danner Shoe Manufacturing Company, P.O. Box 22204, Portland, OR 97222. Telephone (503) 653 2920
Color catalogue, free U.S. and overseas; air mail $2. MC, V.
Father Bill Danner and son Peter Danner run this firm, and the boots they manufacture have a very good reputation indeed. These go from "Urban Walker" through to heavy-duty "Forest Service." Boots for women are in smaller sizes but with materials of the same quality. A new light boot of Goretex has just been introduced. Prices around $100 a pair.

Easy Feet, 7900 Shelbyville Road, Louisville, KY 40222
20-page brochure, 25 cents; overseas $1. MC, V.
A nice catalogue of only comfortable shoes: Earth shoes, Birkenstock sandals, Krone clogs from Denmark, and Marjanes from China Shoes including a suede pair.

Clifford James, High Street, Ripley, Surrey GU23 6AF, England
Color leaflet, free.
About nine pairs of leather shoes at prices between $20 and $30.

18 *Danner Shoe Manufacturing Company* Danner "Lights." New lightweight boots with footbeds of full-grain leather and uppers of Goretex. Boots weigh a third less than comparable leather boots and only a third more than tennis shoes. Price $110 to $115, depending on size of uppers.

19 *Danner Shoe Manufacturing Company* Danner's most popular hiking boot, "Mountain Trail." Described by *Backpacker* magazine as "close to being our ideal shoe." Price about $100.

20 *Kalsø of North America* "Classic Earth Shoe," one of several shoes designed to give the wearer correct posture. Men's sizes in black, men's and women's sizes in light or dark brown, about $48.

21 *Kalsø of North America* "Cool wood sandal" in women's sizes only. About $33.

Kalsø of North America, 2009 E. Kenilworth Place, Milwaukee, WI 53202. Telephone (414) 276 4390
Leaflet, 25 cents; overseas $1. MC, V.
The clumpy-looking Kalso Earth shoe was developed by a Danish yoga teacher, Anne Kalso, who studied the relationship between posture and respiration, and while in a Hindu monastery in Brazil noticed that in the footprint of the Indians, the heel always sank lower than the toes. Back in Denmark she experimented with this principle and after ten years developed the Earth shoe, which does, indeed, leave the heel lower than the toes. The leaflet quotes raves from the wearers and warns that wearers will feel off balance and have stiff leg muscles for a few days while they adjust to the new way of walking.

Kow Hoo Shoe Company, 23 Hennessy Road, Wanchai, Hong Kong. Telephone 5 282 452
Self-measurement chart, free.
I have had three pairs of my old shoes copied by Kow Hoo and can recommend the service to anyone who has a favorite pair of old dress shoes that can't be replaced, or who has trouble finding shoes that fit. I simply put one of my old shoes in a padded envelope and air mail it to Hong Kong along with a letter containing instructions and a personal check. The shoes that Kow Hoo has made me have been fairly flimsy, which is why I only dare recommend them for shoes that won't get a lot of wear. Although, to be fair, the shoes I sent were also fairly flimsy. It may be that in the other leathers and "Deluxe (Superb)" quality—for which you can pay an extra $3—shoes will be stronger.

Many exotic leathers such as Ostrich, Lizard, French Baby Alligator are available, and shoes can be made in your own silk. Golf shoes and boots can be made, and shoes can be copied from any picture you send. Men's shoes start at $52, women's at $45.

Lee Kee, 54 Peking Road, Kowloon, Hong Kong
Leather samples, free. Prices in $.
Men's and women's boots and shoes in the same leathers as at Kow Hoo (above), starting at $60 for West German calfskin. Briefcases and handbags made to order.

A. W. G. Otten, Albert Cuypstraat 102–104–106, 1072 CZ Amsterdam, Holland
Leaflet, free; air mail $1. Prices in $. AE, MC, V.
Wooden shoes used to be worn not at home, but by people who were working and needed protection against dampness or injury. Recently it has been only in Holland that wooden clogs (or *klompen*, as they are called in Dutch) have been worn. A. W. G. Otten sells clogs, both the all-wood kind and the kind that has recently become popular again, wooden soles with leather uppers. The leaflet lists them in blue, white, black, yellow, brown and natural, and prices are about $10 to $15.

Todd's, 5 South Wabash, Chicago, IL 60603. Telephone (312) 372 1335
Brochure, free U.S. and overseas. MC, V.
A few good strong shoes, and excellent Chippewas and Frye boots. Unfortunately photographs are black-and-white, so the handsome Frye boot colors can't be appreciated.

Umbrellas

Stan Novak, 115 West 30th Street, New York, NY 10001. Telephone (212) 947 8466
Color leaflet, free U.S. and overseas.

Canes of every description, from horn-handled to Lucite, including adjustable canes and a brandy cane to fill with alcohol.

Swaine Adeney Brigg and Sons, 185 Piccadilly, London W1V OHA, England
20-page general catalogue, free; air mail $4.
Saddlery and riding equipment catalogue, free.
This very prestigious old firm has been making whips for English monarchs since George III and provides everything necessary for the civilized country life—whips, canes, and drinking flasks.

After six pages of mean-looking whips come things of more general interest: elegant canes, discreetly sober umbrellas in best silk with Malacca handles; many different seat sticks, seat umbrellas and golf umbrellas; hunting and shooting accessories, including silver-plated sandwich boxes; picnic baskets and race hampers; "sporting gifts"—spoons and cuff links with animals on them.

At the end of the catalogue there is an impressive leather section, showing fitted beauty cases, jewel cases, briefcases, gentlemen's fitted dressing cases, writing cases, passport cases and purses.

Uncle Sam Umbrella Shop, 161 West 57th Street, New York, NY 10019. Telephone (212) 247 7163
Price list, free. MC, V.
"Makers and importers of walking sticks, umbrellas and parasols," says this stationery, next to a picture of Uncle Sam carrying an umbrella. Founded in 1866 by a German immigrant and still run by a member of the Simon family, this out-of-the-ordinary store stocks over forty thousand walking sticks and an equal number of umbrellas, only a few of which are shown in the brochure. Traditional canes and walking sticks are available, but clearly, Uncle Sam is happiest carrying, if not a big stick, a Malacca cane or a shillelagh. Umbrellas are $10 and up and come in all the traditional shapes and sizes as well as in giant sizes for doormen or in many colors for golfing. There are also handy folding canes and an umbrella-repair service.

Underwear

Damart Thermawear, 1811 Woodbury Avenue, Portsmouth, NH 03805. Telephone (603) 431 4700
44-page color catalogue, free; overseas, ask for the name of your nearest branch. AE, MC, V.
Damart Thermolactyl insulating underwear, pajamas, warm-up suits. If you suffer from the cold, send for Damart.

DISCOUNT

Please see information on buying at a discount in the How to Buy section.

Louis Chock, 74 Orchard Street, New York, NY 10002–4594. Telephone (212) 473 1929 (closed Friday afternoon and Saturdays, but open Sunday)
Brochure, $1.
Brands stocked: Berkshire and Hanes Stockings; Lollipop, Carter, Vassarette, Duofold briefs for women; Jockey, BVD, Munsingwear, Duofold, Hanes men's underwear; Carter's children's underwear and nightwear; Danskin leotards and tights.

I buy batches of stockings here and have always found the

22

staff helpful. Chock is also very well organized for mail order, which is rare among discount clothing stores. They give 25-percent discount on whatever they sell (although Carol Campion says she bought Duofold here at 30-percent below local prices) so this is a marvelous place to stock up on underwear and hosiery for yourself and anyone else you are responsible for. Underwear also for fat and tall men, but *no* bras or girdles for women. Established 1920.

D and A Merchandise Company, 22 Orchard Street, New York, NY 10002. Telephone (212) 226 9401
List of brands stocked, self-addressed stamped envelope; overseas 1 International Reply Coupon. MC, V.
D and A sells most well-known brands of underwear, and hosiery for men, women and boys. If you know what you want and have someone at home to receive parcels, this is a good place to buy from. D and A sends out just a list of the brands they stock with an order form; you fill out the *exact* details of what you want including brand name, style number and color. They ship C.O.D. (unless you have Master Card or Visa). They say their prices are 25- to 30-percent below department store prices. I found a 28-percent discount when I bought from them, and the postage C.O.D. charge was $1.75 as stated on the order form. Established 1947.

For Men

Bachrachs, 2354 Hubbard Avenue, Decatur, IL 62526
52-page catalogue, free. MC, V.

Britches of Georgetown, 1321 Leslie Avenue, Alexandria, VA, 22301. Telephone (703) 548 0200
Color catalogue, $2; overseas $4. AE, MC, V.
This group of fifteen stores, whose buyers "crisscross the globe . . . in search of the finest fabrics and materials and the newest ideas in technology," publishes pleasing catalogues with background information on the clothes and fabrics featured. Mainly natural fiber in this attractive, if pricey, collection of casual clothes that includes one or two business suits and coats.

Brooks Brothers, 346 Madison Avenue, New York, NY 10017. Telephone (212) MU2 8800
Catalogues three times a year, $2 U.S. and overseas. AE, MC, V.
Brooks Brothers is America's oldest men's clothier, founded in 1818, and one of its best known. Most of Brooks's clothing, including the famous "Brooks Brothers suit," is made for it exclusively, and its catalogue gives an excellent sampling of the store's wares. Brooks's "conservative good taste" is not inexpensive, but prices vary. Cotton shirts can be bought for around $30. Brooks suits are in the more expensive range, and their popular (and in New York omnipresent) alpaca-lined greatcoat costs $250. Brooks's Christmas catalogue has a large choice of gifts, such as luggage, belts, wallets, etc. There is also in each catalogue a section devoted to boys' clothing and catalogues of women's clothes.

Cable Car Clothiers, Robert Kird Ltd., 150 Post Street, San Francisco, CA 94108. Telephone (415) 397 4740
64-page color catalogue $1; overseas, $3. AE, MC, V.

T. M. Chan and Company, Custom Tailor Department, P.O. Box 33881, Sheung Wan Post Office, Hong Kong. Telephone 5 450 875
Brochures, free.

22 *Britches of Georgetown* This pure cotton crew-neck sweater, available in several colors, has recently sold for $32.50; the pure cotton shirt for $24.50; and the pure cotton khaki slacks for $35.

Made-to-measure jackets and trousers in Terylene/wool blends; trousers around $40, jackets $70 to $90. Made-to-measure shirts about $9.

Chipp, Custom Tailors and Furnishers, 14 East 44th Street, New York, NY 10017. Telephone (212) 687 0850
20-page color catalogue, free. Twice a year.
Chipp is one of Madison Avenue's posh clothiers, smaller than Brooks Brothers and, they feel, somewhat less conservative, but in the same league. As would be expected, their clothes are costly, though there are more expensive stores in New York. A full range of men's clothes is listed, most of it the traditional Madison Avenue gray-flannel suit but with a number of more daring departures.

H. Huntsman and Sons, 11 Savile Row, London W1X 2PS, England. Telephone (01) 734 7441
Tour schedule, free. AE, DC, MC, V.
A Huntsman representative tours America each spring with samples of cloth and models of "all types of riding coats, waistcoats, breeches, suits and evening dress wear." He visits thirteen American cities, measuring customers for suits which they will later pick up in London or which will be mailed to them. The Huntsman people feel that considering the workmanship, their prices are very reasonable, and even after duty is paid, compare more than favorably with American prices. Prices for a two-piece suit start at $1130, and for a three-piece suit at $1180.

Hutton's, P.O. Box 85, North Haven, CT 06473. Telephone (203) 239 3702
16-page color catalogue, free. AE, MC, V.

International Male, 2802 Midway Drive, P.O. Box 85043, San Diego, CA 92138. Telephone (800) 854 2795 or (714) 226 8751
Color catalogue, $2. AE, CB, DC, MC, V.
Loungewear such as white braided Moroccan shirts and jogging clothes in silklike fabrics for the flamboyant dresser. The more (but not very) conservative dresser will find a few campaign clothes and Calvin Klein separates.

Henry Poole and Company, Sullivan Wooley and Company, 10–12 Cork Street, London W1X 1PD, England. Telephone (01) 734 5985
Tour schedule, free. AE.
Henry Poole were originally the first tailors established in Savile Row. Each spring and fall a director of the firm tours America with a large selection of new fabric swatches and takes customers' measurements. The measurements are sent back to Cork Street to be made up, and usually the customer comes over to London for a fitting. But suits can be completed without a fitting, in which case any necessary small adjustments can be made by certain American tailors at the expense of Henry Poole.

Paul Stuart, Madison Avenue at 45th, New York, NY 10017. Telephone (212) 682 0320
Color catalogue, $2; overseas $3. AE, DC, MC, V.
My favorite among the New York preppy men's clothes stores, Paul Stuart has a *slightly* more adventurous stock than the others, and by far the most seductive catalogue. The catalogue has gorgeous close-up photographs of textured fabrics and knits, and a meandering philosophical text on each type of clothing. A few clothes for women. Prices high.

SHIRTS

Ascot Chang, 41 Man Yue Street, 2/F Block D, Hung Hom, Kowloon, Hong Kong. Telephone 3 644384
Style sheet, self-measurement chart, fabric swatches, $1; air mail $3. Prices in $.
Reputable thirty-year-old firm makes shirts, shorts, pajamas and robes to measure in pure cotton, $26 and up. Old shirts can be copied. Stanley Marcus (of Neiman Marcus) and Bob Sakowitz (presumably of Sakowitz) are said to shop here.

Harvie and Hudson, 77 Jermyn Street, St. James's, London SW1, England. Telephone (01) 930 3949
Fabric swatches, free.
Nowhere else in the world is there a street like Jermyn Street, crammed with astronomically expensive, ineffably elegant men's haberdashery stores. The mind boggles—who on earth buys himself $50 shirts? If you'd like it to be you, try Harvie and Hudson, a firm with many American customers which will send you swatches of current fabrics—stripes, checks and plain colors in cotton voiles, zephyrs, poplins, broadcloths and oxfords. Price of a made-to-measure shirt about $50 with a minimum order of three shirts.

Hawes and Curtis, 2 Burlington Gardens, London W1X 1LH, England
Notification of New York visit, free. All major credit cards accepted.
"Please note that we are Shirt Makers in London of supreme quality. Our cloths, many of which are woven especially for us and therefore exclusive, are only 100-percent Cotton or Silk; prices for cotton ready-made shirts are from $45, and made to measure from $60.

"We annually visit New York and . . . see clients at the new Hyatt . . . usually for the last week in September, and the first week in October each year, and we advise all clients on our mailing list. Our clientele includes many famous people on both sides of the Atlantic."

Victory Shirt Company, 345 Madison Avenue, New York, NY 10017. Telephone (212) 687 6375
Leaflet, free. AE, MC, V.
Carefully made pure-cotton shirts and pure silk ties for men and women. Shirts cost between $23.50 and $42.50, and Victory points out that the shirts have hand-turned collars, single-needle stitching, split-yoke backs, and are made of excellent cotton. Comparable shirts by other manufacturers are sold through other stores, and cost considerably more, Victory says.

SHOES

Executive Shoes, Box 488, Brockton, MA 02403. Telephone 800 343 1022
28-page color catalogue, free. AE, MC, V.
Wrights Arch Preserver shoes are molded to fit a footprint, including the arch. They are also kept on the last for twice as long as most shoes, says Executive, which makes them keep their shape better.

John Lobb Bootmaker, 9 St. James's Street, London SW1, England

Tour schedule, free. Prices in $.
John Lobb is far and away the most prestigious shoemaker in the world. They have made shoes for at least three English kings and one American president (President John-

son). Each spring and fall a representative tours America in fifteen cities taking measurements of new customers and showing their latest models to old customers. Once measurements have been taken and permanent lasts have been made, customers can order new shoes by mail, with the help of photographs if necessary. Handmade shoes in calf leather start at $765, rarer skins are more expensive.

Alan McAfee, 5 Cork Street,
London W1X 1PB, England. Telephone (01) 734 9010
Color brochure, $1. Prices in $. AE, DC, MC, V.
Very good English leather shoes of every sort for men. Average price $100. "Bespoke customers, or those with 'special requirements' will be quoted for price and time to make by return."

McAfee sent me a photograph of H.R.H. Prince of Wales opening a McAfee box containing a pair of polo slippers (style 52, in case you'd like some too).

Ortho Vent Division, Stuart McGuire, 115 Brand Road,
Salem, VA 24156. Telephone (703) 389 3955
Color catalogue, free U.S. and overseas. AE, DC, MC, V.
Stuart McGuire boasts that their shoes are better than a famous lookalike at twice the price—they even go so far as to photograph the two together. These shoes all have composition soles, with cushioning and leather in-soles and linings at prices around $50.

Richlee Shoe Company, 2 Dyer Street,
Brockton, MA 02403
16-page color brochure, free. AE, MC, V.
Elevator shoes for men.

White's Shoe Shop, W. 430 Main Avenue,
Spokane, WA 99201.
Telephone (800) 541 3786 or (509) 487 7277
30-page brochure, free U.S. and overseas. MC, V.
Excellent, expensive handmade boots with extra-high, strong arches, which make them comfortable for rough country and standing on hard surfaces, in widths AA to EEEE. They can be made to measure, and people with really unusually shaped feet can have lasts made. All makes of men's, women's and children's shoes are repaired.

SPECIAL SIZES

Imperial Wear, 48 West 48th Street,
New York, NY 10036
40-page catalogue, free U.S. and overseas.
AE, BA, DC, MC.
The store for above-average men, with above-average incomes, sells clothes by well-known manufacturers in sizes 46 to 60 regular and long; portlies in regular, short and long, and extra-long sizes 40 to 54. Suits from makers such as Aquascutum, Lanvin and Halston cost between $180 and $300, trousers cost around $40. There are shirts from Excello and Cyril Bartlett; coats (including suede and leather) by Eagle, Lakeland and Zero King; raincoats by London Fog; cashmere sweaters, mohair tuxedos and a couple of pages of boots and shoes.

The King-Size Company, 24 Forest Street,
Brockton, MA 02402. Telephone (617) 580 0500
120-page catalogue, free U.S. and overseas for anyone over 6'3" tall or whose shoe size is from 10 to 16.
Everything for the tall man, thin or fat—from watertight overalls to ruffled dress shirts, including Arrow shirts, Shet-land sweaters, corduroy jackets, insulated sports clothes, work clothes, underwear, pajamas, shoes and boots. Plenty of everything to choose from. Shirts start at $20, trousers at $30.

Women and Children

Johnny Appleseed, 61B Dodge Street,
Beverly, MA 01915. Telephone (617) 922 2040
38-page color catalogue, free. AE, MC, V.

Avon Fashions, Avon Lane, Newport News, VA 23630.
Telephone (804) 827 7000
64-page color catalogue, free. AE, MC, V.

Brownstone Studio, 1 East 43rd Street, New York, NY
10175. Telephone (212) 883-1990
32-page color catalogue, free. AE, MC, V.

Career Guild, 2500 Crawford Avenue,
Evanston, IL 60201. Telephone (312) 492 1400
32-page color catalogue, free. AE, MC, V.

China Rose, 112NE Third Avenue,
Gainesville, FL 32601. Telephone (904) 378 3752
Brochure, 50 cents; overseas surface $1; air mail $1.50.
"Unusual handmade clothing for adults and children" inspired by styles from different times and places. Cindy Leespring makes by hand pure-cotton clothes to order. There are Arabian pants, peasant smocks, Japanese suits and nineteenth-century Kate Greenaway-style dresses. Prices are low; the only drawback is that you have to guess at the final effect as illustrations are black-and-white drawings.

Cleo, 18 Kildare Street, Dublin 2, Ireland.
Telephone (01) 761 421
Color leaflet and swatches, $1. Prices in $.
Cleo sells flamboyant clothes based on traditional Irish styles to boutiques in America and also by mail. Aran knitting appears in all sorts of colors and shapes—as ponchos, full-length hostess skirts, knickerbockers, trouser suits and even as bedspreads. Bright crochet patterns and hand-woven fabrics are used for skirts, vests, capes, hats and bags. And for evening wear there are colorful new versions of tinker's shawls, and the full-length sixteenth-century hooded Munster cloak which used to be worn in southern Ireland.

Collette Modes, 66 South Great George Street,
Dublin 2, Ireland. Telephone 752 188
Color leaflet, free.
Smart classic-tailored suits and coats in Donegal tweeds. Sizes 10 to 16. Collette has a thriving mail-order export business, and I once met a regular customer in New York, who was extremely enthusiastic about the firm.

Esprit, 743 Minnesota Street, San Francisco, CA 94107.
Telephone 800 227 3777
Color catalogue, $1. AE, MC, V.
Esprit was started in 1968 by an ex-model and a couple who had been running a ski and mountaineering business. None of them knew much about the fashion business, but they wanted to make junior clothes with more of a European look (original colors and varied styles) than an American look. The amateurs succeeded and have flourished—they say it is by continuing to challenge the conventional. Anyway, the clothes, shoes and bags they manufacture and sell

through their own catalogue are a delightful change from the classics that are more easily available by mail—these are colorful, casual and novel. Prices mostly under $50.

FBS, 659 Main Street, New Rochelle, NY 10801. Telephone (800) 228 5454
8-page color catalogue, $1; overseas $2. AE, MC.

Sara Fermi Clothing, 11–13 Sturton Street, Cambridge CB1, 2QT, England. Telephone 0223 312 048
Leaflet with swatches, $1. MC, V.
"Fine handmade shirts and nightdresses inspired by shapes from the past and made entirely from natural fabrics." The seven garments illustrated with line drawings on Sara Fermi's leaflet would have seemed odd a couple of years ago; now they are quite in keeping with the New Romantic fashions. Prices go from about $38 for a medieval shirt with lace insets and a nightdress based on the Victorian chemise, to $80 for a dress based on the French and Italian fifteenth-century over-tunic. Lovely fabrics—creamy white voile and spun silk, fine black wool, terracotta and Venetian red Viyella.

First Editions, 340 Poplar Street, Hanover, PA 17331. Telephone (717) 637 1600
24-page color catalogue, free. AE, CB, DC, MC, V.

Anne Harrington Dress Designer, Old Vicarage, Llanybydder, Dyfed, Wales. Telephone 0570 480 719
Leaflet, free.
A descendant of Roger Williams, founder of Rhode Island, left her funky Hollywood boutique for a vicarage in Wales. Instead of sequined jackets for pop stars she now makes demure silk blouses and dresses, with tucks, ruffles and lace; some of the lace is antique. Sizes 8 to 18. Prices start at about $60.

Heather Valley, Brunstane Road, Edinburgh EH15 2QL, Scotland. Telephone 031 669 6161
12-page color brochure, free. AE, DC, MC.
Heather Valley's own made-to-measure tweed skirts with lamb's-wool and Shetland sweaters to match. The designs are all classic, the colors unusual. There are pinks, mauves and dusty blues that the internationally famous manufacturers don't make—you might prefer these. Sweaters cost around $30 each, skirts cost around $75.

Honeybee, 2745 Philmont Avenue, Huntington Valley, PA 19006. Telephone (215) 947 8080
30-page catalogue, free; overseas $3. AE, MC, V.

J. Jill, Stockbridge Road, Great Barrington, MA 01230. Telephone (413) 528 1500
Catalogue, free. AE, MC, V.
A very pretty collection of deliberately old-fashioned, romantic country clothes in pure cotton, silk and wool. Everything is designed by, manufactured by, and only available from, J. Jill.

Knights Ltd., 2565 Third Street, San Francisco, CA 94107. Telephone (415) 826 4614
63-page color catalogue, free. AE, MC, V.

The Landfall Collection, Conway, NH 03818. Telephone (603) 447 2511
32-page color catalogue, free. AE, MC, V.

23

24

25　　　**26**

23 *Esprit* This cotton dress with hand-crocheted inset has recently sold for $34.

24 *Esprit* These hand-embroidered cotton crepe blouses and dress have sold in recent seasons for between $21 and $40 each. *(Photographs by Toscani.)*

25 *Honeybee* This fitted cream blouse and flounced denim skirt have sold in recent seasons for $28 and $35 each.

26 *Honeybee* This cotton broadcloth skirt and top have sold in recent seasons for $62.

27

28

29

**Mark, Fore and Strike, P.O. Box 640,
Delray Beach, FL 33444. Telephone (800) 327 3627**
31-page color catalogue, free. AE, MC, V.

**Nandi Imports, P.O. Box 2719, Petaluma, CA 94953.
Telephone (707) 763 0888**
Brochures, $1; overseas $2. MC, V.
A small collection of cotton clothes made for this firm in
India. Fabrics are Indian, styles are Western. Prices are
low, almost all under $20.

**Noyadd Rhulen, Battle, Brecon, Wales LD3 9RW,
Great Britain. Telephone 0874 89 317**
Leaflet, $1; air mail $2.
A husband and wife, Philip and Poppy Cochrane, have, in
their eighteenth-century Welsh farm, a workshop that produces really charming dresses. Mainly in natural fibers, the
dresses combine simple, loose shapes with dashing color
combinations and fabric contrasts, inspired by patchwork.
Sizes 10 to 18. Leaflet is illustrated only with line drawings.

**Old Pueblo Traders, 3740 East 34th Street,
Tucson, AZ 85726. Telephone (602) 795 0777**
32-page catalogue, $1. MC, V.

**Peachtree Report, 4795-F Fulton Industrial Blvd.,
Atlanta, GA 30336. Telephone (404) 691 7633**
38-page color catalogue, free. MC, V.

**Pennsylvania Station, 340 Poplar Street,
Hanover, PA 17331. Telephone (717) 637 1600**
32-page color catalogue, 50 cents. AE, CB, DC, MC, V.

**Pin Linni Prints, 23 Chapel Street, Camelford,
Cornwall, England. Telephone Camelford 2733**
Brochure with swatches, $1. MC, V.
A studio workshop makes a few clothes for women and
children, each one silk-screened in two colors and rather art
nouveau designs on pure cotton. Everything is available
made-up (prices around $20) or as cut-out-and-ready-to-sew
kits (prices around $15).

**Pitlochry Knitwear, P.O. Box 8, East Kilbride,
Glasgow G74 5QZ, Scotland. Telephone 03552 42080**
Color brochure, free; air mail $1. AE, DC, MC.
Sweaters with matching tweed skirts or kilts, and a few
jackets and dresses. Several can be made to measure. All in
pure wool, with prices around $20 for the sweaters and
around $40 for fully lined skirts. This looks like excellent
value for the money.

**Putamayo, 857 Lexington Avenue, New York, NY 10021.
Telephone (212) 734 3111**
Leaflet, free; overseas $1.50. MC, V.
Brilliantly colored natural fiber clothing from Guatemala,
Mexico, India. Lots of flounces and ribbons. Attractive and
inexpensive.

**La Shack, 19 The Plaza, Locust Valley, NY 11560.
Telephone (800) 645 3524**
31-page color catalogue, free. AE, MC, V.

**Gudrun Sjodens Affar. Regerings Gatan 30–32,
11153 Stockholm, Sweden. Telephone 08 20 34 35**
Catalogue, free. In Swedish. AE, Eurocard, V.
The catalogue of this small firm is in Swedish, so is not easy
to buy from; *please* don't ask for a catalogue unless you are
serious (and have someone to translate). Clothes are simple

27 *Gudrun Sjodens Affar* Pure cotton, waterproofed unlined jacket.
Available in off-white, red, navy, light blue, khaki, dusty pink, and
black. Priced about $80.

28 *Gudrun Sjodens Affar* Pure cotton tricot sweat shirt and pants
in off-white, red, navy, blue, pink, and green. Sizes small to large.
Each about $30.

29 *Gudrun Sjodens Affar* Sweater and skirt in pure cotton jersey.
Colors off-white, navy, red, black, etc. Priced about $22 each.

and up-to-date, in solid colors or stripes (colors are not shown on the catalogue). Prices mainly $25 to $50 for separates, with coats around $200.

Sportspages, 3373 Towerwood Drive, Dallas, TX 75234. Telephone (214) 247 3101
24-page color catalogue, free, AE, MC, V.

The Talbots, 175 Beal Street, Hingham, MA 02043. Telephone (617) 749 7830
74-page color catalogue, free. AE, DC, MC, V.

Ann Taylor, 970 Chaple Street, New Haven, CT 06510.
16-page color catalogue, $2. AE, MC, V.

Trade Exchange (Ceylon), 72 Chatham Street, Colombo 1, Sri Lanka. Telephone 2 5521 24679
Color leaflet, $1.80. AE.
For dramatic kaftans and flowing evening and at-home dresses, you can hardly go wrong here. Handmade batik fabrics have bright colors and bold designs; styles are all loose, therefore easy to fit. Prices are very low . . . only trouble is you must buy six at once.

Trefriw Woollen Mills, Trefriw, Gwynedd, North Wales LL27 ONQ, United Kingdom. Telephone 0492 640 462
Color brochure and swatches, $1; air mail $3. MC, V.
An old mill that used to spin and weave the fleece local farmers brought for their own use now spins and weaves a blend of Welsh and New Zealand wools. A color leaflet shows jackets, coats and capes in traditional Welsh honeycomb tapestry, and there is a list of shawls, blankets, bedspreads, wool fabric by the yard, mohair rugs ($30 each); but the list is not illustrated.

Tuppence Coloured, Brookside Cottage, Stour Provost, Near Gillingham, Dorset, England. Telephone 074 785 630
Brochure with fabric samples, $1; air mail $2.
In the sixties Sally Tuffin was half of the well-known English design team Foale and Tuffin. Now she designs for Tuppence Coloured clothes-by-mail for women and children, which she and Monica Renaudo run from a Dorset village. A far cry from London in the sixties but the clothes, with their pleasing mixture of demure smocking and old-style fabrics in small flower prints, show some of the sophistication that made London so avant garde in those days. Informal clothes for women cost mainly between $60 and $80, with a few available for $20 less as kits. Clothes for children cost $20 to $40, with kits at about a third less. Length of clothes can be adjusted to your measurements.

Water Witch, Department CC, Maine Street, Castine, ME 04421. Telephone (207) 326 4884
16-page brochure with swatches, $1; overseas $2 (refundable). AE, MC, V.
Unusual clothes are made by Catholic sisters from pure cotton batiks, Dutch Java prints, and Liberty of London fabrics. The clothes are sold only in Castine or by mail—not the kind of things you find in department stores.

Wrap Arounds, Route 3, Box 117, Floyd, VA 24091. Telephone (703) 745 2472
18-page catalogue with fabric samples, $1 U.S. and overseas. MC, V.
A community cottage industry in rural Virginia, Wrap Arounds makes by hand clothing that "focuses on fluidity,

comfort and easy care." The clothes are quite sophisticated here with dark-patterned flower fabrics, batiks, and striking designs for wraparound pants, butterfly blouses, cloaks and capes.

SHOES

Chester Beard Shoes, 2716 Colby, P.O. Box 65, Everett, WA 98206 0065. Telephone (206) 259 2716
Leaflet, free U.S. and overseas.
Flat shoes and walking shoes—everything looks very comfortable. This must be the place where the little old lady in tennis shoes gets her tennis shoes.

SPECIAL SIZES

Chico Fabric Design, Box 152, Cohasset Stage Route, Chico, CA 95926. Telephone (916) 342 9178
Brochure with swatches, $2.
Fourteen natural fabrics, mostly simple ones such as gauze, French gabardine, flannel and hand-blocked cotton from Singapore. Susan Lawing also sells roomy Chico work pants for women in sizes up to XL, and Japanese farm clothes.

Hills Brothers, 99 Ninth Street, Lynchburg, VA 24504. Telephone (804) 528 1000
Color brochure, free. MC, V. Shoes for women, sizes AAAA to EE, costing mainly around $30 to $40. Recommended by one of my readers, a customer.

Syd Kushner, 1204 Arch Street, Philadelphia, PA 19107
32-page brochure, free U.S. and overseas. MC, V.
Established in 1898, this firm sells wide-width shoes for women, sizes C to EEE. Low prices.

Lady Annabelle Lingerie, PO Box 1490, Boston, MA 02205. Telephone (617) 242 3825
Color brochure, free; overseas $1. MC, V.
Provocative underwear and nightdresses for the pleasingly plump.

Lane Bryant, 2300 Southeastern Avenue, Indianapolis, IN 46201. Telephone (317) 266 3311
120-page catalogue, free.
80-page "Tall Girl" catalogue, free. AE, V.
After studying the measurements of 200,000 women on the books of an insurance firm, and discovering that 40 percent were overweight, Lane Bryant went into the outsized women's clothes for which it is well known. Unfortunately, in spite of the pioneering start, the clothes are still only clothes to be bought for lack of a more exciting alternative. They are inexpensive and quite a few of the styles are acceptably classic.

There are also catalogues for short women and tall women, listing clothes, shoes and stockings.

Mooney and Gilbert, 31 West 57th Street, New York, NY 10019. Telephone (212) 355 6687
12-page catalogue, free. MC, V.
Specialists in the "long and narrow aristocratic foot, Mooney and Gilbert say they have the largest selection anywhere for the slender heel. All of their shoes and boots are available to 5A width and many to 6A. Prices are between $60 and $70.

**Nierman's Shoes, 17 North State Street,
Chicago, IL 60602. Telephone (312) 346 9797**
16-page catalogue, free U.S. and overseas. AE, MC, V.
Hard to fit? Come to Nierman's where no one is hard to
fit." Women's shoes for very long and narrow and very wide
feet (no in-betweens), in both dressy and comfortable styles.
Also panty hose for the fat and very fat, and boots for thin
and fat legs.

**Piaffe, Department 98, 1500 Broadway,
New York, NY 10036. Telephone (212) 869 3320**
Brochure planned, $2.
Filling a long-time gap, Piaffe, a three-year-old store on
Madison Avenue, is publishing a catalogue of better clothes
for "petites"—women under five feet four who wear sizes 0
to 8. Prices mostly between about $60 to $130.

**Possum, 50 Higham Road, Chesham,
Buckinghamshire, England. Telephone Chesham 7 5 977**
Color brochure, $1; air mail $3.
Possum dresses and skirts with matching knitwear are made
in eleven classic colors and pleasant roomy styles in pure
wool. All the clothes are made to order, so they can be made
in any size at no extra coast. Prices for the separates mainly
between $60 and $80.

**Roaman's, Saddle Brook, NJ 07662.
Telephone (201) 843 8300**
Color catalogue, free. AE, V.
Roaman's says that it tries to bring to the larger woman the
same youthfully styled fashion that is available to the woman who wears a junior or a misses size, and their clothes—in
sizes 14½ to 28½ and 38 to 60—are certainly worth looking
at, with quite a few dresses, trousers and tops that are in
solid colors and simply cut. Dresses cost mostly between $20
and $30, and there are glamorous nightgowns, hostess outfits
and shoes to size 12EEE.

UNDERWEAR AND STOCKINGS

**Dust-Schenck, 37 St. Peter's Street, Bedford, England.
Telephone 0234 554 49**
Leaflets and brochures, $1.50; air mail $5.
An English firm sells the well-known Hanro of Switzerland
dresses and separates in sizes 10 to 22. Of special interest is
the big stock in many sizes of Hanro's delicate pure-cotton
and wool underwear—I have only seen one or two pieces in
the United States and then at prices at least a third higher.

**Frederick's of Hollywood, 6608 Hollywood Boulevard,
Hollywood, CA 90028. Telephone (213) 466 5151**
72-page catalogue, $2. AE, MC, V.
After years on the periphery, Frederick's (like *Playboy*) has
successfully moved into the mainstream of American life.
The lingerie catalogue itself is for the most part illustrated
with incredibly slim and incredibly busty young women, in a
style that is halfway between 1940s pin-ups and the early
fashion drawings of teen-age girls. Satins—or their modern
equivalents, see-throughs—and push-up bras abound, all
with a running commentary that is strictly pre-Women's
Lib. If, by some miracle, you don't have the superhuman
figure required for most of these garments, Frederick's offers
girdles, bras and other devices that will "shape" you
properly, or if this isn't enough, either, to make those dreams
come true, there are falsies "for the girl who can't make it on
her own. . . ." One of the classic American wish books.

**Janet Reger, 12 New Bond Street,
London W1, England. Telephone (01) 493 8357**
32-page color catalogue, $4; air mail $6. AE, DC, MC, V.
An elegant, small but well known shop, Janet Raeger produces a lavish color catalogue of lace-inset underwear and
nightwear. Apart from some pure silk, most things are made
of "high quality" manmade fibers with the effect of satin.
Underwear mainly $45 to $75, with nightdresses and gowns
at over $200.

**J. Simister Design, P.O. Box 10,
Tamworth, Staffs, England**
15-page brochure, $2 including swatches.
Handmade nightwear and underwear, in cotton or a very
wide variety of silks in many colors, lace trimmed. Everything is made to measure. Prices are generally reasonable
with most of the cotton clothes costing under $30, and many
of the silks costing between $30 and $60.

**Victoria's Secret, P.O. Box 31442,
San Francisco, CA 94131**
*Color catalogue, $3 U.S. and overseas surface; overseas air
mail $5. AE, DC, MC, V.*
"Romance . . . a feeling, a glow, a lovely way to live. My
Victoria's Secret private label designs express what's in your
heart . . . romance." Bras, G-strings, slips and kimonos in
"shimmering" fabrics and colors such as "creamy French
Vanilla, vintage Wine or rich Chocolate." Occasionally sug-
gestive but not outrageous, this underwear and nightwear by
well-known manufacturers costs mainly between $25 and
$75.

**Funn Stockings, P.O. Box 102, Steyning,
West Sussex, England**
Price list, 50 cents.
Swatches: silk $3; cotton $3; wool $2.50.

**Visions, Box 239, 557 Willow Road,
Menlo Park, CA 94025**
Price list, 50 cents.
"FUNN is the Company which changed fashion history by
introducing STOCKINGS to a world dominated by: 1. Panty hose 2. in synthetic materials 3. in drab colors . . . Now
Branded Hosiery names have accepted stockings as a fashion, but with their high-speed modern dinosaur machines,
they cannot cope with Natural Fibers." Funn stockings are
very fine and come in lovely pale colors. They've been used
in all sorts of period movies, and are available from the
manufacturers in England at prices between $10 and $17 a
pair, or from California where Visions imports and sells
them for a little more.

DISCOUNT
Please see discount information in the How to Buy section.

**A. Rosenthal, 97 Orchard Street, New York, NY 10002.
Telephone (212) 473 5428**
*Send stamped self-addressed envelope for specific prices.
MC, V.*
Rosenthal has no list of brands stocked, but will send specific prices if you write. They say that they give 20- to 25-
percent discount on women's underwear such as Bali, Christian Dior, Givenchy, Gossard, Lily of France/John Kloss,
Maidenform, Playtex; and Berkshire and Burlington panty-
hose. Actually, I found a 30-percent discount here on the
one price I checked. Established 1943.

Charles Weiss and Sons, 38 Orchard Street, New York, NY 10002. Telephone (212) 226 1717
List of brands or a specific price quote, stamped self-addressed envelope. MC, V.
Charles Weiss will send a very minimal list of women's underwear brands stocked; better to send model number and details for price information. The one price I checked, I found slightly higher here than at other discount stores. Established 1981.

Mendel Weiss, 91 Orchard Street, New York, NY 10002. Telephone (212) 925 6815 or 226 9104
Prices given by mail (send stamped self-addressed envelope) or telephone (Sunday through Friday morning). MC, V.
Discounts on women's underwear and London Fog raincoats of up to 25 percent. Send model number and details for price. Established 1960.

30

Children and Maternity

Baby Love, P.O. Box 127, Laguna Beach, CA 92651
Brochure with swatches, free; overseas $1.50.
This small firm makes three attractive blouses and a dress for nursing mothers. Prices are very low, fabrics are "ethnic," "romantic" or "conventional." There are Velcro side openings for easy nursing.

Clothkits, 24 High Street, Lewes, Sussex, England. Telephone 07916 77111
Color catalogue, free.

Charing Cross Kits, Box 798, Main Street, Meredith, NH 03253. Telephone (603) 279 8449
Color catalogue, $2. MC, V.
Clothkits was started in 1969 by young parents Finn and Anne Kennedy in their own attic. Since then the clothes (which are so distinctive that a couple of dressed-up customers greeted each other with "Hello Clothkits" when they met in deepest Africa) have gathered an ardent following among sophisticated and thrifty English parents.

Most of the clothes are sold as kits with designs printed on fabric and all matching thread and zippers, ready for the customer to cut out and sew. With their striking colors and original patterns, the kits are a real find for people who want to dress their family interestingly at low prices. There are clothes for children up to the age of eleven and women up to size 18, plus ready-made knitwear.

You can buy directly from England or from New Hampshire, where three American women have started an American outpost. The prices are roughly just over a third more expensive if you buy in America, but you do get the convenience of prices in dollars, and no chance of duty.

31

Cotton Cookie Clothing Company, 50 Elm Avenue, Woodacre, CA 94973. Telephone (415) 488 0705
Brochure, $1 U.S. and overseas. MC, V.
Natural-fiber clothes for babies and toddlers: cotton long johns and shirts, Oshkosh overalls, and sheepskin vests.

Cotton Dreams, 999 Laredo Lane #C, Sebastian, FL 32958. Telephone (305) 589 0172
16-page brochure, free U.S. and overseas.
This family firm is dedicated to making available "quality, practical hard-to-find 100-percent cotton and wool family clothing at the lowest prices possible." Some clothes for

30 *Victoria's Secret* Silk chiffon underwear. Clothes change each season, but similar styles are always available.

31 *Clothkits/Charing Cross Kits* Swiss cotton dress comes cut out as a ready-to-sew kit in blended stripes of lilac/blue/pink, red/pink/orange, and other combinations. Can also be made into separate skirt and blouse. Sizes for girls age nine and up, and for women. Priced about $20 to $30.

32

33

34

32 *The Kids Warehouse* Pure cotton Oshkosh overalls stenciled with folk-art designs. Sizes one to ten, at about $19 to $24. All the Oshkosh children's clothes are carried.

33 *Pollyanna Children's Wear* Blouse in wool/cotton mixture with Liberty print. Recently sold in sizes four to eleven years for about $22 each.

34 *Pollyanna Children's Wear* Prisoner pajamas in pure cotton knit for boys and girls ages four to twelve. Recently sold for about $16.

adults, but more for children: French playsuits, pajamas, trousers, Austrian tights, Chinese shoes and Oshkosh overalls for babies and children up to the age of seven.

Cottontails, 1325 43rd Street, Los Alamos, NM 87544. Telephone (505) 662 4558
Brochure, $1 U.S. and overseas.
Clothes in attractive natural fabrics for ages two through ten. Tucks to let out as children grow.

Daisy Chain, The Warren, Great Witchingham, Norwich, Norfolk, England. Telephone Great Witchingham 674
Leaflet, $2.
Traditional, beautifully made hand-smocked dresses and blouses for girls two to eight.

Richard Hanten for Children, 4400 North Scottsdale Road, Scottsdale, AZ 85251. Telephone (602) 949 7349
Catalogue, $1 (refundable) U.S. and overseas. AE, MC, V.
Fairly traditional children's clothes, some imported, some from well-known American manufacturers. There is a little of everything for babies and children up to the age of fourteen, and usually a few pieces that can be monogrammed.

Hopscotch, 65 Pimlico Road, London SW1, England. Telephone (01) 730 7710
Brochure with swatches, $2. AE, DC, MC, V.
Handmade fashionable yet practical clothes such as quilted overalls and ruffled dresses for babies and children, six months to six years. Prices mainly $15 to $25 made-up, and $6 to $16 as kits.

The Kids Warehouse, Brownell Hollow, Eagle Bridge, NY 12057. Telephone (518) 677 8214 (Monday to Friday 9 A.M. to 12 noon only)
Brochure, free U.S. and overseas.
The Kids Warehouse was started by two mothers who found it hard to find children's clothing sturdy enough to hand down from one child to another. They now stock the whole superb Oshkosh overall line, for children in sizes up to 10, and other well-made natural-fiber clothes in good colors.

Laughing Bear Batique, P.O. Box 732, Woodstock, NY 12498. Telephone (914) 679 7650
Leaflet, free U.S. and overseas; overseas air mail $1. MC, V.
Two pages illustrated with black-and-white drawings introduce socks, sweat shirts and infant sets decorated with batik designs of hearts, stars and animals. Designs are cheerful and colors sound good (sky blue with magenta, dusty rose with hot pink, light purple with dark purple). Also tank tops and shirts for adults. Prices are reasonable.

Pollyanna Children's Wear, The Old Coppermill, Coppermill Lane (off Plough Lane), London SW17, England. Telephone 947 7084
Color catalogue, $1. AE, DC, MC, V.
A smallish English organization that designs, manufactures and sells "better designed, more amusing" children's clothes for ages up to twelve. They are well designed and co-ordinated—colors match and tops look good with bottoms. A small collection of medium-priced dresses, skirts, trousers and shirts is put out each spring and fall. Size is determined by the height of the child. Prices for these clothes, which are really very sophisticated and well made, start at about $25 for dresses and for pants.

**The Richman Company, 2627 Finer Road,
Santa Rosa, CA 95401. Telephone (707) 526 4909**
Leaflet, free; overseas $1.
Just a few cotton clothes for children up to the age of six—
overalls, socks, shirts and dresses, most of them dyed by
Barbara Coole Richman in "scrumptious" (her description)
colors such as cider, chocolate, cranberry or new blue.

**☙ Rowes of Bond Street, 170 New Bond Street,
London W1Y 0BN, England. Telephone (01) 409 1770**
Leaflet, free. AE, DC.
Rowes sells its classic English clothes and shoes to the
international set, who pass them around between siblings
and cousins. Dresses tend to be flowered or hand-smocked
($130 and up). Coats and boys' clothes are very traditional
($135 and up), and widely copied by other manufactur-
ers. Clothes can be bought in London or Paris, otherwise
write to Rowes with your requirements, and they will reply
with very inadequate leaflets.

**Gertrude Rueger, Weinplatz 8, 8001 Zurich, Switzerland.
Telephone (01) 211 80 63**
Gertrude Rueger stocks a whole range of children's clothes,
but says that the one with most appeal to American customers is her Swiss dirndl. These dresses, in sizes for ages one
to ten, have white blouses and red skirts with embroidered
black velvet straps. Being 100-percent cotton, they are machine-washable.
   Mrs. Rueger has no catalogue, but here are the prices,
which include surface postage and insurance: ages one to
three, $30; four to six, $35; seven to ten, $40.

**Tigermoth, 166 Portobello Road, London W11, England.
Telephone (01) 727 7564**
Price list, free. March, September.
This small firm sells sophisticated clothes for babies and
children up to the age of eight. A few casual and simple
clothes, some imported from Scandinavia or France, are listed.
The trouble is that the price list is minimal, just a typed
leaflet with one or two drawings, and is not always available.

**Wildflowers, 80 Warren Street, #52,
New York, NY 10007. Telephone (212) 285 2051**
Leaflet, free.
Pure cotton T-shirts, pajamas and dresses and overalls are
silk-screened with humorous circus, animal and flower designs. A very small but nice collection, illustrated with line
drawings.

**The Young Idea, 9 Kingsbury, Aylesbury,
Buckinghamshire HP20 2JA, England. Telephone 880 68**
Catalogue, $1. MC, V.
I've bought lots of Ladybird clothes in my time and found
them far better-wearing and longer-lasting than most of the
American children's clothes I've picked up, so I was terribly
pleased to find this firm, which sells perfect Ladybird
clothes in discontinued lines at bargain prices.
   Young Idea produces four brochures, illustrated with line
drawings, each year. They all show dresses, shirts and pants
for boys and girls up to the age of thirteen, a few baby
clothes (sometimes by the famous British maker Bairns-
wear), sometimes frilly nightdresses and fleeced pajamas,
and sometimes coats. Typical prices in the last brochure I
looked at had dresses and pants for children up to the age of
six and pants for thirteen-year-old boys at $10—not bad,
considering that the clothes are very well made.

35

36

35 *Tigermoth* Finnish pure cotton striped T-shirt and pants in
sizes for babies to six-year-olds. Recently sold separately, or together for about $12. Pure cotton French dress in pale colors such
as dusty green and dusty pink for sizes two to ten years. Recently
sold for about $20.

36 *Tuppence Coloured* (see Women and Children section) Children's clothes in cotton or velvet. Similar styles available ready
made or as kits.

7
COLLECTING

Americana

Hakes Americana and Collectibles,
P.O. Box 1444, York, PA 17405.
Catalogues, four times a year, $2.00 each or $8 subscription; overseas air mail $2.
Hakes sells its wares by mail auction, specializing in Disneyana and other comic-related items, presidential campaign buttons, etc., as well as advertising collectibles and radio premiums.

Art Deco and Art Nouveau

21st Century Antiques, Hadley, MA 01035.
Telephone (413) 549 6678
Catalogue, $3; overseas $5.
A catalogue to delight lovers of Arts and Crafts/Mission movement, art deco and art nouveau: blue and white bakelite radio, $35; silver and black lacquered tray, $25; dragon planter, $75; there is something for every fanciful taste.

Autographs

Walter A. Benjamin, Autographs, Box 255,
Scribner Hollow Road, Hunter, NY 12442.
Telephone (518) 263 4133
Catalogue, free.
Founded in 1887, this is the oldest firm in the United States dealing with autograph letters and manuscripts. Benjamin stocks thousands, ranging in price from a dollar to several thousand. "The Collector," which has been published since the firm began, lists a small fraction of the holdings and appears four to five times a year.

Charles Hamilton, 25 East 77th Street,
New York, NY 10021. Telephone (212) 628 1666
Auction catalogues, free.
Charles Hamilton is one of the country's best-known dealers in autographs and letters. He now sends out his very thorough auction catalogues, in addition to selling directly. Here is a full range of materials, strongest in American history, with Presidents galore.

Butterflies

The Butterfly Company,
51–17 Rockaway Beach Boulevard,
Far Rockaway, NY 11691. Telephone (212) 945 5400
Brochures, $2.
This is the world's largest dealer in butterflies and moths, and its catalogue shows some of them (plus beetles) in full color. These include insects from North America and Europe as well as such exotic places as New Guinea, Australia, Africa and Malaysia.
   The Butterfly Company also sells the requisite equipment, from nets to mounting kits and display cases.

Carousel Animals

**Tobin Fraley Studios, 3246 Ettie Street, #12,
Oakland, CA 94608. Telephone (415) 654 3031**
Catalogue, $5; overseas air mail $9.
Amazing carousel animals, including prancing horses, leaping dragons and lumbering elephants by carvers who are well known in the field. Some animals are stripped, others restored, and others have the old paint. Prices start at $1250, but are mostly higher.

Coins

**B. A. Seaby, Audley House, 11 Margaret Street,
London W1N 8AT, England. Telephone (01) 580 3677**
Monthly bulletins by first-class mail, $35; second-class air mail $24.
Seaby's is the world's largest dealer in coins and medals as well as being Numismatists to the Queen. They have twelve resident coin experts and are the source of many of the field's basic reference works. Their monthly bulletin lists both coins and medals for sale but also runs articles of general interest.

**Spink and Son, 5–7 King Street, St. James's,
London SW1, England. Telephone (01) 930 7888**
Numismatic Circular, ten volumes, one year's subscription, $20.
Spink's, a three-hundred-year-old family firm, is not only mentioned in *The Lost World*, by Sir Arthur Conan Doyle, but they were delighted and amused to find their name dropped by "M" in a James Bond novel: "As Spink and the British Museum agree . . ."

Their illustrated journal *Numismatic Circular* has a catalogue of Greek, Roman, Byzantine, English and foreign coins, war medals and books offered for sale, and it also has articles, reviews, news and correspondence of interest to collectors.

Dolls

**Robin and Nell Dale, Bank House Farm, Holme Mills,
Holme, via Carnforth, Lancashire, England.
Telephone 0524 781 646**
Color catalogue, $3.
Robin and Nell Dale make small painted beechwood stump dolls with arms, for collectors. The dolls are mostly traditional English characters such as Constable Bentham (in 1818 costume) and Admiral Mainbrace (though there is a Pilgrim couple), also circus dolls and nativity sets. Most dolls cost about $25 each, and there is an Alice in Wonderland chess set that costs much more.

**Mark Farmer Company, 38 Washington Avenue,
Box 438, Pt. Richmond, CA 94801**
60-page doll catalogue, $1.
Miniature catalogue, 25 cents.
Very well known to doll collectors, Mark Farmer sells china and bisque doll parts, undressed dolls and dressed dolls, all with an old-fashioned look about them, quite unlike most dolls available. Some are sweet little creatures that are suitable for older children, others are fashion dolls to be elaborately dressed and used as decorations. There is one model

1

2

3

1 *Hakes Americana and Collectibles* A set of six lobby cards for *Hellcats of the Navy,* the only film to co-star Nancy Davis (later to become Nancy Reagan) and Ronald Reagan. Auctioned for $250.

2 *Hakes Americana and Collectibles* Recently auctioned 1930s Disneyana.

3 *21st Century Antiques* Floral-fantasy picture frame in cast iron with brass finish, recently sold for $75. Viennese card tray with two nudes in high relief, sold for $125. *W.F.M.* silver-plated dressing table mirror with depressions for jars, sold for $300.

4

5

6

4 *Eric Horne* Painted jointed wooden dolls in sizes ¼″ high to 8¼″. About $8 to $35. *(Photograph by Graham Ward.)*

5 *Old Time Teddy Bears* Copies of turn-of-the-century teddy bears, 8″ to 25″ high. Prices from $13.50.

6 *Treasure Box Showroom* King Henry VIII and his wives, from the Peggy Nisbet portrait series.

for which you can buy different wigs and different dress patterns, and make a collection of First Ladies. Patterns for dresses, shoe kits, glass domes for displaying the dolls, and collections of miniature furniture are available, and some doll repairs are made.

Ron Fuller Toys, Lexfield, Woodbridge, Suffolk, England
Leaflet, $1.
A charming collection of moving wood and tinplate novelties and souvenirs, painted in bright and attractive colors. Although some wooden boats and airplanes are toys, and can certainly be played with, most of the pieces are like old musical boxes, really to be put on table or shelf to be admired and occasionally worked. Prices start at $14 for an 8-inch plane, and go up to $188 for a circus train and animals.

Eric Horne, 54 Majorfield Road, Topsham, Exeter, Devon EX3 0ES, England. Telephone Topsham 5716
8-page brochure, $1; air mail $2.
Eric Horne makes old-fashioned jointed wooden dolls (undressed) in sizes of ¼-inch high to 8½-inch high, at prices $8 to $35. Christine Horne makes felt-dressed mice, and 4-inch dressed peg dolls in various costumes such as bride and groom, cooks and maids, mother and child and Father Christmas. *But* minimum order is $50.

The Mousehole Workshop, 524 Kinderkamack Road, Westwood, NJ 07675. Telephone (201) 666 1263
Price list, 25 cents; overseas 1 International Reply Coupon.
Four-inch felt mice, dressed as carol singers, angels, Father Christmas, George Washington, a "mousewife" in a mob cap and goodness knows what else. You can even have your family made up as mice, $10 each.

Old Time Teddy Bears, 304 SE 87th Avenue, Portland, OR 97216. Telephone (503) 256 4563
Leaflet, self-addressed stamped envelope; overseas 1 International Reply Coupon.
Karen Walter started making old-fashioned teddy bears after she bought a turn-of-the-century bear in an antique shop, and thought it was more charming than modern ones. She makes them in sizes 4 inches to 27 inches, and in 1981 when 17,000 teddy-bear lovers gathered in Minneapolis, she won the Make a Teddy Bear contest. Prices are reasonable.

Standard Doll Company, 23–83 31st Street, Long Island City, NY 11105. Telephone (212) 721 7787
60-page catalogue, $2; overseas $4. AE, MC, V.
Eyes, legs, arms, faces and wigs are on sale here for doll makers, and for doll dressers there is even more: modern and antique replica undressed baby, toddler, preteen and teen dolls—black, white and Indian. There is also fancy fabric, such as satin lace and tulle, and trimmings, beads and sequins, buttons and buckles and tiny zippers. Patterns to make clothes and rag dolls are available, as well as instruction books.

Treasure Box Showroom, c/o House of Nisbet, Dunster Park, Winscombe, BS25 1AG, England. Telephone 0934 84 2905
Price list and newsletter, free. Prices in $.
This small but well-known company makes Peggy Nisbet dolls—"traditional and historical costumed figurines." There are dolls in national costumes, English and American historical figures, a Williamsburg collection and Victorian dollhouse figures on a one-inch-equals-one-foot scale. Prices under $50 postpaid.

Ephemera

**William Frost Mobley, P.O. Box 333,
551 Mountain Road, Wilbraham, MA 01095**
Catalogue No. 2, $13.
William Frost Mobley, one of the few dealers in ephemera to publish fully illustrated catalogues, describes his own wares better than I can: "A Superlative Selection of American Nineteenth-Century Historical and Advertising BROADSIDES, Trade Cards, Admission Tickets, Letterheads, Billheads, Broadsheets, Song Ballads, Rewards of Merit, Stationer's Labels, etc. Illustrating the Social, Political, and Business History as well as the Development and Flowering of Display Typography and Job printing of the Last Century."

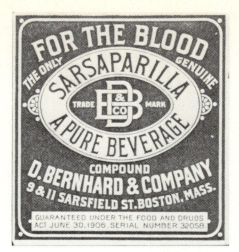

Fossils

**Malick's Fossils, 5514 Plymouth Road,
Baltimore, MD 21214. Telephone (301) 426 2969**
90-page catalogue, $3; overseas $5.
The Malick's catalogue is aimed at those who know exactly what they want and should not be sent for by the rank beginner; but for a serious collector or researcher it is a perfect tool. Malick's lists animal and plant fossils, classified scientifically, artifacts of early man, including not only arrowheads, knives, and the like, all very reasonably priced, but some beautiful terra-cotta figurines from Mexico, fertility figures from Siam, pottery, and so on.

There is also a selection of books related to fossils and artifacts.

For more fossils, see Dover in this section, under Shells.

Hobby Cards

Wholesale Cards, Box 496, Georgetown, CT 06829
Catalogue, $1.
For collectors of hobby cards, a list of the old-fashioned baseball cards as well as nonsports items. There are many sports other than baseball, of course, many recent. The others range from 1940 autographed movie stars to more recent Soupy Sales or even elephant joke cards.

7

Military

**Soldiers Shop, 1013 Madison Avenue,
New York, NY 10021. Telephone (212) 535 6788**
86-page catalogue, $5 U.S. and overseas.
The Soldiers Shop aims to provide military collectors with a wide range of useful and interesting items. They have model soldiers, military uniforms, medals and badges, paintings, over three thousand books, and even ice buckets made to look like drums.

7 *William Frost Mobley* Lithographed nineteenth-century labels. Priced about $3 to $25

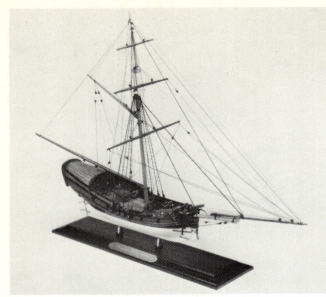

8

9

Minerals

W. D. Christianson, 200 Napier Street,
Barrie, Ontario, Canada. Telephone (705) 726 8713
Price list, free. MC, V.
Mineral specimens ("avidly sought after" by collectors) from all over the world, especially Canada and the United States.

Miniatures

Chestnut Hill Studio, Box 38, Churchville, NY 14428.
Telephone (803) 268 7546
44-page catalogue, $5.25; overseas $7.75.
If you are interested in authentic period pieces in one-foot-equals-one-inch scale, this is an excellent catalogue for you. This family business sells mostly its own designs, and stresses authenticity and scale (even the wood grains are to scale), and everything in the large selection is handmade. Furniture, in most antique styles, is only the beginning of what they offer. There are paintings and rugs and room accessories in the most minute detail: dishes, mirrors, etc. They have sterling silver miniatures for fine dining and cooking. Chestnut Hill is the oldest miniature manufacturer in the United States, and is obviously for the serious and pecunious doll-houser.

Minutiques, 82b Trafalgar Street, Brighton,
East Sussex, BN1 4EB, England. Telephone 0273 681 862
A good source of inexpensive supplies for doll makers and miniature collectors. For doll makers there are heads and parts of all kinds, human hair wigs, straw bonnets, leather shoes and antique clothing. For miniature collectors, realistic building materials and kits to make doll houses (you supply the wood, Minutiques supplies all the fittings and paper and plans), plastic "wood look" furniture, and very nice accessories and doll-house families.

Den Young, 63 Earith Road, Willingham,
Cambridgeshire CB4 5LS, England.
Telephone 0954 60015
Price list, 2 International Reply Coupons; air mail 4 International Reply Coupons.
Den Young makes doll houses and miniatures to order, and he says that his work is in some of the world's finest collections. He is known on radio and television and in the press as one of the foremost craftsmen in the field. He will make any period houses and will even reproduce your own house in a scale of one inch equal one foot. He will also make any piece of furniture from a drawing or photograph or picture cut out of a magazine. His brief price list includes rocking horses, chess sets, fourposters, harps, violins and grand pianos, and he has several chairs for around $12 each. He can also provide sets of stairs, window frames, and set-scene wall boxes.

Models

America's Hobby Center, 146 West 22nd Street,
New York, NY 10011. Telephone (212) 675 8922
Model catalogues: kits to make (1) airplanes, (2) ships, (3) cars. Each catalogue, $1.50; overseas $2.50. HO- and N-gauge train catalogue, $2; overseas $3.
In business since 1931, this firm deals in models for vehicu-

8 *Authentic Ship Models* Bermuda sloop, circa 1740, after Chapman. This model has been built after plans found in Swedish archives and engravings in the Swedish shipwright's book, *Architectura Navalis Mercatoria*. About $440.

9 *Authentic Ship Models* Model ships of oak, mahogany, and Oregon pine with cotton or linen sails and flax ropes are made from original plans. Prices start at about $150 for assembled models, and at about $130 for assembled half models.

lar hobbyists. It carries a complete line of modeling items, and although it has a retail store, its emphasis is on mail ordering. One can buy anything from ready-to-run sets to ready-to-build kits.

Authentic Ship Models, Amsterdam, Bloemstraat 191, 1016 LA Amsterdam, The Netherlands. Telephone 20 24 66 01
80-page color brochure of built model ships, $6 (air mail). Pendants brochure, $4. AE, DC, V.
Magnificent assembled models of beautiful ships. Authentic Ship Models traces the history of the development of the sailing ship with their models of the finest ships of the past. Fifteenth-century Spanish and Portuguese galleons, sixteenth- and seventeenth-century Dutch merchants, eighteenth-century English warships, nineteenth-century American schooners. Prices $130 to $1000, with several American and other simpler ships at around $200.

This firm also makes cast-metal painted and unpainted soldiers and a most striking and unusual collection of pendants based on old sundials. Prices mostly around $40 in bronze and roughly around $90 in silver.

The Black Watch, P.O. Box 666, Van Nuys, CA 91408. Telephone (213) 701 7961
100-page catalogue, $4; overseas $5; air mail $7.50.
Miniature soldiers, both American and imported from England, France, and Scotland. A full selection that ranges from "the ancients" to World War II.

Blenheim Military Models, P.O. Box 39, Brigend, South Wales CF32 8DU, Great Britain. Telephone 011 44 0656 870 477
Color catalogue, $3.
Two ex-antique dealers now run a cottage industry from a tiny village in Wales. They produce toy soldiers, specializing in the late Victorian period when "toy soldiers were in their heyday, and the uniforms were most splendid." Also model soldiers for painting.

Cherry's, 62 Sheen Road, Richmond, Surrey, England. Telephone (01) 940 2454
Price list, $2.
Cherry's, which has become known and thoroughly visited by American model railway buffs, specializes in very high class, second-hand working steam engines of all types, most of them not obtainable in America. Their list gives a detailed description of each model.

Hamblings, 29 Cecil Court, Charing Cross Road, London WC2, England. Telephone (01) 836 4704
No catalogue. Manufacturers brochures, and price quotes in response to inquiries. MC, V.
The largest and oldest established "oo" specialists, and probably the only firm in Great Britain that manufactures, wholesales and retails exclusively model railroad products, parts and accessories. They stock British prototypes which are almost impossible to buy in America; although, strangely enough, there is a demand.

Hobby Surplus Sales, P.O. Box 2170, New Britain, CT 06050
128-page catalogue, $1; overseas (air mail) $2. MC, V.
Kits and supplies for modelers of railroads, boats, cars and planes. Owner says that most supplies are discounted, but I haven't checked.

JMC/Con-Cor, 1025 Industrial Drive, Bensenville, IL 60106. Telephone (312) 595 0210
Catalogues: (1) Model railroading N-scale, (2) Model railroading HO-scale locomotives, (3) HO-scale structures and accessories. Each 80 page catalogue, $3; overseas $6. MC, V.
These large catalogues show the complete range of supplies for people who build model railroads. JMC manufactures and also distributes supplies by many leading manufacturers; they say their goal is to provide *not everything,* but the best available in the industry. The catalogues will tell you what is available. If near a dealer you should buy there; otherwise mail orders are accepted.

The Old Train Shop, 2 Bartholomew Street West, Exeter, Devon, England. Telephone 0392 31548
List of lists, 1 International Reply Coupon. MC, V.
The Old Train Shop supplies, collects and restores old metal toys. They have now become computerized and produce daily updated lists of the old English Meccano, Corgey, Lesney, Triang toys they have in stock, and the spares and replacements for Dinky, Hornby O-gauge, etc. Send an international reply coupon for their master list, which tells how much each of their ten price lists costs.

Polk's Model Craft, 314 Fifth Avenue, New York, NY 10001. Telephone (212) 279 9034
General catalogue planned, $5; overseas $7. MC, V.
Polk's five-story building on lower Fifth Avenue is filled with more model ships, planes, soldiers, railroads, and related impedimenta than I thought existed, and its catalogues, when available, reflect the store's infinite variety. Here are models and kits that replicate reality in such endless detail that model-railroad enthusiasts can choose between different styles of depot stations, not to mention the trains or tracks, or twelve different kinds of refrigerator cars.

Movie Ephemera

Jerry Ohlinger's Movie Material Store, 120 West Third Street, New York, NY 10012 Telephone (212) 674 8474
Price list, self-addressed stamped envelope or 1 International Reply Coupon.
Movie posters, lobby cards, stills, pressbooks—everything for the movie nut. Mostly originals, though some posters are reproduced. Largely American but some European posters are available. Many of the posters are under $10.

Music Boxes

San Francisco Music Box Company, P.O. Box 26433, San Francisco, CA 94126
32-page color catalogue, $1; overseas $2. No catalogue March to August.
A selection of music boxes for children includes tiny wooden merry-go-rounds and skaters that turn as the music plays and Mickey Mouse, Paddington and "Peanuts" boxes. For the more traditionally inclined there are inlaid boxes from Italy, lacquered boxes from Switzerland and feathered birds in gilded cages.

10

11

12

World of Music Boxes, 412 Main Street, Avon, NJ 07717. Telephone (201) 988 6600
46-page catalogue, $1 U.S.; overseas free. MC, V.
A delightfully varied assortment of music boxes. There is a rah-rah page of twenty-seven college songs, "personalized" boxes with any tune you choose and topped with your own photograph, and kits to make your own box or carve a revolving figurine.

Pens

Good Service Pen Shop, 1079 Forest Hills Drive SW, Rochester, MN 55901. Telephone (507) 281 1988
Leaflet, free.
Fountain pen collectors and users will find a stunning array of new and used pens, including over sixty less-common brands, and mechanical pencils. They say that with their complete inventory of parts they can fix most pens.

Paperweights

The Friar's House, Benet Street, Cambridge, England. Telephone 0223 60275
Catalogue, free.
Friar's House sells new English and French paperweights. I found two 1980 St. Louis weights that were also on sale in the United States and found that they cost about 35 percent less in England.

George Kamm Paperweights, 406 West Marion Street, Suit 18, Lititz, PA 17543
Leaflets and price lists, $5 per year; overseas $7.
New paperweights and mainly older ones (1960s and 70s) from the well-known firms as well as smaller ones.

L. H. Selman, 761 Chestnut Street, Santa Cruz, CA 90560. Telephone 800 538 0766
110-page color catalogue, $6; overseas $7; air mail $9.50.
L. H. Selman stocks antique and modern paperweights, as well as books about them. He sells to people who collect them for their decorative value alone, as well as those who buy to invest.

Fine crystal paperweights were first produced in France from about 1840 to 1860; the fad then spread to England, Europe and finally America. Collectors of antique paperweights try to find representative weights from the finest French factories, and sometimes from the English and American.

Modern paperweights, at prices from $60 to $700, are illustrated and described in the informative catalogue, which lists weights from firms such as Baccarat, St. Louis and Perthshire, as well as from individual craftsmen who make signed weights.

10 *The Friar's House* Whitefriars Collection, 1982. Three faceted paperweights. Left, Butterfly; right, Garland of Roses; bottom, Spread of Roses. Each edition 750, price $100 each postpaid.

11 *Albatross Antiques* Rockwell Society 1981 Christmas Plate, "Wrapped Up in Christmas," $25.50.

12 *Kendal Playing Card Sales* American Presidents deck.

Plates

Albatross Antiques, Box 21-CC, Stillwater, MN 55082. Telephone 800 328 1448
Catalogue, free. AE, MC, V.
Collector plates and other ceramic objects. Norman Rockwell, Royal Copenhagen, Bing and Grondahl and many

others. Figurines, Christmas spoons, beer steins, Christmas ornaments; some in new editions, others dating over the years.

13

Playing Cards

Kendal Playing Card Sales, 3 Oakbank House, Skelsmergh, Kendal, Cumbria, England. Telephone 0539 22055
Regular list and Once Only list, free; air mail 50 cents. Prices in $.
Two playing-card collectors sell by mail new playing cards from various countries. Some of the packs sound fascinating even for noncollectors. From Spain there is a deck for about $3 showing the art of preColumbian America, and a reprint of the 1961 Civil War deck with Union and Confederate leaders as the courts, $3.50. There is a Shakespeare set complete with quotations, plenty of royalty, history and humor. There are also magician's packs (seven extra cards), solitaire packs, hand-painted packs from India, and eleven different kinds of tarot cards, including the *Ancien Tarot de Marseille,* the most famous of all. Books about cards too.

U.S. Games Systems, 38 East 32nd Street, New York, NY 10016. Telephone (212) 685 4300
Color brochure, $1 U.S. and overseas.
Tarot cards, which are used for fortune telling, are believed to have originated in Italy in the fourteenth century. U.S. Games Systems sells by mail fascinating reproductions of several of the most famous tarot decks, books about them and also fortune-telling cards and instructions.

14

Shells

Dover Scientific Corporation, Box 6011, Long Island City, NY 11106. Telephone (212) 721 0136
Catalogue of shells, fossils, minerals, Indian artifacts, $1; overseas $2.
Color brochure of shells and minerals, $2; overseas $3.50.
Dover publishes a very satisfactory businesslike catalogue offering fossils, shells, minerals, and Indian artifacts, and books relating to these. There are also polished stones, and larger pieces that are described as potential ashtrays but strike me as much too beautiful to be used as anything but decorations.

The catalogue has an extensive and detailed eight-page list of shells, as well as a number of Indian artifacts such as arrowheads, small pots, etc. Dover says that all its specimens are of top quality and that any purchase can be exchanged within a week of receipt. Dover also offers books on the sciences.

Eaton's Shell and Rock Shop, 16 Manette Street, London W1V 5LB, England. Telephone (01) 437 9391
Collectors price list, free.
Shells, coral, starfish and marine curios from all over the world. Minimum order $40.

Ferguson's Marine Specialties, 617 North Fries Avenue, Wilmington, CA 90744. Telephone (213) 835 0811
Price lists, free.
"Over 35 years in sea shells" states this dealer in shells, both real and artificial. The offerings are, for the most part, real, from the humble at under a dollar to a special selection of "showy" items, such as a large magnifica voluta at $40.

15

13 *U.S. Games Systems* "Chinese Art Treasures." Double-bridge playing cards.

14 *U.S. Games Systems* Hand-painted Indian playing-card deck in hand-painted box. About $150.

15 *U.S. Games Systems* Heron's Tarot of Marseille deck. About $9.

16

17

Stamps

Stanley Gibbons, 391 Strand, London WC2, England

**Stanley Gibbons, 1325 Franklin Avenue,
Garden City, NY 11530**
Price list, free. AE, MC, V.
World-famous for their stamps and authoritative catalogues,
Stanley Gibbons will send lists of stamps, albums, stamp
catalogues, accessories and books that are available.

**Harmers of New York, 6 West 48th Street,
New York, NY 10036. Telephone (212) 757 4460**
Auction catalogues three weeks before auction, $2.
This is one of the world's leading stamp dealers, with
branches in San Francisco, London and Sydney. The firm
runs a series of auctions in each of these cities, each year,
and you can get the catalogue either before or after, with the
prices paid included. Or you can buy directly from each
store. Just about every category of rare and precious stamps
seems to be covered in the catalogue, along with the book
value.

Thimbles

**Shopping Service, 23 Cranbourne Gardens,
London NW11 0JB, England**
Annual brochure, $2.50 (air mail). MC, V.
For thimble collectors, a selection from the world over, including some specially made for the firm. Here are Wedgwood thimbles, Staffordshire enamel, German Vermeil as
well as silver and other materials. Just about every theme
imaginable is illustrated here at prices that range from $3
for a likeness of His Holiness to the twenties for more
elaborate items. Various sets are also available as are accessories, such as stands and sewing kits.

Weapons

**Golden Age Arms Company,
14 W. Winter, Box 28, Worthington, OH 43015.
Telephone (614) 369 6513**
124-page annual catalogue, free U.S. and overseas.
This firm, organized in 1962, sells books on antique firearms, Americana, and antiques in general; reproductions of
muzzle-loading rifles; and pistol parts (kits as well as
parts—and there is generally a savings in the kit price). The
book department has a good selection, not only on guns but
also on Americana and antiques, crafts and Indians.

16 *Dover Scientific Corporation* Chambered nautilus half shell,
$7.50; heart cockle shell, $1; cornucervi murex shell, $25.

17 *Dover Scientific Corporation* Septarian concretion, Utah; 4″ to
6″, $25.50.

8
CRAFTS AND LOCAL PRODUCTS

1

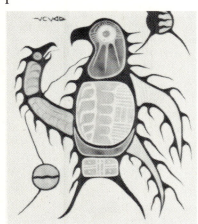

2

3

1 *Iroqrafts* "Loons and Fish" by Richard Bedwash, Ojibwa; 20″ × 26″ signed, numbered print in edition of 100, $90.

2 *Iroqrafts* "Thunderbird Snake" by Richard Bedwash, Ojibwa; 20″ × 26″ signed, numbered print in edition of 100, $60.

3 *Folklore-Olga Fisch* Brightly colored ceramic figures. About $18 to $32.

CANADA

Iroqrafts, Box 3, Ohsweken, Six Nations Reserve, Ontario, Canada. Telephone (416) 765 4206
Catalogue, $1 (refundable, no checks please). Prices in $.
A serious firm that sells traditional and ceremonial Iroquois crafts to museums as well as shops and individuals. Some of the crafts are highly decorative beaded and fringed things: headbands, bracelets and necklaces, tasseled belts, flower-embroidered gloves, fringed and patterned bags. For more serious collectors: hand-sculpted ceremonial false face masks "sold only on the understanding they will not be used in pseudo-Indian ceremonies or other sacrilegious ways" and a whole lot of scarcer items: one-of-a-kind clothes, pillows, quilts, paintings, pottery, full-size canoes, etc.

ECUADOR

Andean Products, Apartado 472 Cuenca, Ecuador. Telephone 82 6171
Color catalogue, $1.
An artisan-owned cooperative that was originally set up with the help of Peace Corps volunteers, it says that its "major longing is to wholesale." Nevertheless, through a color brochure, it does sell to private individuals hand-woven tapestries, chunky hand-knitted sweaters from hand-spun wool, straw Christmas tree ornaments, painted wooden bowls, embroidered clothes, and a few other local crafts. Minimum order $50.

Folklore-Olga Fisch, PO Box 64, Quito, Ecuador. Telephone 231 767
Color crafts brochure, $4.
Color rug brochure, $4.
Olga Fisch was born in Budapest but moved to Ecuador just before World War II. There she became interested in local folk art and helped make Indian crafts into a significant export.

A sophisticated, captivating collection of Ecuadorian crafts is beautifully illustrated in the Folklore brochure: bright and shiny bread-dough figures; richly embroidered cushions and bedspreads; primitive paintings; colorful straw, wood and ceramic animals; and handwoven Salasaca wall hangings. There is also a little Indian jewelry and local clothing, such as embroidered shirts and dresses, handknitted sweaters and felt hats.

ENGLAND

Elizabeth Best, 89 Palmerston Road, London N22, England
Information, 1 International Reply Coupon.
Elizabeth Best makes commemorative pincushions for births, weddings or anything else you might want commemorated. She writes, "I am hardly a firm—just me. I do not have a catalogue as I never make two pincushions the same.

"Christening and birth pincushions are usually covered in voile, and I make them in any size or shape, but I find the most popular are 3½ by 5 inches and 5 by 5 inches. The small one is only suitable for one name, or two short ones, and can have the date on the back or front. This size starts at $36. The large one, either square or diamond, can have three names and time, day and date of birth. I have often been asked to include birth weight, adoption date, Christening date, parents names, etc.!

4   5

6

"Wedding pincushions can be made in the same fabric as the wedding dress and decorated in the colors of the bouquet. I also make anniversary, birthday and Valentine pincushions."

Lydia Corbett, 1 Martins, Dartington Hall, Totnes, South Devon, England
Information, 1 International Reply Coupon; photographs at cost.
Lydia Corbett makes unusual dried-flower collages with the wild flowers she finds in England and France. Her pictures have nothing in common with most dried-flower pictures but are beautifully arranged patterns in color and shape pasted directly onto the glass, occasionally with a cutting of a woman's face, or a butterfly added. The glass has no backing, which gives a translucence that shows the texture of the leaves, and frames are old, which gives the pictures a romantic old-fashioned look, even though the style is new. Pictures are small, up to about 12 by 14 inches including frame, and cost about $40 to $60 depending on size and frame.

Robin and Mary Ellis, Hadstock Road, Linton, Cambridge CB1 6NR, England. Telephone 892 592
Color leaflets: Wooden-Egg Collecting, Pine Treasure House, Round Table, Wood Trays, $1. V.
The leaflets of woodturners Robin and Mary Ellis are lavish with praise for the "subtle color, the smooth texture and the fascinating graining of *natural wood*." They insist that "you cannot place flawless pieces of porcelain on hard, brassy metal, overbearingly floral pressed fiberglass, gaudily printed prints or plastic imitations of anything!" For anyone who agrees with them, they make four trays in rosewood, yew, oak, elm or beech, and legs to go with the trays to handily convert them into little tables. For people even more in love with wood, there are smooth and glossy eggs in exotic wood to be collected and decoratively placed on a wooden platter. On the other hand, for people who don't mind covering their wood, the Ellises make a series of the round tables that are so popular with decorators, intended to be entirely covered with fabric. Low bedside round tables start at just $20, while trays start at about $30.

Global Village Crafts, Roundwell, Street, South Petherton, Somerset, England. Telephone 0460 40194
Catalogue, $1.50; air mail $3. AE, MC, V.
Interior Decor price lists: Indian Interior Decoration, Antiques from the East; Burmese and Thai Lacquer, Indian paintings.
While the Reverend Victor Lamont was training village youth leaders in the Third World, he found a great need for selfhelp in the rural areas. When he returned to England, he started a clearinghouse for information about cheap technology available, but so many of the questions asked were from village cooperatives that wanted to know how to market their products in rich countries, that the Reverend Lamont started an organization to actually sell the goods.

Global Village Crafts consists of a wholesaling branch, a mail-order catalogue, and the original clearinghouse—Rural Communication Services—into which profits from the other branches go.

The organization has been deservedly successful; crafts from such places as Sri Lanka, Upper Volta, Kenya, Guatemala and the Cameroons are chosen with sense and imagination and are appealingly presented in a good-looking catalogue. There is plenty to decorate a house, inlaid boxes, brass lamps, hammocks, baskets and batiks, mobiles, carv-

4 *Folklore-Olga Fisch* Handwoven tapestries made by Salasacan Indians, cost about $33 to $168.

5 *Folklore-Olga Fisch* Silver-plated pins based on archeological motifs. About $12 to $19 each.

6 *Elizabeth Best* Commemorative pincushions, starting at $36 each.

7

10

8

9

11

12

7 *Lydia Corbett* Flower collage 8¼″ by 10″ high, with unusually ornate frame, $50.

8 *Robin and Mary Ellis* Wooden eggs available in sixty-eight different woods. Priced about $4 to $10 each. *(Photograph by Andrew Houston.)*

9 *Global Village Crafts* Rosewood, lacquer, brass, and mother-of-pearl boxes from a large assortment of boxes from many countries. Priced about $4 to $16 each.

10 *Global Village Crafts* Sun and air hammock from El Salvador. About $40.

11 *Global Village Crafts* Six-horse merry-go-round mobile. About $8.

12 *Global Village Crafts* Peruvian *retablos* showing the Nativity. Priced about $20 to $60, depending on size.

13

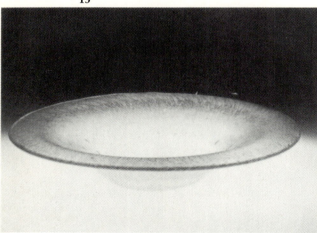

14

ings and decorative toys of all kinds, plus unusual things like do-it-yourself incense kits and Tibetan knives and chopstick sets with wood and metal bowls.

Naturally British, 13 New Row, Covent Garden, London WC2 N4LF, England. Telephone (01) 240 0551
Color leaflet, free.
Opened in 1978 in London's revamped Covent Garden, Naturally British is full of fetching things chosen fussily from craftspeople using "time-honored" traditional methods. The pottery bread crocks, dressed toys, and quilted jackets are presented on the leaflet in a jumble, so the leaflet is appealing but won't be easy to buy from.

Chris Reekie, Old Coach House, Stock Road, Grasmere, Westmorland, England
Brochure, $1.
These handweavers make stoles, rugs, capes from soft and warm mohair in pale tartans and light colors. Prices are very reasonable.

Jeff Samuel, Combe Farm, West Anstey, South Molton, Devon EX36 3NX, England
Details, $1.
"I am not a shop, but a farmer," writes Jeffrey Samuel, "who makes carved sticks, more as a hobby." Sticks are made from hazel, thorn, ash or holly from a valley on the edge of moors; any animal, fish or bird can be carved on the handle, to order, and letters, flowers or leaves can be carved on the shaft. Prices start at about $20 for a fox's head. Ordinary walking sticks and shepherd's crooks are also made.

Peter Tysoe Handmade Glass, 3 Warland, Totnes, Devon, England. Telephone 0803 865 082
Leaflet, $1.
Peter Tysoe, an English glass blower whose work has been shown in galleries in Europe and the United States, also sells glass direct from his workshop. His prices are lower than United States prices for handmade glass. He makes a line of pearly iridescent vases; bowls and plates with faint blue/green and pinkish/purple coloring; ribbed, colored scent bottles and flasks; and clear or colored wineglasses and decanters. Many prices below $40.

John and Jo Withers, Eaten House, 14 Station Road, Madeley, Telford TF7 5AY, Shropshire, England. Telephone 0952 585 131
Leaflet with color photographs, $1.
A husband and wife, silversmith and enameler, make pretty little painted enamel boxes, thimbles and miniature paintings. All of them are hand painted and each design is limited to about twenty-five. Current scenes of birds and flowers are shown on a leaflet, and custom work is happily undertaken. Thimbles are under $10, miniatures under $20 and boxes around $60.

ETHIOPIA

Bethlehem Training Center, P.O. Box 6558, Addis Ababa, Ethiopia. Telephone 18417
Leaflet, $1.
A group of Catholic Good Shepherds are trying to find work for "socially deprived" young women in Addis Ababa. They are teaching needlework and carpet weaving, and have plans for block printing and dyeing. At the moment they are selling by mail handwoven tapestries of Ethiopian scenes, in the natural colors of the local highland sheep wool.

13 *Jeff Samuel* Carved walking sticks at prices from $20.

14 *Peter Tysoe* Pearly glass bowl with slight blue/green or pinkish/purple coloring. About $60.

HOLLAND

Pottenbakkerij 't Spinnewiel,
Zwanenburgwal 62, 1011J9, Amsterdam, Holland.
Telephone 020 240 578
Leaflet in Dutch, free.
Apparently giving a newborn baby a decorated tile is an old Dutch custom. The Pottenbakkerij makes birth tiles with the name, weight and place of birth of a baby worked into a picture of an infant in a crib surrounded by flowers.

HONG KONG

China Products Co., Overseas Service Department,
Lok Sing Center, Yee Woo Street, Hong Kong.
Telephone 5 7908321
4-color catalogues, free.
China Products describes itself as "a big-scale department store with a long history dealing exclusively with general merchandise made in the People's Republic of China. . . . The Overseas Service Department offers services for overseas mail orders, including packing, delivery via posting, shipping both by air and sea as well as receptions for foreign and overseas Chinese visitors to Hong Kong. Best service and high reputation are assured." At the moment, China Products is sending free, lavish, glossy catalogues illustrated with color photographs of a very full range of modern Chinese products. The catalogues will thrill people who like camphorwood chests, palace lanterns, bone carvings, painted vases and figurines, embroidered "beddings" and Mandarin coats. Hurry up and send for the catalogue (but *please* only if you like this sort of thing) as I can't believe they'll go on sending them for free after all my readers start asking for them. No prices are given in the catalogue. You *must* send back the catalogue page indicating what you are interested in, and they will reply with the price in Hong Kong dollars. They will not answer ordinary letters (I tried twice).

Swatow Weng Lee Co., 42 Cameron Road, Kowloon,
Hong Kong. Telephone 3 668716
120-page brochure, free; air mail $3.
This fifty-year-old firm publishes a mail-order catalogue in which they say they will "strive to further elevate our strict standard of service and bring prolonged satisfaction, like it's been before to our clients always." The catalogue, which represents but a portion of their ability to delight, shows a fairly typical Hong Kong selection at typically low Hong Kong prices: women's hand-embroidered polyester nightdress and gown set for about $16.50; men's silk-lined satin brocade dressing gowns for about $30; also women's clothes, gold jewelry and cultured pearls, petit-point handbags, embroidered tablecloths, ivory carvings, porcelain and other Oriental-style decorative objects for the house.

ICELAND

Icemart Mail Order Department,
Keflavik International Airport, 235 Iceland
Color catalogue, $1. Prices in $.
This airport shop sells gorgeous Icelandic knitwear and clothes at prices that are about 25-percent below similar clothes sold in America, after paying postage. Icelandic wool blankets, beautiful long-haired sheepskin rugs, pottery, silver jewelry and Icelandic lumpfish caviar are also sold, and the shop is well used to mail order.

INDIA

Global View, Auro International, Route 3,
Spring Green, WI 53588. Telephone (608) 583 5311
Catalogue, $1 U.S. and overseas.
A business organization that imports handcrafts and clothes from Indian cottage industries. Not the more traditional Indian crafts, but newly designed embroidered and batik cushion covers, white and cream handwoven bedspreads, take-apart wooden puzzle toys, and hand-crocheted lampshades and plant hangers.

Tibetan Self-Help Refugee Center, 65 Ghandi Road,
Darjeeling, India. Telephone 2346
Catalogue, $1.50. Prices in $.
This center was organized in 1959 to give work to the Tibetan refugees who came to India. The main specialty is carpets, and they can make carpets of any design, size and color from the wool of the same sheep that are used in Tibet and from natural dyes imported from Tibet. The rugs shown in the catalogue have angular-flower, bird-abstract and even dragon designs not often seen in the West. The rugs shown are all 3 by 6 feet. Apart from the carpets there is a heavy sweater, two rough wool jackets, fur hats (one a Tibetan soldier's hat), embroidered leather boots, all for extraordinarily low prices. At the end of the catalogue is some metal—a nice brass soup stove, a copper coffeepot (it's called a kettle, but it's coffeepot-shaped) and a copper kettle, all decorated. Tibetan dolls are also for sale, but they are not illustrated, and the Center says that it breeds rare and pure Tibetan Apso dogs. Orders can be booked in advance.

IRELAND

Avoca Handweavers, Ballinacor House, Church Road,
Ballybrack, County Dublin, Ireland. Telephone 853 458
Color leaflet, free. AE, V.
The oldest weavers in Ireland are still at it, and weaving by hand the most beautiful collection of bedspreads, rugs, stoles and scarves; and although the materials and methods are old, the designs are new. Subtle colors and rich textures make the Avoca work really unusual. There are pale bedspreads of brushed and unbrushed wool with cushions to match, violet and blue stoles, brilliantly colored knee rugs, and tawny boucle hats and scarves. Prices are far lower when bought direct from Ireland. Cushion covers and most of the stoles are about $10 each. Bedspreads go from about $50 to about $100.

Cash and Company, P.O. Box 47, St. Patrick's Street,
Cork, Ireland. Telephone 964 411
40-page color catalogue, $2.
Waterford glass, Belleek china, a Foxford rug, a linen table cloth—the usual popular Irish goods, and in addition a few chosen for this catalogue, such as porcelain pigs by Aynesley, china trinket boxes, and nickel-plated brush and comb sets.

D. J. Cremin and Son, Kenmare, County Kerry, Ireland
Color brochure, free; air mail $1.
A small collection of popular Irish products are illustrated in color in this brochure: Aran sweaters, damask and hand-embroidered tablecloths, and Foxford rugs; but most of the catalogue is devoted to Waterford glass and Belleek china at way below United States prices.

15

16

17

15 *Stephen Faller* Foxford pure wool travel rug, 58″ × 68″ in Shadow Check. These rugs are available in several tartans for about $47 each, including surface postage. (Foxford rugs sell for $75 each in New York City.)

16 *Kilkenny Design Workshops* "Ballyhale" handmade glasses. Priced about $10 each.

17 *African Heritage* Necklace of hammered Turkana brass earrings with Arab glass trade beads and coiled brass, $22.

Dublin Woollen Company, Metal Bridge Corner, Dublin 1, Ireland. Telephone (01) 770 301
Brochure, free. AE, DC, MC, V.
Cloth merchants since 1888, Dublin Woollen Company now puts out a neat brochure showing hand- and machine-knitted Aran sweaters, scarves and gloves, and one or two other sweaters. Prices are low; this looks like a good place to buy. They will also send fabric swatches of their handwoven Donegal tweeds, and gossamer tweeds by "Crock of Gold" in luminous colors, and answer specific requests for other Irish dry goods.

Emerald Mail Order, Ballingeary, County Cork, Ireland. Telephone Ballingeary 39
Color catalogue, free; air mail $1. (No catalogue July or August). Prices in $. AE, V.
A typical Irish catalogue with Waterford and Galway crystal and a lot of Belleek, porcelain gift pieces from Aynsley, Royal Worcester, Spode and Wedgwood. A few other goods such as china musical boxes, fruitcake, and knitware are also shown (including lovely Aran cushion covers for about $21.50; they cost twice as much in the United States).

Stephen Faller (Exports), Mervue C.O.C., Galway, Ireland
140-page color catalogue, $1; air mail $2. Prices in $. AE, MC, V.
An all-around selection of popular Irish goods: Aran sweaters, Waterford and Galway crystal, Belleek china, Peterson pipes, tweed hats, Irish linen. Not a vast quantity but a little of each is shown. Also other things such as Nottingham lace tablecloths, Royal Doulton figurines and all the Beswick Beatrix Potter animals.

Kilkenny Design Workshops, Kilkenny, Ireland. Telephone 056 2218
Color brochure, free; air mail $1. AE, MC, V.
Kilkenny Workshops was "Established by the Government of Ireland to advance standards of good design in industry and among consumers." Their color brochures illustrate a distinguished collection of Irish goods that are quite different from the usual fare. Here you have farm shirts and traditional nightshirts, kinsale smocks, Carberry linen and cotton sweaters, leather bags and modern silver jewelry. Also beautiful crafts such as Aran and rough-woven bedspreads, porcelain boxes, pottery and handblown glass.

Helen McGroarty, 7 Grafton Arcade, Dublin 2, Ireland. Telephone 777 508
16-page catalogue, free. MC, V.
A small collection of Aran sweaters, crochet blouses, linen napkins and scarves and hats in Aran and mohair, and mohair rugs.

Mairtun Standun, Spiddal, County Galway, Ireland
Color brochure, free. Prices in $.
Here is a family-run shop without a speck of china or glass in the brochure. Instead, a neat, easy-to-use brochure with color photographs of other Irish things: Aran sweaters, both hand-knit and inexpensive "hand-loomed"; tweed and tartan fabrics; Irish hats; lovely mohair rugs, wraps and scarves; Irish linen, pewter and silver plate; and Irish jewelry in enamel and silver, including the Claddagh ring, which shows whether the owner is fancy-free, according to the way it is worn.

KENYA

**African Heritage, P.O. Box 41730, Nairobi, Kenya.
Telephone 554378
or % African Designs, 175J South Faneuil Hall Marketplace,
Boston, MA 02109**
Catalogue, $2; air mail $5. AE, V.
It is easy to find mass-produced carvings, but hard to find
interesting crafts and decorative objects from Africa. This
firm, started by an American and a Kenyan, has managed.
They sell, through a shop in Nairobi, and also export artifacts imported from various African countries, and objects
made to African Heritage's own design from African materials. Palm-fiber baskets, food containers, musical instruments,
carved animals are sold along with batik gowns, and jewelry
made from old ancient chevron beads, amber, brass, malachite, cow horn and seed pods.

**Kuja Crafts, Hotel Intercontinental, City Hall Way,
P.O. Box 49176, Nairobi, Kenya**
Price list, $2. Prices in $.
A good selection of things from Kenya. Besides the usual
wood carvings there are tie-dyed fabrics, Kitenge and Kanga
material, beaded belts, necklaces, hats, dressed dolls, African
decorated walking sticks, musical instruments from different
tribes, cowhide drums, Masai shields and spears.

MEXICO

**Artesanos, 222 Galisteo Street, Drawer G,
Santa Fe, NM 87501. Telephone (505) 983 5563**
Color catalogue, $1. MC, V.
Lovers of lively and rustic crafts will find plenty in this
catalogue of Mexican goods: Equipales tanned pigskin and
cedar splits furniture, favorite of architects and decorators,
made in the same way since the conquest of Mexico; tin and
brass lamps; decorated mirrors; ceramic tiles and flower
pots; and brilliantly colored hand-blown glass.

SCOTLAND

**Kinloch Anderson and Sons, John Knox House,
45 High Street, Edinburgh, EH1 1SR, Scotland.
Telephone 031 556 6961**
Leaflet, free. AE, DC, MC, V.
A leaflet for standard and "bespoke" kilts, and all the other
bits that make up authentic Highland dress. Also sweaters,
skirts and a little jewelry.

**Scotland Direct, The Bell Tower,
New Lanark, Lanark, ML11 7BR Scotland.**
Leaflets, free. AE, MC, V.
A nice choice of Scottish goods—not quite the usual: ceramic
woodland animals, reproductions of nineteenth-century Scottish landscape paintings, deerskin wallets, bone china thimbles, and silver jewelry.

SENEGAL

**Société Senegalaise Pour la Promotion de L'Artisanat
d'Art, BP 3162, Dakar Senegal. Telephone 21 59 76**
18-page color catalogue, $3. Prices in $.
This won't be the easiest place in the world to buy from,
because although the catalogue is in English, the actual

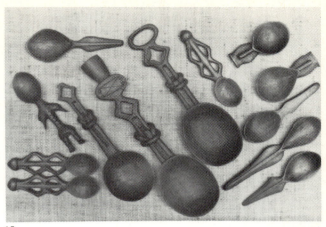
18

19

20

18 *African Heritage* Natural wood hand-carved spoons incorporating traditional African designs and African birds; these spoons, $2
to $6 each.

19 *African Heritage* Kikuyu sisal market baskets in muted natural
colors. Priced about $16 each.

20 *Scotland Direct* Left, traditional Scottish silver loving spoon,
made on the island of Mull, $35. Right, toddy ladle for measuring
spoonfuls of Scotch whiskey. Turned ebony handle and silver bowl,
$78.

21

22

23

language used for correspondence is French. Crafts have been gathered from various Senegalese tribes, and include plain basketwork, traditional weaving, carved ebony wood sculptures, and leatherwork; some of these are rather Westernized. Most interesting, I think, are the batik and embroidered robes (very loose) and especially the gold-and-silver-filigree jewelry, which is not at all expensive.

TAIWAN

Taiwan Handicraft Promotion Center, 1 Hsu Chow Road, Taipei, Taiwan
Color leaflet, free.
"A foundation devoted to the development of handicraft industry in Taiwan" has a clear color leaflet and price list of typical Taiwanese goods, but a minimum order of $50 is required. There are vases in marble, white and blue ceramics; multicolored cloisonné; and brass incense burners, little jade trees, Chinese dolls and on a larger scale, plenty of chests—painted, soapstone inlaid, and Korean style.

THAILAND

Bangkok Dolls, 85 Rajatapan Lane, Maddasan, Bangkok 4, Thailand. Telephone 245 3008
Color brochure, $1. Prices in $.
In the distant past, Thai ladies amused themselves making decorative dolls dressed in classic Thai costumes. In 1957 Mrs. Chandavimol, the wife of a Thai government official, revived the world-famous but degenerating craft and started a small business making really beautiful handmade dolls in classic costumes copied from museum displays. Her most sumptuous dolls represent characters from Thai dance-dramas and are dressed in splendid, glittering costumes, but there are also dolls dressed in working clothes of different Thai regions, with handwoven fabrics and baskets made by the people who made the originals. And there is a group of "cuddly" dolls, also in Thai costumes—the only dolls actually meant for children. Dolls are 8 to 13 inches high and cost between $7 and $28 each.

Rama Jewelry, 987 Silom Road, Bangkok, Thailand. Telephone 234 7521
Ring brochure, free. Crafts leaflet, free.
If you fancy the ornate, Rama sells sterling-silver candlesticks, ashtrays, lighters, cigarette boxes, and cocktail sets, cuff links and tie pins, engraved with Thai designs. The same leaflet has a few other typical Thai products, such as handwoven silks, silk flowers, lacquerware, teak carvings—all made by hand.

T. Seng and Son, 511/9–10 Phetchaburi Road, Bangkok 4, Thailand. Telephone 252 374
Color leaflet, free. Prices in $.
A small assortment of popular Thai goods is listed: princess rings, rings set with birthstones; gold and silver charms; bronze goblets and flatware sets; Thai dolls and Thai silks—twelve solid colors are illustrated. Recommended by a reader, Ane Denmark, who says she has had very satisfactory dealings with T. Seng.

21 *Scotland Direct* Silver jewelry based on the insignia of a Celtic princess, available with amethyst or cairngorm stones. Ring from $44, earrings from $35, bracelet from $126, necklet from $126.

22 *Bangkok Dolls* Cuddly dolls in Thai costumes. Dolls cost $8 to $28, depending on size.

23 *Adobe Gallery* Ceramic Nacimiento by Ada Suina of Cochiti Pueblo. Nacimientos start at $75 for smallest sets. *Photograph by Focus Studio.*

UNITED STATES OF AMERICA

Adobe Gallery, 413 Romero, Albuquerque, NM 87104. Telephone (505) 243 8485
Price list, free U.S. and overseas. Color photographs, $2.
The Adobe Gallery sells local native American art, such as katchina dolls and baskets. By mail they can sell the *nacimientos* handmade of native clay by the Pueblo Indians of New Mexico. There are about seventy-five different styles, sizes and types made, in heights that vary from one to ten inches. Some sets have only the holy family, three pieces; others have the wise men, shepherds, animals, etc. Prices range from $75 to $1200, but the average price for a ten-piece set is $300 to $400.

Arctic Trading Post, Box 262, Nome, AK 99762. Telephone (907) 443 2686
Catalogue, $1 U.S. and overseas.
Howard and Mary Knodel say they are the owners of the last of the old-time trading posts in Arctic Alaska. They travel by ski-equipped airplane, snowmachine and skinboat to twelve coastal Eskimo villages where they trade rifles, down clothing and outboard motors for furs, walrus ivory carvings and eskimo arts. Lovely, carved-ivory cribbage boards, bears, birds and jewelry are shown in the catalogue and many other carvings and crafts such as block prints and skin drawings can be found for you.

Appalachia, 340 Village Lane, Los Gatos, CA 95030. Telephone (408) 354 6700
Catalogue, $2; overseas $3.
Traditional handcrafts of the Southern Appalachian mountains presented in an appealing hand-written hand-drawn brochure. Crafts include rag and handwoven rugs in custom colors, baskets, brooms, carved wooden plates and kitchen utensils, cornhusk dolls and flowers, hand-carved dolls, tin cookie cutters and soft toys, such as Ma and Pa dolls, Raggedy Ann and Andy, and sock monkeys.

Artisans Cooperative, Box 215, Chadds Ford, PA 19317. Telephone (215) 388 1436
16-page color catalogue, $1; overseas $2. AE, MC, V.
This nonprofit organization exists solely to "provide support to rural artisans . . . struggling to survive in areas of our nation where few work alternatives exist." A color brochure illustrates an exceptionally sophisticated collection, including glass Christmas tree ornaments, art nouveau mirrors, silver jewelry, cornhusk flowers, patchwork quilts and cushions, and a quilted velveteen Prussian coat—all looking as though they've been made by art-school graduates, and no doubt many have.

Bear Tribe Medicine Society, P.O. Box 9167, Spokane, WA 99209. Telephone (509) 258 7755
Brochure, free U.S. and overseas. MC, V.
A modern-day medicine society based on the ideas of a Chippewa medicine man is trying to spread their message: "Walk in Balance with Mother Earth." They also sell hides, shells, and a little jewelry, Navajo style wool and acrylic rugs, tipis and a bumper sticker CUSTER HAD IT COMING.

Berea Student Craft Industries, CPO 2347, Berea, KY 40404. Telephone (606) 986 9341
32-page catalogue, $1, overseas $2. MC, V.
Berea students can work their way through college by taking part in extensive and imaginative work programs, many of which involve making crafts. A well-illustrated catalogue shows a lovely collection of brooms, functional pottery, jew-

elry, traditional weaving, wooden games, wrought iron for the fireplace and note cards.

Four Winds Trading Post, St. Ignatius, MT 59869. Telephone (406) 745 4336
Brochure, $1, overseas $2.
Preston E. Miller, Trader, has his post in the Four Winds Historic Village in the center of the Flathead reservation. He gets so many letters from customers with questions that he can't answer them all, but hopes that you can drop by his lodge to play a game of checkers, smoke the pipe or sing some Indian together. Through his brochure he sells mocassins, beaded knife sheaths, tobacco twists, trade silver, trade mirrors, folding knives and blanket coats with beaded epaulets and extra-fancy fringes. Everything is newly made at the post or by Indians in the area, in old styles.

Glass Associates, 410 Plateau, Santa Cruz, CA 95060. Telephone (408) 427 1446
Leaflet, self-addressed stamped envelope; overseas $1.
Tiny clear-crystal humming birds are hand blown by Karina Liikala; she suggests hanging them in flower arrangements, at windows or in Christmas trees, $5 to $9 each including shipping. She also makes what must be a spectacular chandelier of fifty to one thousand humming birds with individual seed lights.

Glass Masters, 621 Avenue of the Americas, New York, NY 10011. Telephone (212) 924 2868
Window Art catalogue, $1. Glassmaster Guild Supplies leaflet, $1; overseas $2. MC, V.
About forty stained-glass pictures are sold with stands or loops so that they can be hung in front of a window for the sun to shine through. Subjects include animals, birds and flowers. Each piece is quite small, up to about 9 inches in diameter, and prices are between $12 and $40. The studio also has a small list of supplies for making stained glass.

Home Co-op, Route 1, Orland, ME 04472. Telephone (207) 469 7961
Catalogue, $1. DC, MC, V.
In June 1970, with a grant of $7,500, Home Co-op began generating work for low-income and unemployed people in Maine who could make handcrafted products. The informal catalogue shows homemade things of all sorts—hand-knit baby clothes, bright-red hand-knit Christmas stockings decorated with snowmen or Santa Claus, Christmas wreaths, smocks and kimonos for women and little girls, woven aprons and place mats, stained-glass ornaments, wooden birdhouses and wooden candlesticks and patchwork quilts.

S. C. Huber Accoutrements, 82 Plants Dam Road, East Lyme, CT 06333. Telephone (203) 739 0772
Brochure, 75 cents.
A lovely little brochure describes the handmade goods of eighteenth- and nineteenth-century design, sold by this center for early country crafts: their own handmade paper, wax candles, hand-spun wools, and handmade soaps; they also stock fabrics, pottery, tin lighting and wooden plates that are similar to the ones used in the country in the last centuries. Herbs and natural dyes and books also stocked.

Mohawk Crafts Fund, 101 East Main Street, Malone, NY 12953
Brochure, 25 cents.
It's good to find a traditional craft alive and unspoiled. This one was helped by a business management class of North Country Community College, which made a class project of

24

helping the basketweavers on the St. Regis Mohawk Reservation.

Doll cradles, knitting, shopping and sewing baskets of black-ash splints and sweet grass, with special fancy shapes to order, are sold through a brochure at prices that are mainly between $4 and $40.

Native Design, 108 South Jackson, Seattle, WA 98104. Telephone (206) 624 9985
Brochure, $1. DC, MC, V.
A wonderful place for basket lovers, this shop has the biggest selection I have seen in a catalogue. The baskets are all made in Africa in traditional designs and come with a label describing the weaving materials and customary tribal use. Choose amongst an Ibunda bark harvest basket, a Zulu serving tray, a bean bowl or a child's lidded lap basket. Over forty baskets in all, at prices mainly between $10 and $30.

Nowetah's American Indian Gift Shop and Museum, Route No. 27, Box 14, New Portland, ME 04954. Telephone (207) 628 4981
Leaflet, self-addressed stamped envelope.
Mrs. Nowetah Timmerman sells an odd assortment of crafts including one hundred wool Indian rugs and blankets in colors or earth tones, leather fringed vests, leather handbags, beadwork, doll-house miniatures and Barbi doll clothes. As her leaflet explains, she does it through lending out home-made catalogues with "*exact* photos in color so that folks can pick and make a selection more easily . . . it would be too difficult to have a printed catalogue made up, as no two Indian rugs, for example, are the same." However, I doubt that Mrs. Timmerman's system can cope with crowds, so you'll probably have to wait when you write to her.

Noisy Crow Papers, 99 Beechwood Hills, Newport News, VA 23602. Telephone (804) 877 2228
Prices and samples, $1; overseas $2.
Beautiful hand-marbled papers are made by an English teacher. Franklin Spoor sells the papers as is to bookbinders and other craftspeople, or made up into sketchbooks and hinged boxes. Although the craft of paper marbling is old, the colors on these papers are rich and clear.

Joan Patton, Sumac, P.O. Box 55, New Lebanon, NY 12125
Leaflet, free; overseas $1.
Joan Patton makes big, strong baskets. All of them are meant for use as hampers, picnic baskets, plant pot containers. They are made of natural rattan and sometimes hand stained in lovely earthy colors.

Pipestone Indian Shrine Association, Pipestone National Monument, P.O. Box 727 (ref. c.c.), Pipestone, MN 56164. Telephone (507) 825 5463
Brochure, free; overseas 50 cents; air mail $1.
The Pipestone Indian Shrine Association is a nonprofit co-operating agency of the National Park Service and provides an outlet for pipestone ceremonial pipes and other pipestone crafts made by local Indian craftsmen. A free illustrated brochure with photographs of representative pipes and other small crafts is available upon request. All items are moderately priced, with small crafts costing under $10 and several pipes under $30.

The Pottery, 10800 East 24 Highway, Sugar Creek, MO 64054
12-page brochure, $1.
Nice functional pottery is made for the kitchen by Ron

24 *Joan Patton, Sumac* Baskets of rattan hand-stained with color. Prices start at $40.

Taylor. Cheese dishes, jugs, casseroles, colanders, spice jars and teapots are all plump and pleasing. Decoration consists of simply one thin band of color.

Qualla Arts and Crafts Mutual, P.O. Box 177, Cherokee, NC 28719. Telephone (704) 497 3103
Leaflet, 50 cents plus 20-cent stamp. AE, MC, V.
An Indian-owned and -operated cooperative, Qualla is trying to keep alive the crafts of the Eastern Band of Cherokee Indians. The main product is beautiful two-color white oak baskets, but a doll, carved bears, and incised-coil pottery are also shown on the leaflet.

Silent Company, 10 Webster Avenue, Glens Falls, NY 12801. Telephone (518) 792 4332
Leaflet, free; overseas $1. MC, V.
If you'd enjoy the silent company of an 1890s swimmer, a man in a hammock, a butcher or Santa Claus, turn to Judi Caselli who creates wired stuffed and embroidered dolls, from the unpromising materials of nylon and fiberfill. She also makes family groups or literary subjects such as Bob Crachet and Tiny Tim, and is happy to make a portrait doll of you or a friend.

Touching Leaves Indian Crafts, 927 Portland Avenue, Dewey, OK 74029. Telephone (918) 534 2859
Brochure, $1 U.S. and overseas.
A full-blooded member of the Lenape Indian tribe sells Lenape beadwork and trade pieces, crafts and reproductions of crafts in glass, plastic, and German silver. She also occasionally has rare Indian corn seeds, which she sells hoping that others will grow and preserve it.

Treasure House of Worldly Wares, P.O. Box 127, Calistoga, CA 90127. Telephone (707) 942 9976
Price list, self-addressed stamped envelope; overseas $1.
Owner Stevie S. Whitefeather says she is a Ponca Indian who was in import, export, wholesaling and jobbing before moving to Calistoga because of the beauty of the Napa Valley. She says, "I have an excellent selection of one-of-a-kind handcrafted items which include American Indian and Native folk art from all over the world." The price list I looked at listed Navajo sand paintings and dolls and crafts from several countries.

West Rindge Baskets, Box 24, Rindge, NH 03461. Telephone (603) 899 2231
Leaflet, free.
The Taylor family has been weaving baskets in the New England way for three generations. If the handle breaks or the bottom splits on a West Rindge basket, the Taylors will fix it for free. Baskets are woven from wide flat strips of ash in several shapes and sizes, wide square ones are called pie and cake baskets, wide flat ones are called garden baskets, tall thin ones are called bottle baskets, and in between there are shoppers, knitters, laundry, porch mail, lunch and picnic and, of course, waste. Prices run from $10 to $20.

Martha Wetherbee–Basketmaker, Star Route 35, Sanborton, NH 03269. Telephone (603) 286 8927
Catalogue, $3.50; overseas $4.50.
Martha Wetherbee, who has been a basketmaker at Shaker Village in Canterbury, New Hampshire, has produced a lovely and informative little booklet about Shaker baskets, which doubles as her catalogue. Her own baskets are careful, even reverent, reproductions for collectors of the communally produced Shaker baskets, a craft the Shakers learned from the brown-ash work of the Indians. Prices for

Martha Wetherbee's baskets start at $45 and go up to around $100.

Wooden Ways, 1529 63rd Street, Emeryville, CA 94608. Telephone (415) 658 4313
Leaflet, free; overseas $1. MC, V.
Janet and Jules Jaffe make elegant square salt and pepper shakers, and buffet boards, in koa, mahogany, oak and walnut inlaid with strips of contrasting wood. Also belt buckles of exotic woods and brass. Designs are new and sleek, not traditional.

WALES

The Teifi Marketing Association, Emlyn Square, Newcastle Emlyn, Dyfed, Wales
Catalogue, $2; air mail $4. MC, V.
A group of people have together produced a catalogue of the crafts they make individually. Illustrated with hundred-year-old photographs, and including a history of the valley, the catalogue is a lovely thing. Hywel Davis makes clogs; Liz Davis makes bird prints; Mike Vaughan Jones makes pottery; Jo Rawlinson makes frame-knitted shawls (and gives knitting courses); Mary Usher makes furry toys. There is also a small electronics firm making a telephone-call light, which you put next to the phone to see, instead of hear, when it is ringing.

9
ELECTRONICS

Audio Equipment

It is a rare shop that gives careful and completely honest advice on audio equipment, so I am delighted to have found two sources—The Assessment Group and Rocky Mountain Audio—that I think will give guidance in a field that is always changing and developing. I hope that both these firms will help people who don't want to do a lot of research with the two questions—how to get the best equipment possible for a certain price, and how to get the equipment that is right for the buyer. People who are willing to do their own research will find *Hi-Fi Choice* useful. It is an English quarterly that devotes each issue to serious reviews of one type of component. Recommended by Clement Meadmore, available from Sportscene Publishers, 14 Rathbone Place, London W1P 1DE, England.

I am also really delighted to have found several sources that give discounts on top audio equipment. It is easy to find discounts on midpriced equipment such as Sony, Pioneer, Technics, Dual and Hajler, but hard to find discounts on "state of the art" (best available) equipment. If you want to check list prices buy *Stereo Directory and Buying Guide* ($2.95 including postage) from Ziff Davies Service Divison, One Park Avenue, New York, NY 10016. It is published each October.

One thing that you should bear in mind, if you are buying audio equipment, is that it seems that in the next few years there may be a changeover to new digital records ("digital" records available as I write are only partly digitally recorded, and are quite conventional). These new records are played by a laser beam, are said to have superb sound, have the added advantage of containing more playing time on a much smaller record, and do not need the delicate surface care that current records need. The new digital records will need a different turntable.

This section has been written with many suggestions and much advice from the sculptor Clement Meadmore, author of *All Sound and No Frills.*

The Assessment Group, Box 1280, Rockville, MD 20850
Questionnaire and advice, $10; overseas $11.
Dr. Steven Frankel sells only advice on what equipment to buy. He sends you a questionnaire, with first a price-range question: How much between $700 and $9000 do you want to spend? Then there are questions about the size of the room, preferred size of speakers, the kind of sound you want. Both Clement Meadmore and I think that the questions are good ones, and the explanations that go with them very useful and helpful in explaining what the equipment is all about. When you return the questionnaire with your answers, you get a list of components, chosen from those currently available, that Steven Frankel thinks best meet your specifications. The examples of advice that Dr. Frankel sent me seemed sensible. As new components are continually being developed, and this service is for people who do not want to read all the literature themselves, this seems to be a good and cheap way of getting information.

Jensens Stereo Shop, 2202 River Hills Drive, Burnsville, MN 55337. Telephone (612) 890 3517
Information, free U.S. and overseas.
Frank Van Alstine specializes in rebuilding good audio equipment so that it will give sound that is equal to that of far more expensive equipment. He does this mainly to Dynaco components, which are no longer being made, but are still available (he'll tell you where). His work is enthusiastically recommended by Clement Meadmore, who, among oth-

1 *Sound Aids* Modified tone arms to get better sound from warped records and to improve cartridge performance. Priced about $90.

ers, considers Van Alstine's innovations brilliant. However, you do need to know a certain amount about audio to understand the information Van Alstine sends out on his work.

Michael O'Brien, 95 High Street, Wimbledon Village, London SW19, England. Telephone (01) 946 1528
Manufacturers' brochures, $2. MC, V.
Michael O'Brien sells top-class hi-fi equipment and also has a personal export service. He says that these components seem to be of special interest to American customers; prices are, very roughly: Quad amplifiers, $650; SME pickup arms, $100; Tannoy speakers, $180.

Sound Aids, 395 Riverside Drive, New York, NY 10025. Telephone (212) 662 9768
Information, free U.S. and overseas.
Sound Aids is the firm through which Clement Meadmore, author of *All Sound and No Frills* (Pantheon Books) sells his own inventions. He modifies existing tone arms on customers' turntables to reduce their mass so that the arm can cope with today's warped records and generally improve cartridge performance. They also sell a cartridge alignment card ($4.50), wooden cassette drawers, and plans to easily make shelves for records from precut plywood and glue.

DISCOUNT
Please see discount information in the How to Buy section.

The Audio Advisor, P.O. Box 6202, Grand Rapids, MI 49506. Telephone (616) 451 3868
Subscription to three catalogues, $1; overseas $2.50. AE, MC, V.
One of the few firms that gives discounts on high-end audio, Audio Advisor publishes a neat little catalogue, offers to give advice, and also sells expensive "audiophile" records at a discount. I found 11- to 25-percent discounts on things such as the Acoustat 3A speakers, Linn Ittok tone arm, and the Nakamichi 682 ZX tape deck, which are very rarely discounted. Audio Advisor offers to beat other price quotes. Established 1979.

Rocky Mountain Audio Research, 5505 Valmont, Boulder, CO 80301. Telephone (303) 447 1900.
Catalogue, $10; overseas $12; overseas air mail $15. MC, V.
Dr. Michael Humphreys sells high-end audio equipment at hard-to-find 15- to 30-percent discounts, and will special order. He publishes a marvelous passionate, outspoken catalogue, in which he delivers his opinion on many components, including troublesome "sacred cows," and he names names when it comes to what he considers blatant rip-offs (but he will sell blatant rip-offs to customers possessed with a "fatal case of stubbornness"). Some of his opinions are controversial (he pans speakers that are generally extremely well reviewed), and he's rather boastful, but I consider his catalogue fascinating.

He suggests various matched systems at prices starting at $720, and will advise any prospective customer who telephones him.

I asked Dr. Humphreys for his suggestion for a $1000 set and he suggests at the moment: NAD 7090 receiver 45/45 watts RMS with Jarris Modification; Rega Planar III turntable with Grace 747 arm; Nakamichi 500 Series or Akai P-90 cassette deck; Rogers LS 3/5A speaker with Clarke Subwoofer. This system includes discounts, it would cost more at list prices. Established 1951.

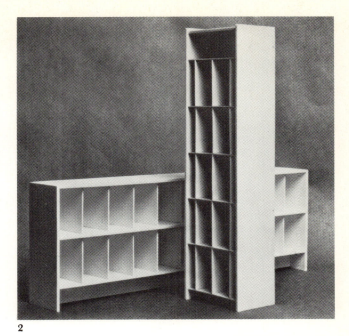

2

3

2 *Sound Aids* With plans and instruction from Sound Aids, pre-cut plywood can be ordered from lumber yard and needs only white glue and masking tape to make record storage shelves. Plans and instructions, $5.

3 *Sound Aids* Wooden storage units hold 68 cassettes each, and can be used as shelf supports and record dividers, $48 each.

**International Hi Fi Distributors,
Moravia Center Industrial Park, Baltimore, MD 21206.
Telephone (301) 488 9600**
Specific prices by telephone (9:00 A.M. to 9:00 P.M.); overseas by mail.
International Hi Fi does not have a catalogue, but says that they have a very large selection of audio equipment. They sell fifty-two well-known midprice brands, and make a big point of having a large stock in their warehouse so that they can ship 90 percent of their orders within twenty-four hours.

**Intersonics, P.O. Box 113, Toyohashi 440, Japan.
Telephone 0532 88 4773**
Specific prices given on request.
This firm sells Japanese components, accessories and Japanese phonograph records at what they say are discount prices (I haven't checked). Specific prices on request.

**J and R Music World, 23 Park Row,
New York, NY 10038. Telephone 800 221 8330**
Catalogue, $2.50. MC, V.
Large shop with mail order sells midpriced audio equipment such as Panasonic, Jensen, Pioneer, Sony etc., at very roughly 20 percent off list prices. Also video equipment.

**Japan Audio Trading, Saikaen Building,
4 33 21 Kamimeguro, Meguro-ku, Tokyo 153, Japan.
Telephone 715 0533**
Price list, $1 (air mail).
Japan Audio specializes in selling brand-name small components that are suitable for air mailing, such as tone arms, cartridges, headphones, tweeters and microphones. Some of the prices I checked were way below United States prices (the Linn Ittock tone arm was $160 below the United States *discount* price, for instance) but others were slightly above (Audio Technics ATH 7 headphones were $6 above the J and R Music World price). So this is an excellent source for the knowledgeable.

**Stereo Discounters, 6730 Santa Barbara Court,
Baltimore, MD 21227. Telephone 800 638 3920**
92-page catalogue, free U.S. and overseas. MC, V.
A group of stores and a mail-order firm that regularly produces catalogues of midpriced audio equipment such as Dual, Hitachi, Pioneer, Sansui, Sony; including, of course, portable sets, car stereo, tapes, etc.

Computers

Personal computers can be used for storing information, budgeting and preparing tax returns, analyzing stocks, developing investment strategies, writing and sophisticated editing. They can also be connected to telephone information services, and, of course, games and educational programs are available.

Computers are not an obvious field for mail order, but detailed catalogues are a good way of finding out what is available. And if you are already an expert, you can find discounts.

**CompuMart Corporation, P.O. Box 568,
Cambridge, MA 02139. Telephone (617) 491 2700**
Catalogue, free U.S. and overseas. MC, V.
A complete and reputable source of hardware and software computer equipment.

**JMC/Con Cor, 1025 Industrial Drive,
Bensenville, IL 60106. Telephone (312) 595 0210**
80-page computer catalogue planned, $3; overseas $6. MC, V.
JMC, which now distributes model railroad equipment to hobbyists, says that they are starting a division that will handle personal computer software, books and related accessories for the most popular brands.

DISCOUNT
Please see discount information in the How to Buy section.

Only for people who already know a great deal about computers, including exactly what they need.

**B. G. Sound, 60 East Ninth Street, New York, NY 10003.
Telephone (212) 674 1185**
Price list, free.
B. G. sells small computers for home use and has very good prices on Apple and Atari Computers, add-on hardware, and financial and data management programs. They say that the list covers only part of what they sell; they can order almost anything in home computers. Almost everything is sold at a discount they say, and their low prices were noted in an article in *New York* Magazine.
Established 1978.

**47th Street Photo, Mail Order, 36 East 19th Street,
New York, NY 10003.
Telephone (800) 221 5858 or (212) 260 4410**
112-page catalogue, $2 U.S. and overseas. Write or telephone with model number for price.
Good prices on Apple computers and Atari computers and programs. However, 47th Street is a general discount store for photographic equipment and gives no advice or information, so this is an address for experts only. Established 1972.

Film and Video Equipment

There are two types of video cassette machines on the market now. Both of them can record television programs, both of them can play the recorded programs back through the television set, and can also play commercial tapes that are compatible with their own system. However, the tapes made on and for one system can not be played on the other system. The two systems are the Beta system, used by Sony and Zenith and others, and the Video Home System (VHS) used by Magnavox, Panasonic, RCA and others.

A newer, and still imperfect, video development is video disk systems which just play and do not record disks that look like records, instead of cassettes. The advantage is that the disks, which are pressed like records, are far cheaper to make and therefore sell at much lower prices.

If you know enough about video equipment to know exactly what you want, you can buy both the machines and the cassettes and games by mail at a discount.

DISCOUNT
Please see discount information in the How to Buy section.

**Dial a Brand, 229–07 Merrick Boulevard,
Laurelton, NY 11413. Telephone (212) 978 4400**
Telephone with model number for price.
Video recorders and cameras only. Established 1970.

Garden Camera, 135 West 29th Street,
New York, NY 10001.
Telephone (800) 223 0595 or (212) 868 1420
Write or telephone (Sunday through Friday 9:00 A.M. to
6:00 P.M.) with model number for a price, U.S. and overseas.
AE, MC, V.
Garden sells film projectors, video recorders, video cameras,
blank tapes and video games. Established 1969.

Foto Electric Supply, 31 Essex Street,
New York, NY 10002. Telephone (212) 673 5222
Write with stamped self-addressed envelope or 1
International Reply Coupon and model number for price (no
prices on telephone), U.S. and overseas. MC, V.
Film cameras and projectors, Video cameras and recorders,
and video games. Established 1961.

47th Street Camera, Mail Order, 36 East 19th Street,
New York, NY 10003.
Telephone (800) 221 5858 or (212) 260 4410
112-page catalogue, $2; or write or telephone with model
number for price. AE, MC, V.
Film cameras and projectors; video cameras and recorders,
blank tapes and accessories. Established 1972.

International Solgo, 77 West 23rd Street,
New York, NY 10010.
Telephone (800) 645 8162 or (212) 675 3555
Telephone with model number for price, U.S. and overseas.
AE, DC, MC, V.
A very good selection of video recorders, games, blank tapes
and Beta and VHS video movies. Established 1933.

4

FILMS AND VIDEO CASSETTES

American Music Warehouse, P.O. Box 3400,
Nashville, TN 31219.
Telephone (800) 323 4243 or (312) 561 2500
Record catalogue, free U.S. and overseas.
64-page video catalogue, free U.S. and overseas. MC, V.
Over two thousand video films, popular feature films, in-
struction films, Spanish soundtrack films, sports, etc. Music
Warehouse says that unlike other catalogues, they list only
popular films that they know are available.

Audio Brandon Films, 334 MacQuesten Parkway South,
Mount Vernon, NY 10550. Telephone (914) 664 5051
Catalogues: (1) 16-mm rental movies for film groups and
schools, (2) International classics, (3) General
entertainment films, (4) Educational; all free.
One of the largest renters of films in the country. The
fascinating catalogues list feature films and shorts from every
film-producing country, including many of the world's great
films. Also specialized shorts, many educational, suited for
classroom use.

Blackhawk Films, Box 3990, 1235 West Fifth Street,
Davenport, IA 52808. Telephone (319) 323 9736
Catalogue, free. MC, V.
Blackhawk sells old Hollywood films (8- and 16-mm). It
has many famous shorts, from Laurel and Hardy to *The
Perils of Pauline,* and also full length classics such as *Intol-
erance* and *The Phantom of the Opera.* Also films from the
twenties through the eighties on Beta and VHS (history, sci-
fi, suspense, Westerns and drama).

4 *CompuMart* NEC printer, Commodore computers, Sanyo monitor, Hewlett-Packard's HP 83. Apple II and III, DEC LS1-11
Systems.

5

Canyon Cinema, 2325 Third Street, #338, San Francisco, CA 94107. Telephone (415) 626 2255
26-page catalogue, $4; overseas $6.
A cooperative group distributing about fourteen hundred films of its three hundred members. The co-op is "open to any film maker with a film of any kind, for the entries are not evaluated. . . ." Rentals are mostly below $20. Films range from "vignettes of the nutty antics of people in a coin-operated automat" to "the black panther is training itself . . . interviews with Huey P. Newton and Eldridge Cleaver. . . ."

Circulating Film Program, Museum of Modern Art, 11 West 53rd Street, New York, NY 10019. Telephone (212) 956 4204
Price list, free.
Classic films (not films about art) for rent, and some also for sale.

Film Classic Exchange,, 1914 South Vermont Avenue, Los Angeles, CA 90007. Telephone (213) 731 3854
Information sheet, long self-addressed stamped envelope. Complete list (30 leaflets) $12; overseas $15.
Film Classic Exchange has been operating since 1921, and has a large library of silent-era films, plus some later films. Films are for sale and for rent, in 8- and 16-mm. Film lists are grouped under subject headings (such as history, social science), also under early studios.

Niles Cinema, 1141 Mishawaka Avenue, South Bend, IN 46615. Telephone (219) 289 2845
72-page catalogue, free U.S. and overseas; 72-page video catalogue, free U.S. and overseas. AE, CB, DC, MC, V.
Sells early films, 16-mm and 8-mm and Super 8; and video cassettes of early films and more recent popular feature films.

Video Dimensions, 110 East 23rd Street, New York, NY 10010. Telephone (212) 533 5999
Leaflet, free U.S. and overseas.
Makes and sells its own video cassettes of "oddball, strange and rare" films (*Hollywood Bloopers, Diabolique, The Cartoon Adventures of Superman*, etc.). Also sells *The Complete Guide to Home Video*, published by Harmony Books, and co-authored by the owner of the store.

Video Shack, 430 West 54th Street, New York, NY 10019. Telephone (212) 489 8130
Catalogue, free; overseas $2. AE, CB, DC, MC, V.
Over 3500 video cassettes and discs for sale—mainly popular feature films, but also some pornography.

Video Yesteryear, Box C, Sandy Hook, CT 06482. Telephone (800) 243 0987
Video Yesteryear, $1.25; Radio Yesteryear, free. Radiola Records, free.
Classic films, mainly twenties through fifties, on video cassettes. Also various fifties television shows on cassettes.

Zipporah Films, 54 Lewis Wharf, Boston, MA 02110. Telephone (617) 742 6680
Brochure, free U.S. and overseas.
Zipporah produces and distributes only Fred Wiseman's controversial and powerful 16-mm documentaries: *High School, Hospital, Juvenile Court*, etc.

5 Sony's new, compact front-loading Betamax VCR SL 2500 incorporates technical innovations originally developed for professional broadcast equipment. Suggested list price is $1,500. Available at discount stores such as Focus Electronics for about $1,059.

10
FABRICS
AND FIBERS

Fabrics

R. Adams, 29/31 Green Street, Burnley,
Lancashire, BB10 1UZ England. Telephone (0282) 33462
Price list, free.
Inexpensive parcels of fabric remnants: cottons, linens, felts, etc., and also patchwork pieces in cottons, velvets and some synthetics. No illustrations; it is pot luck in exchange for low prices.

Argalius, 7 Filellinon Street, Athens, Greece
Leaflet, free.
Argalius sells raw silk by the meter. "PURE NATURAL GREEK SILK spun and woven by HAND . . . it is of the best, the most ELEGANT material for LADIES' and GENTLEMEN'S suits and clothes. . . . They do not wrinkle, the more they are WASHED, the more quality improves; therefore, for years on end you will not get tired of them."
   Argalius will send a swatch if you send an exact description or a swatch the color you want matched. The raw silk is not smooth and shiny like other silk but has a rougher weave. Fabric is thirty inches wide.

Sawyer Brook Distinctive Fabrics,
Box 194, Orford, NH 03777. Telephone (603) 353 9029
Catalogue of swatches $4; abroad ask price, MC, V.
About four times a year Sawyer Brook sends out catalogues with about fifty color-coordinated fabrics for dressmaking, mostly blends and a few natural fibers. Complete Folklore and current Butterick and Vogue patterns are also sold. Free catalogue to anyone who buys $15 worth of fabric.

Carol Brown, Putney, VT 05346.
Telephone (802) 387 5875
Leaflet, 50 cents and self-addressed stamped envelope;
overseas $1.
Fabric swatches on request (to be returned), free. MC, V.
Carol Brown and nephew sell imported natural-fiber fabrics for people who do their own sewing. They manage their shop alone and each mail order requires correspondence, so if too many people write to them service will slow down—be warned.
   The fabrics sound marvelous: Irish tweeds from Avoca, and the Weavers' Shed; Irish blankets in glowing colors to be made into hostess skirts or jackets; heavy unbleached yarn for clothes and upholstery. There are also Indian cottons, printed and plain, Finnish cottons with big bright designs; and Dutch/African cottons made in Holland for the African trade.

Cohasset Colonials by Hagerty, 542HX Ship Street,
Cohasset, MA 02025. Telephone (617) 383 0110
32-page catalogue, $1; abroad $2.
25 fabric samples, $5 (refundable). MC, V.
In this catalogue of kits to make furniture, there are three pages of Colonial-style fabrics, both the lovely, natural rough cottons and sophisticated polished chintzes based on old designs. Fabrics cost between $7 and $9 per yard.

Exotic Silks, 252 State Street, Los Altos, CA 94022.
Telephone (415) 948 8611
Price list, 35 cents; abroad $1. V.
A good, clear price list describes the Chinese, Indian and Thai silks that Deanne Morgan Shute brings back from her biannual trips. Besides the silks, including a batch of whites and natural for batik and dyeing, there are a few cottons

1 *Gill Imports* Crewel fabric from Kashmir, wool embroidery on cotton, $13 to $28 per yard, depending on the amount of embroidery. Bedspreads and cushion covers also sold.

2 *Ethnic Accessories* Folkwear prairie dress pattern, $5.

3 *Ethnic Accessories* Folkwear Edwardian Underthings patterns for camisole, petticoat, and drawers with instructions for sewing; lace and tucking techniques, $5.50.

4 *Ethnic Accessories* Folkwear patterns for infant and toddler clothes from Morocco, Mexico, Turkey, Japan, and Nepal, $6.

5 *Ethnic Accessories* Folkwear pattern for Austrian dirndls with decorative ruching designs and techniques.

and Javanese and Malaysian batiks. Prices are low as the firm does its own importing.

Gill Imports, P.O. Box 73, Ridgefield, CT 06870. Telephone (203) 438 7409
Color leaflet, $1 U.S. and abroad. Swatches, $1 each. MC, V.
Sixteen different crewel fabrics, wool flower embroidery on cream fabric. Prices depend on the amount of embroidery.

Ginger Snap Station, P.O. Box 81086, Atlanta, GA 30366
80-page color catalogue, 50 cents. MC, V.
Calicos, small print and solid color cottons for patchwork. Also kits to make patchwork quilts, and whimsical patchwork pillows, toys and Christmas ornaments. A very good source for the nontraditional quilter.

Imaginations, Marble at Blandin Avenue, Framingham, MA 01701. Telephone (617) 620 1400
Subscription to four sample collections and special offers, $10. Ultra suede samples, $2. MC,V.
Two young women sell the complete range of Vogue patterns, and superior color-coordinated fabrics by mail. For $10 you get four selections of fabric samples a year, and also special offers. The fabrics look good, with plenty of solids and small flower patterns. Tasteful rather than exciting.

Linekin Bay Fabrics, 37 Silver Street, P.O. Box 7346, Portland, ME 04112. Telephone (207) 774 7563
Brochure with swatches, $2.50 U.S. and abroad. MC, V.
Sable brown mohair, ivory alpaca, violet and green tweed—beautiful nubby textured fabrics are woven in this studio. Colors are rich, fibers are all natural, and fabrics have an unmistakably handwoven look.

MacGillivray and Company, Muir of Aird, Benbecula, Outer Hebrides, Scotland PA88 5NA. Telephone 0840 2204
Price list and swatches, free; air mail $2. Prices in $. AE, V.
A popular source for low-priced fabrics, MacGillivray has been selling handwoven Harris tweed by mail for many years and has gradually begun to do other things too. Hand-knitted Harris and Shetland wool socks, hand-knitted Harris wool sweaters, blankets, bedspreads. Fabrics cost about $7–$10 per yard. Recommended by Joan D. Fettes, a reader.

Nizhonie, East Highway 160, P.O. Box 729, Cortez, CO 81321
Leaflet, free (send stamped self-addressed envelope). MC, V.
As the leaflet says, this is an Indian-owned enterprise producing hand-printed (silk-screened) textiles based on Indian patterns. One design is an abstract taken from Navajo storm-pattern rugs, others are based on sand-painting figures, pictographs taken from cliff dwellings, and deer painted on Zai and Zuni pueblo pottery.

Pater Textiles, Rampart Street, London E1 2LD, England. Telephone 790 1937
Price list, 50 cents; air mail $1. March, September.
An old firm that advertises itself as the largest direct-to-consumer textile service in England is recommended by several English women's magazines as a good place for inexpensive fabrics. The newspaperlike price list describes most kinds of fabrics, usually synthetic, including jersey with lurex, raincoat material, anorak material, etc. The prices are almost all $2–$20 a yard.

Rodin, 36 Champs-Elysees, Paris VIII, France
Swatches, free.
This very large fabric shop on the Champs-Elysees, well known to Americans, can sell haute couture silks and wools as well as upholstery fabrics by mail to America. However, their choice is so wide that you have to be very specific in describing what you want, and prices are quite high.

Sew What Fabrics, 2431 Eastern Avenue SE, Grand Rapids, MI 49507. Telephone (616) 245 0834
Catalogue of swatches $5. August, February. MC, V.
Elegant imported natural fiber fabrics, about fifty swatches in each issue. The complete range of Burda patterns.

St. Remy, 156 East 64th Street, New York, NY 10021. Telephone (212) 759 8240.
Color leaflet $1. Swatches (about 70) $5. MC, V.
Traditional French Provençal prints in soft, muted colors on fine Egyptian cotton. Also aprons, bags, herbs, spices, lavender, honey and natural jams imported from France.

Sunflower Studio, 2851 Road B 1/2, Grand Junction, CO 81501
Brochure, $2. MC, V.
An exquisite brochure introduces the surprising work of Constance La Lena. She weaves fabrics and makes clothes in more or less the same way they were made by American village weavers in the eighteenth century. She uses the best, pure natural fibers (cotton, linen and wool), and her dyes have been carefully worked out to give colors as close as possible to the soft eighteenth- and nineteenth-century originals.

The fabrics have evocative names such as tow cloth, dimity, fustian and spotted Chambray. They are utterly plain and simple, with only a few having a woven-in pattern. They can be used for clothes or almost anything in the house.

Jim Thompson Thai Silk Company, 9 Surawong Road, GPO Box 906, Bangkok, Thailand
Price list, free. Swatches on specific request. Prices in $. AE, V.
Gorgeous handwoven, hand-printed Thai silks are among the most astounding bargains I have seen. Iridescent, stylized flower designs, checks and solid colors are all magnificent. Upholstery-weight silks cost $20 a yard, lighter weight silk is about $11 a yard. Silk is also made up into cushion covers, kimonos, luncheon sets, note books and photograph frames. All at low prices, but, alas, there are no illustrations and the minimum order is $50. Swatches can be sent if you say exactly what you want.

Utex Trading Enterprises, 826 Pine Avenue, Suite 5, Niagara Falls, NY 14301
Price list, free.
An importer lists fifty-one Chinese silks with the prices (low) of the fabrics and of swatches.

The Vermont Country Store, Weston, VT 05161. Telephone (802) 824 3184.
96-page catalogue, 25 cents; abroad 70 cents.
Among many other things, the Vermont Country Store sells traditional calico, at about $3.80 a yard, and old-fashioned yard goods "for women and men who sew." Huck towelling, Osinaburg and monks cloth, sheet batiste, and hard-to-find pure *cotton* quilt batting.

See Clothes, Crafts and General sections for more fabrics.

Buttons, Kits, Patterns

Button Creations, 26 Meadowbrook Lane, Chalfont, PA 18914
62-page catalogue, $1. MC, V.
All the buttons that a dressmaker might dream of from basic genuine mother of pearl, wood, leather and pewter to decorated buttons for collectors.

Daisy Kingdom, 217 N.W. Davis, Portland, OR 97209. Telephone (503) 322 9033
16-page catalogue, $1; overseas $3. MC, V.
Fabric swatches, $1; overseas $3.
Kits to make snazzy-looking ski clothes, in contrasting fabrics. The kits come with fabric (uncut), patterns, and all the thread, etc. You do need to know how to sew quite well (be able to make a tailored blouse, or man's shirt, they say). Daisy Kingdom says you save 50 percent of the price of comparable clothes ready-made.

Ethnic Accessories, P.O. Box 250, Forestville, CA 95436
36-page brochure, $1.50 U.S. and overseas.
Ethnic Accessories stocks the entire range of the Folkwear Patterns, inspired by traditional clothes from around the world, and some historical ones. Drawstring pants from Africa, embroidered dresses from Gaza, and quilted coats from Turkey are available, along with Missouri-river boatmen's shirts and Edwardian underthings from the U.S. Also a few other supplies such as lovely-sounding handwoven fabrics from Mexico and Africa.

Frostline Kits, Frostline Circle, Denver, CO 80241. Telephone (303) 451 5600
48-page color catalogue, free U.S. and overseas. AE, MC, V.
Kits to make tents, sleeping bags, packs, outdoor clothing and down comforters. Recommended by Linda Johnson, who has made two of their jackets. She says the materials are top quality, and the instructions are easy to follow. When she telephoned for advice, they were helpful, and when she made a mistake, they replaced the section for free, even though the mistake had been her own fault. However, Jack Stephenson (see Backpacking) tells me that these kits are not necessarily less expensive than similar clothes ready-made.

Past Pattern Replicas, 2017 Eastern S.E., Grand Rapids, MI 49507. Telephone (616) 245 9456
Catalogue, $10; overseas $12. MC, V.
If you are a *really* adept and patient sewer, you can make your own Victorian clothes. Saundra Altman started off by making replicas of the historic clothing in a Grand Rapids museum, while she was a volunteer. She did a lot of reading of old magazines, such as Ladies Home Journal, to learn the correct sewing methods, then traced the original gowns and adjusted the sizes to fit today's figures.

The dresses, which involve tucks, insets, ribbons, lace, ruffles, puffs, billows and lots of work, are very pretty. Also patterns for men's clothing and women's underwear.

Patterns of History, State Historical Society of Wisconsin, 816 State Street, Madison, WI 53706
Leaflet, free.
The State Historical Society of Wisconsin also makes patterns for nineteenth-century women's dresses, and is planning to cover every major style for the period 1832 to 1899. At the moment, there are fourteen patterns at $10 each,

6

7

more severe and not quite as pretty as those from Past Patterns. The society says, "In the tradition of the nineteenth century, these patterns provide the basic cut; use of varied fabric and trimming will produce the kind of costume desired—anything from a house dress to dinner or wedding gown." Sizes 10, 12, 14.

Pearls Company, Box 3088, New Haven, CT 06515
12-page color brochure, $1. MC, V.
Lacy blouses are very popular at the moment—here is a place where you can buy a kit to make a blouse yourself, very inexpensively. About eight pretty blouses to choose from, one dress and some wedding separates, in ecru, black or white polyester lace. These cleverly thought-out kits consist of lace strips, instructions, and anything else needed. All kits cost under $20.

Wood Forms, Foster Hill Road, Henniker, NH 03242. Telephone (603) 428 7830
Leaflet, self-addressed stamped envelope; overseas 75 cents.
Wooden buttons in exotic woods, two styles, three sizes. Buttons can be dry-cleaned or hand-washed.

Dyes

Ajdo Manufacturing Company, 450 Greenwich Street, New York, NY 10013. Telephone (212) 226 2878
Leaflet, free; $1.50 abroad.
Ajdo, established in 1902, sells to professionals. They manufacture dyes that are used in batik, tie-dye, fabric painting, block and screen printing on every kind of fabric. Ajdo's price list and instruction leaflets are unnervingly scrappy, but the firm is highly recommended by Robin Weinberg, a friend of my daughter, who says it's the best dye source in New York, and has the most amazing colors.

Cerulean Blue, P.O. Box 5126/G, Seattle, WA 98105. Telephone (206) 625 9647
12-page catalogue, 50 cents U.S. and abroad. MC, V.
A nice, informative price list of natural and better synthetic dyes of many kinds; fabrics for dyeing; silk thread for sewing, and books.

Mr. C. D. Fitz Hardinge-Bailey, St. Aubyn, 15 Dutton Street, Blankstown, NSW 2200, Australia
Price list, $1 (U.S. stamps accepted).
Fleece wools price list and samples, $13.
The natural dyes sold by this firm are produced mainly for use in the firm's own weaving, but they also sell their dyes to customers, and leading institutions such as the Smithsonian, throughout the world.

Wide World of Herbs, 11 Catherine Street East, Montreal H2X 1K3, Canada. Telephone 842 1838
Price list, free.
A very complete supply of dried-plant material, natural dyes and mordants.

See Spinning section for more dyes.

6 *Frostline Kits* Aztec vest of down-filled nylon taffeta, available ready made or as a ready-to-sew kit, about $39.95. The kit is available with bands in contrasting colors (royal blue with green and navy, red with navy and tan, etc.).

7 *Pearls Company* Kit of lacy strips in black, white, or ecru, to make blouse "Laury," $18.95.

Knitting

R. S. Duncan and Company, Falcon Mills, Bartle Lane, Bradford, West Yorkshire BD7 4QJ, England. Telephone (0274) 576702
16-page color catalogue with samples, $2. MC, V.
Each year R. S. Duncan and Co. puts out a splendid catalogue illustrating in color some attractive knitting patterns for children, adults and fatties, with actual samples of most of England's best-known yarns: Falcon, Jaeger and Sirdar at prices that they say are below normal retail prices in the United Kingdom.

Holmfirth Wools, Briggate, Windhill, Shipley, Yorkshire BD18 2BS, England
Catalogue of yarn samples, $1.
A good selection of yarns in the usual commercial colors for hand and machine knitting, in pure wool and wool/synthetic mixtures. Baby wools, crepe, lurex and Twilleys stalite, which is good for crochet.

Manos del Uruguay, 35 West 36th Street, New York, NY 10018. Telephone (212) 564 6115 or (800) 223 8915.
Yarn samples, about seventy shades, but not all for knitting, $3; overseas $3.50.
Knitting book with nineteen patterns, $6 postpaid; overseas $7. AE, MC, V.
Gorgeous hand-spun, kettle-dyed yarn from an Uruguayan co-op. Yarn intentionally varies in color and thickness to give a striated effect, and knits up into thick, sporty sweaters, or can be used for weaving. Nineteen knitting kits for sweaters, hats and baby blankets are sold, but you have to buy the knitting book to see them.

Snowflake, N-1315 Nesoya, Norway
Color catalogue, $1, air mail $2. Prices in $.
Snowflake has a thriving business exporting kits to make traditional pure-wool Norwegian sweaters. The kits contain instructions in English and everything you need: "the very best, soft and lovely Norwegian wool," knitting needles, pewter buttons or clasps.

Elizabeth Zimmerman, Meg Swansen, 6899 Cary Bluff, Pittsville, WI 54466. Telephone (715) 884 2799
Price list and sample card, $1 U.S.; sea mail $2.
Two designers sell subtly colored imported yarns—Canadian fisherman and "homespun," Scottish Shetland, Finnish Sumoi—and unspun, undyed wool from Iceland. They send a biannual newsletter with an original knitting pattern in each issue to customers who have bought over $10 worth of yarn.

Also see Yarn section.

8

9

Lacemaking

Lacis, 2990 Adeline Street, Berkeley, CA 94703. Telephone (415) 843 7178
Price list, $1; abroad $2. MC, V.
Kaethe and Jules Kliot collect and sell lace, and also the supplies for lacemaking. They have linen lace threads and equipment for battenburg, bobbin, filet, net and all kinds of lacemaking, and tatting.

8 *Manos del Uruguay* Kits to knit sweaters with hand-spun kettle-dyed yarn start at about $36.

9 *Snowflake* Kits to knit traditional Norwegian sweaters, jackets, hats, and gloves. Sweater kits start at about $25.

10

11

10 *Rainbow Gallery* Complete needlepoint kit for *The Unicorn in Captivity*, from the fifteenth-century tapestry in the Cloisters Collection, Metropolitan Museum of Art, New York, for $75.

11 *Eva Rosenstand* Typical children's Christmas calendar, with rings for small gifts—one for each day from December 1 to 24. Linen, yarn, rings, and cross-stitch chart, sold together.

Needlework

Art Needlework Industries, 7 St. Michael's Mansions, Ship Street, Oxford, OX1 3DG, England
Six knitting brochures and yarn samples, $2.50.
Ten English needlepoint brochures and yarn samples, $2.50.
This is by far the most scholarly and serious of these needlework shops, and the owner, Heinz Edgar Kiewe, has spent over forty years writing books and researching historical designs. He makes a few nasty cracks about "prefabricated bargain-basement kits" and says his kits are not for neurotics who want to finish something overnight but require discipline, respect and love from the embroiderer.

Mr. Kiewe has gathered many of his unpublished designs from customers, including one allegedly embroidered by Mary Queen of Scots, and another said to have been worked on by Marie Antoinette in prison.

The knitting brochures include wool samples, illustrations and descriptions of Aran sweaters, jackets and hats. Also Icelandic, mohair, Shetland, camel's-hair and cashmere sweater kits.

Needlecraft House, Main Street, West Townsend, MA 01474. Telephone (617) 597 8989
52-page color catalogue, $1; abroad $2. MC, V.
Crewel and needlepoint kits for pictures and cushions, also tablecloths to embroider. Mainly quiet flower and plant designs. Pure wool yarns, low prices and custom finishing.

Peacock Alley, 650 Croswell Street, S.E., Grand Rapids, MI 49506. Telephone (616) 454 9898
36-page brochure, $2 U.S. and abroad.
Pillows, coasters (favorites with beginners), belts and luggage-rack straps (favorites with teen-agers, who use them as guitar straps), children's picture frames, eyeglass cases, brick covers for doorstops or book ends, pincushions and several rugs, mainly in modern designs.

Rainbow Gallery, 13615 Victory Boulevard, Suite 245B, Van Nuys, CA 91401. Telephone (213) 787 3542
24-page color brochure, $1 U.S. and abroad; $2 abroad (air mail).
Imported kits to make copies of famous tapestries and picturse such as Leonardo Da Vinci's *The Last Supper*.

Eva Rosenstand Corp., P.O. Box 755, Kennebunk, ME 04043

Eva Rosenstand, Clara Weaver, Ostergade 42, 1100 Copenhagen K, Denmark
Color brochure, $3. Prices in $.
This firm sells pretty, fresh Danish designs for embroideries, tablecloths, placemats and tapestries. The designs are light and colorful with only a few traditional designs and with lots of wild-flower bouquets. Unlike most of the other needlework firms in this section, Eva Rosenstand sells charts instead of trammed or painted canvases, which means you have to count out the design yourself when embroidering.

The catalogue also shows an appealing collection of cheerful Christmas kits for tablecloths, babies' bibs, cards, mobiles and tree decorations over which cavort bouncy elves, angels, children, snowflakes and stars. Mounting kits, hangers and sewing accessories are on sale too.

Royal School of Needlework, 25 Princes Gate, London SW7 1QE, England. Telephone (01) 589 0077
12-page price list, $3; air mail $4.
This famous institution was founded in 1872 by a daughter of Queen Victoria with the aim of "restoring ornamental needlework to the high place it once held among the decorative arts." Now, the school teaches highly specialized techniques, restores needlework and lace, executes important needlework commissions. By mail, they sell books and suplies for all sorts of needlework, embroidery transfers and a few kits. They also paint canvases to order, and will interpret photographs of homes and gardens, including the family pets.

Seldon Tapestries, 9 Stanwick Road, London W14, England. Telephone (01) 602 3586
Brochure, free; air mail $2.
How about a needlepoint picture of your dog, house, hobbies or favorite landscape? Seldon Tapestries specializes in carrying out customers' own ideas. Write to them with your suggestion and they will quote you a price for a picture on a wall hanging, bedhead, handbag, belt, tray cover, cardtable top, rug, etc. They also have an interesting collection of ready-made kits.

Sudberry House, Box 895, Colton Road at Exit 71, Old Lyme, CT 06371. Telephone (203) 739 6951
22-page color catalogue, $2.50 U.S. and abroad (refundable).
Wooden objects on which to mount needlepoint: trays, footstools, mirrors, and magazine racks, pen sets, cheeseboards. Lots of ideas for what to do with all the needlework after your house becomes over cushioned.

Jane Whitmire, 2353 South Meade Street, Arlington, VA 22202. Telephone (703) 684 8036
16-page brochure, $1 U.S. and abroad.
A graduate of Chicago Art Institute traveled with her army husband, collecting needlework and folk art. She has now adapted some of the designs into a lovely collection of crewel and needlepoint featuring Byzantine horses, Coptic cupids and other exotica. Most unusual is a collection of cushions with Oriental rug designs, gold beads, copper and brass threads and silk highlights.

Herrschners, Stevens Point, WI 54481. Telephone (715) 341 0604
80-page color catalogue, free. MC, V.

The Stitchery, 204 Worcester Street, Wellesley, MA 02181
48-page color catalogue, $1. AE, MC, V.

Lee Wards, Direct Marketing Division, 840 North State, Elgin, IL 60120. Telephone (312) 888 5800
84-page color catalogue, free.

The World of Stitch and Knit, Inc, P.O. Box 709, Framingham, MA 01701. Telephone (617) 877 0606
Catalogue, free. MC, V.
These four catalogues all have cheerful and colorful needlework, fiber and sewing projects of all sorts to decorate the house, including Christmas decorations and things for children's rooms (Lee Wards also sells other crafts, and miniatures). Many synthetic yarns and very low prices.

12

13

14

12 *Royal School of Needlework* William Morris "Flower Pot," crewel embroidery kit, 20 inches square. About $45.

13 *Seldon Tapestries* Rug kit, available in nine pieces or in one, with the design painted on the canvas and wools.

14 *Jane Whitmire* William the Conqueror's boat, taken from the Bayeux Tapestry. Crewel embroidery in red, blue, and green on dark linen, 15″ by 30″, $35.

Rugs

**Braid-Aid Fabrics, 466 Washington Street,
Pembroke, MA 02359 0603**
94-page catalogue, $2; abroad $3. MC, V.
A very thorough and complete catalogue of materials, supplies and books for making hooked and braided rugs, with some quilting fabrics also.

Heritage Hill Patterns, Box 624, Westport, CT 06881
16-page catalogue, some color, $1.50; abroad $2.
Patterns, fabrics and Paternayan yarns to make hooked rugs (with yarn or fabric) and needlepoint rugs. Designs a little fresher than most hook rug designs, which tend to be rather conventional.

Screen Printing

**NAZ DAR Company, 1087 N. North Branch Street,
Chicago, IL 60622. Telephone (312) 943 8338**
130-page screen printing catalogue, free; abroad $2.
All inks, equipment and supplies needed for silk screening, from beginners' kits to enormous drying racks for professionals. Instruction books too. Recommended by Mary Lou Weaver, a reader.

Spinning

**Brandy Creek Farm, R.R. 1, Valcourt,
Quebec, J0E 2L0, Canada**
Price list and samples, $2.
Margrit Multhaupt raises registered Angora goats, and sells the untreated mohair "in the grease to spinners." Prices are international auction prices.

**Romni Wools and Fibres, 3779 West 10th Avenue,
Vancouver, British Columbia V6R 2G5, Canada.
Telephone (604) 224 7416**
Price list for goods and yarn samples, free.
Raw wools, mohair fleece and equipment for spinners. Silk, cotton, linen, and wool, and mill end yarns for knitters and weavers.

**Straw into Gold, 3006 San Pablo Avenue,
Berkeley, CA 94702. Telephone (415) 548 5241**
164-page catalogue, $2.50 U.S. and overseas; overseas airmail $3.50. MC, V.
An entrancing catalogue of supplies for spinning, including an excellent assortment of dyes, and unusual yarns, also supplies for basketry, and a great booklist. A *wealth* of information and instruction is given in the catalogue. Recommended by my friend Tom Englehardt.

Weaving

Harrisville Designs, P.O. Box 283, Harrisville, NH 03450
Brochure and samples, $4 U.S. and abroad.
This is what John Colony says about his firm: "We operate in close conjunction with a larger effort by local people to revitalize the village of Harrisville without altering its essential character as a nineteenth-century mill town. . . . Our objective in Harrisville Designs is to make the highest-quality yarns and supplies available to handweavers at reasonable prices."
According to a weaver and teacher I talked to, they succeed remarkably well. She says that the looms are very nice and excellent value for the money (there is a four-harness loom with a weaving width of 22 inches which costs $215 as a kit). She recommends the natural yarns and the dyed wool yarns, which are in good and vivid colors.

**Robert C. Nelson, Rural Route 2, Box 540,
Rands Pond Road, Newport, NH 03773**
Leaflet, free U.S. and abroad.
Robert Nelson has developed two wooden waist looms, which he makes himself. They are small and cheap (between $10 and $15) and handy. You tie one end of the yarn to a table or chair, the other around your waist, and according to the width of the loom you have, you can weave cloth from 12 to 18 inches wide. When you finish, the whole thing is easy to fold up and put away. The loom can also be carried around, as it weighs just a few ounces.

**The Pendleton Shop, 465 Jordan Road,
Sedona, AZ 86336. Telephone (602) 282 3671**
Leaflet, self-addressed stamped envelope U.S. and abroad; samples $1.50 U.S. and abroad.
Mary Pendleton runs the Pendleton Fabric Craft School in "the heart of the red rock country," where you can take courses for from one to six weeks in handweaving and non-loom weaving, creative stitchery, Navajo weaving and macrame. Weaving supplies are sold: a Navajo loom, hand-spun Navajo yarn, and folding looms made of birch hardwood.

**Schacht Spindle Company, 2526 49th Street,
P.O. Box 2157, Boulder, Co 80306.
Telephone (303) 442 3212**
Leaflet, free; sea mail $1; air mail $2.
Looms and accessories: an inkle loom, a tapestry loom, and a good four-harness table loom.

**School Products, 1201 Broadway, New York, NY 10001.
Telephone (212) 679 3516**
Catalogue, $1.
One of the largest suppliers of weaving equipment in the country, School Products sells Artcraft and Leclerc looms.

Yarns

Many yarns can be used for either knitting or weaving. The sources below have either especially unusual and lovely yarns, or yarns at lower prices for the quality. There was a time when you could find better colors and better prices by buying from abroad. Now, it is possible to find interesting hand-dyed American yarns, but yarns of similar quality are still less expensive when bought from abroad, even after paying for postage.

**Barbouris Handicrafts, 56 Adrianov Street,
Athens 116, Greece, Telephone 324 7561**
Sample cards, $2.
Hand-spun yarns at low prices. Thirty-three-pound minimum.

**Cambridge Wools, P.O. Box 2572,
Auckland, New Zealand**
Price list and samples, $1.
Yarns for knitting and weaving, and fleece for spinning. Low prices.

**William Condon and Sons, P.O. Box 129,
Charlottetown, Prince Edward Island, C1A 7K3, Canada**
Brochure and yarn samples, 50 cents. Prices in $.
Beautifully colored wool yarns for knitting and weaving at
half U.S. prices. Weavers should stick to the two-ply and up
as the single ply do not weave well.

**Craftsman's Mark Yarns, Tone Dale Mill, Wellington,
Somerset, England. Telephone (082) 347 7266**
Sample cards, $5.
Exclusive yarn and fleece in lovely natural colors. "Best in
the world," says one of my advisers.

**Ed-U-Tex Kits, 5445 S.W. 14th Avenue,
Portland, OR 97204**
Samples, $1 and long self-addressed stamped envelope.
Soft-spun single yarns, hand spun in Oregon, for knitting,
crochet and weaving: pure wool, wool/silk, yak, camel, cash-
mere, mohair, natural or hand dyed to order.

**Cheryl Kolander, 276 North Myrtle,
Myrtle Creek, OR 97457. Telephone (503) 863 6330**
Samples, $5 U.S. and abroad.
Fantastic selection of silk yarns, natural and hand dyed with
natural dyes.

**Stavros Kouyoumoutzakis, 166 Kalokerinou Avenue,
Iraklion, Crete, Greece**
Samples, $1. Prices in $.
Yarns from Cretan and Australian wool, in thin, medium
and two-ply, at about half U.S. prices.

**Les Filatures de Paris, 75 Rue Lecourbe,
75015 Paris, France. Telephone 16 6 434 54 00**
Samples, $1.
Good assortment, many cotton yarns, and wool from finest
boucle to very thick yarn. Lovely, subtle colors.

**Norsk Kunstvevgarn, Arnevik,
N-4890 Grimstad, Norway. Telephone 041 462 87**
Samples, $4.
In twenty-eight beautiful, clear, vivid colors, wool yarn for
two-ply knitting, needlepoint and weaving.

**Rammagerdin, Hafnarstr. 19, P.O. Box 751,
Reykjavik, Iceland**
Color brochure, yarn samples, free. Prices in $. AE, MC, V.
Icelandic Lopi yarn in natural colors at about half the price
of Lopi bought in the U.S.

**Richard Sans Sicar, 6 Rue de la Republique,
81270 Labastide-Rouairoux, France. Telephone 98 01 18**
Samples, $6; air mail $9. Text in French.
Fleece also cotton, linen and wool yarns. You really need
French for this one, and you must buy within two weeks of
receiving samples.

Paula Simmons, Box 12, Suquamish, WA 98392
Small sample cards of hand-spun yarn in solid colors, $1.25.
Paula Simmons and her husband spin yarn to order. The
customer chooses the yarn size, the texture and the color
shade (though all the yarns are natural colors) in solid
shades, heathers or tweeds. The yarn costs $1.35 an ounce.
The Simmonses do all their own wool processing—sheep
raising, shearing, wool washing and carding, spinning and
weaving.

**Textere Yarns, College Mill, Barkerend Road,
Bradford BD3 9AQ, England. Telephone Bradford 22191**
Samples, $2.
Textere Yarns, in the middle of the English textile industry,
sells a wide variety of yarns at extremely low prices. Sam-
ples change according to what is available.

**The Weavers Shop, King Street, Wilton, Nr Salisbury,
Wiltshire SP2 0AY, England. Telephone 2733**
Price list and samples, $2.
The Wilton Royal Carpet Factory sells to weavers the same
yarns that are used in their famous carpets (80-percent
wool, 20-percent nylon, two-ply, mothproofed). They also
sell very inexpensive long ends of unsorted yarn in mixed
colors.

Woodsedge Wools, P.O. Box 464, Kingston, NJ 08528
Price list, $1; abroad $3.50.
Hand-spun yarns from the farm's own sheep, bred especially
for their hand-spinning qualities. Colored, undyed yarns
(black, brown, gray, tan) are a specialty. Also vegetal-dyed
mohair yarns, and exotic imported yarns. Wonderful source,
sample cards available.

11 FOOD

Food bought by mail is usually no cheaper than food bought locally, but buying by mail is a way of getting hold of unusual ingredients and delicious specialties that you may not be able to find in your own district. It is also a marvelous way of giving presents, and most of the firms below can produce really tempting and beautifully wrapped packages.

As compared to other products, it is hard to tell the quality of a food through the information given in a catalogue. I have tried to be selective rather than comprehensive and choose only firms that I believe sell especially good food.

Please note that food catalogues are revised frequently, so there is often a delay while they are printed.

Notable Food Shops

Dean and DeLuca, 121 Prince Street, New York, NY 10012. Telephone (212) 254 7774
Catalogue planned, free.
The shop started in the loft district, SoHo, by Joel Dean and Giorgio DeLuca has quickly become one of New York's renowned food shops. The owners care passionately about food ("We want people to relate to foods as the miracles they are") and say they will only stock foods they believe in ("... our aim is to enable our customers to see even the lowliest foods anew"). But their appreciation of the lowliest does not mean they don't discriminate. Quite the contrary, they are very fussy. When in the store I asked for a garlic press, I was definitely glared at (no unnecessary gimmicks). They stock more fresh foods than most famous food shops—fruits and vegetables, pâtés, pies, etc., yet also have the exotic and hard-to-find double-yolk eggs from Maine, sun-dried tomatoes from Tuscany, their own Provençal fruits in alcohol.

Dean and DeLuca have been talking about a mail-order catalogue for about a year now. If you are interested in very expensive, very good food, put your name on their list.

E.A.T., 867 Madison Avenue, New York, NY 10021. Telephone (212) 879 4017
$1 to be put on mailing list for monthly leaflets. AE.
Eli Zabar, the youngest of the Zabar brothers who own the hugely popular food and kitchenware emporium Zabar's (see Kitchen section) went up-market and opened a sparkling white and pale wood shop on the posh East side.

Eli says he is a zealot for quality, and is constantly experimenting and "training the palate of his customers to his own sense of taste." And indeed, it is Eli Zabar who was among the first to stock Norwegian smoked salmon, who has *fresh* white truffles in season, whose cheeses are described as "most exceptional" by *The New York Times,* and who stocks the jam (Fouquet) that was voted number one in the *New York* magazine jam-rating session. However, before you reach for your pen, let me add that prices are very high, some would say outrageously so.

Fauchon, 26 Place de la Madeleine, Paris VIII, France. Telephone 742 6011
Catalogue, free. In French. AE, DC.
Fauchon is France's Fortnum's (see below) with the difference that when in 1970 Maoist students looted Fauchon and distributed their goodies to the poor, Fauchon refused to prosecute. When Emily Pankhurst and the suffragettes smashed Fortnum's windows, Fortnum's merely sent a hamper of delicacies to sustain them in prison.

The catalogue austerely and simply lists the many foods that they import and export, some of which will be no great

1

2

1 *Fauchon* Sweets, preserved fruits, and chocolate.

2 *Fortnum and Mason* "Buckingham," Fortnum's largest Christmas hamper, which includes caviar, champagne, and 62 other foods, $711 postpaid within Great Britain. Hampers can be made up to order with a choice of 84 different foods.

treat to Americans—"Rice Krispies" and "Coco Pops," for instance. However, everything is neatly divided into categories, so it is easy to find things that one could hardly find anywhere else, such as Nopalitos Finos (Feuilles de Cactus en escabeche) and kiwi-fruit jam.

The foods most popular with American mail-order customers are goose liver; truffles; glazed chestnuts; preserves; chocolates; white peaches; French asparagus; mustards of all sorts; snails; dried mushrooms (morilles, cepes, chanterelles); pâtés (hare, thrush, baby wild boar, deer, pheasant, partridge, blackbird, and lark). There is plenty to delight any serious cook or eater, and everything is beautifully packaged.

🎀 **Fortnum and Mason, Piccadilly, London W1A 1ER, England. Telephone 734 8040**
Color Christmas catalogue, free; air mail $2. September. No catalogue January to August. AE, DC, MC, V.
Started in 1707 by Hugh Mason and William Fortnum (royal footman with excellent connections at the palace), Fortnum's has purveyed food to royalty and top people ever since. They are thoroughly experienced in mail order to Englishmen abroad; officers in the Napoleonic wars would rely on their hams, tongues, butter and cheese. Queen Victoria sent Florence Nightingale crates of concentrated beef tea through Fortnum's.

Now Fortnum's has expanded into a small department store, and the lavish, sybaritic Christmas catalogue has a little of the best of everything. The food pages are magnificent, with full-color photographs of caviar and pâté, English and Scottish cheeses, salmon, nuts, desert fruits, and crystallized fruits prepared exclusively in France, ginger and honey, handmade chocolates, and of course, the hampers—famous as Christmas gifts complete with champagne and cigars. And if you are looking for presents and have money to fling carelessly away, you can choose from a "safe" rather than an original array of crocodile briefcases, velvet slippers, satin pillows, pewter bar accessories, cut-glass and silver plate. But remember the Fortnum's label is a costly one.

General

Maison Glass, 52 East 58th Street, New York, NY 10022. Telephone (212) 755 3316
114-page color catalogue, $3. AE, CB, DC, MC, V.
This eighty-year-old New York firm was offering a full range of delicacies well before the gastronomy explosion turned every major department store into a competitor. Their catalogue is very comprehensive, offering as full a range of prepacked food, also game, smoked meats and fish, natural American honeys, etc., largely imported, as can be found in the country. Prices are high, but then not that many catalogues offer half a dozen forms of truffle or a page of different vinegars. Fancy gift baskets and accessories.

Imported

CHINESE

China Bowl Trading Company, 80 Fifth Avenue, New York, NY 10011. Telephone (212) 255 2935
Price lists, brochure, free.
Suppliers of ingredients needed for Chinese cooking, from herbs to dried mushrooms. The Company also sells various canned sauces and flavoring, as well as noodles and other classic staples.

EAST EUROPEAN

Paprikas Weiss, 1546 Second Avenue, New York, NY 10028. Telephone (212) 288 6117
64-page illustrated catalogue, $1 annual subscription. MC, V.
Paprikas Weiss, along with its competitor, H. Roth and Son, is known to many food lovers as the leading importer of food and cooking utensils from what used to be called Middle Europe. A rich selection of over ten thousand items are in their catalogue. Just about any food that you can think of from that part of the world is amply represented: sheets of strudel dough, prune butter (Lekvar), Hungarian ham or salami, dried mushrooms and poppy seeds. Their catalogue also has a vast selection of cooking, coffeemaking and, particularly, baking utensils.

H. R. Roth and Son, 1577 First Avenue, New York, NY 10028. Telephone (212) 734 1111
Catalogue, free. AE, DC, MC, V.
H. Roth and Son, a very nice neighborhood food and utensil shop, was started by the present owner's Hungarian great-grandmother. The catalogue has such delicacies as crystallized rose petals, violets, mint leaves and mimosa; fresh almond paste; honeybread for grating; baking chocolate; Lebkuchen and honey cake spice. Also dried and candied fruits, nuts, freshly ground spices.

Unusual imports include foods from Brazil, Holland and Indonesia, and utensils such as baskets to make potato or noodle birds nests, a Dutch pancake kit, and a Mexican tortilla press.

FRENCH

J. A. Demonchaux Company, 827 North Kansas, Topeka, KS 66608. Telephone (913) 235 8502
Price list, 25 cents.
Imported delicacies from France, including such hard-to-find things as crystallized fruit, marrons glacées and fancy pâtés. Somewhat less expensive but less comprehensive than Maison Glass.

GERMAN

Bremen House, 220 East 86th Street, New York, NY 10028. Telephone (212) 288 5500
12-page price list. Issued free twice a year. AE, MC, V.
Bremen House has been one of the central shops of New York's German neighborhood, Yorkville, for as long as I can remember, and at Christmas time, with its piles of *Stollen*, marzipan and chocolates, it is thronged by thousands who long for the traditional German *Weihnachten* goodies.

In addition to these sweetmeats, other ingredients for German cooking are available from Bremen. Imported cheese and smoked meats, jams, even imported vegetables are listed. Bremen is a good source of other imported foods that Germans import back home: a wide variety of Scandinavian seafood—herring, anchovies, etc.; French cheese; honey and other delicacies.

3

4

5

3 *Gazin's* Grinders for sea or rock salt and for peppercorns. About $9.95 each.

4 *Gazin's* Creole praline sauce with pecans, for ice cream, pancakes, and waffles. About $3.99.

5 *San Francisco Bay Gourmet* Triple strand of braided California garlic has 24 bulbs and loop for hanging. Priced about $17.50.

INDONESIAN AND DUTCH

Mrs. De Wildt, 245-A Fox Gap Road, R.D. #3, Bangor, PA 18013
Price list, free.
The best place in America to get Indonesian food and spices that also has an extensive stock of Dutch food. If you like the classic Indonesian Rijsttafel dinner here are all the requisite ingredients, from *sambal* (hot pepper pastes) to *krupuk udang* (shrimp tapioca wafers that are deep-fried and then served with rice). All sorts of spices are listed, as well: wild-lime leaves and dried-lily flowers.

ITALIAN

Balducci's, 424 Avenue of the Americas, New York, NY 10011. Telephone (212) 673 2600
Leaflet, free. AE.
A well-known Italian food shop, Balducci's mail offerings appropriately stress such delicacies as Italian cheeses, olive oils and dried mushrooms, as well as nougat (*torrone*), *amaretti* cookies and the traditional holiday *panforte*, a kind of hard fruitcake. However, nonItalian treats are also available, from caviar to air-freighted Swiss chocolates.

Manganaro Foods, 488 Ninth Avenue, New York, NY 10018
Brochure, free.
Since 1893 Manganaro's, a less fashionable shop than Balducci's, has sold food from Italy: salami, proscuitto, *scungli* (conch), *calamares* (cuttlefish), *baccala* (dried cod), pasta of all sorts, Italian cheeses, and Italian desserts such as *panettone, torrone, colomba* and *amaretti*. Manganaros also sells the special kitchen implements needed to make your own pasta.

MEXICAN

Tia Maria, 4501 Anapra Road, Sunland Park, NM 88063. Telephone 800 854 2003, X 909
Catalogue, free. AE, MC, V.
Tia Maria firm manufactures and sells Mexican foods, ready-made or ingredients: chiles, canned or ground as well as various sauces and relishes that will turn eggs, for instance, into *huevos rancheros*.

MIDDLE EASTERN

Sultan's Delight, 409 Forest Avenue, Staten Island, NY 10301. Telephone (212) 720 1557
Price list, free. MC, V.
Sultan's Delight gives a broad reading to its name, since its catalogue lists not only Middle Eastern foods but costumes and accessories for belly dancers. Here are all the basic ingredients for cooking, such as tahini and vine leaves, including spices in pound lots and olives available very cheaply in three- and five-pound packs. Candies, pastries, Halawa, Turkish coffee—all the traditional treats at very reasonable prices. Also henna by the pound, Arabic headdresses and musical instruments, and kitchen utensils such as Turkish coffeepots and cups.

ORIENTAL

**Pacific Trader, 19 Central Square, Chatham, NY 12037.
Telephone (518) 392 2125**
Price list, $1 (refundable). MC, V.
A very complete and inexpensive source of Oriental groceries. Ingredients not only for Japanese and Chinese meals,
but Indonesian and Middle Eastern as well. A nice, neat list
of Oriental groceries, at prices that are slightly lower than I
find locally for Chinese, Japanese and also Indonesian and
Middle Eastern cooking. Vine leaves stuffed with rice, tahini
and hummus; cellophane noodles, at least eight different
kinds of noodles, soy sauces, straw mushrooms, rose and
orange flower water, canned mangoes, lychees and lots more.

SPANISH

**Moneo and Son, 210 West 14th Street,
New York, NY 10011. Telephone (212) 929 1644**
Catalogue, $2 U.S. and overseas.
A very complete list of ingredients for Spanish, Mexican and
South American cooking. There is a $25 minimum, but as
much of the food is in tins, it is possible to lay in a good
stock at one time.

American Regional

**Gazin's, 2910 Toulouse Street, P.O. Box 19221,
New Orleans, LA 70179**
Catalogue, free. MC, V.
Creole products, made by Gazin's and by local suppliers:
praline sauce, cane syrup, gumbo and jambalaya mixes.
Here are the ingredients for many Creole recipes, from dried
red beans to hot pepper jelly. Gazin's also sells some incredibly rich sounding fruitcakes, including date and pecan cake,
pineapple apricot cake and a chocolate almondine Creole
recipe that sound exceptionally tempting.

**The Great Valley Mills, 101 South West End Boulevard,
Quakertown, Bucks County, PA 18951.
Telephone (215) 536 3990**
Price list, free. MC, V.
Great Valley Mills sells a number of foods, a few of which
it produces itself, such as flours and meals, cracked cereals,
pancake and waffle mixes. Among the local specialties there
are Pennsylvania Dutch smoked ham and turkey, sausage
and scrapple; Pennsylvania Dutch apple and peach butter,
preserves, relishes and honeys.

**Maria's, 111 Stratford Road, Winston-Salem, NC 27104.
Telephone (919) 722 7271**
Catalogue, free; overseas air mail $2. MC, V.
This firm offers a selection of gourmet treats: coffees, teas,
spices, cheese, nuts, chocolates and the like, all very attrac-
tively packaged in simple wooden baskets, terra-cotta pots,
cloth pouches, none of which are extravagantly priced. Indeed, some of the prices—the little wooden crates of chocolate cordials or locally hand-dipped chocolates, for instance—are remarkably reasonable. A good place for
presents.

**San Francisco Bay Gourmet, 311 California Street,
San Francisco, CA 94104**
General gift catalogue, $1 (refundable). MC, V.
The San Francisco Bay Gourmet produces a cheerful cata-

6

7

8

6 *San Francisco Bay Gourmet* Wicker basket of California dried,
nut-stuffed, and glacé fruits. Priced about $13 to $17, depending on
size.

7 *San Francisco Bay Gourmet* Flavored, ground chocolate for chocolate drinks; almonds in white chocolate; and roasted almonds
dipped in dark chocolate and cocoa dusted. About $8 each.

8 *San Francisco Bay Gourmet* Little bag with twelve assorted
chocolate bars. About $16.

logue specializing in California- and Southwest-produced foods, and out-of-the ordinary gift packs. Sourdough bread from San Francisco is mailed on Mondays, fresh from the bakers; Napa Valley jam is made from the same grape varieties that are used for wine; and nineteen-inch garlic braids come from the Santa Clara valley. Sonoma Jack cheese, dry salami, Northwest salmon, pistachio nuts, dried and fresh fruit, San Francisco chocolate are all sold too.

Senor Murphy Candymaker, P.O. Box 2025, Santa Fe, NM 87501. Telephone (505) 988 4311
Leaflet, free. MC, V.
Local, Mexican-influenced candies: pine nut brittle, pine nut candies and roasted, salted pine nuts.

Sugar's Kitchen, P.O. Box 41886, Tucson, AZ 85717. Telephone (602) 299 6027
Leaflet, free.
Western delicacies, from California dried brown mushrooms to hot pepper sauce. Some unexpected specialities, such as nectarine chutney; others, such as Arizona mustards and relishes, are "no salt."

Henry and Cornelia Swayze, Brookside Farm, Turnbridge, VT 05077. Telephone (802) 889 3737
Price list, free U.S. and overseas.
Maple syrup, straight from the farm, made by very serious producers who liken the work to winemaking. As a result, they specially blend complementary flavors, since each batch of syrup differs in taste. The syrup that doesn't live up to their high standards is sold to commercial packers.

Vermont Country Store, Weston, VT 05161
96-page catalogue, 25 cents; overseas 75 cents. MC, V.
Some really good New England foods are included at the end of this general catalogue; real maple sugar and syrup; pickles relishes and jams make use of local fruits and vegetables, and local favorites such as rum plum jam, cranberry conserve and rose hip jelly are sold. A friend tells me that the stone ground grains, and nine different flours (including yellow corn meal, oat and rye flour and buckwheat) are excellent, and so are the Vermont cheddar, stone ground whole grain bread, fruit cake, tea and fresh ground coffee.

Willis Wood, R.F.D. 2, Springfield, VT 05156
Price card for cider jelly and maple syrup, free.
I found this cider jelly in my local health food shop. After complaining loudly about the price, my family fell for it. They eat it with cold chicken; I eat it with bread and lots of butter. It has a wonderful sharp taste—I'll never eat jam again.

Apparently the firm has been around making boiled cider and cider jelly since the 1880s. The owners, Willis and Tina Wood, say that the jelly has absolutely nothing added so is good for natural food addicts and diabetics, they also say it is expensive because it is concentrated. It's a delightful and unusual local specialty.

Meats

Amana Society Meat Department, Amana, IA 52203. Telephone (319) 622 3113
Leaflets, free.
The Amana colonies, or villages, are a settlement of German Protestants who came to America in the nineteenth century and who have retained a communal arrangement similar in some respects to the Mennonites. The Amana meats are available nationally by mail, and their smoked meats and sausages come highly recommended. One of my most enthusiastically gastronomic friends is eloquent about their summer sausage, which resembles salami. Smoked bacon is available in slabs of seven pounds at an enormous saving over local prices. Assortments and smaller quantities are available.

Colonel Bill Newsom, 127 North Highland Avenue, Princeton, KY 42445. Telephone (502) 365 2482
Leaflet free, U.S. and overseas; overseas air mail 60 cents.
Virginia-style, hickory-smoked country ham, which means that the ham is uncooked, crusty and salty; it needs soaking before cooking. Colonel Bill's hams seem to be many people's favorites and were recommended to me by food writers Evan and Judith Jones, who say that some people find country hams too dry ard strong. So be prepared, if you haven't tried one before.

Gaspar's Sausage Company, Faunce Corner Road, P.O. Box 436, North Dartmouth, MA 02747. Telephone (800) 343 8086
Brochure, free. MC, V.
Gaspar makes its own Portuguese-style sausage, hot or mild. Assorted imported delicacies are also available.

Gould's Country Smokehouse, River Road, Piermont, NH 03779. Telephone (603) 272 5856
Leaflet, free. V.
Corncob-smoked ham, precooked, with more of a smokey flavor than the Virginia-style hams. Recommended by food writers Evan and Judith Jones.

Menuchah Farms Smokehouse, Route 22, Salem, NY 12865
Price list, free.
This very small concern produces smoked meats that have been praised by New York food writers James Beard, Craig Claibourne and Mimi Sheraton. I like their honey-and-brown-sugar-rubbed smoked chicken, which freezes beautifully and makes one of the few really good meals that requires no work whatever.

Schaller & Weber, 22-53 46th Street, Long Island City, NY 11105. Telephone (212) 721 5480
Leaflet, free.
Schaller & Weber proudly claims that theirs is the only American-made product ever to win the highest prizes at the Utrecht International Exposition, and even without that endorsement, I would agree that theirs are among the best wursts available in America. Their catalogue lists some eighty varieties of the most popular of all German foods, from the various sausages (knockbauern, bock and weisswursts) to liverwurst and bolognas (which bear no relation at all to what is sold in supermarkets under that name), as well as Westphalian smoked hams and other goodies.

Usinger's Famous Sausage, 1020 N. Third Street, Milwaukee, WI 53203. Telephone (414) 276 9100
Leaflets, free.
Mimi Sheraton, of the *New York Times*, has described Usinger's "variations on the liverwurst theme" a "gastronomic triumph." This is one of the few firms that uses a minimum of preservatives and natural casings. Usinger's was started in 1880, is still using the original German recipes, and has a really good reputation for their German-style sausages and luncheon meats.

There is no shortage of firms that sell steaks by mail, mainly for gifts. In 1980, *New York Times* food critic Mimi Sheraton tasted and rated sirloin strips and filet mignons from eleven meat-by-mail firms around the country. She found that all the meats lived up to promised weight and size; but decided that, as the meats have to be frozen for shipping, there is little point in buying meat by mail if you have access to a good butcher, who sells "choice" meat. Fresh "choice" (officially second-best) tastes better than frozen "prime" (officially top-quality) she found. However, the meat can make a welcome gift, as long as there is someone to receive and refrigerate the meat when it arrives. These were Mimi Sheraton's two preferred firms for quality and good shipping:

Signature Prime,
Division of New City Packing Company,
147 South Water Market, Chicago, IL 60608.
Telephone (800) 621 0397 or (312) 829 0900
Color catalogue, free. MC, V.
Besides the beef, which has a superb beefy flavor, according to Ms. Sheraton, Signature sells other meats, domestic and wild fowl and game, including wild elk, buffalo, western antelope, llama and wild goat ("roast a whole leg and watch your guests as they savor its delicate flavor").

United American Gourmet Fare,
4545 South Racine Avenue, Chicago, IL 60609.
Telephone (800) 621 0222;
or Illinois residents call collect (312) 927 9300
Color catalogue, free. AE, MC, V.
The beef Ms. Sheraton describes as having excellent flavor with a texture bordering on toughness reminiscent of pre-World War II steaks from grass-fed beef with its slightly fibrous graining; United also sells lamb, smoked pork, prepared and partially cooked chicken, and seafood.

Fish

George Campbell & Sons, 18 Stafford Street,
Edinburgh EH3 7BE, Scotland
Price list, free (specify what you are interested in).
This elegant fishmonger and game dealer ("It is our earnest desire to be of service to our customers") is over a hundred years old and is "supplier of fish and poultry" to Her Majesty the Queen. For local customers they have snipe, golden plover, wood cock, quail, and venison fresh or frozen all year around.

For mail-order customers they have boneless findons, smokies, and kippers which, they say, "are very popular with Americans of Scottish descent"; and also smoked Scotch salmon: "We send our own caught and smoked salmon by air or air freight to all parts of the world." Prices are far lower than United States prices for the best Scotch salmon.

Caviarteria, 29 East 60th Street, New York, NY 10022.
Telephone (800) 221 1020 or (212) 759 7410
Price lists, free. AE, DC, MC, V.
This store became famous by offering fresh caviar at bargain prices and their current list shows how you can save up to $450 by buying your Beluga by the kilo. Smaller quantities are available, as are cheaper caviars and other delicacies. Foie gras, smoked salmon, American caviars and even dried mushrooms and truffles, some at better prices than elsewhere.

Josephson's Smoke House and Dock, 106 Marine Drive,
P.O. Box 412, Astoria, OR 97103.
Telephone (503) 325 2190
Catalogue, free. MC, V.
Northwestern salmon, smoked or pickled at prices about two thirds of those for Nova Scotia and even less than Scotch; still less if you buy the larger size: ten pounds will cost you a mere $10 a pound. Josephson uses the Scandinavian recipes for smoking and curing salmon. Canned fish are also sold and attractive wooden gift boxes may be ordered, at a premium.

Murray's Sturgeon Shop, 2429 Broadway,
New York, NY 10024. Telephone (212) 724 2650
Price list, free.
A tiny shop and the pride of the neighborhood, Murray's has been complimented in *The New York Times* for its excellent smoked salmon and red caviar. It is known to all as a prime source for these plus whitefish, sable and other preserved fish. Murray's uses express or air freight for orders, but has a minimum order of $50.

Ritchie of Rothesay, 37 Watergate,
Rothesay, Bute, Scotland. Telephone 3012
Price card, free.
A family firm on the Isle of Bute that has been air mailing their own bland, cured, smoked salmon to fastidious American gastronomes since a mention in *The New York Times*. A two-pound side of salmon is their minimum order, currently $40 postpaid—an excellent price.

Saltwater Farm, Warrel Lane, York Harbor, ME 03911.
Telephone (207) 363 3182
22-page catalogue, free; overseas $1.50. AE, DC, MC, V.
Saltwater Farm is the country's leading purveyor of live lobsters, a complicated business that concentrates on shipping from eight to twenty lobsters (with or without clams) by air freight to lobster lovers throughout the country. Lobsters average 1⅛ pounds, and cost roughly $40 for four (plus shipping). Clams are $48 for two pecks, but somewhat less if bought in conjunction with the lobsters.

When Saltwater Farm started, over thirty years ago, lobsters were shipped by rail, and railway employees would ice down lobster barrels every few hundred miles (far better service than I can remember ever getting on the Boston & Maine), but now the jet age allows the firm to send its lobsters all over the world, and also to import smoked salmon from Ireland, which it sells along with a number of other delicacies not native to Maine, such as crab. The catalogue also lists various lobster-eating accessories and a number of related items.

Summer Isles Foods, The Smokehouse,
Achilumbuie, Ullapool, Ross-shire, Scotland IV26 2YG.
Telephone 085482 353
Price list, free.
Managing director Keith Dunbar writes: "We specialize in producing gourmet foods using traditional recipes for preparing spicy and/or herbal brines for curing our meat, fish and poultry before smoking over select hardwoods—some of which come from a Highland spinning-wheel maker and some from a cooperage where they produce oak casks for maturing whisky.

"Our raw materials are the best of Highland produce from our local crofts, glens and rivers. Our gentle brine curing and lengthy traditional smoking produce really distinctive flavors and taste.

"I have two assistants and we do all the work ourselves—

so we are quite small and aim to give a friendly personal service."

A friend of mine who writes on cookery and who (lucky person) has tasted smoked salmon from most of the British houses, says that the Summer Isles salmon is unusual, spicier than the blander cures, and is very good. There is a $50 minimum for sales to the United States.

Cheese

Cheese of All Nations, 153 Chambers Street, New York, NY 10007. Telephone (212) 732 0752
Price list, $1. AE, DC, MC, V.
Cheese of All Nations is the best source that I have found for buying imported cheese by mail, and their catalogue will be a relief to beleaguered cheese lovers who have opened packets and cans of foreign cheese only to be disappointed by the results. Very few stores have an adequate supply of good imported cheese, and none, I should think, can match this one.

Crowley Cheese, Healdville, VT 05147. Telephone (802) 259 2340
Leaflet, free U.S. and overseas. MC, V.
The Crowley family has been making cheese for sale since 1824, and have occupied their current factory since 1882. Their natural Colby cheese is still made according to the old Vermont process, cutting and raking the curds by hand and using old-fashioned crank presses. The result is that Crowley Cheddar bears little resemblance to store-bought cheese. It comes in three- and five-pound wheels, mild, medium or sharp, and is very highly recommended. All sorts of cheese lovers consider it Vermont's best.

Hidden Acres Cheese Farm, Joe and Mary Eichten, 16705 310th Street, Center City, MN 55012
Price list, free U.S. and overseas.
Two professors from the University of Minnesota went to Holland to study cheesemaking, then returned to teach the methods to American farm families. Joe and Mary Eichten were two of the students, and have been very happy to turn from the uncertain business of selling milk to the enjoyable task of making cheese. They now use the raw milk from their seventy cows to make all natural Gouda, Swiss and Muenster with no additives, preservatives or artificial color.

Ideal Cheese Shop, 1205 Second Avenue, New York, NY 10025. Telephone (212) 688 7579
Price list, free.
Evan and Judith Jones recommend Ideal as a good cheese shop that sells domestic and imported cheese by mail. Evan Jones has written, among other books, an enjoyable book of information and recipes—*The World of Cheese,* published by Alfred A. Knopf.

Kolb Lena Cheese Company, 301 West Railroad, Lena, IL 61048. Telephone (815) 369 4577
Leaflet, free; overseas $1.
Kolb Lena, an American firm, makes widely praised European-style cheese such as Camembert, feta, and mozzarella, besides American cheeses. Their Brie was recommended to me by food writers Evan and Judith Jones. The Brie has also been praised by James Beard, who has written "if properly aged and stored, [it] is a match for most of the great French Bries."

Maytag Dairy Farms, Box 806, Newton, IA 50208. Telephone 800 247 2458 or (515) 792 1133
Brochure, free U.S. and overseas.
When in the thirties Maytag was wondering how to use the milk from their prize-winning Holstein-Friesian herd, they heard that Iowa State University had developed a new method of making American blue cheese. Maytag decided to use the process, had its first cheesemaker trained at the university, and built a plant and caves especially to make the blue. They now make raw milk cheddar, Swiss and Edam too. A cheese-loving friend of mine says the others are all right but the blue is superb. It is of the creamy not crumbly kind.

Morningland Dairy, Route 1, Box 188, Mountain View, MO 65548. Telephone (417) 496 3817
Price list, self-addressed stamped envelope; overseas $1.
Two couples, Jim and Margie Reiners and Robert and Donna Roman are running a farm by rotating crops, soil building, composting manure and using no herbicides or pesticides—they are also dreaming of a herd that eats only hay and no grain. Meanwhile they make raw milk cheeses from cow's milk and goat's milk. They say that as the cheese is natural, each batch is different, but all are good. I bought some of their goat cheese, which is "cheddar" type (rather different from French goat cheeses) and liked it.

Sugarbush Farms, Woodstock, VT 05091. Telephone (802) 457 1757
Leaflets, free.
Sugarbush is a small business started in the way that so many city dwellers dream of—by a couple who left New York, took their savings and bought a farm. They make maple-syrup products from their own trees and have a smokehouse for their own cheeses. Their all-natural Cheddar is so famous that it has been written up glowingly in *Gourmet* magazine and *The New York Times* food section.

Herbs and Spices

Aphrodisia Products, 282 Bleeker Street, New York, NY 10014. Telephone (212) 989 6440
126-page catalogue, $2.50; overseas $5. V.
A really helpful catalogue describes the uses of the herbs, spices and essential oils sold by this store. There is a *very* complete stock of herbs and spices for cooking, including herbal extracts in liquid form, and ingredients for Chinese, Indonesian and Indian cooking.

Deva, P.O. Box C, 303 East Main Street, Burkittsville, MD 21710. Telephone (301) 473 4900
Natural-fiber clothes brochure, free.
Wild herbs list, free.
Will Endress and friends collect and sell wild herbs for cooking and health uses. He chooses only wild plants because they are stronger and more vital. The herbs are completely free from any sort of contamination, and are not stored for long before selling. He sells them through craftsfairs, and through Deva, a cooperative group.

Charles Loeb–Mr. Spiceman, 615 Palmer Road, Yonkers, NY 10701. Telephone (914) 961 7776
Catalogue, free. MC, V. Minimum order $10.
This firm sells spices in bulk, saving you, they say, at least half the price charged in stores for those tiny jars.

The Spice House, 1102 North Third Street, Milwaukee, WI 53203. Telephone (414) 272 0977
Descriptive price list, $1.
If you want spices, don't miss this engaging, long, typed price list. "The cast" (as they call themselves) make an effort to buy the very best varieties of each spice, and provide lots of information about them in their catalogue. They are not purists, sell bouillon cubes and dehydrated garlic, but they obviously love spices. They make their own mixes, including several salt-free ones, and have gift packs.

9

Natural Foods

Erewhon Natural Foods, 236 Washington Street, Brookline, MA 02146. Telephone (617) 738 4516
16-page catalogue, free. MC, V.
A little Boston shop started fifteen years ago by Michio and Aveline Kushi, Erewhon is now a large company whose goods are sold in health-food stores throughout the country and in Europe and Japan. A good range, the expected cereal, pastas, nut butters, fruits spreads and herb teas are sold, but also Japanese sea vegetables, Japanese macrobiotic ingredients, sesame oils, miso and the like. Also certain perishables, such as bread and exotic root vegetables, which have been found to survive shipping, can be bought by mail.

Maryse et Daniel Favre, Agriculteurs Biologiques, Village de Guarguale, 20128 Grosetto, Prugna, Corsica. Telephone 95 24 21 80
Price list, in French, self-addressed envelope and 1 International Reply Coupon.
I got this friendly note from the Favres:

> We are a young couple, 26, 29 years old working on a 6 ha. ground for two years.
> We are not born here in Corsica but came five years ago and settled here in a non habited valley. This valley was very rich fifty years ago (seven water mills in a 6 km. distance). People produced everything they needed to eat and we want to discover again this agriculture of self-living but with modern ways so that it doesn't not seems too difficult . . .
> We sell our own produce to build our house bigger and to arrange our property better (walls, green houses etc.). We are small and want to stay so and to live a wonderful and long life.
> We write a lot to friends among the world and are happy to take the time to do it. Why not you? Bye, bye.

Their produce consists of pickled vegetables and fruits, including mushrooms, cherry tomatoes in herbs and vinegar, and black and white figs in vinegar. Also black olives a la Greque and sun dried fruits (figs, peaches and raisins).

Jaffe Brothers Natural Foods, P.O. Box 636, Valley Center, CA 92087. Telephone (714) 749 1133
Price list, free U.S. and overseas.
Although grains and beans are also sold, it's the fruit and nuts that are particularly interesting. The nuts, sold in five-pound lots, are a third to almost half off the prices at my local nut shop, as well as the big mail-order firms. There are lots of tempting organic dried fruits, including tropical ones such as pineapples, mangoes and papayas.

Nichols Garden Nursery, 1190 North Pacific Highway, Albany, OR 97321. Telephone (503) 928 9280
Catalogue, free. MC, V.
In addition to selling a very wide choice of herbs and spices,

9 *Sugarbush Farms* Three-pound wheel of natural Vermont white cheddar cheese, aged for a year. Priced about $15.35.

Nichols has a number of gastronomic aids. Here, for instance, is one of the few catalogues to offer yogurt cultures. There is a page of herbal teas and various other health foods such as carob drink, natural chicken broth, etc. In addition to this, Nichols sells a number of macrobiotic foods, various sea vegetables and dried Japanese vegetables.

Walnut Acres, Penns Creek, PA 17862.
Telephone (717) 837 0601
Catalogue, free; overseas $1.
The Walnut Acres catalogue is the most complete of any of the natural-food suppliers that I have seen. The name refers to an actual farm, 360 acres of it, which has been growing and shipping whole foods since 1945. It started in a practically classic fashion with a couple, the Keenes; inspired by Gandhi and others who urged a back-to-the-soil movement, they left college teaching to farm.

The actual catalogue is just about comprehensive, listing not only the usual grains, fruits and nuts, but bread, meat, fish, eggs, vegetables, cookies, even bottled water. Walnut Acres also sells a large selection of vitamins and natural cosmetics, and even laundry detergents and cleaners free of phosphates and NTA.

If you're a serious user of natural foods, or have friends who are, then it makes sense to buy in bulk. These prices offer considerable savings.

Nuts

Fresno Trading Company, 4222 West Alamos, Box 9869, Fresno, CA 93794. Telephone (209) 442 4855
Catalogue, free U.S. and overseas. V.
California nuts, handsomely packaged in wood and glass by a firm that started with pistachios and branched out. A few other items, such as Granny Smith apples or dried fruit bars.

Koinonia, Partners, Route 2, Americus, GA 31709.
Telephone (912) 924 0391
Brochures and leaflets, free.
Koinonia Partners is one of those remarkable utopian adventures that shine through America's past. Started as a Christian communal farm in 1942, it sought to establish a peaceful example and help its neighbors to introduce scientific farming methods. Koinonia stresses aid to those nearby and helped to start a series of local industries. These include pecan shelling, the making of fruitcakes, candy, pottery and various sewing enterprises. Among the products that can be bought by mail are fruit cakes and pecans, nut granola, peanuts, soy bean and soy grits.

Sunnyland Farms, P.O. Box 549, Albany, GA 31703.
Telephone (912) 883 3085
Catalogue, free. MC, V.
Roasted and salted cashews, pecans, pistachios, macadamias and peanuts; raw almonds, brazils, filberts, pecans, peanuts, and walnuts for roasting at home, or cooking. Also candied pecans, pecan brittle, pralines and fruitcake.

Young's Pecan Sales Corporation, P.O. Drawer 5779, Florence, SC 29502. Telephone (803) 662 2452
Price list, free.
Plain pecan halves and pieces, at much lower prices.

Fruit

Barfield Groves, P.O. Box 68, Polk City, FL 33868.
Telephone (813) 984 1316
Brochure, free.
The Barfields sell boxes of citrus fruits—oranges, grapefruits and tangerines, grown in their own groves. "The dependable way to gracious giving," they say.

Harry and David, Bear Creek Orchards, Medford OR 97501. Telephone (503) 766 2121
Color catalogue, free. MC, V.
Harry and David is famous for the "Fruit of the Month Club," through which you send some lucky person from three to twelve boxes of fruit that arrive periodically throughout the year.

Laflin Date Gardens, P.O. Box 757, Thermal, CA 92274.
Telephone (714) 399 5665
Color brochure, free; overseas 25 cents; air mail $1. MC, V.
Specialists in the famous Medjool dates, this shop sells many other varieties, as well as date cakes, bread and dates for cooking. Gift-boxed or in much, much cheaper bulk packs.

Baked Foods

Baldwin Hill Bakery, Baldwin Hill Road, Phillipston, MA 01331
Price leaflet, free. Wholesale. Minimum order twelve large loaves (bread freezes well).
A research physician and a landscape architect met while working at Erewhon Food Company and together got interested in the idea of making and selling a really good bread. They were inspired by tasting a loaf a friend had brought back from Lima bakery in Belgium. After trying to learn how to make the bread by mail, Hy Lerner and Paul Petrosky actually went to Belgium and worked as apprentices.

In the bread they developed, only organically grown whole wheat, sea salt and untreated deep well water are used. The dough is kneaded slowly and leavened with a natural sourdough made from wheat and pure water only. The loaves are baked over a wood fire in a traditional brick oven. The result is a firm dark bread that keeps well. ("Dark and delicious" says a friend of mine.)

Collin Street Bakery, Box 79, Corsicana, TX 75110.
Telephone (214) 872 3951
Leaflet, free U.S. and overseas.
This fruit and nut cake is recommended by Sabina D. Jordan, who hasn't tasted it but says her Texan friends say it is as fruity and nutty as can be. If you buy it, you'll join Mr. and Mrs. Zubin Mehta, H.R.H. Princess Marguerite de Bourbon d'Orleans, Mrs. Cornelius Vanderbilt, Jr., and the Sincere Company of Hong Kong, among others. Clearly a lot of companies use the firm to polish off a gift list in one fell swoop, and the cake in its Olde Christmas tin gets sent to about 192 countries a year.

Elizabeth the Chef, St. Mary's Road, Sydenham Farm Industrial Estate, Leamington Spa CV31 1JP, England.
Telephone 0926 311 531
Color brochure, free.
This British firm specializes in traditional Christmas cakes,

fruitcakes, Christmas puddings as well as cakes shaped into holiday figures.

Lebkuchenfabrik E. Otto Schmidt, Zollhausstr. 30, 8500 Nurnberg 50, Germany
Leaflet, free. In German.
A reader who has been buying from them for several years enthusiastically recommends the Lebkuchen, traditional German spice cookies made by this firm. She says that Lebkuchen of the classical Nuremberg variety is one thing a home-baker usually doesn't do as well as the Lebkuchen factories. The recipes are carefully guarded secrets, and cookbooks have only simple-minded recipes; New York's are never fresh and have outrageously high prices.

My informant says this firm is not as well known as the famous Haegerlin and Singer but definitely offers better merchandise at lower prices. Lebkuchen are liable to get stale, so Otto Schmidt recommends sending only the seven-pound assortment in the metal box to the United States.

Matthews 1812 House, Box 15, Whitcomb Hill Road, Cornwall Bridge, CT 06754. Telephone (203) 672 6449
Leaflet, free.
Plenty of firms sell rich fruitcakes by mail, but the most appealing leaflet I have seen comes from Deanna Matthews of Matthews 1812 House. The business is just over a year old, and was started by a young mother who likes natural foods, and wanted work that she could do at home. She makes two cakes, a Fruit and Nut, and a Brandied Apricot, and they are really health foody—nothing but fresh eggs, cream, honey, brown sugar, dried fruit, brandy and wheat flour; no candied fruit, rinds, peels, fillers; and, of course, no preservatives. She sends out a sample of her Fruit and Nut cake with each leaflet, the piece I got was very apricoty, and rather tart.

Moravian Sugar Crisp Cookies, Route 2, Box 427, Clemmons, NC 27012. Telephone (919) 764 1402
Brochure, free; overseas $1. Minimum order $9.50.
These paper thin cookies have lemon, sugar, ginger, chocolate and butterscotch flavors, and have been highly praised by critics. Tin containers assure freshness and various gift assortments are ready-made.

Pepperidge Farm Mail Order Company, Box 119, Route 145, Clinton, CT 06413
Color catalogue, free. AE, MC, V.
In recent years Godiva chocolates have become known as the ultimate in fancy chocolates. They are expensive, wrapped in gold paper, sold on Fifth Avenue, and the original Belgium chocolates had a fine reputation. In fact, the chocolates sold in the United States are made here, and the firm is owned by Campbells soup. You can buy the chocolates along with sweet and rich Pepperidge Farm cookies and cakes in various gift combinations, through the Pepperidge Farm mail order catalogue.

Wolferman's Original English Muffin Company, 3306 Wyoming Street, Kansas City, MO 64111. Telephone (816) 756 0900
Brochure, free. MC, V.
Apparently Kansas City, which is known in gastronomic circles primarily as the birthplace of Calvin Trillin, the *New Yorker*'s famed food critic, is also known as the source of the best English muffins available. Wolferman's highly praised offerings are available per se, or in fancy gift packs, or on a monthly plan.

10

10 *Matthews 1812 House* Fruit and nut cake and brandied apricot cake. One-half-pound (oblong) cake, $12. Three-pound (round) cake, $21.

11

12

13

Preserves

Hickins, R.F.D. 1, Black Mountain Road, Brattleboro, VT 05301. Telephone (802) 254 2146
Price list, self-addressed stamped envelope; overseas 2 International Reply Coupons.
This farm sells its highly praised fresh produce to visitors but also has a nice selection of preserves to sell by mail. Jams, jellies, pickles—the usual categories but with some tempting variants, such as pickled tarragon kohlrabi, unsweetened wild blackberry jam.

Plumridge, 33 East 61st Street, New York, NY 10021. Telephone (212) 371 0608
Leaflet, free. AE, MC.
"Confections for the Carriage Trade—Established 1883," states the leaflet listing these extremely expensive sweets for the rich. Plumridge started out supplying gift baskets of fruit to passengers on steamships, "as gifts from some of New York society's leading families." The seasonal nature of the fruits led the firm to develop substitutes such as candied fruits and delicious spiced nuts, for which the firm is best known. Plumridge makes its own jams and jellies, and sells an appealing mixture of dessert fruits, apricots, dates, prunes and figs. Baskets and other gift assortments are also available; many gifts for babies or children. Minimum order $25.

The Soap Box-Crabtree and Evelyn, Box 167, Woodstock, CT 06281
Color comestibles catalogue, $2 (refundable).
Color cosmetics catalogue, $2 (refundable).
This firm was established a few years ago to produce naturally based toiletries, and traditional foods. Their foods may not be better than those of other specialty food firms, but they are infinitely more gorgeously packaged, making them very good for presents: gingerbread men and almond shortbread; plum walnut brandy, and greengage preserve; jasmin petal jelly and gooseberry chutney; fruit syrups, fruit vinegars and scented honeys—everything is irresistably exquisite and available individually or in gift crates.

The Silver Palate, 274 Columbus Avenue, New York, NY 10023. Telephone (212) 799 6340
Price list and newsletter, $2 a year U.S. and overseas.
Two young women have made a startling success of their tiny shop selling their own foods. At first take-out dishes for people to reheat at home and now also packaged foods sold with the Silver Palate label through posh shops and catalogues around the country. Their special approach has been fanciful and imaginative foods, cooked in small "home-cooked" batches, and distinctive packages. They make such novelties as blueberry vinegar, pink pepperberry oil, plum chutney, mixed spices and peppers to put in a pepper grinder. They are one of the few firms making brandied fruits and sweet sauces that really look and taste homemade. A good place for original food gifts (a "nibbler's" hand-stenciled basket of pickled wild cherries, basil mustard, pesto walnuts, and duck pâté, for instance). And although prices are high, most things on the price list cost under $10.

11 *The Soap Box-Crabtree and Evelyn* Peach preserves and amaretto with almonds. Eight-ounce jar about $5.

12 *The Silver Palate* An assortment of nuts, spices, and preserves.

13 *Chocolaterie Confisserie Brosshard* Boxes of praline chocolates in 1982 cost (including airmail postage to the U.S.): 10 ounces, $16; 1 pound, $20; 2.2 pounds, $35.

Chocolate

Making good chocolate, like making good wine, is a complicated business. Much of the work is done not by retail chocolate shops but by big chocolate manufacturers.

Chocolate beans grow in pods on trees around the equator and, like coffee beans, differ greatly in flavor and quality. Some beans are tasty, scarce and expensive; others are cheaper and taste more ordinary, depending on stock, climate and soil. Chocolate manufacturers buy beans in thirty-thousand-pound lots through commodity brokers. The manufacturers roast, grind, "knead" and flavor the beans. Depending on the mixture of beans used and the treatment at different stages, subtly different chocolates are produced. This is what the chocolate makers known to the public buy. In some cases the shops listed below have their own blend made to order; in other cases they may mix several chocolates besides adding their own flavoring and their own fillings.

Bailey's, 26 Temple Place, Boston, MA 02111.
Telephone (617) 426 4560
Price list, free U.S. and overseas.
Bailey's ice cream parlor and chocolate shop is over a hundred years old and is well known in Boston. They have a worldwide mail-order business at bargain prices (compared to the New York shops). Chocolates have traditional American jelly centers, cream centers such as banana and lime, chewy centers such as marshmallows, etc. Jellies, gum drops, rock candy, mints and every fudge imaginable are also sold.

Karl Bissinger French Confections,
4744 McPherson Avenue, St. Louis, MO 63108.
Telephone (314) 361 0647.
Color chocolate brochure, free.
Mint and sugar-cube leaflet, free. (Not available November or December). MC, V.
A tempting catalogue with a wide selection including liquer-flavored "creme" chocolates, pecan bark, cocoa almonds and chocolate desert shells for filling yourself. For more ambitious givers, there is a candy-of-the-month plan, in which you give three-to-twelve-months' worth of gifts with different chocolate each time.

There's a separate leaflet of decorated and monogrammed mints and decorated sugar cubes.

André Bollier, 5018 Main Street,
Kansas City, MO 64112. Telephone (816) 561 3440
Leaflet, fall, $1 (refundable). MC, V.
A Swiss family makes chocolate truffles, pralines and fondants with heavy cream, pure ingredients, and Swiss recipes. Shipped only in cooler weather, October to April. Excellent reputation. Lower than New York prices.

♣ **Charbonnel et Walker, 29 Old Bond Street,**
London W1, England. Telephone (01) 629 4396
18-page color brochure, $2.
A posh little shop in Old Bond Street selling chocolates in lacy, velvety, flowery boxes—most suitable for a romantic gesture. There are two gratifying services: One is a foil-covered chocolates with letters on top that can be used to spell out a message. The other service is that centers are numbered so you can choose your own favorites (and avoid whatever you don't like). As well as chocolates, you can buy Marzipan Amandé in the Lubeck tradition, Marzipan Gingembre, marzipan with assorted nuts, crystallized pepper-mint creams, crystallized ginger, glacéed pineapple, marron glacé, burnt or sugared almonds, etc.

Chocolaterie Confisserie Brosshard,
Stadthausstrasse 145, 8400, Winterthur, Switzerland
Prices, 1 International Reply Coupon.
Confisserie Brosshard sells by mail boxes of their praline chocolates: "All chocolates are made in our own hause."

Confisserie-Schatz,
Getreidegasse 3, A-5020 Salzburg, Austria
Price list, free. Prices in $.
Salzburger Mozartkugeln are filled with pistachio marzipan and hazelnut nougat and coated with chocolate in the form of a ball. I can happily report, having received a free sample, that they are *very* rich and *very* delicious. Each one is wrapped in silver foil with a rather blurred picture of Mozart on it and packed in a box which shows an old engraving of Salzburg and is tied with a ribbon with the colors of the Austrian flag. They cost, including surface postage (it takes about five weeks), $10.50 for a minipackage (15 pieces); $18.50 for maxi (32 pieces). A suitable present for a musical gourmet or a greedy music lover.

Harbor Sweets, P.O. Box 150, Marblehead, MA 01945.
Telephone (617) 745 7648
Catalogue, free.
Harbor Sweets is best known for its "sweet sloops," which were invented when Connie Strohecker was trying to make what her husband claims is the best chocolate recipe in the world: chocolate-covered homemade almond butter crunch. She ran out of dark chocolate, tried white milk coating, and found that the results looked rather like sailboats. Since then the Stroheckers have also started making Marblehead Mints (dark chocolate and peppermint crunch) and sand dollars (butter caramels and pecans) all handmade. I recently bought some sand dollars and loved them.

Hershey's Chocolate World, Mail Order Department,
Park Boulevard, Hershey, PA 17033.
Telephone (717) 534 4912.
Color leaflet, free. MC, V.
Hershey's Chocolate World, which entertains and educates 1.5 million visitors annually by giving them an automated tour showing the story of chocolate, also sells amusing chocolate souvenirs: a giant Hershey bar a foot and a half long and nine inches wide, and a giant Kiss. Other edibles include Kisses in jars and in an old-fashioned box of chocolates.

Kron Chocolatier, 764 Madison Avenue,
New York, NY 10021. Telephone (212) 472 1234
Price list, $1. AE, MC, V.
Kron has become very famous in recent years not just for the taste of its chocolate but for their shapes. Chocolate legs (female), torsos (!), tennis rackets and other more innocent shapes seem to have a wide appeal, though the price of these items is very high indeed. So is the cost of Kron's excellent chocolates, just about as high as you can pay in New York but at least very tasty (and the packaging, wooden crates and shiny papers, is nice). For some reason, Kron's baking and cocoa chocolates and powders are much more reasonably priced.

14

Li-Lac Chocolates, 120 Christopher Street, New York, NY 10014. Telephone (212) 242 7374
Price list, free; overseas $1. AE, DC, MC, V.
This small shop, started in 1923, still hand makes its chocolates daily in the building. Walnut creams, hazelnut butter truffles, chocolate-covered fruits, French mints and more, are all sold at prices that are somewhat lower than at the other New York handmade chocolate shops.

Teuscher Chocolates of Switzerland, 620 Fifth Avenue, New York, NY 10020. Telephone (212) 246 4416
Leaflet, free. AE, MC, V.
Teuscher makes the best chocolate I have ever tasted, and, according to *New York Times* food writer Mimi Sheraton, "many connoisseurs" like them too. The chocolates are made and packaged in Zurich, Switzerland, and flown in once a week.

The chocolates have an extremely rich, melting quality which, according to Teuscher owner Mr. Bloom, comes partly from the flavor of Swiss milk and partly from the fact that the chocolates have no additives or preservatives whatever. The eleven varieties of truffles are most famous.

Milton York Candy Company, Box 416, Long Beach, WA 98631. Telephone (206) 642 2352
Price list available only September through March, free. MC, V.
In 1882 a young candymaker, Milton York, started his business with a tent, an open fire, and recipes he had learned during his apprenticeship in Portland, Oregon. Twelve years later, he built a shop and a home on the same spot, and thirty-six years later, he built the shop that is still there. Several of the candies are also made from the original recipes; Ragged Robins, pecans and caramels dipped in dark or light chocolate, and chocolate layers with almonds, for instance. Chocolates are made by hand with butter and cream and no preservatives, so they are shipped only September through May.

Coffee and Tea

Caravansary, 410 Townsend Street, San Francisco, CA 94107. Telephone (415) 777 5591
Brochure, free. AE, MC, V.
A wide choice of coffees, including a number I've not seen elsewhere: Armenian, Yemeni and Ethiopian blends, all richer and stronger than most coffees. Peruvian and Mexican are also available, as well as decaffeinated.

The Coffee Connection, P.O. Box 455, Cambridge, MA 02138. Telephone (617) 492 3716
Price list, free. MC, V.
This firm buys and roasts its own coffees and ships the freshest lots of an impressive variety of beans. You can place a standing order for regular mailings.

Schapira Coffee Company, 117 West Tenth Street, New York, NY 10001. Telephone (212) 675 3733
Price list, free.
Schapira has been roasting its own coffees and blending its own teas since 1903. They sell a very good variety including water-decaffeinated (a third of their sales are by mail order) and also coffeemaking equipment (for this you have to write with a model number).

14 *The Coffee Connection* Coffees and teas are available on standing order to arrive every one, two, three, or four weeks, and are charged to customer's MasterCard or Visa.

**Simpson and Vail, P.O. Box 309,
Pleasantville, NY 10570. Telephone (212) 349 2960**
Annual catalogue, free. MC, V.
"Purveyors of gourmet teas and coffees," this firm specializes in unusual teas, handsomely packaged. Decorated cannisters, or an authentic brick made of pressed China tea. The catalogue also lists a coffee- or tea-of-the-month club, sending packages of either in twelve varieties throughout the year.

**Whittard and Co., Ltd., 111 Fulham Road,
London SW 3 6RP, England. Telephone 01 589 4162**
Price list, free. AE, DC, MC, V.
Ninety-year-old Whittard sells teas and coffees: "All blended teas are blended at our premises, and all coffees are roasted daily here." An American customer writes to me lovingly of their "honest, straightforward, careful, personal" service; their dozens of China, India and Sri Lanka teas; their coffees from all the best farms in all the best places "at their peak and 100% true"; and says they handle mailings like "masters of old." Indeed, they cater to the world's most respected people, my informant says; "I doubt if you could drag it out of them if you had a dungeon with a rack in your basement . . . but you may be sure that someone in the shop has been busy with a special mailing to Monaco, Palm Springs, San Francisco, Abu Dhabi, the "city within the city" in Rome, and that revered palace. . . . "

Heublein [Farmington, CT 06032; Telephone (203) 233 7531], *Christie and Sotheby Park Bernet (Antiques section) run auctions for fine wines for which it is possible to put in absentee bids.*

**Morell and Company, 307 East 53rd Street,
New York, NY 10022. Telephone (212) 688 9370**
Catalogue, free. April, October, November.
My favorite wine catalogue is produced by energetic and publicity-receiving Peter Morrell. He is especially interested in California wines, so besides the imports he has a very good selection of wines from there. The catalogue is informative; and lower prices are frequently offered on new arrivals and at the beginning of the season. They will send their catalogues anywhere inside the country.

**Tele-Wine, Wine by Wire, 10 East 39th Street,
New York, NY 10016.
Telephone (800) 223 2660 or (212) 685 2100**
Information, free. AE, MC, V.
If you feel a sudden urge to send someone a bottle of champagne, you can now do it through Tele-Wine, who, for $35 will send a bottle of domestic champagne or two bottles of domestic or imported wine anywhere in the United States (or to capitals in Europe). You can choose the wine (or they can help), and it will be delivered by one of the participating stores throughout the country. You pay with a credit card.

Wine

Wine lovers who would like to try a wider range or more interesting wines than are available locally will be happy to hear that several states allow you, under certain conditions, to receive wine for your *personal* use (not resale).

It is illegal to mail alcoholic beverages, but they may be shipped by commercial carrier to permissible destinations. (The commercial carriers, United Parcel Service, Federal Express, etc., have their own regulations. Basically they will accept shipments from licensed dealers with accounts.)

The legal department of the trade association, The Wine Institute, 165 Post Street, San Francisco CA 94108, has compiled a very useful *Survey of Restrictions on Interstate Shipments to Unlicensed Individuals for Personal Use Wine and Brandy.* It gives details of laws and regulations governing what wine you are allowed to bring in with you and what you are allowed to have shipped in from other states and from abroad.

If you live in a state not listed below, direct wine shipments are at the time of writing forbidden, but whether your state is listed below or not, it is worth finding out if it is legal to have wines delivered for you to a friendly local licensee (shop or restaurant).

If you live in one of the states listed below, contact your State Alcoholic Beverage or Liquor Control Commission. You may be allowed to receive shipments of wine for your own use in certain amounts and *under certain conditions* (which, except for states appearing in italics, entails getting a permit and sometimes paying taxes): Alabama, *Alaska,* California, Connecticut, *District of Columbia,* Hawaii, *Illinois,* Massachusetts, *Michigan, Missouri,* New Jersey, Ohio, *Oklahoma,* Pennsylvania, *Rhode Island,* South Carolina, Vermont, Washington.

1 *Tulipshow Frans Roozen* A view of the nursery and show garden where a thousand varieties of spring flowers can be seen from April 10 to May 15.

2 *Henrietta's Nursery* Orchid cactus strictum, a good hanging plant, $2.50.

3 *Richters* Bergamot "Panorama," an exceptionally handsome, fragrant herb, attracts bees and humming birds. The leaves and flowers make a tisane, and young leaf tips and flowers can be used in salad for taste and appearance. About $1 per packet.

4 *Richters* French marigold "Harmony," preferred variety for insect control. Root secretions control soil worms, nematodes, that attach to plant roots; and repulsive odor of leaves discourages above-ground insects. About 60 cents per packet.

A permit is not needed for importing bulbs or seeds into the United States, but it *is* needed for plants and should be obtained before plants are ordered. Write to Permit Unit, United States Department of Agriculture, Animal and Plant Health Inspection Service, Federal Building, Hyattsville, MD 20782. Ask for the "Application for Permit to Import Plants or Plant Products under Quarantine No. 37." You will be sent a simple form on which you list the plants you are going to order and, after you return it, a mailing label which you forward to the nursery with your order.

Canadians who want permits write Agriculture Canada, Plant Quarantine Division, K. W. Neatby Bldg., Ottawa, Ontario K1A OC6, Canada. But in this section it is safer to assume that U.S. nurseries will not ship to Canada unless they are willing to sell "overseas."

African Violets

Buell's Greenhouses, P.O. Box 218 CC, Weeks Road, Eastford, CT 06242. Telephone (203) 974 0623
Price list, 25 cents plus self-addressed stamped envelope; overseas $1.

Lyndon Lyon Greenhouses, 14 Mutchler Street, Dolgeville, NY 13329. Telephone (315) 429 8291
16-page color brochure, 50 cents.
"African violets, Gloxinas and their relatives," including miniatures for terrariums. Plants are listed but not illustrated on the Buell price list. Lyndon has a partly illustrated brochure.

Bulbs

P. DeJager & Sons, 188 Asbury Street, South Hamilton, MA 01982. Telephone (617) 468 1622
64-page color catalogue, free. June. MC, V.
This is the place for a good selection of imported Dutch bulbs. The firm has its own nurseries and offices in Holland. There are large sections in the catalogue of daffodils, narcissi and tulips, and also some hyacinths, snowdrops and other lovely small flowers. Prices on most bulbs are now as low as, or lower than, bulbs bought direct from Holland.

Mrs. J. Abel Smith, Orchard House, Letty Green, Hertford, England. Telephone Hatfield 61274
Price list, free.
Mrs. Abel Smith grows and raises daffodil bulbs on her own land; she has over one hundred varieties including many prize-winners. Overseas orders should be in by mid July.

Tulipshow Frans Roozen, Vogelenzang, Holland. Telephone 02502 7245
28-page color catalogue, free. June. Prices in $.
A colorful, well-illustrated catalogue displays some of the choice tulips and other flowering bulbs grown by this three-hundred-year-old family firm. It is very easy to buy here, the catalogue comes out in June, bulbs are sent in October. Quality of the bulbs is good (I've bought some), and the prices on a few hyacinths and botanical tulips, for instance, are about 15-percent below U.S. prices, after paying postage.

Van Bourgondien, Bros., P.O. Box 9, Babylon, NY 11702. Telephone (516) 669 3500
50-page color catalogue, free. AE, MC, V.
Dutch-grown and domestic bulbs. One of the few firms in the U.S. that carries the rare fall-blooming Crocus Sativus, the source of saffron.

J. B. Wijs & Zoon, Singel 508, 1017 AX, Amsterdam, Holland. Telephone 020 22 12 16
Brochure, free. April.
Another source of popular bulbs from Holland. Like Tulip-show, it concentrates on basics.

Cacti and Succulents

Beahm Gardens, 2686 Paloma Street, Pasadena, CA 91107. Telephone (213) 792 6533
Mimeographed list, 50 cents, U.S. and overseas.
Beahm Gardens specializes in Epiphyllum, sometimes known as orchid cactus, which is misleading because there is no relationship to orchids beyond the fact that both have extraordinary flowers. These very decorative and unusual plants are simple to grow, Beahm Gardens says.

Desert Plant Company, P.O. Box 880, Marfa, TX 79843. Telephone (915) 729 4943
40-page catalogue, $1; overseas $2.
About thirty cacti of the Southwest are photographed and described in this catalogue. Cacti are picked in the field and cost around $1 each. Handmade, hand-painted, three- to four-inch bowls and planting pots made in Mexico for the cacti are also sold.

Henrietta's Nursery, 1345 N. Brawley, Fresno, CA 93711 5899
50-page catalogue, $1; sea mail $2.
Henrietta's has specialized in cacti and succulents for twenty-five years. The yearly catalogue is chatty, full of pictures and fairly descriptive. Over two thousand species are listed, and books on cacti and succulents are for sale.

Holly Gate Nurseries, Billingshurst Lane, Ashington, Sussex RH20 3BA, England. Telephone (0903) 892 439
Unillustrated price list, $1. V.
Holly Gate specializes in cacti, succulent and bromeliad seeds and plants, and has a very large overseas following, much of it American. They attribute this in part to the number of plants they sell that are available nowhere else and also to the competitiveness of their prices.

Quinta Fdo Schmoll, Cadereyta de Montes, Qro, Mexico. Telephone 42
Price list, free. Prices in $.
This cactus farm has a typed list of the many cactus plants and seedlings for sale. There are no descriptions, just names and prices, but if the names don't mean anything to you, ask for offers number one or two—both of which are ready-chosen assortments. Prices start at $20 for seventy seedlings, including postage (you can also get smaller quantities). Anyone interested in show plants can write for additional information.

Clematis

Fisk's Clematis Nursery, Westleton, Saxmundham, Suffolk, England. Telephone 263
40-page color catalogue, $2; air mail $3.
These specialists consider clematis the most beautiful and rewarding of all climbing plants. The catalogue has a selection of perfectly hardy wild species, which are good for covering unsightly objects such as garages and fences.

Dahlias

Halls of Heddon, West Heddon Nurseries, Heddon on the Wall, Newcastle upon Tyne NE15 0JS, England. Telephone Wylam 2445
Leaflet, $1.
Specialists in chrysanthemums and dahlias, Halls sells dahlia tubers, November to February, and has been exporting to specialists, exhibitors and gardeners for sixty years.

Groundcover

Prentiss Court, P.O. Box 8662, Greenville, SC 29604
Leaflet, free. MC, V.
A small firm sells over seventy hardy groundcover plants, bare root and 2½- to 3-inch pots, at bulk order prices. The leaflet stresses the fact that the lower prices mean customers can buy enough plants for good coverage.

Herbs

Borchelt Herb Gardens, 474 Carriage Shop Road, East Falmouth, MA 02536
Price list, self-addressed stamped envelope.
A listing of culinary and medicinal herbs with cryptic comments—garlic chives ("very tasty"); horehound ("used in cough drops").

Richters, Goodwood, Ontario L0C 1A0 Canada. Telephone (416) 640 6677
54-page catalogue, $1; overseas $2. MC, V.
A marvelous herb/seed catalogue. It has an enormous selection of culinary herbs (eight different basils, nine different parsleys), medicinal herbs (nine different comfreys), herbs for dyeing, and rare and exotic herbs (some used in religious ceremonies). Now they've added seeds for unusual vegetables (Chinese vegetables, cardoon, purslane, roquette, etc.), wildflower seeds, alpine flower seeds, organic plant foods, natural insect controls and a good book list.

Well Sweep Herb Farm, 317 Mt. Bethel Road, Port Murray, NJ 07865
30-page price list, 50 cents.
Herb plants are listed here (no description or growing information). Natural, not dyed, dried flowers are sold in bunches, or specially chosen for arrangements.

House Plants

The Banana Tree, 715 Northampton Street, Easton, PA 18042. Telephone (215) 253 9589
Price list, 25 cents or stamps; overseas 40 cents.
The Banana Tree sells tuberous bulbs and exotic rhizomes, such as peacock ginger from Burma and seeds to grow plants such as the Chinese fly-catching vine with "long peculiar insectivorous flowers."

Logee's Greenhouses, 55 North Street, Danielson, CT 06239. Telephone (203) 774 8038
102-page catalogue, $2.50; overseas $6.
Logee's, started in 1892 by the father of the present owners, specializes in tropical plants. The catalogue gives brief descriptions of most plants and has photographs of just a few. Begonias, geraniums and herbs are grown and sold in profusion, and there are also cacti and succulents, vines, oxalis and a section listing "choice plants for the home and conservatory." A great deal to choose from.

Irises (Peonies, Day Lilies)

Gilbert H. Wild and Son, Department TCC-1982, Sarcoxie, MO 64862
96-page catalogue, $2; overseas $4.
This one-hundred-year-old, family-run business is a major source for peonies, irises and day lilies. Collections are listed, as well as culture information.

Ivy

The Garden Spot, 4032 Rosewood Drive, Columbia, SC 29205
Price list, self-addressed stamped envelope; overseas 1 International Reply Coupon.
"Rare and choice ivies for the collector and/or gardener" are grown by the Garden Spot. They quickly get new and fresh varieties that are offered in England and Asia, and ship all year around.

Magnolias

Gossler Farms Nursery, 1200 Weaver Road, Springfield, OR 97477. Telephone (503) 746 3922
8-page price list, 50 cents U.S. and overseas.
This firm specializes in magnolias and "companion" plants. The unillustrated price list contains many varieties exclusive to Gossler.

5 *Peter Paul's Nurseries* Sundew Drosera spathulata, carnivorous sundews attract gnats, flies, and other insects, which stick to the plant when they touch it. About $3.

6 *Peter Paul's Nurseries* Carnivorous Venus's-flytraps have finger-like cilia around the edges of the leaves. When flies, moths, or bugs are attracted to the plant, tiny trigger hairs on the surface of the leaf sense them, and the leaf snaps shut. Bulbs, six for $1.95 to two for $3.50, depending on size.

Miscellaneous Specialties

Dutch Mountain Nursery—"Berries for the Birds," 7984 N. 48th Street, Route 1, Augusta, MI 49012. Telephone (616) 731 5232
Price list, 25 cents; overseas 50 cents.
For thirty years this firm has been professionally handling

plants which attract birds. Their list is informative—it tells you what tree or shrub you can plant where to attract which kinds of birds.

Kester's Wild Game Food Nurseries, P.O. Box V, Omro, WI 54963. Telephone (414) 685 2929
26-page catalogue, $1 U.S. and overseas, MC, V.
A catalogue of plants that provide food for wildlife.

Peter Paul's Nurseries, Department A91, Route 4, Canandaigua, NY 14424. Telephone (716) 394 7397
4-page catalogue, 25 cents; overseas 3 International Reply Coupons. MC, V.
For the more advanced gardener of carnivorous or insectivorous plants, there is Peter Paul's, which in sixteen years has built up a good reputation. The concise, businesslike catalogue contains the standard selection of these plant oddities, as well as some rare ones.

Mushrooms

The Kinoko Company, P.O. Box 6425, Oakland, CA 94621. Telephone (415) 562 3671
Leaflet, free; overseas $5.
Dried Velvet stem, tree oyster and Shiitake mushrooms are available (dried or fresh) in a few places but are very expensive. Dr. Henry Mee has done Chinese food lovers a great kindness in inventing a way of growing mushrooms easily at home. He has produced a sort of log made of organic materials, which is injected with spores and incubated. The logs produce a total harvest of two to three pounds, not huge, but the mushrooms have a strong flavor, and are used sparingly anyway.

Orchids

Acres of Orchids, Rod McLellan Co., 1450 El Camino Real, South San Francisco, CA 94080. Telephone (415) 871 5655
20-page color catalogue, $1.50 U.S. and overseas. MC, V.
Acres of Orchids represents the third generation of a family business specializing in the orchid. Listings include many species, both common and rare.

Organic

Butterbrooke Farm, 78 Barry Road, Oxford, CT 06483. Telephone (203) 888 2000
Price list, free; overseas 50 cents.
Butterbrooke Farm Seed cooperative started with Tom and Judy Butterworth just producing additive-free food for themselves. They gradually started supplying seeds to friends, gardening clubs and church groups, and have now become known to gardeners around the country. Their seeds are all chemically untreated, open pollinated seed of rapidly maturing strains and they really try to keep prices down (as I write prices are 25 cents and 45 cents a packet), partly by producing a very inexpensive price list, as you'll see.

7

8

7 *The Kinoko Company* Shiitake mushroom log. After 6 weeks Shiitake mushrooms grow for several months. About $14.95.

8 *The Kinoko Company* Ling Zhi Tea Mix tea made from three mushrooms. Said to have a mildly earthy taste with mellowy sweet mushroom aroma—three bags about $10.

9

**Gothard, P.O. Box 370, Canutillo, TX 79835.
Telephone (505) 874 3125**
Brochure, free.
Gothard presents its own answer to crop pest control. Since 1959 it has been selling *Trichogramma*, little wasplike insects which become parasites to the eggs of insects that destroy crops. Bothard claims that *Trichogramma* will not feed on vegetation or destroy other beneficial insects.

**Johnny's Selected Seeds, Albion, ME 04910.
Telephone (207) 437 9294**
56-page catalogue, free U.S. and overseas.
An impressively serious and well-written catalogue. Rob Johnston, Jr. (Johnny) supports "organic" methods, and his seeds are untreated, although seeds grown by both organic and nonorganic methods are sold. Seeds are tried each year under northern growing conditions and the grounds have the shortest, coolest growing season of any seed company in the U.S.

The catalogue lists only vegetables, and has a sophisticated selection of the usual and unusual. Johnny encourages customers to save their own seeds, will swap his seeds for heirloom varieties, and offers to answer gardening questions by phone or mail if you send a self-addressed stamped envelope.

**Oak Cottage Herb Farm, Nesscliffe, Near Shrewsbury,
Shropshire SY4 1DB, England. Telephone Nesscliffe 262**
Price list $1; air mail $2.
Compost-grown herbs, dye plants and old cottage garden plants. Ruth Thompson says that she sends seeds and large orders overseas.

**Sanctuary Seeds, 2388 West 4th Street,
Vancouver, British Columbia, V6K 1P1, Canada**
32-page brochure, $1.
A small family firm grows untreated traditional (nonhybrid) vegetable and herb seeds, some of them in bulk quantities. Their friendly catalogue is sprinkled with stories and sayings, and they like to get poems, prayers and advice from their customers.

**Vermont Bean Seed Company, Garden Lane, Bomoseen,
VT 05732. Telephone (802) 265 4212**
32-page catalogue, free; overseas $2.50. AE, MC, V.
A complete line of vegetable seeds; the specialty is beans, peas and corn. The largest selection in the world, they say. Seeds are not treated with fungicide.

Plants, General

**Alpengrow Gardens, Micaud & Company,
13328 King George Highway,
Surrey, British Columbia V3T 2T6, Canada.
Telephone (604) 584 9392**
32-page price list, $1.
Alpengrow has grown alpines, flowering shrubs and dwarf conifers for many years, and the catalogue lists a number of rare plants unavailable elsewhere. Their slow-growing conifers are, they feel, their most interesting offering. Nearly everything in their catalogue can be imported to the United States.

**Blackthorne Gardens, 48 Quincy Street,
Holbrook, MA 02343. Telephone (617) 767 0308**
38-page catalogue, $2 (refundable).
A big and partly illustrated catalogue full of enthusiastic

9 *Blackthorne Gardens* Prizewinning Lemon Royal Bowl Strain lily, large fragrant blooms in lemon yellow. Bulbs $4.25 each.

descriptions on nice thick paper offers lilies, rare bulbs, species, wild flowers, alliums, hostas and clematis.

**Bodnant Garden Nursery,
Tal y Cafn, Colwyn Bay LL28 5RE, Wales.
Telephone 0492 67 460**
Price list, 1 International Reply Coupon.
This is one of the very beautiful gardens run by the National Trust, the private group that preserves a number of the United Kingdom's stately homes and gardens. A number of ornamental trees and shrubs are available by mail at very reasonable prices. Bodnant has recently decided to start propagating uncommon trees, shrubs, herbaceous plants and alpines. They invite suggestions and requests.

**Endangered Species, 12571 Redhill, Tustin, CA 92680.
Telephone (714) 730 6323**
24-page price list and four newsletters, $4. MC, V.
A husband and wife who like unusual plants propagate some that are not easily available commercially, others that are endangered, and others that they find particularly useful or beautiful, for landscaping, bonsai or containers.

**Hillier Nurseries, Ampfield House,
Ampfield Nr Romsey, Hampshire 505 9PA, England.
Telephone 0794 68733**
Price list of trees, shrubs, fruits, roses, hardy perennials and alpine plants, $1; air mail $3. DC, MC. V.
Founded in 1864, and nurserymen and seedsmen to the Queen Mother, Hillier is one of the most impressive botanic establishments in the world. The firm cultivates some fourteen thousand different plants and publishes, as one botanist put it, "an absolutely essential reference work . . . available at an absurdly low cost." This is how the Hillier catalogue describes it: ". . . contains representative descriptions of approximately eight thousand woody plants, which we believe to be the most comprehensive publication of its kind ever published."

   Hillier recommends that export orders be shipped in their most dormant season, November to February. They are perfectly willing to handle small export orders of only one or two plants (as well as larger ones, of course), but for small orders they charge $30 for the extra work involved in special packing and documentation.

**Wayside Gardens Company, Hodges, SC 29695.
Telephone (803) 374 3387**
150-page color catalogue, $1; available December to June only. AE, MC, V.
Wayside Gardens sells a wider variety of plants by mail than any of the other nurseries. They publish enormous, fully illustrated, detailed and fairly instructive catalogues which are well worth the outlay of $1.

**White Flower Farm, Litchfield, CT 06759 0050.
Telephone (203) 567 0801**
Year's subscription to two color catalogues and one leaflet, $5. MC, V. (No shipping to Canada)
Although this famous catalogue of perennials and shrubs is no longer written by W. B. Harris, the creator of the nursery, it is still an informative delight to read. Plants are expensive, but there is a good, sophisticated selection with nice touches and suitable presents such as wild strawberry plants, buffalo grass for flavoring vodka, jasmine vines to perfume a room in winter, and hanging pottery planters.

10

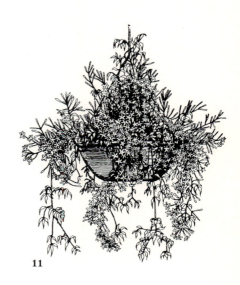

11

10 *Endangered Species* Succulents: E. tortirama with thick, twisted green arms and spikes at the corners of the twist—rooted cuts, $10; E. groenwaldii with pale cream turnip caudreax surmounted by tightly twisted marble purple arms and mustard yellow flowers, $24.

11 *White Flower Farm* One-year-old jasmine plant perfumes a room with fragrant white flowers in January and February. One plant with stoneware pot and hanger, $36. One plant without pot, $12.

12

13

14

12 *R. Harkness and Company* Rose "Mountbatten" (Harmantelle) used in the royal wedding bouquet on 29 July 1981. A 1982 introduction.

13 *Roses of Yesterday and Today* "Alfred de Dalmas"—low growing, 2½′ moss rose. Very pale pink, very fragrant.

14 *Sutton Seeds* Some of the seeds and seed collections available.

Rhododendrons

**The Greenery, 14450 N.E. 16th Place,
Bellevue, WA 98007. Telephone (206) 641 1458**
Price list, $1.
A small nursery sells rhododendrons, minimum order $25.

Rock Plants

**Rakestraw's Perennial Gardens and Nursery,
G-3094 S. Term Street, Burton, MI 48529.
Telephone (313) 742 2685**
24-page price list, $1.
A tidy brochure describes rare rock-garden plants and perennials. Just over fifty sedums, and a few suggestions on starting a rock garden are given. Other hard-to-find yet easy-to-grow perennials are listed, and Rakestraw's says that if you are looking for anything unusual that isn't on their list, they may be able to find it for you.

Roses

**David Austin Roses, Bowling Green Lane, Albrighton,
Wolverhampton WV7 3HB, England.
Telephone Albrighton 2142**
60-page brochure, free.
Specialist growers of shrub and old-fashioned roses, Hybrid Tea and Floribunda Roses. An admirable catalogue with sober descriptions, hints, and suggestions for small gardens, poor soil, north wall climbers, hedges, and inexperienced rose gardeners.

**R. Harkness and Company, The Rose Gardens, Hitchin,
Herts SG4 0JT, England. Telephone Hitchin 4027**
36-page color brochure, $1; overseas $2. V.
Started by Robert Harkness in 1882, this is still a family firm and Peter Harkness says that although the paperwork is tedious, those who love roses have far more choice from English nurseries than American ones. Minimum order $50.

**Jackson and Perkins, Medford, OR 97501.
Telephone (503) 776 2000**
40-page color catalogue, free.
One-hundred-year-old Jackson and Perkins is the world's largest grower of roses, and the best known. Their catalogue has roses of every sort, as well as a few berries, vegetables and flowering trees.

**E. B. Legrice (Roses), Norwich Road, North Walsham,
Norfolk NR28 0DR, England**
24-page color catalogue, free. V.
A good assortment of roses is grown by this sixty-year-old firm, which sells special collections of miniatures, scented, and easy-to-grow roses. Also wild and old-fashioned roses.

**Mini-Roses, P.O. Box 4255 Station A, Dallas, TX 75208.
Telephone (214) 946 3487**
16-page price list, free.

**Nor East Miniature Roses, 56 Hammond Street,
Rowley, MA 01969**
16-page color brochure, free; overseas $1.
Two sources of miniature roses; Nor East has a smaller

stock but the catalogue is illustrated, and there is a page of microminis for people who like to go to extremes.

Roses of Yesterday and Today, 802 Brown Valley Road, Watsonville, CA 95076. Telephone (408) 724 3537
78-page catalogue, $1.50; overseas $3. MC, V.
This nursery grows and sells "old, rare and unusual roses." A well-produced and extremely readable catalogue has black-and-white photographs of roses, enthusiastic descriptions, plenty of advice and instruction, and quotations from customers as well as literature about the beauty of the roses. Irresistible.

Seeds

GENERAL

First, the big mainstream seedsmen. *But note that these catalogues appear in January and tend to sell out.*

W. Attlee Burpee Company, 300 Park Avenue, Warminster, PA 18974. Telephone (215) 345 1071
164-page color catalogue, free.
Established in 1876, at a time when most seeds were imported from Europe, Burpee started experimenting in America, before the government did. Still a leader in the field, with a vast selection of seeds, and first-rate service.

Henry Field Seed and Nursery Company, Shenandoah, IA 51602. Telephone (712) 246 2110
100-page color catalogue, free. MC, V.
A general line of garden seed, field seed and nursery stock.

Joseph Harris Company, Moreton Farm, Rochester, NY 14624. Telephone (716) 594 9411
90-page color catalogue, free U.S. and overseas.
This well-known, hundred-year-old firm has many of its own varieties, and produces an excellent and informative catalogue.

George W. Park Seed Company, P.O. Box 31, Greenwood, SC 29647. Telephone (803) 374 3341
125-page color catalogue, free. AE, MC, V.
Park claims they offer the largest selection of flower seeds in the country, but they also have a general selection of vegetables and some Southern varieties.

Stokes Seeds, 737 Main Street, Box 548, Buffalo, NY 14240
Catalogue, free.
An outstanding catalogue, intended for market gardeners, but appreciated by everyone else for the detailed information on its stock. Untreated seeds are marked UT.

Sutton Seeds Ltd., Hele Road, Torquay, Devon TQ2 7QJ, England. Telephone Torquay 62001
128-page color catalogue, free. MC, V.
England's most famous seed company is strong on grass seed and publishes a very good catalogue.

Thompson and Morgan, P.O. Box 100, Farmingdale, NJ 07727. Telephone (201) 363 2225
100-page color catalogue, free. January. MC, V.

This English firm claims to have the reputation of listing more seeds in their catalogue than anyone else in the world. Americans get a shortened version, but it does contain interesting vegetable and flower seeds.

MISCELLANEOUS SPECIALTIES

Here are the specialized seedsmen. They carry the unusual seeds not on sale in garden shops, and more varieties within their specialty than you'll find in the big catalogues.

Allwood Brothers, Clayton Nurseries, Hassocks, Sussex, England
24-page catalogue, free. V.
A marvelous shop for carnation and pink lovers, Allwood specializes in selling by mail. Worthwhile for American buyers, according to Allwood, are carnation, pink and dianthus seeds, many of which are not generally available in America.

Robert Bolton & Sons, Birdbrook, near Halstead, Essex CO9 4BQ, England
General catalogue, free. December.
Sweet-pea list, free. August.
"Bolton's, The Sweet Pea Specialists, Awarded 336 Gold Medals," states the letterhead, and each August a special sweet-pea list is published. A general seed catalogue is available each December with a full range of flower and vegetable seeds. The sweet peas include the standards plus a constant stream of new varieties.

John Brudy Exotics, Route 1, Box 190, Dover, FL 33527. Telephone (813) 752 2590
30-page brochure, $1 (refundable); overseas $2.
Seeds to create unusual indoor plants—some for hanging plants, others for bonsai, other plants intended to appeal to "connoisseurs" that have to be ordered ahead, as they do not store well.

Chiltern Seeds, Bortree Stile, Ulverston, Cumbria LA12 7PB, England
184-page price list, $1; air mail $2.
A descriptive listing of seeds from unusual plants, shrubs and trees not usually grown from seed. Chiltern says that plants grown from seed are likely to be disease-free, and in cases where plants are delicate, don't have the transplant trauma. Many eucalyptus shrubs, Regal polyanthus, and seeds imported from Australia, the Canary Islands, South Africa (and California).

J. A. Demonchaux, 827 North Kansas, Topeka, KS 66608. Telephone (913) 235 8502
Price list, free.
Seeds for good French vegetable varieties often quite different from American versions, also for vegetables popular in France: several chicories, endives, two sorrel, purslane, etc.

L.S.A. Goodwin and Sons, Goodwin's Road, Bagdad, Sth 7407 Tasmania, Australia. Telephone 002 686 233
Price list, 60 cents U.S. postage stamps or 4 International Reply Coupons; air mail, $1.50 in U.S. postage stamps or 8 International Reply Coupons.
List with one packet of Regal Polyanthus Primrose seeds, $3 in U.S. bills.
Mr. Goodwin says that his lists are used by universities, national parks, trust gardens, and nurseries all over the world. He sells tree, shrub, vegetable and flower seeds

(many of them rare), which include sought-after Australian varieties.

M. Holtzhausen Seed Import/Export Burton House, Trinity Street, St. Austell, Cornwall PL25 5LT, England
112-page catalogue, $1; air mail $2.
Unusual annuals and perennials for the open garden.

Horticultural Enterprises, P.O. Box 340082, Dallas, TX 75234 0082
Leaflet, free.
For Mexican-food lovers, seeds for thirty different peppers, green tomatoes, Jicama, plus chia, Cilantro and Epazote herbs. A list of recommended books on Mexican cooking is included on the leaflet.

J. L. Hudson, Seedsman, P.O. Box 1058, Redwood City, CA 94064
120-page catalogue, $1; overseas $2.
An interesting firm that sells an enormous variety of unusual American and imported seeds. Many endangered species seeds, and an exchange whereby you get credit for unusual seeds you donate. Not for the lazy, many of the seeds are hard to grow.

Le Jardin du Gourmet, Box 42A, West Danville, VT 05873
Leaflet, 50 cents; overseas $1.
Culinary wonders from the plant world: shallots for eating and seeds for unusual vegetables such as corn salad, sorrel, chard and purslane. The well-known French seeds by Vilmorin are sold here.

Kitazawa Seed Company, 356 West Taylor Street, San Jose, CA 95110. Telephone (408) 292 4420
Price list, free U.S. and overseas.
Japanese and some Chinese vegetable seeds, a nice collection. Edible burdock, Japanese radish, pickling melon, bitter melon and more.

P. Kohli and Company (Near Neelam Theater), Park Road, Srinagar, Kashmir 190009, India
Price list, 5 International Reply Coupons.
P. Kohli supplies private individuals and firms around the world with hardy wildflower seeds and bulbs, seeds for ornamental and flowering trees, shrubs, climbers and conifers (he boasts of sending bulbs to Holland). The seeds are collected from temperate and alpine regions of Kashmir and Western Himalayas. Mr. Kohli says that his little known, exquisite, exotic wildflowers are becoming popular with keen gardeners throughout the world because of their "great garden merits." In addition to their beautiful flowers, many possess medicinal properties." A wonderful source—I particularly like the sound of *Nepalensis:* "a prostrate beauty with many rosy-red flowers in late summer."

Midwest Wildflowers, Box 64, Rockton, IL 61072
26-page catalogue, 50 cents.
Seeds of plants native to the Midwest are hand-collected and packaged, and the packages are sold for 50 cents each. The catalogue is more like a storybook—each seed listing includes all known facts and folklore for that plant and detailed culture instructions.

The Redwood City Seed Company, P.O. Box 361, Redwood City, CA 94064. Telephone (415) 325 7333
28-page price list, 50 cents; overseas $1.
"A catalogue of useful plants" lists seeds for unusual vegetables, dye plants, fruit and nut trees, and garden and medicinal herbs. Engaging text with historical comments on many of the plants.

Clyde Robin, P.O. Box 2855, Castro Valley, CA 94546. Telephone (415) 581 3467
80-page color catalogue, $2; overseas $3; air mail $4. MC, V.
This firm specializes in wild-flower and wild-tree seeds and has over fifteen hundred varieties. The listings are concise; culture information is included, as well as many words of encouragement and adages interspersed throughout. The firm handles books on the subject and some supplies.

F. W. Schumacher Company, Horticulturists, 36 Spring Road, Sandwich, MA 02563. Telephone (617) 888 0659
26-page catalogue, free U.S. and overseas.
"Seeds for Nurserymen and Foresters" is the title of this firm's catalogue, and it is obviously professionally oriented. The listings are nondescript and mostly in Latin only. Schumacher carries a general line of tree, shrub, azalea, rhododendron and fruit seeds.

Seed Savers Exchange, Kent Whealy, Rural Route 2, Princeton, MO 64673
Yearbook, $3; overseas $5.
"The yearbook is not a catalogue, and we are not a seed company," says founder/editor/publisher/writer Kent Whealy. This is an organization of serious gardeners who want to preserve varieties of vegetables that are in danger of being lost. A member is anyone who has heirloom (or foreign or unusual or outstanding) vegetable or food crop seed varieties to offer. Anyone else can write to members listed in the yearbook and offer $1 for the offered seeds. The typed yearbook makes interesting reading.

Watkins Seeds, P.O. Box 468, New Plymouth, New Zealand
Catalogue, $1; air mail $2.
Adventurous gardeners may wish to try some of these attractive-looking New Zealand flower and vegetable seeds.

Terrariums

Arthur Eames Allgrove, P.O. Box 459, North Wilmington, MA 01887
8-page catalogue, 50 cents.
Hardy native wild flowers, ferns and groundcovers, and a good assortment of plants for terrariums.

Tools and Equipment

By Hand and Foot, P.O. Box 611, Brattleboro, VT 05301. Telephone (802) 254 2101
Leaflet, $1 U.S. and overseas (refundable). MC, V.
A group of people interested in tools "dependent on human energy" have tested tools for scything, chopping wood, and moving heavy loads. They sell only the tools that worked

best, sell them at reasonable prices, and provide plenty of information to go with them.

Gardenwork, The Dell, Catherine de Barnes, Solihull, West Midlands B92 0DE, England. Telephone 021 705 5131
Leaflet, free; air mail $1.50. AE, B.
A few carefully chosen traditional and unusual tools for the garden including the excellent Trigagrip hand tools. Watch it though—one or two are imported from the U.S. Mr. Densham says he learned about the correct use of the right tools the hard way, as a contractor looking after large gardens.

A. M. Leonard, 6665 Spiker Road, Piqua, OH 45356. Telephone (513) 773 2694
76-page catalogue, free. MC, V.
Established in 1885, Leonard's has the biggest supply of garden equipment available by mail. The range will appeal to serious gardeners and to professionals.

Smith and Hawken Tool Company, 68 Homer, Department 064, Palo Alto, CA 94301. Telephone (415) 324 1587
34-page catalogue, free U.S. and overseas. MC, V.
Smith and Hawken hand garden tools are made in England by Bulldog, one of the oldest producers in the world. The catalogue is impressive and enticing—it is illustrated with line drawings and written informatively by people who know and care.

Sudbury Laboratory, 572 Dutton Road, Sudbury, MA 01776. Telephone (617) 443 8844.
Color leaflet, free U.S. and overseas. AE, MC, V.
The world's largest manufacturer of soil test kits says that their tests are simple to use and can make dramatic improvements in your crops. Various kits, including a "houseplant survival kit" are sold, plus other things such as fertilizers and animal repellents.

Trees

Bountiful Ridge Nurseries, P.O. Box CC 250, Princess Anne, MD 21853. Telephone (800) 638 9356
50-page catalogue, free U.S. and overseas. AE, MC, V.
This excellent firm specializes in fruit trees, nut trees, ornamental trees and berry plants. As a family business they are proud of their selection and they promise quality stock. Enormous number of varieties to choose from—thirty-five types of peach trees, for instance, and colonial apple trees, too. Good service.

Henry Leuthardt Nurseries, Montauk Highway, East Moriches, Long Island, NY 11940
52-page brochure, $1 (refundable).
The art of training fruit trees into flat, symmetrical shapes was developed in Europe for decorative purposes and to take advantage of small spaces. Henry Leuthardt says that his trees produce especially large and excellent fruit because of the extra exposure to the sun, and because the trees are grafted onto proper stock. Hard-to-find dwarf fruit trees, berry plants and hybrid grapes are stocked.

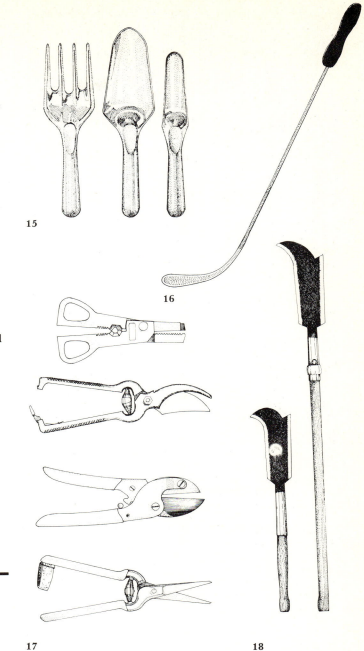

15 *Smith and Hawken* Trigger Grip—prize-winning tools that will not rust, break, bend, or corrode. Gleaming finish makes them easy to see in the garden and a "trigger" under the handle makes them useful for people with a weak grip or arthritis. Available individually or as a set for about $14.

16 *Smith and Hawken* Jungle Knife, an extremely useful hand cutter that is sharpened on both sides so that it cuts in both directions as you swing it back and forth in front of you. Cuts close to trees and fences but also easily clears large areas of weeds. About $6.

17 *Smith and Hawken* Flower gatherer with thorn remover, classic pruner, heavy-duty pruner, and grape harvester for grapes, fruit, flowers, and close-in cutting. Priced about $8 to $20 each.

18 *Smith and Hawken* Yorkshire Bill Hook for trimming, pruning, clearing brush and thickets, stripping fallen trees, and splitting wood. About $40 or $46, according to length of handle.

19

Musser Forest, P.O. Box 340, Indiana, PA 15701. Telephone (412) 465 5686
40-page color catalogue, free U.S. and overseas.
Trees of all kinds, the largest stock in the United States, hedges, windbreaks, and groundcovers.

Southmeadow Fruitgardens, Lakeside, MI 49116. Telephone (616) 469 2865.
112-page catalogue, $8; overseas $9. Price list, free; overseas $1.
Unusual fruit trees, bushes and vines, including over two hundred apples, many gooseberries and rare grapes. The big catalogue includes histories of the varieties.

Stark Brothers, Louisiana, MO 63353. Telephone (800) 325 4180
Color catalogues, free. MC, V.
The largest and best-known fruit specialists publish full-color catalogues with small selections of their standard size and dwarf fruit trees.

Water Gardens

Lilypons Water Gardens, 1899 Catocat Road, Lilypons, MD 21717. Telephone (301) 874 5133
50-page color catalogue, $3; overseas $4; air mail $6.
Take one look at either of these catalogues and you'll immediately want to set up a water garden in your bathtub or backyard, depending on your situation. This gorgeous, clear catalogue shows an extraordinary variety of lilies, old and new varieties of lotus, green plants for the pool and some magnificently exotic fish. Equipment to make a simple polyethylene-lined pool, waterfall and fountain, a pool filter, and scavengers such as bullfrogs, tadpoles and snails to keep ponds and lakes clear are all for sale, and so are supplies for indoor aquariums.

Paradise Gardens, 14 May Street, Whitman, MA 02382. Telephone (617) 447 4711
40-page color catalogue, $1.50; overseas $2. MC, V.
An equally appealing but smaller catalogue has fish, hardy and tropical plants, some unusual scavengers, fountains and waterfalls.

Wild and Native Plants

Gardens of the Blue Ridge, P.O. Box 10, Pineola, NC 28662. Telephone (704) 733 2417
42-page catalogue, $2.
Wild flowers and native plants of the southern Appalachians, hardy native orchids, evergreen trees and shrubs.

Yerba Buena Nursery, 19500 Skyline Boulevard, Woodside, CA 94062. Telephone (415) 851 1668
Price list, free.
Two hundred and fifty species of plants that are native to California, including uncommon ones. Also native and exotic, hardy and tender ferns. Just listings, no descriptions.

19 *Lilypons Water Gardens* "Gladstone," one of the largest pure white hardy water lilies, $15.95. Pink, red, yellow, blue; fragrant, night-blooming, and miniature lilies are also sold.

13
GENERAL DEPARTMENT STORES AND MAIL-ORDER HOUSES

The catalogues of the mail-order firms in this section are very useful for finding out what is available, and contain many practical goods at lower prices (Sears' tools, for instance, are universally praised for their value). They often do a better job than more glamorous and looks-obsessed firms. A clothes pattern cutter who has worked for all sorts of manufacturers has told me that whereas the famous designers care about a general effect, she has been really impressed at the meticulous care firms such as J. C. Penney take with fit.

If you depend on the mails to do your shopping, then department store catalogues will be very useful. Each store produces several catalogues a year, usually showing clothes for men and women, linen, gifts. Some stores also show furniture, kitchen appliances and tableware. Of course, department stores do charge list prices, so on brand name goods you may be paying more than you need, however, most stores have sales, and send out sale catalogues.

Getting hold of the catalogues is a problem; some stores make it simple by selling their catalogues (and advertising their Christmas catalogues in the fall). Other stores say that they will send a catalogue to any one who asks for it "if the letter gets to the right department," i.e. Direct Mail or "Catalogue." I have found that if you open a charge account with a department store (no charge unless you don't pay your bills on time) you are likely to get their catalogues for free. Write to the Credit Department of each firm for an application form. (The credit departments of Abraham & Straus, B. Altman, Bergdorf Goodman, and Lord & Taylor have told me that they consider applications from overseas customers for charge accounts.)

Where there is no catalogue price given in this section, it is because I couldn't get any information out of the stores. All the stores do produce catalogues, so ask them yourself or watch out for advertisements.

Abraham and Straus, 420 Fulton Street, Brooklyn, NY 11201. Telephone (212) 875 7200
Several clothes and home-furnishing catalogues a year.
A complete department store, with, like most department stores, fairly traditional taste in furniture.

Aldens, 5000 West Roosevelt Road, Chicago, IL 60607. Telephone (312) 854 4141 or (800) 435 6947 (for orders)
402-page color catalogue, $1. MC, V.
Not as large as the biggest mail-order firms, Sears and Montgomery Ward, Alden's sells mainly clothes, with a certain amount for the house in the way of soft furnishing, kitchenware and brand-name small appliances. Publishes about thirteen catalogues a year including sale catalogues, and one for the "full figure."

B. Altman and Company, 361 Fifth Avenue, New York, NY 10016. Telephone (212) 689 7000
Fourteen catalogues a year. AE.
Notable for its Beaux Art interior, the only one of its kind to remain fairly unspoiled in a New York department store. The ground floor still has dark wood counters, chandeliers and a quietly respectable atmosphere. The catalogues, too, show good things without the razzmataz of the more publicity-conscious stores.

Bergdorf Goodman Company, 754 Fifth Avenue at 58th Street, New York, NY 10019
96-page catalogue.
The reason that Bergdorf Goodman, the poshest of the New York department stores, has an air of such luxurious intimacy is that when it was built, next to the Plaza Hotel, the site

was considered so far uptown as to be a mad gamble, and was accordingly designed so that it could be divided and leased off as small boutiques in case of disaster. The location turned out to be an excellent one, and the small rooms have continued to give a feeling of genteel privacy, quite unlike that of the other large clothing stores. Bergdorf claims to have been the first store to introduce really high-quality ready-to-wear women's clothes and to coax their customers out of the fitting rooms.

There are four catalogues a year of women's clothes in sizes 8 to 14 from most of the Bergdorf departments.

Bloomingdale's Advertising Department, 1000 Third Avenue, New York, NY 10022
Several catalogues a year.
Bloomingdale's, which started off in 1872 announcing itself as the "Great East Side Bazaar selling Clothes and Corsets," has become the liveliest and the most design-conscious of the large New York stores, and the one with the most ardently articulate customers—well-known writers drool in print over the delights of Saturday afternoons spent browsing in Bloomie's.

The catalogues, like most of the other catalogues from department stores, do not concentrate on clothes but have a wide variety of medium prices and often brightly colored things for the house. The Christmas catalogue has clothes for men, women and children, also posh chocolates, plum puddings and imported cookies; and sleekly modern, useful yet decorative objects for the rest of the house.

Marshall Field, and Company, P.O. Box 7199, Chicago, IL 60680. Telephone (312) 781 1050
Several catalogues a year. AE.
Marshall Field, the splendid Chicago store with a Tiffany dome, was once the largest department store in America. For a while the store's motto was "Give the Lady what she wants," originally said by Marshall Field to a quarreling clerk, and the firm is still known for its extensive customer service. Catalogues have mainly clothes and sales, but there is a Christmas catalogue which adds fairly inexpensive gifts to the medium-priced clothes.

Garfinkel's, Attention Mail Order Department, 1401 F Street, N.W., Washington, DC 20004. Telephone (202) 628 7730
Six fashion, sales and gifts catalogues, $3 U.S. and overseas. AE, MC, V.
Mainly clothes and sales catalogues, from Washington's largest department store; also Christmas catalogue with gifts and food as well as fashions.

Gimbels, 1275 Broadway, New York, NY 10001. Telephone (212) 564 3300
Several catalogues of furniture, housewares and clothes a year.
"Fairness and Equality of All Patrons, whether they be Residents of the City, Plainsmen, Traders or Indians" was an early Gimbels's advertisement. For many years Gimbels and Macy's were neck-and-neck competitors with their low prices, but now Macy's has copied Bloomingdale's and got somewhat grander, leaving Gimbels looking more staid. Nevertheless, Gimbels's catalogues of clothes, furniture, appliances and housewares contain plenty of color and good design.

Gump's, 250 Post Street, San Francisco, CA 94108. Telephone (800) 227 3135
Four color catalogues, $2 for series. All major credit cards accepted.
Gump's was started by Solomon Gump in the gold-rush days, when it sold gilded mirrors for the saloons, and picture frames and gilded cornices and later pictures for the newly rich. Solomon's son, A. Livingston Gump, enlarged the stock and brought in more and more of the Asian art which has remained typical of the store to this day.

Now Gump's specializes in jade, Oriental antiques, and modern, mostly European gifts. They also carry jewelry, art, clothes, modern and antique silver, reproduction and antique European furniture, and the largest selection of famous-name glass and china in the West. The catalogue shows things from almost all the departments, with a distinct leaning toward the traditional rather than the modern.

Harrods, Knightsbridge, London SW1X 7XL, England
Linen catalogue, free. Gift catalogue, free. Food Hall catalogue, free. Catalogues available October through December only. AE, DC, V.
Harrods, the biggest store in Europe and the most famous department store in the world, started as a little grocery shop bought by Henry Harrod in 1849. At that time, the district, Knightsbridge, was a rough one, notorious for its highway robberies. Luckily for Henry, the Great Exhibition of 1851 in Hyde Park was good for the neighborhood and Harrods prospered with its new customers.

But, of course, it's not as a neighborhood store that Harrods has become internationally known and a first stop for most tourists. Although not a fashion leader, the shop, with its 214 departments, is famous for its comprehensive, varied, good quality and expensive stock, British-made and imported.

There is a special export department which sends huge quantities of goods abroad a year—smoked salmon, gazebos, lace handkerchiefs and all breeds of dogs and cats worldwide. Harrods will happily open an account for overseas customers, and claims to be able to supply customers with anything they want. But don't get your hopes up, I have found Harrods as unresponsive to small queries as any other large store. However, they do publish two free catalogues, available October through December each year. One catalogue of expensive linen has sheets imported from Italy, France, Portugal, Spain, Switzerland, and the United States of America; imported tablecloths and towels; and a colorful collection of cotton, wool, pure mohair and pure cashmere British blankets.

A gift catalogue contains jewelry, scarves, leather, clothes and children's toys. With the gift catalogue comes the Food Hall catalogue, illustrating hampers, hams, smoked salmon, pâté, caviar and chocolates (including liqueur chocolates). Anything not suitable for export is so marked. If you'd like the Harrods label, there are several small gifts, such as brandy butter, Scottish shortbread in a tin, a decorated jar with Harrods tea bags.

Lord and Taylor, 424 Fifth Avenue, New York, NY 10018. Telephone (212) 391 3300
Seven catalogues a year.
One of the most elegant New York department stores, Lord and Taylor promoted American dress designers when the French were considered the only couturiers worth bothering about. Although the store sells furniture (with some lovely antiques), home furnishings, and clothes for men and children, the catalogues are mainly of women's clothes, except for the Christmas gift catalogue, which adds a few clothes and small things from other departments.

I. Magnin, Dept. 500, Oakland, CA 94612. Telephone (415) 834 1373
Five catalogues a year, $2; overseas $4; air mail $10. AE.
Started by Mary Ann Magnin, this was the first (and only?)

department store started by a woman. For years Magnin, a famous clothes store, lived by the precept of Mary Ann's son Grover: "Nothing is forgotten as quickly as price, if you back it up with quality and style." The store still produces lavish catalogues, mainly of clothes, but scattered with a few gifts such as cashmere blankets, fur throws, and imported foods.

Neiman-Marcus, P.O. Box 2968, Dallas, TX 75221. Telephone (800) 527 5800 [Texas (800) 492 5510]
Christmas catalogue, $2; seventeen catalogues throughout the year, $5; overseas $15.
Neiman-Marcus was started in 1907 as a luxury clothing store. Over the years the Marcus family, which has stayed very much in charge, has added more and more goods and departments until it has the widest range of any American department store—in the luxury brackets, that is. Although slightly more moderately priced goods have been added over the years, the store still revels in its reputation for scandalous extravagance, flaunts its nouveau oil-rich customers, and manages to attract attention to itself each year for gift suggestions on the "bare line of credulity," as the president says, such as his and her camels, submarines, and aquariums with real pearls instead of sand.

Unlike many of the catalogues for the ultrarich, which show expensive *and* hideous products, these are cleverly done with simple graphics and lovely color photographs, and listing goods which, antique Indian carousel horses and Japanese aviaries notwithstanding, are often simple. In the catalogue I looked at, clothes, jewelry, household goods, food and toys were covered. I painstakingly counted and found sixty-seven items for $20 or under.

J. C. Penney Company, P.O. Box 2056, Milwaukee, WI 53201
Two large catalogues, spring, fall, also sale catalogue, $2. To receive them regularly you must buy regularly. MC, V.
J. C. Penney doesn't manufacture but has about 85 percent of its products made to the company's own specifications and sold under its own brand name. The goods are often tested by *Consumer Reports* and do creditably (obviously my remark is too general and you should look up specific items before buying). Although Penney's doesn't have quite as broad a range of equipment as its competitors Sears, Roebuck and Montgomery Ward (it doesn't sell large household appliances such as dishwashers and ovens), it is the third-biggest mail-order firm in the country.

PUB (Paul U. Bergstroms AB), Box 7836, Export Department, S-10398 Stockholm, Sweden. Telephone 22 40 40
Leaflets for glass, flatware and souvenirs, $1.50 for all. Prices for all of these in $.
PUB is a large cooperative department store in Stockholm with a very efficient export service. They have no general catalogue, so you have to write and ask about any Swedish thing you are trying to track down. They mainly sell to America stainless-steel tableware and Swedish glass: Orrefors, Kosta and Skruf at well below American prices and a few Swedish souvenirs such as dolls and painted Dalecarlian horses.

Quelle International, P.O. Box 999, Oceanside, NY 11572. Telephone (516) 536 4357
750-page color catalogue, $4. Spring, fall.
I recommend Quelle, Germany's largest mail-order house, which is streets ahead of its competitors in standards of design. Whatever the section, their goods are easier on the

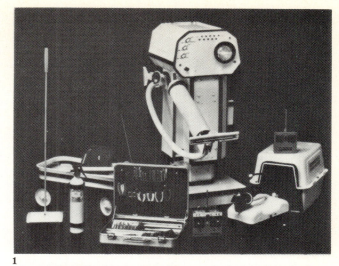

1 *Neiman-Marcus* ComRo I Domestic robot that operates by remote control or pre-programmed micro-computer. Will open doors, serve guests, take out trash, bring in newspaper, walk the dog, fetch, haul, dust, pick up after kids and pets, and more. Fitted with wireless telephone, smoke alarm, vacuum, cigarette lighter, digital clock, black-and-white television, and more. Offered for sale Christmas 1981, $15,000. On the lower right is ComRo pet, "Wires," with carrying case; runs around, lights up, wags its "tail," blinks, squeaks, and sells very well at $650.

2 *Neiman-Marcus* Colorful hot-air, collapsible, portable dirigible. It is 120' long, has a 72-horsepower engine, travels up to 25 miles an hour, and has room for two passengers and a picnic hamper. Sold in 1979 only, with flying instructions, for $50,000.

3 *Neiman-Marcus* A pinewood and acrylic black sheep for any family without one, sold in 1981 for $275.

4

5

eye than the goods in similar catalogues from other countries.

Quelle has an office in the United States, advertises here, and although the catalogue is in German, it comes with a complete translation for the clothes and linen sections (the most popular in America). Very clear instructions, including a full table of exchange, are included, so there is virtually no calculating to do.

In other sections there are bicycles with motors, kitchen gadgets and bright-enameled saucepans, toys, Christmas decorations, and a marvelous food section with all sorts of German candies and cookies packed for Christmas and wrapped for hanging on the tree. There is also furniture, and in fact almost anything that an American mail-order house would have, Quelle has too. You're bound to find several things you want here.

Sakowitz, 1111 Main Street, P.O. Box 1387, Houston, TX 77001. Telephone (713) 759 1111
76-page color catalogue, $2.50. AE, MC, V.
Mainly clothes, (ram's head blazer buttons to Russian lynx-belly coats), but also gifts such as champagne toothpaste and ostrich-skin desk sets.

Saks Fifth Avenue, Folio Collections, P.O. Box 5138, F.D.R. Station, New York, NY 10022
Several catalogues a year.
Saks Fifth Avenue, perhaps the most famous of the New York department stores, sells mainly clothes and linen through their catalogues. Their Christmas gift catalogue is chastely elegant, with excellent color photographs and gifts that rarely cost less than $25.

Schiphol Airport Shop, P.O. Box 7501, 1118ZG Schiphol Airport, Amsterdam, Holland. Telephone 020 5172497
Occasional catalogue free.
Unfortunately Schiphol only very occasionally publishes catalogues. A shame because their prices on brand-name goods tend to be lower than even other airport shops. If you enjoy foraging, write with specific details (and model number if possible) to ask about pens, watches, medical and nautical equipment, clothes by Burberry, Gucci, Hermes, etc., and electronic appliances and photographic equipment. Although I doubt whether these last, except possibly for European brands, will cost less than at U.S. discount stores.

Mail Order Department, Shannon Free Airport, Ireland
60-page catalogue, free; air mail $1. Prices in $.
Shannon Airport has a famous tax-free shop with a vast and superbly organized mail-order business and a very efficient catalogue showing popular brand-name items at greater savings than any other shop, and including an estimate of the American duty you'll have to pay on each item.

The goods on sale are always things that have proved popular and include English china, Irish porcelain, Irish lace and linen, Irish jewelry, Peterson pipes, knitwear (although the selection is smaller than at the English knitwear shops, their prices for Pringle are several dollars lower), Viyella blouses and robes (at half their New York prices), Irish rugs and rug coats, mohair and mohair coats, and even golf balls. Shannon will also undercut on imports—French perfume, Swiss army knives, etc.

Spiegel, 1061 35th Street, Chicago, IL 60609. Telephone (312) 986 1088
Catalogue, $3. AE, MC, V.
Unlike the other big mail-order houses, Spiegel now sells brand-name goods, and in most areas has more sophisticated design than they do. The catalogue has mainly clothes, with

4 *Sears, Roebuck and Company* A 19″ color television set capable of receiving the twenty hours of captions now being broadcast for weekly regular programs. This set for the hard of hearing is available only through Sears, and costs about $600. For more information about the set, contact Dept. 703, Public Relations, at Sears. For more information about captioning contact National Caption Institute, 5203 Leesburg Pike, Falls Church, VA 22041. Telephone (800) 336-3444.

5 *Oy Stockmann* Candleholders by Wartsila. Finnish glass is available from Stockmann at well below American prices.

well-known names such as Liz Claibourne and Jones New York for women, Wrangler and Hanes for men; a nice kitchen department carries Leyson pots, Cuisinart and Simac appliances. Other well-known small appliances and some furniture and furnishings also stocked.

Stechers, 27 Frederick Street, Port of Spain, Trinidad
Leaflet, free.
Stechers, which claims to be almost a landmark for Caribbean tourists, has been widely written up in the American press as a great spot for bargains. They handle internationally known glass, china, watches, perfumes, stainless steel, pewter, binoculars, etc. They will send you a leaflet listing the manufacturers they handle and then will give you their price for any specific thing you ask about. If they do not have what you want in stock, they can order it.

Oy Stockmann AB, Export Service, P.O. Box 220, Helsinki 10, Finland. Telephone 176 181
Manufacturers brochures, $5. AE, DC, MC, V.
Stockmann, the big Finnish department store and the biggest show in Helsinki, is a wonderful mail-order source for anyone interested in modern design. For $5 they'll send an assortment of manufacturers' brochures: Arabia china, iittala glass, Jurko wooden toys, Aarika wooden decorations, karhu ski equipment, Finella enamel kitchenware, Muurame furniture. Be absolutely sure you tell them if you have a special interest, because the selections of brochures they send vary. All the smaller things are much cheaper if bought from Finland. Tell Stockmann what you want, and they will send you an invoice in your own currency which includes transportation costs. The glass and china is far cheaper bought direct from Finland; medium-sized things such as palaset cubes are about the same in both places once you add transportation costs.

Sears, Roebuck and Company, Department 744, Sears Tower, Chicago, IL 60684. Telephone (312) 875 2500
Main catalogues, May, July, September. American customers should order the main catalogue ($2) from their nearest distribution center and specialized catalogues from the above address.

Far East customers should order it from:

Sears, Roebuck and Co., D/742, 2650 East Olympic Boulevard, Los Angeles, CA 90051

European customers from:

Sears, Roebuck and Co., D/742E, 4640 Roosevelt Boulevard, Philadelphia, PA 19132
Main catalogue free to military personnel; $5 to others overseas. Specialized catalogues are free: Office Equipment and Supply catalogue, Men's Apparel Catalogue of Big and Tall Sizes, catalogue of uniforms, Western catalogue, Home Improvement catalogue, Accessories and Supplies for Automobiles and Trucks, Accessories for Mobile Homes, Recreation Vehicles catalogue, Fishing and Boating, Home Care and Convalescent Needs catalogue, Power and Hand Tool catalogue, Farm and Ranch catalogue, Mother and Baby needs, Hunting, Winter Sports Apparel and Equipment.

Montgomery Ward, P.O. Box 6778 Montgomery Ward Plaza, Chicago, IL 60680
American customers can get catalogues from nearest center or the above address.

6

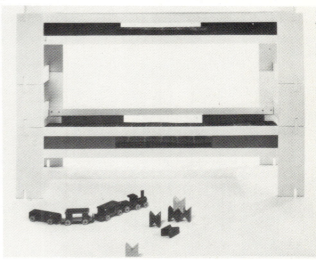

7

8

6 *Oy Stockmann* "Fox and Geese" and "Mill Game," small games for travelers, also available in larger coffee-table size. Two of the decorative wooden objects made by Aarikka and available at Stockmann.

7 *Oy Stockmann* Bunk bed designed by Pirkko Stenros. The complete "Muurame" range of natural birch and painted modular furniture designed by Pirkko Stenros is available for prices below U.S. prices.

8 *Oy Stockmann* Reindeer Lapp slippers in adults' and children's sizes, and hand-knitted Lapp mittens.

Montgomery Ward, Baltimore, MD 21232
is the address where would-be customers in Africa, Eastern Canada, Central and South America, Europe, the Middle East and Caribbean can get catalogues.

Montgomery Ward, Oakland, CA 94616
Would-be customers living in Asia, Mexico, the Pacific Islands and Western Canada should write to this California address for catalogues.

Catalogues cost $2 U.S. and overseas (refundable).
A true reader's guide to the Sears and Montgomery Ward catalogues would end up being a book about America as it is today, for there are few documents as basic and indicative of our consumer society as these vast telephone-directory–type books.

Given the literally thousands of items sold, the question is what to choose when one has access to competing department and other stores. The answer for me has been to read the catalogues with the *Consumer Report's Buying Guide* next to me and to see which of the specially made appliances rate best. In the case of most large appliances, such as clothes dryers, the Sears and Montgomery Ward makes will be among those listed as acceptable and should be considered along with competitors'. It makes sense to use these catalogues when comparison-shopping for articles in any of a number of practical categories, though in certain areas, such as furniture, these firms manufacture only the most traditional items, and in others, such as general books and records, they are out of the running altogether.

DISCOUNT
Please see discount information in the How to Buy section.

Best Products Company, P.O. Box 26527, Richmond, VA 23261. Telephone (804) 261 2197
440-page color catalogue, $1. MC, V.
Best sells brand-name goods at a discount. It is the only general discount firm I have seen that has a really complete fully illustrated color catalogue, and is therefore an excellent address for people who do not want to go to the bother of researching the model number that most discount firms need. They give a list price for their goods, which I have found to be accurate in my spot checking, and then their own price which is generally 20 to 30 percent lower. They stock jewelry, glass and china, kitchenware, small appliances, luggage, office and photography equipment, electronics, hardware, automotive and sports equipment, children's furniture and toys. The only trouble is that they do not have as wide a selection in any field as the specialized discount firms, nor do they always carry the very top brands. Established 1957.

Whole Earth Access, 2990 7th Street, Berkeley, CA 94710. Telephone (415) 848 3600
144-page catalogue, $3; overseas $4.50; overseas airmail $6. MC, V.
I have seen only some page proofs of this catalogue, but it looks as though it will be a good one. Kitchen equipment, tools and clothes have been chosen with an eye to quality and durability. Kitchen things such as the Hobart Kitchen Aid, Henckel knives and the Champion juicer; and clothes such as shirts and jackets by Woolrich, pure cotton jeans by Lee Rider and boots by Timberland are stocked. There is plenty of information about the goods, and many but not all of them are sold at a discount. List price and Whole Earth Access price are both given. Established 1980.

These gift catalogues all sell smaller objects for the house and person, and seasonally largely change their stock. *Many of them buy, sell and trade their lists of customers, so if you buy by mail from these or similar firms, you are bound to be flooded by other similar catalogues without even asking or paying for them.*

I have divided the catalogues into groups: The group that sells mainly things that cost under $20 nowadays has fewer of the Lord's-Prayer-on-a-pewter-thimble type of thing, and more just-what-I-needed gadgets for the house. In the over-$20 group, although styles vary from modern to traditional, and prices from quite to very expensive, goods tend to be carefully chosen and fashionable.

1

2

1 *Happy Things* Washing grains that blend cereals and nut kernels with fine oils, in hand-thrown ceramic jars and rush baskets. Pots about $8 each, refills about $3.

2 *Happy Things* Little Scribbler notepads decorated with Victorian children; in soft colors. Set of five, about $1.

Mostly Under $20

Abbey Press, Hill Drive, St. Meinrad, IN 47577. Telephone (812) 357 8011
48-page color catalogue, $1. MC, V.

The Added Touch, 132 Trafalgar Road, Oakville, Ontario Canada L6J 3G5
30-page brochure, free U.S. and overseas. MC, V.

Bruce Bolind, 100 Bolind Building, P.O. Box 9751, Boulder, CO 80301. Telephone (800) 972 5858
80-page color catalogue, $1. MC, V.

Harriet Carter, Department 21, North Wales, PA 19454. Telephone (215) 368 3366
96-page color catalogue, free. AE, MC, V.

Joan Cook, 3200 S.E. 14th Avenue, Fort Lauderdale, FL 33316. Telephone (305) 761 1600
112-page color catalogue, free. AE, MC, V.

Egertons, Lyme Street, Axminster, Devonshire EX13 5DB, England. Telephone 0297 32742
Catalogue, free; air mail $2. AE, DC, MC, V.

Enticements, 777 Irvington Place, Thornwood, NY 10594. Telephone (914) 747 1411
28-page color catalogue, free. AE, MC, V.

Happy Things, 48 Millgate, Newark, Nottinghamshire, England. Telephone 0636 72624
44-page catalogue, $1. MC, V.

Jenners, Princes Street, Edinburgh, Scotland. Telephone 031 225 2442
32-page color catalogue, free (October to Christmas only). AE, MC, V.

Mencap, 123 Golden Lane, London EC1Y 0RT, England. Telephone (01) 253 9433
32-page color catalogue, free.

National Canine Defence League Promotions, 10 Seymour Street, London W1H 5WB, England. Telephone (01) 935 5511
16-page brochure, free.

New Hampton, 340 Poplar Street, Hanover, PA 17331. Telephone 800 621 5809
64-page color catalogue, free. AE, DC, MC, V.

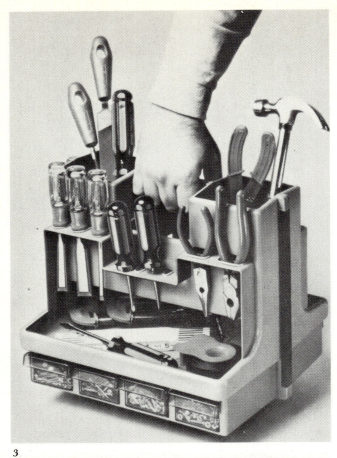

3

4

3 *Lillian Vernon* Tool caddy for storing and carrying tools has won European design award. Priced (without tools) about $16.95.

4 *The Nature Company* Glass oil lamps designed by Jon Wolfard, may be filled with odorless or scented oil. About $28.50 to $37.50, depending on size.

**Spencer Gifts, 590 Spencer Building, Atlantic City, NJ 08411.
Telephone (609) 645 3300**
48-page color catalogue, free. MC, V.

**Jean Stuart, Stuart Building, Pleasantville, NJ 08232.
Telephone (609) 927 4688**
64-page color catalogue, free. AE, MC, V.

Lillian Vernon, 510 South Fulton Avenue, Mount Vernon, NY 10550. Telephone (914) 699 4131
100-page color catalogue, free. AE, MC, V.

Mostly Over $20

**Horchow Collection, P.O. Box 340257, Dallas, TX 75234.
Telephone (800) 537 0303 [In Texas (800) 442 5806]**
Year's subscription, $3; overseas $6. AE, MC, V.
I believe that Rocher Horchow published the first, and still most famous, exclusively mail-order gift catalogue to make it big with the upper classes,—his Horchow Collection, produced in the early seventies. The lavish catalogues, with their high-quality paper, type, and color photographs, have been widely copied. Things sold continue to be a lively mixture of the modern and traditional, gathered from around the world—$12 Appalachian hearth broom to $600 portable hi-fi system. According to a Horchow survey, customers tend to be mature and well-heeled women, as many live in cities as countryside, and more read *Better Homes and Gardens* than any other magazine. The chances are that if you fit that description you are already getting one of the Horchow catalogues (new additions include *Trifles* and *Grand Finale*) if not, you are in for a treat.

American Express Merchandise Sales, 125 Broad Street, New York, NY 10004. Telephone (800) 353 3000
50-page color catalogue, free. AE.

Boston Proper, Mail Order, 180 Bodwell Street, Box 78, Avon, MA 02322. Telephone (617) 580 2210
36-page color catalogue, free. AE, MC, V.

**Brentano's, Department 1408, Ashbury Park, NJ 07712.
Telephone 800 228 2028**
52-page color catalogue, $2.50. AE, MC, V.

**Chris Craft, Route 7, Manchester Center, VT 05255.
Telephone (802) 362 3141**
44-page color catalogue, free. AE, MC, V.

Collector's Guild, 601 West 26th Street, New York, NY 10001. Telephone (212) 741 0400
32-page color catalogue, free; overseas $2. AE, DC, MC, V.

Columbus Collections, 1755 Lynnfield, Suite 157, Memphis, TN 38119. Telephone (901) 683 4100
35-page color catalogue, free U.S. and overseas. AE, MC, V.

Arnold Craven, P.O. Box 7408, 2410 East Kivett Drive, High Point, NC 27408. Telephone (800) 334 3061
34-page color catalogue, year's subscription, $3; overseas $1; overseas air mail $2.

Creme de la Creme, 908 North Ernst Court, Chicago, IL 60611. Telephone (800) 621 6105
19-page color catalogue, free. AE, MC, V.

**Barbara George Collection, P.O. Box 2156,
Edison, NJ 08837. Telephone (201) 561 7890**
30-page color catalogue, free. AE, MC, V.

**Charles Keach, 4030 Pleasantdale Rd., N.E.,
Atlanta, GA 30340. Telephone (404) 449 3100**
Color catalogue, free. AE, MC, V.

**Marco Polo, Box 481-C, Portsmouth, NH 03801.
Telephone (603) 436 8338**
16-page color brochure, $1. MC, V.

**The Nature Company, P.O. Box 7137,
Berkeley, CA 94707. Telephone (415) 524 8340**
32-page color catalogue, free. AE, MC, V.

**Papillon, 2930 Amwilder Court, Atlanta, GA 30360.
Telephone (404) 449 6186**
21-page color catalogue, $1. MC, V.

**Propinquity, 8941 Santa Monica Boulevard,
West Hollywood, CA 90069. Telephone (213) 652 2933**
30-page color catalogue, free. AE, MC, V.

5

Humorous Catalogues

These firms sell inexpensive jokes, tricks and humorous gifts
for "when you care enough to send the tackiest" as Wretched Mess says. From "all-time-favorite" Delux dribble
glasses, and "chicken sheet" note pads to Mickey Mouse
watches, and not forgetting the famous "whoopee cushion,"
these catalogues have delighted millions of the young and
young-at-heart. Great places to find presents for difficult
pre- and early adolescents.

**The Game Room, 2100 M Street, Washington, DC 20037.
Telephone (202) 775 1894**
*56-page color catalogue, U.S. and overseas $1; overseas air
mail $2. AE, MC, V.*

**Johnson Smith Company, 35075 Automation Drive,
Mt. Clemens, MI 48043. Telphone (800) 228 5440**
Catalogue, free. MC, V.

**The Wretched Mess Catalogue, P.O. Box 1526,
Mountain View, CA 94042**
16-page catalogue, 25 cents, MC, V.

6

Country Style

These catalogues have decorative objects and small pieces of
furniture for the house in the now popular "country style,"
from apple dolls, blue-spattered stoneware, to vaguely Early
American phone centers and record storage boxes.

**Buffalo Peddler Catalogue, Box 110,
Buffalo, NY 14224-0110. Telephone (716) 675 4856**
18-page catalogue, $1. MC, V.

**Country Loft, South Shore Park, Hingham, MA 02043.
Telephone (617) 749 7766**
40-page color catalogue, free. AE, MC, V.

7

5 *Propinquity* Collectors' dolls with loops for hanging, $12 to $14
each.

6 *Propinquity* Betty and Bimbo vase, candle holder, music box,
book ends, mugs, and money box. Priced $7.50 to $35.

7 *Propinquity* Painted tin serving tray, $8.50; hen porcelain teapot
and mugs, $45; hen salt and pepper shaker, $12; tea towels to
match tray, four for $18.

8

9

Faith Mountain Herbs, Department CC, Box 366, Sperryville, VA 22740. Telephone (703) 987 8824
27-page catalogue, 50 cents. MC, V with minimum order of $15.

Furniture Crafts, Main Street, Box 489, Stoneham, MA 02180. Telephone (617) 438 4963
31-page color catalogue, $1. MC, V.

Jennifer House, New England's Americana Marketplace, New Marlboro Stage, Great Barrington, MA 01230
96-page color catalogue, 25 cents. AE, MC, V.

Old Guildford Forge, 1840 Boston Post Road, Guildford, CT 06437. Telephone (203) 453 2731
80-page color catalogue, 50 cents. AE, DC, MC, V.

Perkins Country Collection, Village Road, Jackson, NH 03846. Telephone (603) 383 9612
32-page color catalogue, $1. AE, MC, V.

Sturbridge Yankee Workshop, Blueberry Road, Westbrook, ME 04092. Telephone (207) 774 9045
48-page color catalogue, 50 cents.

8 *Faith Mountain Herbs* Fragrant herb wreath contains golden yarrow, nutmeg, cinnamon sticks, bay, sage, rosemary, thyme, and eucalyptus, and is dotted with red peppers against a background of statice and artemisia. Priced about $36.

9 *Faith Mountain Herbs* Cream stoneware horticulture mugs, with decorations taken from seventeenth-century prints. A set of six about $24.

10 *Perkins Country Collection* Apple head doll inspired by an early American folk art. Bread lady 15″ high, $65. Sewing lady also available, $65.

10

15
HOBBY AND PROFESSIONAL EQUIPMENT

The catalogues in this section are among the most useful of all. Many of the firms sell superb, professional-quality equipment that is not available at the local hardware or craft supplies store. Some of the firms sell perfectly ordinary but hard-to-find supplies. (I got a letter this very week from a man who lives in the middle of Manhattan complaining that lamp parts have "disappeared from the New York scene".) Most of the firms were started by people who first used the tools, and although they supply specialists, the catalogues are written as carefully and clearly as though the customers were complete beginners. If you have ever been curious about any of the following occupations, send for a catalogue. The catalogue will tell you what you need, give you an idea of what is involved in the practice, and almost always have an excellent booklist to help you go further.

Architecture

Charrette Corporation, 31 Olympia Avenue, Woburn, MA 01858
170-page catalogue, $3.50; abroad $10. MC, V.
Started nineteen years ago by two recently graduated architects, Charrette is the only business in the world to specialize in supplies for architects. Here you can find everything necessary for design, presentation and modelmaking, as well as lots of other supplies of interest to designers, artists, and anyone who regularly draws or drafts. The catalogue is very pleasantly laid out and easy to look through. The quality and design of the stock is excellent. Goods go from desks, chairs, storage systems and lights through instruments, paints and papers and include hundreds of special products.

Art

Arthur Brown, 2 West 46 Street, New York, NY 10036. Telephone (212) 575 5555
224-page catalogue $2; abroad $5. Pen brochure, free.

Grand Central Artists Materials, 18 East 40th Street, New York, NY 10016. Telephone (212) 679 0023
224-page black-and-white catalogue, $2. AE, MC, V.
All of these firms send out the same large catalogue, which is particularly strong in the fields of commercial and graphic art. In addition to a very full range of first-rate imported paints, papers and brushes, they also carry such specialized items as retouch colors, hyplar mediums, drafting and drawing tables, templates, perspective aids and other tools of this kind.

For the less professional, the catalogue contains everything from press-on lettering, plain cards and envelopes to make greeting cards, and photograph frames, to office furniture, etc.

Grand Central has a large custom-framing department and will either do framing there or give advice to home framers. For these there are metal-section and wooded frames as well as Plexiglass box and slip frames.

New York Central Art Supply Company, 62 Third Avenue, New York, NY 10003. Telephone (212) 473 7705
Main 224-page catalogue, $3. Fine art papers and handmade papers, $2. All printmaking supplies, $2. Canvases, paints and easels, $2. Calligraphy supplies, $1. AE, DC, MC, V.

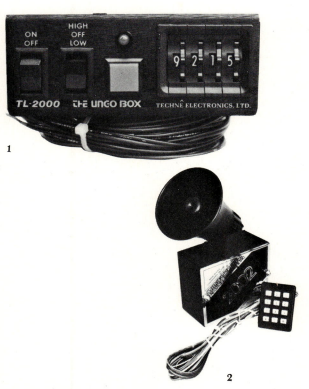

1 *Louisville Lock and Key* "The Ungo Box," one of two electronic (as opposed to mechanical) car protection devices sold by Louisville. So sensitive that it detects a window being tapped. When a thief enters the car or opens the trunk, the horn is sounded and the ignition disabled. If an attempt is made to disarm the Ungo Box, a full cycle alarm sounds for one minute then automatically re-arms. Priced about $289.

2 *Louisville Lock and Key* "Crimestopper" sounds its siren and disables the ignition when thief enters or opens hood or trunk of car. The mechanical motion detector protects against towing. Louisville considers this the best system in its price range. About $199.95.

3

4

5

**Falkiners Fine Papers, 4 Mart Street,
London WC2E 8DE England. Telephone (01) 240 2339**
Price list of papers and sample books, free.
A good collection of European and Japanese handmade papers for bookbinding, calligraphy and printmaking, mold and machine-made papers for artists and printmakers. Prices of paper samples are given on the price list.

**Gill Mechanical Company, P.O. Box 7247,
Eugene, OR 97401. Telephone (503) 686 1606**
Leaflet, free U.S. and abroad.
Invented by a man who hated the way his wife squeezed the toothpaste, the Tube Wringer is also used by dentists and artists to get the last expensive drop out of tubes. Recommended by photographer Nikki Ekstrom.

**Graphic Chemical and Ink Company,
728 North Yale Avenue, P.O. Box 27,
Villa Park, IL 60181. Telephone (312) 832 6004**
40-page catalogue, free U.S. and abroad.
A very good and instructive catalogue of printmaking supplies, mainly for etching with the firm's own inks, plus all Hanco's. Silk-screening supplies too.

**T. N. Lawrence and Son, 2–4 Bleeding Heart Yard,
Greville Street, Hatton Garden,
London EC1N 8SL, England**
Price list, free.
Famous old firm makes engravers' blockwood blocks, and sells tools and materials for wood engraving, wood and line cutting, and etching, including a good assortment of English handmade papers.

DISCOUNT
Please see discount information in the How to Buy section.

**Pearl, 308 Canal Street, New York, NY 10013.
Telephone (212) 431 7932**
Catalogue $2.50. MC, V.
Pearl advertises 20 to 30 percent off list prices on all their brand-name paints, plus Osmiroid and Waterman pens, and easels, tables, etc. They also have some supplies for most crafts. However, there is a $50 minimum for mail order. Established 1938.

**Utrecht Linens, 111 Fourth Avenue,
New York, NY 10003. Telephone (212) 777 5353**
28-page catalogue, free.
Utrecht Linens manufactures its own acrylics, oils, tempera, watercolors, canvas and stretchers, so their prices are low. The firm was originally well known for its canvases; its paints came later and are good buys. House-brand prices are roughly 30 percent below better-known brands. A few well-known brands are stocked at about 10 percent below list prices. Established 1949.

Automotive

**Louisville Lock and Key, 317 Wallace Center,
Louisville, KY 40207. Telephone (502) 589 4127**
26-page catalogue, $3 (refundable); overseas, $4; overseas air mail, $5. MC, V.
A good and thorough catalogue of antitheft devices to protect

3 *Oldstone Enterprises* A rubbing taken from a miniature of a gravestone in the Old Burying Ground, Boston. "Mother" Goose is said to have written the nursery rhymes.

4 *Pourette Manufacturing Company* Gold-sprayed silver foil designs for decorating candles.

5 *Soldner Pottery Equipment* Soldner electric wheel. Light and movable yet stable with a half-splash pan for easier clean-up, and an expanding frame to fit different heights comfortably. A new version for people in wheelchairs has recently been designed, and wheels are available as kits. Priced $440 to $660.

the different parts of a car, or the whole car, and its contents. From a $50 fuel lock that cuts off fuel, stranding the driver, to a $300 electronic motion sensor; there are all sorts of possibilities for thwarting thieves. This catalogue describes the options (including what *not* to buy) and locksmiths Gary Smith and Paul Graham will recommend what is best for your car and your parking habits.

J. C. Whitney and Company, 1917 Archer Avenue, P.O. Box 8410, Chicago, IL 60680
220-page catalogue, free. MC, V.
Parts and accessories "for all makes, years and models . . . for all cars, vans, trucks, motorcycles and recreational vehicles." A basic catalogue with everything needed for car, truck and machine repairs. Recommended by Orville Schell and Stephan Wilkinson.

DISCOUNT
Please see discount information in the How to Buy Section.

J. Robert Tire Connection, 1313 St. Paul Street, Baltimore, MD 21202. Telephone (800) 638 4770, or in Maryland call collect (301) 252 8732
Brochure, free. MC, V.
The Tire Connection tells me that prices on car accessories vary according to area, so people in "competitive areas" will be able to find tires at below list price locally. The Tire Connection says they sell tires and accessories at 20 to 40 percent below "list" price. Tires are mainly better quality radial tires—such as Michelin, Continental, Pirelli, Kleber and B. F. Goodrich—and tires for unusual sizes, foreign makes and high speed. They also sell custom wheels by Koni and KYB, shock absorbers for domestic and foreign cars, and quartz halogen lights. Established 1920.

Basketry

H. H. Perkins Company, 10 South Bradley Road, Woodbridge, CT 06525. Telephone (203) 389 9501
Brochure, free.
You'll find plastic and natural cane, reed, rush and grass at this supplier, together with kits to make doll cradles, sewing baskets, stools and mail baskets. Books and bulletins on raffia work, weaving with cane and reed, and wood finishing are listed.

Beekeeping

The Walter T. Kelley Company, Clarkson, KY 42726. Telephone (502) 242 2012
66-page catalogue, free U.S. and abroad.
Walter T. Kelley got his first beekeeping book in 1908 when he was eleven, and by 1924 he was a full-time beekeeper, manufacturer and seller of beekeeping equipment. Now he has a large beehive factory, sends goods all over the world, and puts out a catalogue that can provide everything you need to follow in his footsteps (in a more modest way, of course).

Bookbinding

Basic Crafts Company, 1201 Broadway, New York, NY 10001. Telephone (212) 679 3516
16-page catalogue, $1, abroad $2. MC, V.
Basic Crafts provides bookbinding tools and supplies for individual craftsmen, schools and libraries. Their catalogue is also good for beginners; it shows kits, and instruction books and pamphlets besides several kits for papermaking and marbling.

Brass and Stone Rubbing

Oldstone Enterprises, 77 Summer Street, Boston, MA 02110
Leaflet, free.
Rubbing is the cheapest and healthiest (it takes place out of doors) of hobbies. Genevieve Jacobs, the manager of Oldstone Enterprises, describes it as "the art of transferring any textured surface to a piece of paper or fabric." You do it by taping paper over the surface to be rubbed and then rubbing the paper with special wax in whatever color you like until the imprint appears. The most elegant things to rub are gravestones in New England, but manhole covers, company plaques, grillwork and all sorts of other things are popular too and, cleverly mounted, can make beautiful decorations.

Candlemaking

Pourette Manufacturing Company, 6818 Roosevelt Way, N.E., P.O. Box 15220, Seattle, WA 98115. Telephone (206) 525 4488
68-page catalogue, $1 (refundable) U.S. and abroad. MC, V.
The largest and oldest supplier of candlemaking equipment has a huge selection of molds, both plain and fancy, as well as equipment to decorate the candles with, holders of various kinds, and books and pamphlets on the subject—and, of course, basic waxes, wicks, dyes and perfumes.

Caning

Frank's Cane and Rush Supply, 7244 Heil Avenue, Huntington Beach, CA 92647. Telephone (714) 847 0707
Brochure, 50 cents; abroad $1. MC, V.
If the seat on your antique bentwood rocker needs recaning and you just heard an estimate of $30, then Frank's Cane and Rush Supply may be your salvation. This firm deals in everything you need to do it yourself and the catalogue gives helpful advice.

Ceramics

Soldner Pottery Equipment, P.O. Box 428 (Seventh and Main), Silt, CO 81652. Telephone (303) 876 2935
Leaflet, free U.S. and abroad.
Paul Soldner, a potter and trustee of the American Crafts

6

7

Council, has designed four wheels and a clay mixer. Wheels start at about $420 for a knock-down kit for a kickwheel, and go up to about $660 for the "professional model" electric wheel.

Westwood Ceramic Supply Company, 14400 Lomitas Avenue, Industry, CA 91746. Telephone (213) 330 0631
96-page pottery-supplies catalogue, $3; abroad $5. MC, V.
This large firm sells J. J. Cress electric kilns, Walker pug mills, and Shimpo wheels, and has a large supply of clays, glazes, tools and books.

Clockmaking

Selva Borel, 347 13th Street, P.O. Box 796, Oakland, CA 94604. Telephone (415) 832 0356
64-page color catalogue, $2; abroad $4. MC, V.
Imported German parts to make and repair clocks. Also a few kits to reproduce old German clocks.

Mason and Sullivan Company, 39 Blossom Avenue, Department 4514, Osterville, MA 02655. Telephone (617) 428 6933
24-page brochure, $1 U.S. and abroad. AE, MC, V.
Here you can get the complete kits or assorted parts and plans to make about twenty reproduction clocks. The catalogue is well laid out, with a bit of information about the original of each model and a list of prices for the parts or the whole kit for each clock. Prices run from about $65 for a Connecticut cottage clock kit to about $290 for all the parts needed to make an 89-inch-high Aaron Willard grandfather clock in cherry. One of three books for beginners explains how clocks and watches work and how to repair them; the other two deal with woodwork and staining and finishing wood.

Conservation

Talas, 130 Fifth Avenue, New York, NY 10011. Telephone (212) 675 0718
Price list, $5; overseas $6.
A unique source of specialized bookbinding and preservation materials. Besides aids to preserving leather, papers, photographs, fabrics, etc., there is wallpaper cleaner, limousine car polish, label remover, concentrate soap solution for getting dirt out of uneven surfaces and more of interest to mere householders.

Decoupage

Laffer Industries, P.O. Box 335, Sandusky, OH 44870. Telephone (419) 626 5220
16-page catalogue, $1 U.S. and abroad.
Sixteen pages of plain wooden boxes, trays, candle-holders, napkin rings, picture frames and about fifty other things to decorate either by painting or by decoupage, which is the art of decorating by covering a surface with cut-outs. Varnish, applicator and instruction books are for sale.

6 *Mason and Sullivan Company* Regulator clock modeled after the Seth Thomas No. 2 Regulator sold in the 1860s and 1870s. Blueprints and instructions to make this clock are available for $3.25, or kits without the movement are on sale at various prices, starting at $103.

7 *Electroni-Kit* Small and inexpensive electronic kits for beginners.

Electronics

Allied Electronics Corporation, 401 East Eighth Street, Fort Worth, TX 76102
Catalogue, $1; overseas $3. MC, V.
Allied is the Sears of the electronics world and its catalogue is a professional reference tool which any amateur can use. Here are both the leading brand names and a large choice of Allied's own products. The catalogue starts with semiconductors and integrated circuits and goes on to list tens of thousands of items from banana jacks to walkie-talkies.

Electroni-Kit, 388 St. John Street, London EC1V 4NN, England. Telephone (01) 278 0109
Leaflets, Electroni-kits and Chip Shop kits, $1. MC, V.
Introductory kits to teach teen-agers and beginners about electronics. Chip Shop kits have complete components to make burglar alarms, lie detectors, etc. Ex-System kits are more elaborate and can be used for many different experiments. Chosen by England's Design Council for an electronics exhibition at the London Science Museum.

Heath Company, Benton Harbor, MI 49022. Telephone (616) 982 3571
98-page catalogue, free. MC, V.
The Heath Company was started in 1918 by Edward Bayard Heath, a flying enthusiast, who sold a plane "ready to fly" or in various stages of completion. The plane has long since been dropped from the books, but this respected and now enormous firm specializes in ready-to-assemble kits of electronic equipment. There are kits for beginners who can change a light bulb but don't know a volt from an ohm or a transistor from a capacitor, says Heath. Over four hundred kits, including intercoms, car and boat equipment, radios, color television sets and much more.

Jensen Tools, 1230 South Priest Drive, Tempe, AZ 85281. Telephone (602) 968 6231
62-page catalogue, free; overseas $2. AE, MC, V.
Jensen, the best-known firm in its field, manufactures and sells a very good range of tools for electronic work. Recommended by Henry Lanz of Garret Wade.

Flower Arranging

Dorothy Biddle Service, Dept. CC, Greeley, PA 18425–9799. Telephone (717) 226 3239
Leaflet, 25 cents; overseas air mail $1.
Rodney Biddle, son of Dorothy Biddle, has been running this firm of supplies for flower arrangers since 1936 and has built up a good stock of basic equipment: several kinds of holders, of course, including some that are specially suitable for artificial flowers, as well as pebbles and moss to hide the holders, a gadget to fix and clean the holders, sticky tape, clay and ties for the plants, clippers, gloves, sprayers, tool kits and containers for tiered, hanging and floating arrangements and arrangements around candles. Also mixtures to preserve flowers and clean artificial flowers, and books and calendars with illustrations of arrangements and instructions.

Ikebana International, CPO Box 1262, Tokyo, Japan. Telephone 293 8188
Explanatory leaflet, free.
A nonprofit international organization for people interested in *ikebana* (Japanese flower arranging) with chapters all over the world. If you are interested in joining, write to the head office and find out whether there is a chapter near you. If there is, you can join, whether you are a beginner or more experienced. A year's Regular Chapter Membership costs around $10. Each chapter varies in its activities, but most have flower-arranging classes, demonstrations and study groups. People who do not live near a chapter can become Members At Large for around $10, pay their yearly dues directly to the head office in Tokyo, and receive a magazine, newsletter and an illustrated step-by-step manual in flower arranging.

Ran, c/o Sogetsu School 2–21, 7-Chome, Minato-Ku, Tokyo, Japan. Telephone 03 (408) 1126
34-page color catalogue, $5.50 surface; air mail $6.50. AE.
Sogetsu is the most modern of the leading *ikebana* schools, and through them you can buy everything you need for Japanese flower arranging (or plain flower arranging). A wonderful selection of simple and unusually shaped containers in many colors; "scissors," which are actually special little shears; over thirty shapes and sizes in "needlepoint" metal flower holders; and plenty of illustrated, instructional books and magazines in both Japanese and English. Also notebooks, calendars and postcards decorated with photographs of arrangements.

Furnituremaking

Home Workshop Supplies, P.O. Box 10, Islington, Ontario M9A 4X1, Canada. Telephone 239 2641
64-page catalogue, $2 (refundable). MC, V.
If you want to build modern furniture or remodel a kitchen, but are not interested in traditional jointing methods, Home Workshop Supplies will be a godsend. This firm offers fittings from Europe that have been developed to join man-made materials, such as particle board, and knock-down furniture. Fittings include concealed cabinet hinges that neatly align doors, extra-strong bed brackets that eliminate the need for mortising, a "magic" wire that is a simple and invisible way of fitting shelves to bookcases and cabinets, a self-assembly polyvinyl-chloride system to make drawers without glue, and a lot of other problem solvers.

For kitchen building or remodeling, Home Workshop Supplies offers sliding brackets, pull-out cupboard fittings, extension tables, a built-in ironing board, a fold-out mixer stand and the like to make a really well-organized kitchen. Nice, clear descriptions explain the products and give instructions on their use.

General Crafts

Dick Blick Company, P.O. Box 1267, Galesburg, IL 61401
40-page catalogue, $2. MC, V.
"Dick Blick ships quick" is the slogan of this firm located far from any major city but whose crowded catalogue of art and craft supplies shows that theirs is a very successful mail-order business. Blick specializes in materials needed for the graphic arts but stocks a wide variety of other supplies for all the crafts now so popular, and Blick has kits, specific materials, larger equipment and furniture. Whether you are an amateur or professional, this is a basic list to consult. Prices tend to be lower than at the more specialized firms,

8

9   10

8 *Grey Owl Indian Craft Company* Sioux imitation eagle war bonnet kit, all the materials necessary. About $14.95.

9 *Grey Owl Indian Craft Company* Floral beaded woodland costume made of different black velvet beadwork panels. Available separately at about $12.95 each.

10 *Grey Owl Indian Craft Company* Handmade Venetian trade beads, 30 cents to $4.90 each.

and less expensive equipment is stocked along with the better-known brands.

Nasco Handcrafters, 1 West Brown Street, Waupun, WI 53963. Telephone (414) 324 2031
378-page catalogue, $1; $2 abroad. MC, V.
A big catalogue of basic supplies, some manufactured by this firm, for most crafts: art and graphics, ceramics, jewelry making, enameling, candlemaking, macrame, needlework and weaving.

Indian Supplies

Del Enterprises, Box 248, Mission, SD 57555. Telephone (605) 856 4817
Catalogue, $1; abroad $3.
This firm sells supplies for American Indian beadwork and has a beautiful collection, one of the best, they say, of fancy "trade beads." Patterned beads in glass and metal are photographed close up and well described, and the firm has recently started manufacturing reproductions of old-style goods that are hard to find: brass beads, brass "hawk bells," brass shoe buttons, genuine bone beads and "hair pipes."

Grey Owl Indian Craft Company, 113–15 Springfield Boulevard, Queens Village, NY 11429. Telephone (212) 464 9300
146-page catalogue, $1; abroad $2. MC, V.
Here are kits and supplies to make American Indian costumes of all kinds. Prices are low, but the goods are not especially authentic—plastic imitation beadwork and plastic Iroquois face-mask kits can be found. There is a lot of everything, however, including tools and accessories such as Plasticine—to change the shape of a nose—and makeup and body paint.

Jewelry and Lapidary Equipment

California Crafts Supply, 1096 Main Street, Orange, CA 92667. Telephone (714) 633 8891
Catalogue, $1.50; abroad $2. MC, V.
Plain, down-to-earth catalogue lists basic supplies for silversmithing, lost-wax casting, forged brass jewelry, plastic projects and contemporary leathercraft. Although the catalogue doesn't contain as much as some of the others, it does have the simple necessities, including books, and is well organized and agreeable to look through.

Clear Creek Trading Company, P.O. Box 1250, Idaho Springs, CO 80452. Telephone (303) 567 4987
48-page catalogue $5; abroad $7.
Catalogue of glorious beads and things for necklaces (also macrame): pottery, pasta (the rage of St. Tropez), bone and shells, "medicine bottle" beads from Africa, "glass flower" beads from Japan, mystical amulets from India, silver dragons from China. Peacock and partridge feathers, semiprecious stones, silver- and gold-filled clasps, and books on beading and macrame. Enough to inspire *anyone.* This hand-drawn catalogue is recommended by Carol Campion, a reader.

Deepak's Rokjemperl Products, 61, 10th Khetwadi, Bombay 4, India. Telephone 388031
Price list, free. Prices in $. Illustrated leaflet (rather blurry photocopied pages), $2 or 2 International Reply Coupons.
Under the above name this firm sells cut and polished gemstones, beads, bead necklaces, silvery filigree jewelry and small ivory carvings. From the same address and from the same price list, but under the name Shah's Rock Shop, the same firm sells rough gemstones.

Geo-Sonics, 102 West Lincoln Street, New London, IA 52645. Telephone (319) 367 2255
40-page catalogue, free. MC, V.
The Geo-Sonics division of Geode Industries has manufactured vibratory machines for tumbling for twenty years. A professional catalogue illustrates tumblers plus machines for drilling, cutting, polishing and engraving. They say "no other firm takes more time to correspond with its customers, helping to solve tumbling problems."

International Import Company, P.O. Box 747, Stone Mountain, GA 30086. Telephone (404) 938 0173
56-page price list, free U.S. and abroad. October.
Besides writing monthly articles for *Modern Jeweler*, George A. Bruce, the owner of International Import Company, is a picturesquely named Ordinary Fellow of the Gemological Association of Great Britain. A list of about 3,000 of the 100,000 precious and semiprecious stones in stock is published each October and gives customers an idea of which stones are available in what sizes, weights, shapes and prices. As the specific stones listed are sold, close substitutes are sent. The list is matter-of-fact and the descriptions abbreviated.

New Central Jewelry Store, 67 Main Street, Colombo, Sri Lanka. Telephone 28895
Price list, free.
Dealers in Sri Lanka gems, this firm sells blue sapphires, yellow sapphires, star sapphires, star rubies, cat's-eyes; also semiprecious stones such as aquamarines, amethysts, garnets, moonstones and topaz.

Leather Work

Leathercrafters Supply Company, 25 Great Jones Street, New York, NY 10012. Telephone (212) 673 5460
Color catalogue, $2. MC, V.
Leathercrafters stocks cowhide bags and belt leather, Western and Canadian latigo, English kip and hide skins, and leather for clothes such as chamois, suede, deerskin, antelope and elk. They stock Osborne tools, and also cleaners, preservatives, Fiebling dyes, finding, cobbler sandal supplies, and books.

MacPherson, 730 Polk Street, San Francisco, CA 94109. Telephone (415) 771 1900
126-page catalogue, $2; abroad $3. MC, V.
Supplies for leather work, including Osborne tools and quite a bit for shoemaking and repairing.

Magic

Lewis Davenport, 51 Great Russell Street, London WC1B 3BA, England. Telephone (01) 405 8524
254-page book catalogue, $12. 24-page "Children's Magic and Close-Up Magic," $3.
For children, parents and professionals—"tricks of infinite jest that will bewilder the brain." This third-generation family firm (there is a photo of Betty Davenport lifting a white rabbit from a top hat) supplies snappy routines to professional conjurers all over the world, but also manufactures humbler pranks: stinky scent, goofy teeth, dirty nose drops, and squirting chocolate suitable for party favors or "the man who likes pocket tricks (and who doesn't?)" at lower prices than comparable articles in America, they say.

D. Robbins and Company, 70 Washington Street, Brooklyn, NY 11201
72-page Professional Magic brochure, $1. 74-page Magic Tricks brochure, $1.
"E-Z magic" is the D. Robbins trademark, and there are plenty of simple stunts for under $5 in the catalogue of "practical tricks for stage-club-parlor." All the favorites that delight children are listed and illustrated in the oddly old-fashioned style that magic catalogues seem to keep to. About forty books are sold on all aspects of magic and tricks.

Natural Sciences

Watkins and Doncaster, Four Throws, Hawkhurst, Kent, England. Telephone Hawkhurst 3133.
52-page catalogue, $4. MC, V.
The letterhead says that this ninety-eight-year-old firm sells "the finest equipment for all the Natural Sciences." R. J. Ford adds that it is cheaper for Americans to buy their products direct rather than through American firms. There is the necessary equipment for the study and practice of botany, dissection, geology, onology and taxidermy, and being specialists in entomology, Watkins and Doncaster can provide exclusive entomological items such as moth traps, which, they say, they alone manufacture.

Reverse Glass Painting

E. & S. Robinson Associates, Gage Road, Wilton, NH 03086
Brochures, long self-addressed stamped envelope.
Tinsel painting, a variation of the popular Victorian hobby of reverse glass painting, involves painting on glass with transparent and opaque oil colors and glitter. The Robinsons sell instructions and decorative old patterns collected by William L. Crowell, a great uncle. Painted glass can be used for pictures, trays, tables. Other patterns sold here are for painting tin, and wooden furniture.

Rubber Stamps

A new graphic craze, popular with children and adults alike. Useful for making cards, wrapping paper, and generally communicating. Said to be addictive.

All Night Media, Box 227, Forrest Knolls, CA 94933. Telephone (415) 488 4963
32-page catalogue, $1.25.
About four hundred original humorous stamps, many designed by co-owner Robert Blomberg. Especially suitable for children, making cards and wrapping paper. Irresistible animal alphabet and numbers.

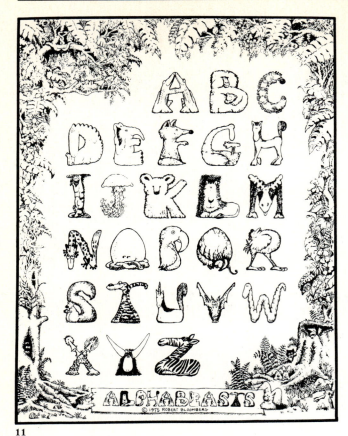

11

12

11 *All Night Media* Rubber stamps. © Copyright by All Night Media.

12 *Rubberstampede* Rubber stamps. © Copyright by Rubberstampede.

Bizarro Rubber Stamps, P.O. Box 126, Annex Station, Providence, RI 02901–0216
20 page catalogue, $1.50; abroad $2.50.
One of the oldest and best-known firms has mainly forties and earlier designs, also a grab bag of "cheap way to support the habit" stamps that cost about one third of the usual price.

Elbow Grease, P.O. Box 25056, Richmond, VA 23260
20 pages, $2.
About a hundred stamps, 80 percent of which have been drawn by the owners in rather odd, sophisticated period styles.

Good Impressions, 1126 Avery Street, Parkersburg, WV 26101. Telephone (304) 422 1147
20-page catalogue, $1; abroad $1.50.
About two hundred stamps with turn-of-the-century designs, including some ornate words: "Fragile," "Thank You," etc.

Hero Arts, P.O. Box 5234, Berkeley, CA 94705. Telephone (415) 654 4080
24-page catalogue, $1.50 U.S. and abroad.
About three hundred stamps in a mixture of styles, including Alice in Wonderland stamps.

Mary Alice Scenic Stamps, 2453 Echo Park Avenue, Los Angeles, CA 90026. Telephone (213) 663 2862
6-page catalogue, $1.50; abroad $2.
Five large pages show about five hundred turn-of-the-century images, and several alphabets, two decorative.

Nature Impressions, 1007 Leneve Place, El Cerrito, CA 94530. Telephone (415) 527 9622
18-page brochure, $1.25; abroad $2.
Quite different from the other rubber-stamp catalogues, Nature Impressions contains no funny stamps, but original, accurate and rather respectful impressions of animals and a few plants.

Rubberstampede, P.O. Box 1105, Berkeley, CA 94701. Telephone (415) 843 8910
56-page catalogue, $2 U.S. and abroad (refundable).
About 350 rubber stamps, including many animals, a dragon alphabet, and many messages such as "Deceased," and "Boom."

St. Simon Society, 178 Fifth Avenue, New York, NY 10010. Telephone (212) 255 5990
16-page catalogue, $1; abroad $2.50.
Several styles, messages such as "Never talk dirty to your parakeet," cute stamps by Kimble Mead, and a cat alphabet.

Science

Edmund Scientific, 101 East Gloucester Pike, Barrington, NJ 08007. Telephone (609) 547 3488
164-page catalogue, free U.S. and abroad. AE, DC, MC, V.
Norman Edmund, an amateur photographer, started Edmund Scientific in 1942 when he found it was hard to get the experimental lenses he needed. The firm continues to make available the kind of somewhat technical equipment more easily available to professionals, and individuals, schools, colleges and industrial customers all get the same catalogue.

Astronomy is the specialty, but the catalogue is altogether

a marvel. Professionals and what Edmund calls "serious amateurs" will find useful tools and unusual equipment for the lab, photography, electronics and many other fields. But frivolous amateurs will also find plenty—party givers will find silver balloons, giant balloons and helium, strobe lights and an instant party kit that "transforms any room into a maze of color." Children will find motorized models to build; the health conscious will find jogging pacers and blood pressure gauges; the energy conscious will find solar radios; and everyone else will find "Products for Scientific Living": NASA-developed lightweight space luggage, wine-chilling gadgets, cordless-bath whirlpools and the like.

13

Sculpture

Sculpture House, 38 East 30th Street, New York, NY 10016. Telephone (212) 679 7474
48-page catalogue, $2.
As the catalogue announces, here you can get tools, materials and accessories for casting, wax modeling, wood carving, stone carving, plastic sculpturing and ceramic sculpturing. This fifty-year-old firm says it produces the world's most complete line of products for sculptors and also does custom casting, restoring, etc. Books on sculpturing and potting are also sold.

Alec Tiranti, 70 High Street, Theale, Berkshire, England. Telephone 302 775
Sculptor's catalogue, $2.
The London business of Alec Tiranti was started in 1895 by John Tiranti, a master carver from Turin. The firm is now run by the founder's grandson and sells tools for stone and wood sculpting and supplies for clay modeling, all made to the firm's own design either in its own workshops in Berkshire or imported from craftsmen in Italy.

14

Short-Wave Radio

Radio West, 3417 Purer Road, Escondido, CA 92025. Telephone (714) 741 2891
36-page brochure, free U.S. and abroad. MC, V.
A selection of the best short wave radio equipment. "We are picky," they say. Also a little advice for the newcomer and the confused, and an invitation to write or call with more questions.

Stained Glass

Whittemore-Durgin Glass Company, Box 2065 DF, Hanover, MA 02339. Telephone (617) 871 1743
Complete literature package, 50 cents U.S. and abroad. AE, MC, V.
This firm claims to be the only source of supply in the world for all materials, patterns, tools, etc., for the production of stained-glass windows, lampshades and ornaments. There are many sources of supply, they say, but nowhere else is everything available under one roof.

13 *Edmund Scientific* Astroscan 2001 beginner telescope, quick to set up, has an especially wide, bright field to make finding celestial objects easier. About $229.95.

14 *Edmund Scientific* Spottingscope, designed for terrestrial use, offers a magnification range which binoculars can not, focuses down to 25 feet, and gives unusually sharp images. It is lightweight and adapts to a standard camera tripod. Priced about $250. Good for birdwatching, boating, etc.

15

16

Stenciling

Adele Bishop, Box 557, Manchester, VT 05254
Color catalogue, $2. AE, MC, V.
Not just furniture, but almost anything can be stenciled—floors, window shades, letter boxes, table mats and certainly fabrics. Adele Bishop has easy-to-use transparent stencils; special brushes for controlled and subtle color tones; special paints, including new ones for fabrics; and beautiful early American patterns. Hard to resist.

Surplus

Airborn Sales Company, 8501 Steller Drive, P.O. Box 2727, Culver City, CA 90230. Telephone (213) 870 4687
92-page catalogue, $1 U.S. and abroad.
Established in 1945, Airborn has a good selection of aircraft, automotive, marine, hardware, and industrial components. They sell new and used surplus, and manufacture and distribute other lines too.

C and H Sales Company, 2176 East Colorado Boulevard, Pasadena, CA 91107. Telephone (213) 681 4925
112-page catalogue, free U.S. and abroad.
C and H sells only new surplus. Aircraft instruments, generators, motors, optics, transistors and more are stocked.

Palley Supply Company, 11630 Burke Street, Los Nieros, Los Angeles, CA 90606. Telephone (213) 692 7501
Catalogue, free.
The largest "surplus" store in America has 7½ acres of government and industrial "excess inventory" goods, of which a portion is listed and illustrated in their big catalogue. Hydraulic equipment is, they say, their biggest business, and they have a complete line of hydraulic pumps, motors, cylinders, valves, hose, accumulators, filters and test stands; they do overhaul/repair work as well. Field telephones and telephone wire are also popular with forestry services and on farms. Palley says that universities and governments buy from them, and many small businesses have been launched by incorporating Palley stock into their finished products.

Tatooing

Spaulding and Rogers Manufacturing, Route 85, New Scotland Road, Voorheesville, NY 12186. Telephone (518) 768 2070
48-page catalogue, $3; abroad $8.
Spaulding and Rogers have manufactured tatoo guns and equipment for twenty-five years. Their catalogues contain all supplies, including "sets to get you started" for beginners, and amazing designs of dragons, wrathful serpents and tigers, skulls and girls.

15 *Adele Bishop* Stencil sheets for decorating fabrics, furniture, and other surfaces cost between about $9 and $20 a set.

16 *Spaulding and Rogers Manufacturing* Designs for tattooing.

Tools

Brookstone Tool Company,
127 Vose Farm Road, Peterborough, NH 03458.
Telephone (603) 924 7181
Tool catalogue, free U.S. and abroad.
Gift catalogue, free U.S. and abroad. AE, MC, V.
Brookstone is one of the best-loved American mail-order
companies. The catalogue, subheaded "Hard to Find Tools
and Other Fine Things," is famous for its unusual tools and
useful gadgets. But it is by no means only aimed at burly
do-it-yourselfers; even the least active among us will find
something they want (a fake light socket to hid jewels? a
horn with a mile-wide shriek? a three-day candle for power
failures?). Somewhere among the television rotators, plastic
bag sealers, self-draining hoses, no-mess cheese graters, security door locks, snap clips to hang appliances, ear stoppers—
somewhere is the perfect present for almost every difficult
person.

McKilligan Industrial Supply Corporation,
435 Main Street, Johnson City, NY 13790.
Telephone (607) 729 6511
800-page catalogue, $5 (refundable on $100 order). MC, V.
"Our Catalogue is Thick, Our Service is Quick," announces
McKilligan. It is hard to imagine a handy person who won't
find something he or she needs or wants in this whopping
catalogue. Supplies for foundry, plumbing, gardening, electrical work, electronics and crafts are all here, plus shop
furniture and tools, of course. Certainly, a valuable reference
work to anyone maintaining or repairing a house, and looking for right tool to do the job.

DISCOUNT
Please see discount information in the How to Buy section.

Silvo Hardware,
2205 Richmond Street, Philadelphia, PA.
Telephone (215) 423 6200
174-page catalogue, $1; overseas $3. MC, V.
Brand-name tools at low prices, with a wide range of tools
for home building and maintenance: power tools, automotive
tools, supplies for plumbing and plastering, plus professional
drain cleaners, weatherstripping and the like. Good selection
and quality, fair prices and service, according to toymaker
Jack Dohany, who buys all his tools by mail.

J. Simble and Sons,
76 Queens Road, Watford, Herts WD1 2LD, England
76-page catalogue, $2; air mail $3.
A good selection of brand-name British tools from staplers to
sawbenches. Simble has an active worldwide export service.

U.S. General Supply Corporation,
100 Commercial Street, Plainview, NY 11803.
Telephone (516) 576 9100
196-page catalogue, $1. MC, V.
U.S. sells a huge range of brand-name tools at significantly
lower prices than they go for at hardware stores. Jack
Dohany says these are the lowest prices he has found on
brand-name tools, although the firm is not strong on woodwork tools.

Winemaking

Presque Isle Wine Cellars,
9440 Buffalo Road, Northeast, PA 16428
40-page catalogue, free. MC, V.
Presque Isle Wine Making Cellars has a good reputation
and puts out a small, businesslike catalogue of supplies for
home winemaking, but is the only firm that does not sell kits
for beginners. They think that part of the pleasure of winemaking is in using your wits to determine what is and is not
needed. Instead of kits they offer beginners advice and information.

Semplex of U.S.A.,
4805 Lyndale No., Minneapolis, MN 55430.
Telephone (612) 522 0500
22-page catalogue, free U.S. and sea mail.
Semplex of U.S.A. is the agent for a very reputable English
firm, and the catalogue is a good basic listing of winemaking
supplies and American and English books about making
beer and wine.

Dr. George Green, with characteristic thoroughness, is work-
ing towards producing a superb wine in New York State
and has already won several medals for the wine he makes
with his own grapes. He suggests the following sources for
serious winemakers:

Foster Nursery Company, 69 Orchard Street,
Fredonia, NY 14603
A Guide to American and French Hybrid Grape Varieties,
$1.50.
This nursery sells grape vines, and produces an extraordi-
narily practical booklet describing grape varieties, with notes
on their culture.

The Wine Lab, 1200 Oak Avenue, St. Helena, CA 94574
Price list, free.
For the knowledgeable, a list of winemaking supplies. No
descriptions or explanations. The Wine Lab gives classes for
home winemakers, bonded winemakers and classes in "sen-
sory evaluation."

Wood Carving

Carl Heidtmann, Box 140245,
D-5630 Remscheid 1, Germany
Brochure, 3 International Reply Coupons.
Excellent wood-carving tools at prices below equivalent
American prices.

Ashley Iles, East Kirkby, Spilsby, Lincolnshire, England
Leaflet, $1.
Very good hand-forged wood-carving tools sold individually
and in sets at comparatively low prices.

Woodworking

Many of the best tools are not sold at the local hardware
store but are only available by mail. Jack Dohany, a professional toymaker who buys his tools by mail, very generously
sent me comments on his favorite sources. His notes are
scattered below and in the general tool section.

17

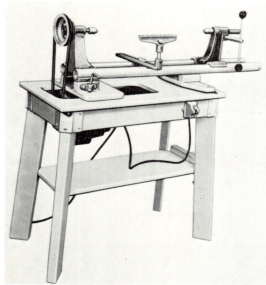

18

17 *Gilliom Manufacturing Company* A kit with metal parts, plans, and instructions to make this 18″ band saw is available for about $167.99. Plans and patterns cost only $4.

18 *Gilliom Manufacturing Company* A kit with metal parts, plans, patterns and instructions to make this combination lathe–drill press, disc sander, tool grinder, is available for about $74.99. Plans and patterns only cost $4.

**American Machine Tool Company,
Fourth and Spring Street, Royersford, PA 19468.
Telephone (215) 948 0400**
Leaflet, free. MC, V.
The American Machine Tool Company manufactures bench power tools for home workshop enthusiasts who want something more than the portable power tools that people use for "fix-up" jobs around the house, yet not as expensive as the bigger, fancier more nearly automatic tools that some home workshop enthusiasts buy. There is a small market for simpler, less expensive tools, and A.M.T. reaches it by mail order and says that by eliminating "expensive gingerbread," they keep most of their prices low.

Conover Woodcraft Specialties, 18125 Madison Road, Parkman, OH 44080. Telephone (216) 548 3481
24-page catalogue, $1 U.S. and abroad. MC, V.
Conover sells something very unusual: cast-iron, heavy-duty industrial machinery equivalent in weight and mass to similar American machinery, such as Powermatic, but at far lower prices. The machinery is from Taiwan, and Conover says that they took two years to find machinery of the quality they wanted. Suggested by Henry Lanz of Garret Wade, who says he hasn't bought here, but has heard good things about the machinery. Smaller tools also sold, which Jack Dohany says are of very good quality.

Albert Constantine and Son, 2050 Eastchester Road, Bronx, NY 10461
100-page color catalogue, $1.
Constantine's was founded in 1812 by a neighbor of Duncan Phyfe's, Thomas Constantine, an authority on mahogany who was engaged by the Vice-President to make mahogany desks and chairs for the Senate. They now sell lumber, fine woods and veneers, mainly by mail, and have an astonishing range of woods, many that I had never even heard of. Then, besides wood, they have other things that are needed for specific projects: moldings for framing pictures, hardware such as handles and hinges for furniture, lamp parts, shelf brackets, plenty of different wood finishes and tools. The catalogue ends with 101 suggestions for "things to do in shop and home," and tells you where in the catalogue you'll find the appropriate supplies.

**Craftsman Woodservice Company,
1735 W. Courtland Court, Co. Addision, IL 60101.
Telephone (312) 629 3100**
144-page catalogue, 50 cents. MC, V.
Domestic and foreign hardwoods, veneers and all other hard-to-find supplies for working with wood: lamp parts, frames, instrument kits, upholstery supplies, etc.

Frog Tool Company, 700 West Jackson Boulevard, Chicago, IL 60606. Telephone (312) 648 1270
Catalogue, $2; overseas $3, overseas air mail $6. MC, V.
Traditional hand-working tools, a good selection, including tools for building log cabins. A well-chosen, well-described list of books on woodcraft includes subjects such as furnituremaking and refinishing, boat building, toymaking, and restoring old buildings. Good selection, prices and service, and very good quality according to Jack Dohany.

Gilliom Manufacturing Company, 1109 North Second Street, St. Charles, MO 63301. Telephone (314) 724 1812
Brochure, $1 U.S. and overseas. MC, V.
Gilliom's makes and sells good kits for amateur woodworkers to build woodworking machines. The firm supplies the metal parts and plans, the customer uses his

own wood, and the resulting power tools cost far less than ready-made ones.

Leichtung, 4944 Commerce Parkway, Cleveland, OH 44128. Telephone (216) 831 6191.
80-page catalogue, $1 for two-year subscription. MC, V.
Leichtung is comparable to Frog so far as service and prices go, but is best known for its Lervard Danish workbenches, including a folding model for people without room for a permanent workshop. The catalogue contains a slightly smaller collection of good tools (Bracht chisels and gauges, for example) plus a few other ingenious small fixtures for the home, such as extra strong hangers to store heavy objects on the wall.

Parks Woodworking Machinery Company, 1501 Knowlton Street, Cincinnati, OH 45223
Leaflets, free.
For wood- and metal-cutting band saws and planers, Parks, a ninety-year-old specialty firm, makes saws and planes. Some are for commercial use, but the twelve-inch planer is manufactured for home use. Quality and prices both high.

Garret Wade Company, 161 Avenue of the Americas, New York, NY 10013. Telephone (212) 695 3358

Lee Valley Tools, 2680 Queensview Drive, Ottawa, Canada. Telephone (613) 596 0350
100-page color catalogue, $3 U.S. and overseas; overseas air mail $6. AE, MC, V.
These two branches of one firm produce a prize hand-tool catalogue, full of beautiful photographs and careful explanations of the uses of the contents. Traditional hand woodworking tools and supplies are sold. Some, such as moulding planes, mortise chisels, cranked neck and paring chisels, and veneering tools, are no longer made in the U.S. Besides the hand tools, there is Inca machinery from Switzerland, Arundel lathes from England, a complete range of Japanese woodworking tools, and high-quality wood finishes. The catalogue will delight anyone who loves tools. The only trouble, says Jack Dohany, is that the photographs are *so* excellent that the actual tools can look disappointing when they arrive, although they are perfectly fine.

Woodcraft Supply Corporation, 313 Montvale Avenue, Woburn, MA 01888
Tool catalogue, $2.50; abroad $3.65. Projects catalogue, $1; abroad $1.50. AE, MC, V.
Similar, but not identical to Garret Wade, Woodcraft has a very good selection of very high quality woodworking tools. Jack Dohany thinks the selection and quality is about the best, here. There is also an excellent projects catalogue for people who want kits.

Woodline the Japan Woodworker, 1731 Clement Avenue, Alameda, CA 94501. Telephone (415) 521 1810
30-page catalogue, $1.50 U.S. and abroad. MC, V.
Very fine woodworking tools imported from Miki, Japan, a toolmaking center for five hundred years. The highest grade steel is used in these tools, and it has an extremely hard cutting edge that stays sharp longer, although it is brittle and needs more care than the lower quality steel usually used in woodworking tools. Japanese kitchen knives are also shown in the catalogue. Superior Western tools are not in the catalogue, but are also stocked: Record and Stanley metal planes, Henry Taylor and Ashley Isles carving tools, Hirsch chisels and gauges, Fuller countersinks and bits, Primus wooden planes and Inca woodworking machinery.

19

20

21

19 *Woodcraft Supply Corporation* Kit to make Washington dollhouse, has precision die-cut pieces of mahogany plywood, to be assembled without tools, screws, or nails. House is on a scale of 1″ = 1′. Priced about $43.50, postpaid.

20 *Woodcraft Supply Corporation* This kit to make an electric guitar can be assembled in two hours. Everything needed is included. About $225, postpaid.

21 *Woodcraft Supply Corporation* Kits to make natural wood lampshades that cast a warm light cost between $24 and $32 each. Easy to assemble, no tools are needed, and everything, including the electrical parts, is provided.

1

2

3

1 *Brook Hill Linens* Pillows in old and new lace threaded with satin ribbons start at $15 for the smallest size. Bedspreads can be made to match.

2 *Cabin Creek Quilts* This wall hanging is a sampler of the different quilt patterns available as pillows and as bedspreads. Pillows start at $20, baby quilts at $45, quilts in single size at about $170.

3 *Annie Cole* Hand-knitted pillows in traditional old designs start at about $40 for the smallest size. Bedspreads can be knitted to match.

Appliances

OVERSEAS ELECTRICITY

American electrical appliances are normally made to run on 110 volts/AC. If the electricity in your area is different (say, 220 volts) turn to one of the shops in this book that specializes in dual-voltage appliances made to work with your electricity. I am told by the stores that almost all the appliances are available in versions that can be used overseas. If you cannot find what you want in a dual-voltage version, you should remember that some appliances can be used with different electrical current simply by using an adaptor. Things with motors such as electric shavers, food mixers, refrigerators, vacuum cleaners, and floor polishers are usually easy to convert. Equipment with heating elements, or with timing devices such as clocks, automatic washing machines, cookers, and most types of record players and tape recorders, are hard to convert.

DISCOUNT
Please see discount information in the How to Buy section.

I have taken to buying all my appliances at a discount by mail or telephone, and trying to persuade my friends to do the same. To buy at a discount you do need to know exactly what you want, including the model number. This can be done by window shopping, sending for manufacturers' brochures, finding someone who already has an appliance you are considering, or (my favorite method) by consulting *Consumer Reports*. *Consumer Reports* not only tests appliances to find out which ones work best in various ways, but also gives model numbers and list prices. A year's subscription to *Consumer Reports*, eleven issues and the *Buyer's Guide*, costs $14; in Canada $15; other countries $16. Write to *Consumer Reports*, P.O. Box 1949, Marion, OH 43305. The December *Buyer's Guide* alone, which is a volume of compressed listings from back issues, costs $3.50 postpaid U.S. and overseas (sea mail). It's available from *Consumer Report* Books, Box C-719, Brooklyn, NY 11205.

Bondy Export Corp,
40 Canal Street, New York, NY 10002.
Telephone (212) 925 7785.
Send model number and self-addressed stamped envelope (overseas 1 International Reply Coupon) for price information by mail only. MC, V.
Bondy has a wide selection of appliances, but will only send things weighing less than 50 pounds out of New York State. I have found them reliable about giving prices by mail, and when I bought two appliances from them (with certified check) they delivered promptly both times. They say that they specialize in appliances for overseas. Established 1950.

Dial-a-Brand,
229–07 Merrick Boulevard, Laurelton, NY 11413.
Telephone (212) 978 4400 or (516) 352 4447
Give model number for price by telephone only.
Dial-a-Brand sells only by telephone. They sell all *large* household appliances such as dishwashers, clothes washers and dryers, ovens, refrigerators and air conditioners. They also sell televisions and video recorders but do not sell any office machines or small appliances. I bought from Dial-a-Brand a very good Freidrich air conditioner for $395, while

the firm I used to buy from was charging the list price of $559. I was lucky with delivery to my area, so I got the conditioner within a few days, and paid C.O.D. with a certified check. A friend of mine just bought a color television set at $100 below list price, also with prompt delivery. Established 1967.

Focus Electronics,
4523 Thirteenth Avenue, Brooklyn, NY 11219.
Telephone (212) 871 7600
Send model number for price information by mail, U.S. and overseas. MC, V.
Focus has an all-around selection of major brands of large and small appliances for the house, plus audio, video, television and photographic equipment. They ship all over the world and sell dual voltage appliances. I have found Focus good at quoting prices (they scribble the price on your own letter). I ordered a Sony Walkman from them and there was a delay of over three weeks before I got it; they say that they do not send goods bought with personal noncertified checks until the checks have cleared. Established 1970.

Foto Electric Supply,
31 Essex Street, New York, NY 10002.
Telephone (212) 673 5222
Send stamped self-addressed envelope or International Reply Coupon and model number for price by mail only, U.S. and overseas. MC, V.
I have found Foto Electric good at giving prices by mail although they will not do it over the telephone. They sell major household appliances, television, video and photography equipment, and send dual voltage goods around the world. Established 1961.

International Solgo, Attention Oscar Rosenberg,
77 West 23rd Street, New York, NY 10010.
Telephone 800 645 8162 or (212) 675 3555

International Solgo of Long Island,
1745 Hempstead Turnpike, Elmont, NY 11002.
Telephone (516) 354 8815
Write or telephone with model number, U.S. and overseas. AE, MC, V.
International Solgo insists that they sell "everything" in the way of large and small appliances, plus electronics and some luggage, jewelry, etc. I have found them better at giving prices over the telephone (they didn't answer two of my letters) when they generally seem to check to see whether they have whatever I'm asking about in stock. I ordered a vacuum cleaner and a Cuisinart from them by mail (with certified checks) and in both cases they sent them within the week. President Oscar Rosenberg says that they specialize in 110–220 multivolt merchandise and are helpful to overseas customers. Established 1933.

LVT Price Quote Hotline,
P.O. Box 444, Commack, NY 11725–0444.
Telephone (516) 234 8884 or (212) 784 0014
Catalogue $2.00 or telephone between 9 A.M. and 2 P.M. for prices.
LVT does not like to be called a "discount" firm, but says that they make their "best offer," which is below list prices. They sell a very wide range of goods from organs and major appliances, through CB radios, and all the usual electronics and telephone equipment, down to home-security and health-care supplies. The catalogue only has some of the goods they sell, with list prices. You must telephone (not write) for the LVT price. Established 1976.

Bedroom and Bathroom

BEDSPREADS

Brook Hill Linens, 698 Madison Avenue,
New York, NY 10021. Telephone (212) 688 1113
Color brochure, $1; overseas $2. AE.
A romantic, softly colored collection of pillows in old and new lace threaded with satin ribbons. Prices $15 to $75 depending on size. Bedspreads in the same style, can be made to order.

Blowing Rock Crafts, Goodwin Weavers, P.O. Box 314,
Blowing Rock, NC 28605
12-page brochure, $1. MC, V.
Bedspreads, tablecloths and drapery fabrics are made in four traditional American patterns, in the South "Honeycomb," "Lovers Knot," "Morning Star" and "Whig Rose."

Cabin Creek Quilts, Box 383, Cabin Creek, WV 25035.
Telephone (304) 595 3928
Leaflet, some color, free. MC, V.
This organization was started in 1970 by a VISTA volunteer with five women in Cabin Creek, a thirty-mile hollow in the mountains of West Virginia, and now has over a hundred quilters all over the state. Eight different-patterned quilts in four sizes each are made at prices from $170 to $405 for single size. Baby quilts start at $45, pillows at $20, and there are also children's vests, placemats, tablecloths, aprons, shoulder bags, and wall hangings for children's rooms, all in patchwork and just a few cloth dolls and puppets.

Annie Cole, 4 St. Simon's Avenue, Putney,
London SW15 6DU, England
Brochure, $1; air mail $2 (refundable).
Fascinating and unusual fine cotton bedspreads handknitted in traditional old designs. Annie Cole's new firm has already exported to Neiman Marcus, but with her knitters' interests at heart she is glad to sell by mail and cut out the middleman. Prices for pram covers and feather-filled cushions very reasonable, for this sort of work, at under $50.

The Freedom Quilting Bee, Route 1, Box 43-A,
Alberta, AL 36720. Telephone (205) 573 2225
Leaflet, $1 U.S. and overseas. MC, V.
This is what the manager, Estelle Witherspoon, says about this cooperative composed of black women: "The Quilting Bee started in 1965, immediately after the Selma Freedom marches. A civil rights worker saw beautiful quilts on the lines in rural areas and suggested that the people sew quilts for marketing. A small business was started, it grew, a larger sewing center was built. Presently we have about twenty women working daily. We do a mail-order business and also sell quilts through a representative in New York. Our sewing ladies have used their salary (small) to improve their homes and improve the family's standard of living . . . the Bee has been the means of much improvement in this poverty area of Alabama. We are still poor people."
The quilts are made in five designs that come from a 140-year tradition in Alabama's Black Belt area. They are made in all basic colors and you can choose the main color you'd like. Prices: $235 for a single, $260 for double and $340 for king-size.

4

5

Golden Ram, P.O. Box 246, Christiansburg, VA 24073. Telephone (703) 382 0049
12-page catalogue, $2 U.S. and overseas.
Handwoven bedspreads in American eighteenth-century Colonial overshot patterns. Your own colors can be matched, and hand-spun, hand-dyed yarns can be used.

Pembroke Squares, 8 Pembroke Square, London W8 6PA, England
Brochure, $1.
Pembroke squares has revived the English country craft of crochet bedspreads, which, they say, were popular with Victorian brides. The authentic Victorian designs have been gathered from all over England and are made up in white or beige machine-washable cotton, which dyes well. They can also be made in a huge range of colored wools and in any size to order. Prices about $170 to $330, but then the spreads are instant heirlooms.

Sunshine Lane, Box 262 C, Millersburg, OH 44654
Color brochure, $1; overseas $2. One color photo, $5 (refundable); book of sixty color photos, $35 (refundable). MC, V.
Handmade quilts in traditional patterns. The catalogue shows about fifteen designs, but quilts can also be made in any color, size, and design that you choose, or copied from a sketch or a picture.

COMFORTERS

If you use a European-style comforter instead of blankets (like the Germans and Scandinavians) you can more or less avoid bedmaking, as the comforter just needs shaking and spreading. Down is better than feather filling, it is warmer for the weight, and longer-lasting than feathers. The comforter should be bought large, with a good overhang to stop cold air creeping in, and should have interior (baffle) walls, to prevent the down from bunching. There should *not* be sewn-through stitching to keep down in place because this will create colder patches along the seams. These comforters are used inside sheets (rather like a large pillow case), and down and feather comforters should be washed absolutely as rarely as you can bear (and not dry-cleaned).

If you have been tempted by the idea of comforters, but put off by the high price, you will be pleased to hear that down sleeping bag manufacturer Jack Stephenson (see backpacking section), who knows a lot about insulation, thinks that manmade Polarguard works just as well as down for comforters. The good lightness/warmth ratio, and the ability of down to spring back after being tightly packed, are not crucial on a bed. On the other hand, the fact that Polarguard does not bunch up, and can be machine-washed, are advantages. Jack Stephenson also suggests two light comforters, rather than one, so that one can be taken off in warmer weather. *Country Ways* has a very cheap and easy kit to make a Polarguard comforter; *Eastern Mountain Sports* and *Recreational Equipment* have comforters with manmade Hollofil (good too, only it bunches, unlike Polarguard). Sears also has very large selection of comforters at much lower prices yet of comparable weight and warmth.

Country Ways, 15235 Minnetonka Boulevard, Minnetonka, MN 55343. Telephone (612) 935 0022
Catalogue, free U.S. and overseas. MC, V.
Kits to make snow-shoe furniture, window blinds, outdoor clothing, country musical instruments, and even a small wooden sailing boat. But the easiest kit of all, and it is really

4 *Pembroke Squares* Hand-crocheted bedspreads copied from Victorian designs start at about $150.

5 *Feathered Friends* European down comforter in a case can be used without sheets and blankets to simplify bed making. Prices start at $259 for twin-bed size.

easy, is the Polarguard comforter, which costs a mere $30 for a king-size, if you provide your own fabric.

Feathered Friends, 155 Western Avenue, W. Seattle, WA 98119. Telephone (800) 426 2724 or (206) 282 5673
16-page color catalogue, $1 U.S. and overseas.
Down comforters, pillows and pure cotton sheets. Everything is expensive, but the catalogue is a good one which tells you exactly what you are getting.

Scandia Down, 1011 Madison Avenue, New York, NY 10021. Telephone (212) 734 8787
Brochure, free; overseas $1, overseas air mail $2. AE, MC, V.
Scandia Down is a large firm which sells professionally made down comforters, in five sizes including bunk-size. Scandia Down makes covers from various brightly colored famous-brand sheets, and also sells bottom sheets and pillowcases to match (though they do not, unfortunately, sell fitted bunk-size sheets).

For kits to make your own comforters, see Frostline in the Sports Equipment and Clothes section.

J. Schachter Corporation, 115 Allen Street, New York, NY 10002. Telephone (212) 533 1150
Catalogue and swatches, $1. Prices given by mail or telephone, U.S. and overseas. MC, V.
Schachter sells bed and bath linen at a discount (Martex, Dan River, Spring Mills, Stevens, St. Moritz, Wamsutta) including linen designed by Calvin Klein and Marimekko. But Schachter is best known for its custom-made comforters in down (even rare and expensive eiderdown from the eiderduck; feathers; synthetic fiber; or lambswool). Comforters can be made to any size, and any way you want and so can pillows. Schachter also remakes and re-covers customer's own comforters.

DISCOUNT
Please see discount information in the How to Buy section.

Eldridge Textiles, Harris Levy and *Rubin and Green* (Linen section) all sell Northern Feather comforters at a discount (when I compared prices, their prices were 30 to 40 percent below the prices charged for the same comforters by the New York department stores).

LINEN

F. Braun and Company, 717 Madison Avenue, New York, NY 10021. Telephone (212) 838 0650
Brochure, free. Available January and August only. AE, DC, MC, V.
A luxury linen shop that stocks pure-cotton and flannel sheets, linen placemats, will fit sheets to any size bed, and monogram everything. The brochure is available in January and August only.

Limericks, (Linens), Limerick House, 117 Victoria Avenue, Southend on Sea, Essex SS2 6EL, England. Telephone 0702 43486
Color brochure, free. MC, V.
"Postal shopping for everything in the linen cupboard"—an excellent source for the thrifty and nimble-fingered. Limericks has a wide range of basics, including all-wool blankets by prestigious Early of Witney, at prices at least 25 percent below U.S. prices. Also all the materials for making your own towels, sheets, and down comforters.

Moselys, 738 Lincoln Road Mall, Miami Beach, FL 33139. Telephone (305) 538 3637
Color catalogue, free. AE, DC, MC, V.
Forties glamour for the bed and bath: satin comforters appliquéd pillows and monogrammed everything.

Porthault, 57 East 57th Street, New York, NY 10022. Telephone (212) 688 1660
Color catalogue, $2.50. AE, MC, V.
Very famous for its flowery sheets, actually made by Porthault, which are loved by the rich and the grand (and available in cotton, cotton voile, linen and silk), this French firm also makes night gowns and dressing gowns, matching bathrobes and towels, and posh table linens. *Extremely* expensive.

Pratesi, 829 Madison Avenue, New York, NY 10021. Telephone (212) 288 2315
8-page color brochure, $2 U.S. and overseas. AE, MC, V.
Exquisite and also *extremely* expensive sheets and towels, and less exquisite table linens made by Pratesi in Italy. White sheets with lilac lace borders, beige silk with silk lace, or less romantic, more tailored, plain sheets with embroidered raised satin stripes are among the prettiest and all have comforters to match. Pratesi has unusual pewter colored towels and bathrobes with fine gray stripes.

Scintilla Satin Shop, 4802 North Broadway, Chicago, IL 69640. Telephone (312) 728 2590
Color brochure, free U.S. and overseas.
Acetate and polyester satin fashions for the bedroom, from black and purple sheets to monogrammed boxer shorts, you can add a lot of shine to your bedroom.

Lucy Stewart's Private Stock, 24 Union Wharf, Boston, MA 02109. Telephone (603) 523 4313
6-page color catalogue, $1; overseas $2. MC, V.
Cotton flannel sheets, all-wool blankets, and down pillows. Natural fibers only, for the bed in high quality and rather high prices.

The White House, 51–52 New Bond Street, London W1Y 0BY, England. Telephone (01) 629 3521
Occasional 20-page color catalogue, free. AE, V.
As a London *Times* journalist wrote recently: "If I ruled the world (and nanny ruled the ironing board) all children everywhere would be dressed at the White House." But the White House is not only for children. Embroidered sheets, pure-linen face towels, lace-trimmed handkerchief sachets are quite as popular with rich parents as the muslin nursery sets. And the problem for the seventy-five-year-old shop is not finding customers, but finding goods of high-enough quality—the work and demanding standards are not popular with young needlecraft apprentices, so many goods are imported from Belgium, France and Switzerland.

6 *Laura Ashley* Tiny prints on pure cotton fabrics in soft colors are available by the yard or on bedspreads, curtains, tablecloths, and smaller things for the house.

7 *Hippo Hall* Matching sheets, fabrics, and wallpapers are available in these and other designs for children.

8 *David Mellor* Child's set for ages three to ten. Stainless steel with acetal resin handles in red, yellow, black, or cream. Dishwasher safe. Priced about $15.

DISCOUNT
Please see discount information in the How to Buy section.

There is no need to wait for white sales, all these stores sell brand-name sheets and towels at a discount all year around. I have often compared prices, and I have found the discounts steady. Recently, for instance, Macy's was having a sale on Fieldcrest Royal Velvet towels, and charging $11.50 for the bath size (their regular price is $13.50); at the same time, these stores were charging $9.50 for the same towels, same size. I always buy here.

Eldridge Textile Company, 277 Grand Street, New York, NY 10002. Telephone (212) 925 1523
No catalogue, gives specific prices by mail.
Sheets (and towels if made), by Burlington, Fieldcrest, Martex, J. P. Stevens, Wamsutta. Including designs by Bill Blass, Christian Dior, Grace Kelly, Jordache, Calvin Klein, Mary McFadden, Vera and others. Established 1939.

Franco Textile Company, 294 Grand Street, New York, NY 10002. Telephone (212) 226 9413 and (212) 226 3370
No catalogue, prices given by mail U.S. and overseas or telephone (3:00 to 5:30 P.M. best time, Sunday through Thursday only). AE, MC, V.
Sheets (and towels if made) by Cannon, Fieldcrest, Martex, Springmaid, Wamsutta. Including designs by Bassetti, Bill Blass, Mary McFadden, and Marimekko. Comforters. Established 1965.

Homework Design Corporation, 281 Grand Street, New York, NY 10002. Telephone (212) 226 4644
No catalogue, specific prices given by mail and telephone (Monday to Friday 9:00 A.M. to 5:00 P.M.). AE, MC, V.
Sheets (and towels if made) by Cannon, Martex, Jakson, J. P. Stevens, Wamsutta. Including designs by Bill Blass, Angelo Donghia, Christian Dior, Calvin Klein, Marimekko, Yves St. Laurent. Comforters, bathroom accessories, shower curtains and rugs also sold. Established 1980.

Harris Levy, 278 Grand Street, New York, NY 10002. Telephone (212) 226 3102
No catalogue, specific prices given U.S. and overseas by mail and telephone (Monday to Friday, 9:00 A.M. to 5:00 P.M.). AE, MC, V.
Sheets (and towels if made) by Burlington, Fieldcrest, Dan River, Springmaid, J. P. Stevens, Wamsutta. Also sheets for children, imported sheets, blankets, comforters, bedspreads and curtains. Monogramming service. Established 1894.

Rubin and Green, 290 Grand Street, New York, NY 10002. Telephone (212) 226 0313
No catalogue. Send self addressed stamped envelope for specific prices by mail.
Sheets (and towels if made) by Cannon, Martex, Dan River, Springmaid, Wamsutta. Sheets and comforters can be made in any size to order. Established 1945.

Curtains and Cloths

Laura Ashley, Department 41, C.S.B. 5308, Melville, New York 11747. Telephone (800) 526 6383
Annual subscription to catalogue and several brochures, $3. AE, MC, V.
If you stumble upon one of Laura Ashley's small shops, you may think you've made a personal discovery of an exclusive

boutique. In fact this chain of over eighty small shops has been around for over twenty years, and immensely popular for most of that time. The distinctive Ashley look of natural fabrics, tiny Victorian prints, gathers and tucks and dusty subtle colors was first manifest in a line of clothes, which immediately became a craze with young English women. Now it has spread to charming things for the house: cozy sprigged lampshades; flowery cotton tablecloths; fabric-covered address books; bouquet-covered dinner ware; quilted bedspreads; tiles and wallpaper and made-to-measure curtains. If you want to introduce some sweetness into your decorative schemes, you'll find plenty here, in colors such as lavender, terra-cotta, sage green and burgundy.

Canadiana Curtains, 205 Dunlop Street East, Barrie, Ontario, Canada L4M 1B2. Telephone (705) 737 3940
Brochure with swatches, free U.S. and overseas. V.
Fringed, ruffled, lace or plain—traditional curtains in standard or made-to-measure sizes, with tablecloths, lampshades, duvet covers to match. All in solid colors or simple squares.

Clothcrafters, Elkhart Lake, WI 53020. Telephone (414) 876 2112
Leaflet, free U.S. and overseas.
This small company started out making filter cloths for the Wisconsin cheesemakers in 1936. In 1978 they added some pure-cotton products for the house, such as white shower curtains and chef's aprons, real-cotton cheesecloth, and seamed flannel sheets that are half or one third of the price of the imported ones sold by Lucy Stewart and others.

Constance Carol, P.O. Box 899, Plymouth, MA 02360. Telephone (800) 343 5921
32-page catalogue, free, MC, V.
Swatches, $4.
Tab curtains, which Constance Carol says are the most authentic and appropriate curtains for Early American homes, are the specialty here. There are many different fabrics, but the look is generally simple and tailored. Wooden and wrought-iron rods for hanging the curtains are also sold, and ingenious curtain cranes, which take the curtain back against the wall.

Country Curtains at the Red Lion Inn, Department CC, Stockbridge, MA 01262. Telephone (413) 298 3921
Brochure, free.
This popular, twenty-five-year-old firm makes a nice variety of "country" style curtains, in standard sizes only. Ruffled or tailored, in unbleached cotton, gingham, flower-sprigged, or even hand-stenciled permanent press. Plenty to choose from.

Hippo Hall, 65 Pimlico Road, London SW1, England. Telephone (01) 730 5532
Color brochure, $2.
An exceptional firm that makes matching bed-linen fabric and wallpaper for children. Designs include active animals in interesting scenes: frogs, mice, rabbits, elephants and hippos; hearts; balloons and lollipops; football players and airplanes; and an amusing animal alphabet. Fabric is $15 to $25 per meter (one yard, three inches).

Just Gingham Etc., 44 Pimlico Road, London SW1, England. Telephone (01) 730 2588
Color leaflet, $3. AE, V.
Cover everything: toaster, bread basket, ironing board, lamp, clothes-hanger and tissue box with gingham and Broderie Anglaise or all-white Anglaise. Just Gingham makes fresh and pretty things for the house in sixteen shades of checked gingham.

Kainuun Pirtti Oy, Varastokatu 2, 87100 Kajaani 10, Finland. Telephone 986 38800
Color catalogue, $3.50 (air mail).
For the sauna, handwoven towels and slippers in natural linen and beautifully colored stripes; for the house, handwoven tablecloths, travel rugs and "Raanus" striped tapestries which are inspired by folk art and can be used as bedspreads. None of these typical Finnish handwoven things are easily available outside Finland.

Puckihuddle Products, Oliverea, NY 12462. Telephone (914) 254 5553
24-page color catalogue, $1; overseas $1.50; air mail $2.50. AE, MC, V.
Old-fashioned country charm for the house. Patchwork, lace, and quilting on bedspreads, pillows, tablecloths and accessories. An outstanding collection, recommended by Carol Campion, a reader.

Flatware and Silver

Graham Jackson, 48 Beauchamp Place, London SW3 1NX, England. Telephone (01) 584 9128
Leaflet, free. MC, V.
Silver-plated flatware from Sheffield in two qualities, both of which can be washed in the dish washer. Pieces can be bought individually or in sets and prices start at about $25 for a five-piece place setting.

David Mellor, 4 Sloane Square, London SW1W 8EE, England. Telephone (01) 730 4259
Catalogue, $1; air mail $4.
David Mellor, Sheffield silversmith, cutler and designer, has a complete kitchen shop in London. By mail he sells the good-looking modern flatware he has designed and made. Patterns include chunky "Provencal" in rosewood and stainless steel and hand-forged "Embassy" in sterling silver, which was originally commissioned for use in British embassies. Mellor says that the Sheffield Cook's knives, penknives, scissors and hunting knives, "all of superb quality," have proved to be of special interest to American mail-order customers.

Panken and Thorn, 207 East 84th Street, New York, NY 10028. Telephone (212) 249 8108
These appraisers, whose main business is appraising and buying estates, also sell used sterling silver. If you are looking for a few pieces or a complete set of used sterling flatware, let them know.

S. Samran Thailand Company, 302–308 Petchburi Road, G.P.O. Box 740, Bangkok, Thailand. Telephone 281 4539
10-page brochure, free; air mail $1. Prices in $.
Bronze tableware is a Thai craft that is very popular with tourists; it is a beautiful light gold color, but like silver, it must be polished. Samran is a leading maker. Complete sets of tableware, in teak wood chests, cost $60 for six-place settings, $75 for eight, and $165 for twelve. There are ten patterns, and handles may be plain bronze, decorative bronze with Thai "angels" on the ends, rosewood or buffalo horn (buffalo horn should not be machine-washed). Tea sets and bar sets also for sale; also sugar bowls and salt and

pepper shakers, fondue sets, candlesticks, bottle openers and lots of other little things at very reasonable prices.

DISCOUNT
Please check discount information in the How to Buy section.

Never buy sterling silver flatware without checking the prices at these stores, and don't allow your friends to either. This is one of the areas where manufacturer's suggested list prices have almost nothing to do with the prices usually charged. Even department stores which charge "list price" for almost everything, charge less than "manufacturers' suggested list prices." In 1981, the *New York Times* ran an article on silver prices, and found that Carl's House of Silver and Michael C. Fina (below) were selling a four-piece place setting of Groham's Chantilly sterling silver flatware for half the price that was being charged at a New York department store. I compared prices on four-piece place settings by Kirk-Steiff, Lunt, and Gorham, and found that you would save $100 *or more per place setting*, if you bought at these stores instead of at New York department stores.

Carl's House of Silver, 86 West Palisade Avenue, Englewood, NJ 07631. Telephone (201) 568 5990
Occasional catalogue, free.
This store sells sterling and silver plate by all the well-known manufacturers, and also gifts and some imported china. Produces occasional catalogues, and gives prices by mail and telephone in answer to specific requests. Established 1950.

Michael C. Fina, 580 Fifth Avenue, New York, NY 10036. Telephone (212) 869 5050
Catalogue, $2. AE, DC, MC, V.
This Fifth Avenue store (second floor) says they have the largest display of silver in New York. They sell sterling silver, silver plate, flatware and holloware; also china, watches, luggage, pens all by well known manufacturers. Most prices are said to be discount prices, and I checked the sterling silver flatware, which certainly was. Gift wrapping, and repairs. Established 1940.

Fortunoff, 681 Fifth Avenue, New York, NY 10022. Telephone (800) 223 2326 or (212) 758 6660
Occasional catalogues, free.
Fortunoff sells sterling silver holloware and flatware, silverplate and stainless-steel flatware, by all the leading manufacturers. They will give prices in answer to specific requests by mail or by telephone (Monday to Saturday 9:00 A.M. to 6:00 P.M., Sunday 12:00 P.M. to 5:00 P.M.). Established 1930.

Jean's Silversmiths, 16 West 45th Street, New York, NY 10036. Telephone (212) 575 0723
Send details for price by mail only.
This small and dusty-looking shop, sells all the leading brand-name sterling silver flatware and holloware, and says that they stock over a hundred current and discontinued patterns. If you want a discontinued pattern they don't have, they'll register your request on a file card and let you know when it comes in. They specialize in sterling silver, and stock both new and used. They give prices in answer to specific requests by mail but not by telephone. Established 1910.

See stores in Discount Glass and China section for discounts on Christofle and Jensen flatware.

Furniture

MODERN AND MISCELLANEOUS

Alpha Design Studio, 613 South 21st Avenue, Hollywood, Fl 33020. Telephone (305) 920 8999
16-page catalogue, $2.
Lots of acrylic: lamps galore, picture frames, desk sets, bud vases, candle holders and more. Acrylic furniture and objects can be made to your specifications.

Arise Futon Mattress Company, 37 Wooster Street, New York, NY 10013. Telephone (212) 295 0310
21-page color brochure, $2 U.S. and overseas. AE, MC, V.
Suddenly Japanese-inspired furnishings have appeared in the United States, and stores selling futon mattresses and furniture to go with them have proliferated. Futons, which have been used for hundreds of years in Japan, are not only an inexpensive and attractive way to furnish a home, but are also supposed to provide healthy support for the body during sleep.

Arise belongs to a sculptor, Art Weider, who says he introduced futons and Japanese quilts to America in the seventies. The firm sells, in strong solid colors, the cotton batting mattresses and pillows that can be combined in various ways to make beds, chairs and sofas. The traditional way is to put them straight on to the floor, but Art Weider has designed cubes and frames in clear- or color-lacquered wood that can be combined harmoniously with the futons, if you prefer Western furniture. Down comforters, meditation pillows, tatami mats and Shoji screens are also sold.

Bedlam Brass Beds, 19–21 Fair Lawn Avenue, Fair Lawn, NJ 07041. Telephone (201) 796 7200
Color catalogue, $3; overseas $4. Replacement parts, $1; overseas $1.25.
Mainly brass beds in traditional and modern designs but also coffee tables, end tables and mirrors in brass.

The Bedpost, 795 Bethel Road, Columbus, OH 43214. Telephone (614) 459 0088
Brochure, $1.95; overseas $2.50. MC, V.
The Bedpost people say they sell hundreds of styles of waterbed frames, and their leaflet shows a few of the most popular styles. If you have seen a frame elsewhere give them the name, or a picture and they'll give you a quote. Their beds cost $300 to $350 delivered anywhere in the continental United States and come complete with mattress, heater and everything you need.

J. & D. Brauner, 298 Bowery, New York, NY 10012. Telephone (212) 477 2830
50-page brochure, $2 U.S. and overseas. AE, MC, V.
Butcher block in all shapes and sizes is listed, as well as cutting boards and lazy Susans, shelves, storage cabinets, wheeled serving work carts and about twenty tables that nod at different styles. Expanding tables and chairs are also for sale, and there are a few newly added parquet tables. Butcher-block tops for kitchen counters can be made to order with cut-outs for sink and cooking top; minimum length, three feet.

Christopher Design, 1901 South Great Southwest Parkway, Suite 214, Grand Prairie, TX 75051. Telephone (214) 641 8850
Brochure, free.
A beautifully printed little brochure introduces a few pieces of willow furniture "outstanding examples of expert rustic

craftsmanship . . . crafted in exactly the same manner by successive generations." Prices start at $90 and go to $400 for a double chaise longue with a natural canvas seat cushion.

Conran's, 145 Hugenot Street, New Rochelle, NY 10801. Telephone (914) 632 0515
114-page color catalogue, $3. AE, MC, V.
The catalogue from this international chain of stores will be a godsend to anyone who likes modern design in the house, but doesn't want to spend too much money on it. Terence Conran, author of the popular *House Book,* opened his first London store in the sixties. He was the first person to successfully sell, not the glamour and drama of modern Italian and French design, but the homey look of an up-to-date country cottage. Favorite Conran materials are humble: pine, cotton, earthenware, rope and rush. Colors are bright, shapes are simple, and prices are low.

Even though similar furniture can now be found in other stores, the Conran catalogue is really useful because it has an attractive version of just about everything you need for the house from a toothbrush holder (pine or plastic) to a cupboard, including furniture, lights, lamps, linen, rugs and mats, paints, wall papers, fabrics and kitchen supplies.

Country Workshop, 95 Rome Street, Newark, NJ 07105. Telephone (201) 589 3407
16-page catalogue, $1; overseas $2.50. MC, V.
Country Workshop has been making modern ready-to-paint furniture and selling it by mail since 1950. The designs, although more graceful than much unfinished furniture, are unadventurous. You can get most basic pieces to furnish an apartment in either maple or walnut. Each piece comes in an enormous number of sizes, which can be combined in various ways. Inexpensive yet durable, the chests I bought here twenty years ago are still going strong.

Creations Drucker, 166 Rue Gerard de Seroux, 60320 Bethisy St. Pierre, France
Color leaflet, free. Prices in $.
If you feel nostalgic for bygone days in French cafeterias, or have an eye for the odd, you might like the Drucker terrace furniture. The mixed rattan chairs (for dining not reclining) are not often seen around these days. Prices mainly around $200 each, with an extra 20 percent for insurance and transportation to New York.

Deutsch, 196 Lexington Avenue, New York, NY 10016. Telephone (212) 683 8746
72-page catalogue, $2.
This firm imports a big selection of sophisticated but expensive rattan furniture. There are beds, sofas, chests of drawers, tables, swings, bar carts and mirror frames in enough different styles to please people who want sparse, modern shapes, as well as those who want curly Victorian ones. This is the place for a canopy bed, a rickshaw or a gazebo.

H.U.D.D.L.E., 3416 Wesley Street, Culver City, CA 90230. Telephone (213) 836 8001
Catalogue, $2. MC, V.
Jim and Penny Hull, who started H.U.D.D.L.E., wanted to rethink furniture for city living, avoid waste and keep prices down. Their early furniture was made from recycled products. Now there is less talk of recycling, but the furniture is still more colorful, more imaginative and cheaper than most.

Much of the furniture is for children; there is a baby bed that converts to a single bed, and several bunks, which can be arranged in different space-saving combinations, including bed above and a desk and a chest of drawers below. For

9

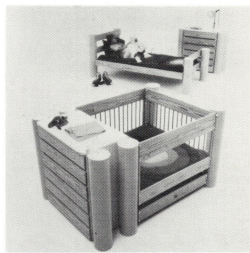

10

11

9 *Arise Futon Mattress Company* Futon mattress used as a sofa. Priced about $91 to $150, depending on stuffing. Ash coffee table about $159.

10 *H.U.D.D.L.E.* Toobline baby bed with dresser, $698. The crib converts into a twin bed.

11 *H.U.D.D.L.E.* "Art Gym." One piece that can be used as an easel, a slide, or a puppet theater. About $139.

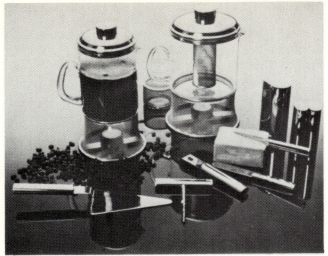

12

13

14

12 *Illums Bolighus* Tea and coffeepots designed by Signe Person-Melin for Boda Nova. Also sugar shaker, salt and pepper shakers, butter knife, bottle opener, and cake knife.

13 *Lyon Hammocks* Pure cotton hammocks in rainbow shades from Yucatan. Priced $53 to $90.

14 *3 Falke Mobler* Bar cabinet 8068 in oak, teak, or rosewood. Prices start at about $970 in teak (without the refrigerator).

the rest of the house, there are shiny silver plant holders; brightly colored fabrics in big, bold designs; sleek, prize-winning bathroom towel rails; and a huddle couch: a sort of conversation pit cum bed, for a more relaxed life-style. "It will change the way you sit, change the way you sleep, maybe even the way you live."

Ikea, 1224 Dundas Street East, Mississauga, Ontario, Canada L4Y 2C1. Telephone (416) 279 9331
Ikea, 4351A No. 3 Road, Richmond, B.C., Canada V6X 2C3. Telephone (604) 273 2051
100-page color catalogue, free.
Friends of mine furnished an entire summer cottage in Maine by mail from Ikea in Sweden. They are delighted with their goodies and have joined the Swedes and non-Swedes who have *fervently* recommended this store to me. Apparently this now-enormous enterprise was started by a man who wanted to make very inexpensive, very good furniture. He managed it with spectacular success, and the big plant and shop outside Stockholm have become a favorite weekend excursion goal—people drive out, dump their children in the Ikea nurseries, eat in the Ikea restaurant, wander around looking at the chair and carpet torturing machines (everything is tested to see how it will stand up), buy something, and drive home with it strapped on top of the car.

Ikea now has branches in Canada and publishes an English-language catalogue with prices in Canadian dollars, so it is much easier for Americans to order. There is furniture for every room, including plenty for children's rooms, natural wood kitchen cabinets, wooden bed frames and pure cotton sheets, colorful window shades and wallpaper and unusual smaller things in pine, such as a medicine cabinet with a lock, planters, cassette racks, vanity mirrors and shelves. A good source for people who want inexpensive modern furniture.

Illums Bolighus, Amagertov 10, Copenhagen, DK 1160, Denmark
64-page color catalogue $5 (air mail).
Illums Bolighus is known throughout the world for the most comprehensive collection of modern Scandinavian Design, and its open store is a brilliant modern version of the old turn-of-the-century department store design.

Much of Illums's business is now done overseas, and I was told when I visited them that they have a flourishing trade even in Russia, where they are called on to furnish whole buildings of offices rented there by foreigners. The catalogue is, I'm sorry to say, aimed at people who want to furnish a whole building, and is strong on conference tables. However, there is a sampling of rosewood dining tables, leather chairs, lamps, flatware, china and rugs besides a page of Bjorn Wiinblad's whimsical pottery, which does make the catalogue a worthwhile investment for Swedish design lovers.

Isabel Brass Furniture, 120 East 32nd Street, New York, NY 10016. Telephone (800) 221 8523
Color catalogue, $4; overseas $5. AE, MC, V.
Isabel claims to be the only brass-bed factory that sells by mail nationally. Brass frames are made in all sorts of styles from "single sleigh," which, with cushions, can be used as sofas, to four posters. You can buy just the bed head to attach to your own iron frame, or the whole thing.

Leathercrafter, 303 East 51st Street, New York, NY 10022. Telephone (212) 759 1955
32-page leather-chair brochure, $1. MC, V.
About thirty leather chairs are shown in this little brochure.

Almost all the designs are based on well-known shapes—the director's chair, the butterfly chair, the officer's chair, many of them for between $75 and $175. Others are outright copies of the classic modern chairs by famous designers, often at less than half the price of the originals.

Lyon Hammocks, 41 Galen Street, Watertown, MA 02172. Telephone (617) 923 2261
Leaflet, 25 cents; overseas $1. AE, MC, V.
Hammocks don't have to be just for lying in and reading under a tree, you can use them for sitting, and even sleeping in, inside the house too. Lyon imports cotton hammocks from the Yucatan in beautiful rainbow shades, or various colors with white.

Murphy Door Bed Company, 40 East 34th Street, New York, NY 10016. Telephone (212) 682-8936
Leaflets, 50 cents.
The Murphy Door Bed Company is alive and well and still selling Murphy beds by mail. Their beds, which space-savingly fold up flat against the wall with the bed made up, cost from $193 without the mattress, and any mattress can be used. On to that price you must add the cost of building a closet, if you want a disguise.

Natural Selection, P.O. Box 303, Stevens Point, WI 54481
34-page color catalogue, free. MC, V.
Natural Selection, a division of Herrschners, a subsidiary of Quaker Oats, sells modern furniture that is "multifunctional and affordable"—tables fold, sofas turn into beds, and file cabinets can be used as end tables. Some of the pieces arrive knocked-down, and prices are generally low.

Plexi-Craft Quality Products, 514 West 24th Street, New York, NY 10011. Telephone (212) 924 3244
Catalogue, $2.
Lots for the house in clear Plexiglass: tissue boxes and trays to telephone caddys, plant stands and dining tables. Custom orders a specialty.

Scan Co-op Contemporary Furnishings, 8406 Greenwood Place, Corridor Industrial Park, Savage, MD 20763. Telephone (301) 953 2050 X 224 or 225
Occasional leaflets, free.
Scan was recommended to me by a friend who bought a leather couch there several years ago, and said that Scan's prices were so much lower than other stores' that it made you mad (at the other stores). I haven't been able to compare prices because I haven't seen the same pieces elsewhere, but Scan's are certainly moderate.

The firm is a twenty-two-year-old member owned co-op, which buys in bulk, spends less than is usual on advertising, and says that they regularly check prices in other stores and sell at 20 to 30 percent lower prices.

Designs are mainly what we think of as contemporary Scandinavian, in teak, rosewood and walnut, but there are still newer chrome and painted wood pieces. Every piece of furniture needed in a house is stocked, but it is not all shown on the occasional flyers that are published.

Shinera, P.O. Box 528, Dept 1F, Boston, MA 02102. Telephone (800) 343 2997
24-page color catalogue $2.50; overseas $3.50. AE, MC, V.
Quiet simplicity and beauty, says Shinera, have long been recognized in the Orient as essential elements in furnishing. Cotton is now being recognized by the furniture industry to provide cool breathability in the heat, and insulation against cold. Shinera makes all cotton Japanese-inspired futons and floor cushions and provides comforters and pure cotton sheets. There are also low cherrywood tables, stools, aper-screens and lights—to help make the home into the restful, nurturing, aesthetic refuge from everyday pressures that Shinera believes it should be. Covering fabrics come in beautiful solid colors, and elegant Japanese flower designs. Prices are low, and Shinera's approach looks like a good one for the agile and impecunious.

3 Falke Mobler, Falkonercentret, DK-2000, Copenhagen F, Denmark. Telephone 01 87 30 30
Catalogue, $20 (refundable); leaflets, free.
This large firm (which has furnished the General Time Corporation building in Stamford besides several hotels around the world) has its own workshops and makes a wide range of furniture all in "Danish Modern" styles. Some of this is shown in the catalogue.

Mr. Ole Faarup, the president of the firm, says that they also stock furniture by famous Danish architects such as Hans Wegner and Arne Jacobson, which is hard to find in the United States. They also stock furniture by the leading Italian firms B & B, Cassina, Saporiti, and by Knoll, generally only available through designers in the United States. Mr. Faarup says that Americans can save by buying furniture from these manufacturers from 3 Falke Mobler. I tried to compare prices on Knoll just when prices were going up and got the impression that the furniture was about half New York price including shipping to New York, if bought from 3 Falke Mobler. *Well* worth looking in to, but *please* do your own price comparisons.

Twinoaks Hammocks, Route 4, Box 169, Louisa, VA 23093. Telephone (703) 894 5125
Leaflet, free. MC, V.
Ropelike (actually propylene) hammocks and hanging chairs are handwoven in the traditional Southern way by Twinoaks; a backpack's hammock costs only about $14. The sale of hammocks supports two kibbutzlike communities inspired by B. F. Skinner's Utopian novel *Walden II*, and started in the sixties.

Vermont Tubbs, Forest Dale, VT 05745. Telephone (802) 247 3414
Color catalogue, free.
Vermont Tubbs, who make snow-shoes, also make furniture out of snow-shoe materials for inside and outside. The furniture was originally designed for camping and boating, but admirers of the light and portable pieces have been using them all over the place—pool, tennis court, children's room, beach house, etc.—according to Vermont Tubbs. The furniture, made from New England hardwoods and tanned rawhide, and finished with urethane, makes an interesting change from the usual porch furniture.

Charles Webb, 7 Thorndyke Street, Cambridge, MA 02138. Telephone (617) 491 2389
Catalogue, $2.
A good source for people who like well-designed and unobtrusively modern wood furniture. A group of twenty-five cabinetmakers make most basic furniture in white oak (with cherry and walnut on request) cribs, trundle beds, filing cabinets, several kinds of storage, tables and sofas with loose cushions. Charles Webb writes "the pieces are of exceptional durability . . . the design attempts to put (them) beyond the vagaries of taste."

The Workbench, 470 Park Avenue South, New York, NY 10016. Telephone (212) 481 5454
40-page color catalogue, $2.
The Workbench has the largest store on the East Coast devoted to modern furniture, and they sell solid, inexpensive things, much of it in Scandinavian-inspired styles made of teak and oak. If you are tired of those woods, look at the butcher-block desks, glass-and-chrome dining tables, and bentwood and Italian cane chairs.

Bill and Jenny Young, R.D. 2, Chester Springs, PA 19425
Leaflet, $1 U.S. and overseas; overseas air mail $2.
Bill and Jenny Young design and make colorful and amazing beds for children. There are bunkbeds disguised as double-decker buses, doll houses, or Pennyslvania Dutch barns; and singles as cars, boats or fire engines. Although the beds have been written about all over the place, they are available only by mail from the Youngs. Prices between $525 and $750.

REPRODUCTION FURNITURE

Ashley Furniture Workshops, 3a Dawson Place, London W 2, England. Telephone (01) 289 1731
12-page color catalogue, $1; air mail $2. Prices in $.
Excellent handmade leather furniture, the popular Chesterfield sofa and all sorts of interesting reproductions such as hooded hall porter's chairs, sedan chairs, the Winfield steel and leather rocker and a folding campaign chair. *New York Magazine* and *The Old House Journal* furnished offices here, and I bought a Chesterfield by mail myself. I found the firm reliable, and experienced in export. Chesterfields now cost about $2300 landed in the United States.

Biggs Mail Order Department, 105 East Grace Street, Richmond, VA 23219. Telephone (804) 644 2891
80-page catalogue, $5.
This two-hundred-year-old firm makes a complete range of reproduction eighteenth-century furniture in solid mahogany including upholstered pieces and beds. They have exclusive reproductions from Independence, National Historical Park, Thomas Jefferson Memorial Foundation and Old Sturbridge Village. Styles include simpler Queen Anne from the early part of the century, more elaborate carved Chippendale, and then lighter inlaid and veneered Hepplewhite and Sheraton from the later part of the century.

Cathay Arts Company, P.O. Box 95801, TST, Kowloon, Hong Kong. Telephone 3 666 193
48-page catalogue with some color, free; air mail $3. Color leaflet, free (air mail).
This firm sells both wholesale and retail, and publishes a magnificent catalogue with photographs, many in color, of a wide range of teak and rosewood Oriental furniture "for those who appreciate the finest." There is furniture for every room, and some of it is very splendid. Besides sets for living and dining rooms as well as bedrooms, there are bars, hi-fi cabinets, silver chests, ottomans, serving trays, screens and planters. Sizes range from little jewelry boxes (in nineteen different designs) to enormous display cabinets with lighting and scenic inlay decorations. Reader Sandra Harada says that she ordered carved Rosewood furniture from Cathay and had to wait eight months for delivery, but the furniture is beautiful.

15 *3 Falke Mobler* Italian "De Sede" three-seat sofa in leather, $2591.

16 *3 Falke Mobler* "Dux" natural wicker chair with white cotton cushions, $663; ottoman to match, $275.

Classic Garden Furniture, Audley Avenue, Newport, Shropshire, England. Telephone 0952 813 311
Catalogue, $6 (air mail).
This small factory makes cast-iron furniture with methods that haven't changed for over a hundred years. There are charming Victorian-style conservatory chairs and "girl's head" pub tables, but perhaps more suitable for export are bramble bench ends ($90)—you supply the wood slats; the "boy and snake" umbrella stand; Punch and Judy door stops; or the Lion and Unicorn footscrapers. A very good selection of iron fireplace accessories.

Craft House, Williamsburg, VA 23185. Telephone (804) 229 1000
200-page catalogue, some color, $8.95; overseas (surface) $11. AE, MC, V.
In 1926 John D. Rockefeller, Jr., set up a nonprofit foundation to preserve the historic buildings and a large part of the Colonial capital of Virginia. By the 1930s so many visitors had asked where they could buy accurate reproductions of the eighteenth-century furniture on display that the Foundation decided to start a program of reproducing appropriate pieces, and made arrangements with manufacturers in several fields.

The large and educational catalogue will fascinate anyone interested in antiques or reproduction furniture and interiors. It contains not only pictures of the multitude of reproductions but also background information on the originals, a history of eighteenth-century furniture and decoration, and also of Williamsburg. Cotton, linen, silk and damask fabrics and wallpaper are also sold. Lights, mirrors, fireplace accessories, candle holders, and a good collection of china and pottery and glass from primitive tavern glasses and wine bottles to elegant air-twist stemware. There is pewter and silver, and for any one who would just like inexpensive knickknacks, a section called a "Potpourri of Gifts" lists brass trivets and door stops, decorated tiles, party invitations and note cards.

Cornucupia, Mail Order Center, P.O. Box 44, Westcott Road, Harvard, MA 01451–0044. Telephone (617) 456 3201
Brochure, $2; overseas $3. MC, V.
A nice informative brochure illustrates largely handmade Colonial furniture: two tables, two hutches and a lot of Windsor chairs. The pine and cherry furniture is oiled and waxed (you can save 10 percent by doing this yourself); the pine can be stained to match a sample you send, but the Corrys won't touch the cherry as they say there is an "especially warm corner reserved in hell for people who stain that lovely wood."

Gerald Curry, Pound Hill Road, Union, ME 04862. Telephone (207) 785 4633
12-page catalogue, $2 U.S. and overseas; air mail $4.
Lone cabinetmaker Gerald Curry's catalogue shows chairs and beautiful chests authentically reproduced from quality eighteenth-century American originals. Mainly Chippendale, in French polished solid mahogany at prices between $400 and $2500. He likes custom work too for other furniture which he does at similar prices.

Martin Dodge, Southgate, Wincanton, Somerset, BA9 9EB, England. Telephone (0963) 323 88
38-page color catalogue, $5; air mail $10.
Martin Dodge, a third-generation cabinetmaker, started his business with the idea of making the "finest in English furniture, made to traditional master standards from selected

17

18

17 *Bill and Jenny Young* Racing car bed, about $525.

18 *Ashley Furniture Workshops* Seven-foot-long Chesterfield sofa with button seat. Available in different leathers and with chairs to match. Priced about $2300 landed in the United States.

19 *Fortune Arts and Furniture* Hand-carved soapstone inlaid screen. Coromandel, lacquer, and soapstone screens are available, prices start at about $180.

20 *Orleans Carpenter* Swing-handle, oil-rubbed cherry wood boxes. Copies of boxes made by Shakers from the end of the eighteenth century until 1955. Priced about $24 to $30.

21 *The Bartley Collection* Butler tray table with eleven-piece top. Kit about $279.

materials by authentic methods." The methods aren't totally authentic, as advanced adhesive and machining techniques are used, but this is one of the few places where you can get high-quality solid mahogany furniture in the most luxurious styles of the past. Adam, Chippendale, Regency and Sheraton are represented, and there are intricately inlaid, and painted Regency pieces. Chairs mainly $250 to $400, tables $200 to $1500.

Fortune Arts and Furniture, 159 Ocean Terminal, P.O. Box 9606, TST Kowloon, Hong Kong. Telephone 3 721 6066
80-page color catalogue, $2; air mail $5. All major credit cards accepted. Prices in $.
A clear, fully illustrated catalogue shows a good range of Chinese furniture from traditionally constructed Siamese rosewood pieces, to intricate soapstone and mother-of-pearl inlaid, hand-decorated and coromandel pieces. There are small boxes, reproduction antique porcelain, and many screens. Prices are far lower than similar furniture bought here, so this is an outstanding source for people interested in Chinese furniture.

Fundação Ricardo do Espirito Santo Silva, Largo das Portas do Sol 2, Lisbon 2, Portugal
Photographs on request, free.
This unique museum and school of decorative arts was founded by a Portuguese banker who was anxious to keep alive the arts rapidly being taken over by machinery. In twenty-three workshops, experienced craftsmen and trainees rigorously copy furniture—using the original techniques—in the purest styles and periods of the past, mainly French. A bookbinding department reproduces bindings from the sixteenth-century to the Romantic period—the Fundação was completely responsible for restoring Madame du Barry's library at Versailles.

As for prices—the Rockefellers, the Rothschilds and the palaces of Fontainebleau and Versailles shop here. If that doesn't put you off, write and tell them what kind of things you are interested in and the Fundação will give you information that "falls upon those."

Guild of Shaker Crafts, 401 West Savidge Street, Spring Lake, MI 49456. Telephone (207) 785 4633
Catalogue, $2.50.
Guild of Shaker Crafts was started by the Shaker authority Mrs. Edward Deming (Faith) Andrews, who, with local craftsmen, started making careful copies of specific pieces of Shaker furniture. This catalogue and the furniture, accessories and sewn goods all have an extremely appealing "modest plainness."

Tables cost between $450 and $950, stools $50 and $300. Much of the catalogue is devoted to smaller accessories, candle stands, a candle box, a mirror, a towel rack, a spool chest, a sewing table, trays, oval boxes, picture frames (these can be made to order), handloomed throws, gardener's coats and ladies' smocks, a child's apron and bonnet.

A. Gargiulo & Jannuzzi, 80067, Sorrento, Naples, Italy. Telephone (081) 781 041
Color leaflet, free. Prices in $.
The oldest inlaid wood work factory in Sorrento has a color brochure of its amazingly intricate French style handmade furniture for those who "desire to obtain imitation antique furnishings that have been made with care and attention." Woods are rosewood, mahogany, walnut, briar. Prices for boxes, little tables, and chests including shipping costs are low, and they say, "There is no problem if you wish to

order by mail . . . as soon as the order is received, it shall be filled and sent."

Historic Charleston Reproductions, 105 Broad Street, Charleston, SC 29401. Telephone (803) 723 8292
56-page catalogue, $3.50; overseas $6. AE, MC.
The Historic Charleston Foundation, which since 1947 has been saving, preserving and restoring buildings in Charleston, South Carolina, has had various manufacturers reproduce furniture and decorative objects from private Charlestonian collections. Baker has reproduced eighteenth-century furniture, including decorated Adam, Hepplewhite, Sheraton, Regency, Directoire and Empire pieces that are a rarity in the United States. There are also lamps, fabrics and beautiful smaller things that would make lovely presents: pewter, china, seventeenth-century prints and needlepoint kits.

Charlotte Horstmann and Gerald Godfrey, 104 Ocean Terminal, Kowloon, Hong Kong. Telephone 3 677 167
Catalogue planned $3; air mail $5. AE, V.
Charlotte Horstmann, an antique porcelain specialist, and Gerald Godfrey, a jade specialist, opened an antique shop over twenty-five years ago. Since that time they have become leading decorators in Hong Kong and they have Ming-style rosewood furniture made to their own specifications. There is no catalogue in print as I write, although one is being planned, but I have seen an earlier catalogue of their new furniture, which was a model of simplicity and clarity.

Martha M. House, 1022 South Decatur Street, Montgomery, AL 36104. Telephone (205) 264 3558
42-page catalogue, some color $1; overseas $2; air mail $5. MC, V.
Martha House says that practically all the Victorian furniture being produced in the world today is being manufactured in Montgomery, where there are four large factories. Their large catalogue shows chairs, sofas, a few chests, small tables and a headboard based on the heavy ornate Victorian styles which, they say, were originally made for the stately mansions of the aristocratic South. The wood is solid mahogany, tables have wood or marble tops, and the upholstered pieces are covered in velvet, brocade, tapestry or brocatelle. Prices run from around $100 for footstools, plant stands and small coffee tables to around $900 for sofas.

Abelardo Linares S.A., Plaza de las Cortes II, Madrid 14, Spain
No catalogue.
This famous Spanish antique shop in the middle of Madrid makes such authentic-looking reproductions out of old dry walnut, oak and mahogany that one can't help wondering whether they are being passed off as genuine somewhere. (Linares says they have been supplying American dealers for many years.) Most of the pieces are large carved Spanish chests and tables, but perhaps of more general interest are the reproduction lanterns, a few of which are small enough to go by mail. There are also mirrors with ornate carved frames gilded in real gold leaf to be made in any size.

Majestic Furniture Company, Peninsula Hotel, Shopping Arcade BW2, Kowloon, Hong Kong. Telephone 666 544
Color leaflet, free. AE, V.
The Majestic Furniture Company shows a little of each kind of popular Chinese furniture in their color leaflet: simple teakwood chests and desks, heavily carved tables and

bars, inlaid screens and end tables. They will also custom-make furniture to your own specifications.

Thomas Moser, Cobb's Bridge Road, New Gloucester, ME 04260. Telephone (207) 926 4446
36-page catalogue, $3 U.S. and overseas. MC, V.
The Thomas Moser workshop produces handsome cherrywood furniture, each piece made by one man, in styles that have "moved towards the contemporary although our whole collection is still squarely rooted in Shaker and other traditional form." Traditional methods of joinery are used, rubbed oil and wax finish is used, pieces are never stained. Custom reproduction and modern furniture is also made.

Orleans Carpenter, Box 107-C, Rock Harbour Road, Orleans, MA 02653. Telephone (617) 255 2646
Brochure, 25 cents. MC, V.
Colonial and Shaker reproductions, mainly oil-rubbed, a trestle table, a hutch table, a cedar chest, a mirror and some round boxes and trays.

Victorian Reproductions, 1601 Park Avenue South, Minneapolis, MN 55404. Telephone (612) 338 3636
Furniture catalogue, $5; overseas $10.
Lighting catalogue, $5; overseas $10. MC, V.
Victorian furniture reproduced in Honduras mahogany, bathroom fixtures in hand-rubbed oak, and oddities such as Victorian solid-brass mechanical doorbells, decorative copper lightning rods, and cast-iron planters.

Yesterday's Yankee, Lover's Lane, Lakeville, CT 06039. Telephone (203) 435 9539
Brochure, self-addressed stamped envelope; overseas 1 International Reply Coupon.
"Reproductions of Yankee ingenuity" stained or painted pine furniture of humble origin, all very "American country." There are five tilt-top tables, two dressers, and a Connecticut chest. Any of the furniture can be monogrammed.

KITS

These firms sell furniture as kits, ready for you to assemble and finish yourself. There are great advantages to buying furniture as kits. Not only is it much less expensive than buying equivalent pieces readymade; also the furniture is well constructed, with mortise and tenon joints, and dovetailed drawers; and is delivered faster than much readymade furniture. To assemble the furniture, you need hammer and screwdriver, but no special tools, and intelligence but no experience. Notice that prices and appearance of the furniture depends partly on the kind of wood used.

The Bartley Collection, 747 Oakwood Avenue, Lake Forrest, IL 60045. Telephone (312) 634 9510
24-page color catalogue, free.
The Bartley Collection, generally considered a "top of the line" furniture-kit manufacturer, has been most flatteringly reviewed by *Workbench* magazine and others. The firm was started by Kenneth Bartley Boudrie who found that antique furniture was too expensive for him, and available reproductions were modified in design and flimsily constructed.

The Bartley eighteenth-century reproduction furniture is mostly copied from pieces in the Henry Ford Museum. It is made in solid cherry or Honduras mahogany, and is expensive. Prices about $100 to $1400 (and about double, sold assembled and finished), but the furniture can be put togeth-

22 *Cohasset Colonials* Four-poster canopy bed in maple and pine, with post turnings copying originals at the Yankee Peddler Inn, Holyoke, Massachusetts. Kit costs about $232 for twin size and $255 for queen size.

23 *Cohasset Colonials* Pumpkin pine hutch cabinet. Kit about $289.

er by novices, and when finished is of better quality than most ready-made furniture generally available.

Cohasset Colonials by Hagerty, 542HX Ship Street, Cohasset, MA 02025
32-page catalogue, $1; overseas $2. MC, V.
25 fabric samples, $5 (refundable).
A collection of kits for making seventeenth- and eighteenth century American furniture. Each piece has been exactly copied from an original in a museum or private collection, and there is an appealing range of graceful and simple pieces for every room: a fairly easy looking project is the Colonial mirror, $51, with the molding taken from an early-seventeenth-century courting mirror in the Wadsworth Atheneum; the kit contains single-shock silvered glass to give that hand-blown look, and also handwrought nails. The kits are of rock maple, and almost knot-free Eastern white pumpkin pine. They come sanded and ready to assemble with hardware, glue, sandpaper and stain.

You can also buy pewter reproductions of collector's items, and fabrics adapted from old designs.

Shaker Workshops, P.O. Box 1028, Concord, MA 01742. Telephone (617) 646 8985
15-page catalogue, 50 cents; overseas $2.
The Shaker Workshops was started in 1971 by three men, one of whom, a historian, had previously been buying and selling antique houses, and another of whom, an art historian, had been the curator of a Shaker village. The Workshops manufactures reproductions of specific pieces of Shaker furniture, both ready-made and in kits, and several pieces can be seen in Shaker museums and villages.

The furniture is, of course, beautiful, delicate and plain. The kits of maple and knotless pine (which cost about one third less than the finished pieces) contain all the materials needed. There is a trestle table at $310—benches, stools, rocking chairs and several smaller pieces, such as hanging shelves, mirrors, cupboards, candle holders, hurricane lamps and bowls.

The Western Reserve, Antique Furniture Kit, P.O. Box 206A, Bath, OH 44210
14-page brochure, $1.
A few pieces of furniture and more shelves, boxes, scoops and sconces in pine, poplar, maple, cherry or walnut. Everything is available finished and assembled, or as kits, hand-made and test assembled to order, sanded and ready to finish. Prices are very low. A few pieces are on sale in The Shaker Museum, Chatham, New York and Shaker Historical Society, Shaker Heights, Ohio.

Yield House, North Conway, NH 03860. Telephone (603) 356 3141
72-page color catalogue, $1. AE, MC, V.
Inexpensive kits to make Colonial and country-style furniture in knotty pine.

DISCOUNT
Please see discount information in the How to Buy section.

A great deal of money can be saved by buying American brand-name furniture through the stores that specialize in selling it at a discount. When I compared prices on a king-size Sealy Posturpedic mattress, I found that Jones was selling it at 43 percent below a New York department store's price and $151 below the store's *sale* price. Richard B. Zarbin was offering the same mattress at $103 below the store's sale price, freight *prepaid*. The problem is that these firms do not have catalogues, so you *must provide model number, and, when applicable, fabric number and grade.*

Jones Brothers, P.O. Box 991, Smithfield, NC 27577. Telephone (919) 934 4162
No catalogue, price information if you give model number.
When I wrote to Jones, they replied with a very helpful pro-forma invoice giving retail price, their own discount price and an estimated shipping price on the furniture I had asked about. Established 1946.

Mallory's, P.O. Box 1150, Jacksonville, NC 28540. Telephone (800) 334 1147
Leaflet, $1; overseas $2. Manufacturers brochures listed on leaflet.
Mallory's has an informative leaflet, listing the brand-name furniture they sell, giving delivery information, and offering for sale manufacturers' brochures with discount price lists. They sell furniture, lamps, accessories, Oriental carpets, bedding, bedspreads, and clocks. Established 1948.

James Roy Furniture Company, 15 East 32nd Street, New York, NY 10016. Telephone (212) 679 2565
Leaflet, free U.S. and overseas. AE, MC, V.
The James Roy leaflet only lists the almost two hundred brands of furniture and furnishings (including *all* brand-name carpets) on which a third off retail prices is guaranteed. If you write with a model number, you'll get a slow reply with a handwritten price and estimated delivery date. The price they gave me on the Sealy Posturpedic mattress was way below the New York department store's *sale* price. This firm has been mentioned several times in the media for its low prices. Established 1946.

Stuckey Brothers Furniture Company, Stuckey, SC 29554. Telephone (803) 558 2591
No catalogue, in answer to a model number (and model and grade of fabric if applicable) will give price U.S. and overseas. V.
Established 1930.

Richard B. Zarbin and Associates, 225 West Hubbard Street, Chicago, IL 60610. Telephone (312) 527 1570
In answer to a model number (and model and grade of fabric if applicable) Zarbin will send you the list price, and tell you what percent discount they give including prepaid freight.
Established 1969.

Glass and China

No one but a reckless spendthrift should buy imported expensive glass and china in America. Most of it sells for half the American prices in the country where it is made, so with little effort (but some patience) quite a lot of money can be saved.

The glass and china business seems to be one of the best organized foreign-mail-order activities; several of the shops say they have been at it for over twenty years. Goods are expertly packed, and on the rare occasions when something arrives broken, most of these shops will immediately replace the article simply on your say-so.

I compared prices recently on Wedgwood's "Turquoise Florentine" five-piece place setting, and found that Gered,

24

24 *Shaker Workshops* A faithful rock maple copy of the rocker made by the Mt. Lebanon Shakers. Kit costs about $125, assembled and finished about $268. Maple candlestand. Kit about $42.

25

26

27

London, was selling it for $100 less per place setting than Bloomingdale's New York, regular price, and $63 per place setting below Bloomingdale's sale price. Spode's "Christmas tree" three-piece buffet set was selling for $39.95 at Carl's House of Silver, New Jersey, and only $22.45 including shipping to the United States at the Reject China Shop in London.

Bennington Potters, 324 County Street, Bennington, VT 05201. Telephone (802) 447 7531
Color brochure, $1 U.S. and overseas.
Bennington Potters was started by David Gill after World War II. He didn't know, at the time, that Bennington pottery was also the name of the highly sought after stoneware produced in Bennington around 1800, and the name has caused numerous misunderstandings with visitors who turn up expecting wares in the old style.

The Gills make sleek, functional modern stoneware that is cast or molded, not thrown individually on a wheel, in four solid colors—white and three shades of brown. Complete dinner, tea and coffee services are made, casseroles, gourmet cookware (snail dishes, corn dishes and bread/pâté pans) and mugs in the same style complement the place settings.

China Pottery Arts Company, 11 Ta Tu Road, Peitou, Taipei, Taiwan. Telephone 891 5111
166-page color catalogue, $6. Prices in $.
The magnificently presented catalogue introduces China pottery with a trumpet blast: "Mr. K. C. Jen, for the purpose of reviving and developing Chinese culture, making human life more pleasant and colorful, and promoting the mutual comprehension of those particularly in favor of Chinese culture, founded this company on February 10, 1958." The introduction goes on to say that the company manufactures Chinese classical pottery reproductions of different dynasties and that the designs, glazes and colors are patterned after pottery, porcelain and bronze articles in local museums. Much of the catalogue shows dignified bases decorated with flowers or Chinese scenes at prices mostly between $20 and $100, but there are also functional pieces—punch bowls, tea sets, lamps, and elephant tables, and "all designs and colors can be changed to meet your preference."

Chinacraft, Parke House, 130 Barlby Road, London W10 6BW, England. Telephone (01) 960 2121
Catalogue planned, free. Specific prices on request.
Chinacraft is running low on catalogues, and is not sure when new ones will be out. However, I include them because they have the widest range of British glass and china, and are very experienced in mail order.

Fabrica Sant'Anna, Calcada da Boa Hora 96, Lisbon, Portugal
52-page catalogue in Portuguese, $5.
This large firm has done *"grandes"* works for clients in Portugal and abroad and finishes the catalogue with a list of them—mostly municipal offices, hotels, embassies and palaces. But don't be daunted, their catalogue shows plenty of unusual antique style ceramic objects for private homes in prices that are way below equivalent pieces bought in the United States: plates, mugs, jugs, jars, nameplates, candlesticks and table lamps hand painted in flowery folk art styles. For more ambitious decorators there are fountains, benches and decorative panels, from a twelve-tile, eighteenth-century gentleman on a horse to a whole wall-sized view of old Lisbon which is now pleasing guests in a Brussels hotel.

25 *Chinacraft* Royal Worcester "Hyde Park," an Italian Renaissance design raised in 24-carat gold. Five-piece place setting, about $165 (this five-piece place setting costs $350 in the United States).

26 *Fabrica Sant'Anna* Seventeen-inch handmade and hand-painted platter. About $39.

27 *Fabrica Sant'Anna* "Artistic panel" of hand-painted tiles. About $40.

**Frosig, Norrebrogade 9, DK-2200
Copenhagen, Denmark. Telephone 01 39 9000**
*Manufacturers' brochures: Bing and Grondahl, Royal Co-
penhagen, Bjorn Wiinblad, free; air mail $2.*
Frosig has the very attentive Mrs. Buddig looking after
American customers, who, she says, have been writing her
long and interesting letters for the past twenty-five years.
The numbers of American customers have increased enor-
mously, not through advertising but through the "mouth-to-
mouth" method—not surprisingly, as you will see. Royal
Copenhagen porcelain is sold here in both first and second
quality, but the high standards of Bing and Grondahl makes
it possible for them to stock and sell only its second-quality
porcelain, for the defects are very hard to see. Prices are
consequently splendidly low for their porcelain figurines,
misty-colored flowered vases, and pale blue scenic ashtrays.

**Gered, 174 Piccadilly, London W1 0PD, England.
Telephone (01) 734 7262**
*Wedgwood and Spode 20-page color brochures, free. Prices
in $. AE, DC, MC, V.*
If you definitely want Wedgwood or Spode, write to Gered;
they show more table settings from these companies than
anyone else.

**Leather and Snook, 167 Piccadilly,
London W1V 9DE, England. Telephone (01) 493 9121**
*Royal Crown Derby, Royal Worcester, Royal Doulton,
Minton, Webb Corbett Crystal manufacturers' brochures.
AE, DC, V.*
Leather and Snook sends out manufacturers' brochures from
several firms and specializes in Royal Crown Derby.

**Limoges-Unic, Ventes par Correspondence,
12 Rue de Paradis 75010, Paris, France.
Telephone 770 5449**
23-page catalogue in French, $3 (refundable).
Limoges-Unic puts out a large and luscious color catalogue
for their busy mail-order service. Elegant French Limoges
porcelain by leading manufacturers with impressively literary names—"Balzac," "Colette," "Corneille," "Gide,"
"George Sand," etc.
  Glass by Baccarat, Lorraine, Val St-Lambert, and modern
glass by Daum, including their household objects.
  Also French silver, which is a grayer color than most
silver, and silver plate. But I compared one or two prices on
the famous French "Cristofle" silver plate, and prices seem
to be about the same as list price in New York. Try Jompole, New York, for lower prices on Christofle.

**Nordiska Kristall, Kungsgatan 9,
S-111 43 Stockholm, Sweden. Telephone 08 10 43 72**
Orrefors catalogue, $1. Prices in $.
This fifty-year-old firm in the center of Stockholm sells the
best Swedish crystal by Orrefors and Kosta-Boda. The catalogue shows a splendid assortment of possible gifts: perfume
bottles, ice buckets, bells, smoker's sets, candle holders, hur-
ricane lamps, chandeliers, decanters, bowls, vases, ashtrays
and purely decorative pieces. This firm also has over sixty
different stemware patterns in stock. Swedish glass is considerably cheaper when bought direct from Sweden, and is a
really good buy.

**Porsgrunn Porselen, Karl Johansgate 14,
Oslo 1, Norway. Telephone 02 412 900**
Leaflet, free; air mail $1. V.
I got a rather misspelled letter from this shop, whose card
announces that it is a "store specializing in Norwegian

28

28 *Leather and Snook* Olde Avesbury by Royal Crown Derby.
Fine English china sells in England for about half United States
prices.

29

30

31

29 *A. B. Schou* Royal Copenhagen Blue fluted salad bowl, $64 (this bowl sells for $130 in New York). The whole Royal Copenhagen Blue fluted range is available at about half United States prices.

30 *A. B. Schou* Clear or opal white vase designed by Alvar Aalto for Iittala, $48 (this 6¼″ vase sells for $87 in New York).

31 *A. B. Schou* Royal Copenhagen Blue Flowers shell-shaped candy dish, $34; candlestick, $28; vase, $22.

porcelain." They tell me that "as a ruel our broshures will always be available," and they sent me a leaflet illustrating "very intresting Norwegian Mounten Flora porcelain." This is a coffee set with each of twelve place settings prettily decorated with a different mountain wild flower and described on the back in Norwegian and English. A plate and a cup and saucer together cost just around $24.

Reject China Shop, 33/34/35 Beauchamp Place, London SW3, England. Telephone (01) 584 9409
12-page color catalogue, $3 (or write for a price quote).
Reject China Shop is well known to overseas tourists visiting London. They sell china by leading manufacturers that has been "rejected" for flaws in glazing, coloring or pattern. No chipped or cracked china is sold, and the shop says that the flaws are hard to see. Aynesley, Coalport, Spode, and Royal Worcester are stocked, and Galway Crystal by Wedgwood. Also the very popular, newer earthenwares, Midwinter and "Botanical Garden" by Portmeirion. If you know what you want, don't bother with the catalogue (which has no prices) but ask for a price quote. Regular china is also sold, so *always* ask whether price given is for "reject" china, and compare with other English firms.

Rosenthal Studio-Haus, Dr Zoellner, Leopoldstrasse 44, 8 Munich 23, Germany
No catalogue.
This Rosenthal is very well known to tourists and mailorder customers for its full stock of Rosenthal glass, china and flatware. They haven't answered my letters lately but reader Charles Flynn assures me that they are still there, and selling by mail at prices way below American ones. If you want some Rosenthal, try them.

Saxjaers, 53 Købmagergade, 1150 Copenhagen, Denmark
Leaflets, free.
Commemorative plates by Bing and Grondahl, Royal Copenhagen and other European manufacturers, at prices about 40 percent below United States prices.

A. B. Schou, Skandinavisk Glas, 1 Ny Ostergade, 1101 Copenhagen, Denmark
Catalogue, $3. AE, MC, V.
A. B. Schou specializes in low prices on selected "giftwares" such as porcelain figures, commemorative plates, bowls, vases and candlesticks by famous European glass and china manufacturers. The firm is recommended by a generous reader who has sent me a detailed account of his favorite glass and china shop: " . . . an OUTSTANDING firm in Copenhagen . . . I have had extensive dealings with A. B. Schou since 1969. Experience convinces me of their quality of integrity, attention to orders, willingness to help with items not featured in their regular catalogues and brochures . . . and the fact that they are just plain kind, fine people. . . . A. B. Schou's merchandise is all 'first quality'; I have never received an article of 'second sorting' from them." The reader also did some price comparisons for me and found that at a time when the Orrefors vase was selling for $145 in the United States, Schou was charging $68 including postage and insurance. He also had compared then current prices on Lladro figurines:

	A. B. Schou	U.S.A.
Angels "4961," "4962"	$27 postpaid	$ 47.50
Valencian Girl	$59 postpaid	$ 95
Soccer Player	$40 postpaid	$ 70
Japanese Girl	$73 postpaid	$130

John Sinclair, 266 Glossop Road, Sheffield S10 2HS, England. Telephone 742 750 333
Leaflet, free. Prices in $. AE, V.
This firm sells collector's plates and mugs, figurines and special issues produced by the leading European china and glass manufacturers. Every three months or so they send leaflets to their customers.

Steuben Glass, Fifth Avenue at 56th Street, New York, NY 10022.
Telephone (800) 223 1234 or (212) 752 1441
224-page color catalogue, $5. Christmas. AE, DC, MC, V.
In the 1930s the Steuben glass operation was reorganized, and from being an undistinguished and financially unsuccessful firm, became an internationally known producer of crystal. The transformation was mainly brought about by Arthur Houghton, Jr., a great-grandson of the founder of Corning (which owns Steuben), who felt that the glass should no longer be designed by the glassmakers themselves, but by outside designers.

A sculptor was brought in as the principal designer, and over the years Steuben has made less functional glass and more expensive "art objects" and "presentation pieces." Presidents Truman and Eisenhower started a tradition of presenting Steuben glass to heads of state, and pieces are in the collections of over seventy countries. Pieces range from small, smooth animals to pieces with elaborate, stylized engravings. Some pieces cost less than $100, but most prices range from $100 into the thousands.

Rowland Ward (East Africa), P.O. Box 40991, Nairobi, Kenya. Telephone 25509 Nairobi
Leaflet, free. AE, DC.
A gallery of African art, by mail sells glasses, decanters, jugs and punch bowls engraved with big-game animals (lion, elephant, buffalo, giraffe and sable antelope). The glasses are available singly or in sets, and each glass costs between $18 and $39. The glasses are manufactured in, and mailed directly from, Bavaria. (But they take three months to reach you from the time that Rowland Ward gets your order).

DISCOUNT
Please see discount information in the How to Buy section.

I have found that you save far more by buying imported glass and china from the countries where it is made. But if there are no foreign sources for what you want, check prices at these discount firms.

A. Benjamin and Company, 82 Bowery, New York, NY 10013. Telephone (212) 226 6013
Specific price given if you send stamped self-addressed envelope. No prices given over the telephone.
Benjamin sells silver, glass and china at a discount. I have not checked the china and glass discounts, but I have generally found that British glass and china is far less expensive if bought direct from Britain. However, this may be a good place to buy Noritake, Val St. Lambert. Minimum order $50. Established 1946.

The Jompole Company, 330 Seventh Avenue, New York, NY 10001. Telephone (212) 594 0440
Leading brands of stainless steel and sterling flatware (also Christofle silverplate) and American and imported glass sold at a discount. Arabia, Lenox, Mikasa, Noritake, Rosenthal, Villeroy and Boch, Val St. Lambert and other brands are stocked. Established 1913.

32

33

34

32 *A. B. Schou* Royal Copenhagen vase, $60.

33 *A. B. Schou* Glass by Lalique, Paris. Anemone candlestick $135 (this candlestick costs $235 in USA). Anemone vase, $145 (this "flacon" costs $260 in the United States).

34 *A. B. Schou* Lladro figures: "Girl with Lamb," $83; "Children with Angry Goose," $131.

35

36

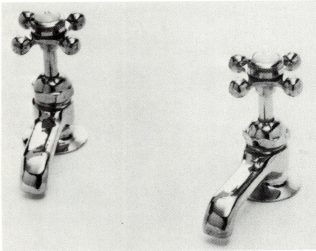

37

35 *Almost Heaven Hot Tubs* Hot tubs of redwood or Honduras mahogany, including Jacuzzi whirlpool, start at $1895.

36 *Horton Brasses* Reproduction handles: Chippendale (1749), Hepplewhite (1700–1800), Victorian (1841–1900).

37 *The Renovators Supply* Solid brass Victorian-style faucets with porcelain caps. About $38.50 a pair.

Rogers and Rosenthal, 105 Canal Street, New York, NY 10002. Telephone (212) 925 7557
Send self-addressed stamped envelope for specific price.
Discounts on sterling silver flatware and holloware, American and imported china and glass such as Ginori, Haviland, Limoges and Val St. Lambert. Special orders are taken for manufacturers not stocked. Established 1947.

Treasure Traders, P.O. Box N-645, Bay Street, Nassau, Bahamas. Telephone (809) 322 8521
Specific prices on request.
Treasure Traders give 30 percent off Georg Jensen and Christofle flatware. Similar discounts on Orrefors, Rosenthal, Baccarat crystal, and china such as Richard Ginori, Rosenthal and Royal Worcester.

Hardware and Bathroom Fixtures

Almost Heaven Hot Tubs, Route 5C, Renick, WV 24966. Telephone (304) 497 3163
Color brochure, free U.S. and overseas.
A small firm that manufacturers hot tubs from redwood or Honduras mahogany. Get the complete system here from them, including Jacuzzi whirlpool pumps, and the whole thing will arrive at your door in several cartons. With a friend and a rubber hammer to help, it can be assembled within a day, says Almost Heaven.

Ball and Ball, 463 West Lincoln Highway, Exton, PA 19341. Telephone (215) 363 7330
52-page catalogue, $4; overseas $6. MC, V.
This family firm manufactures reproduction hardware fittings. Ball and Ball claims that theirs are "brasses for those who know the originals"; they have indeed made hardware copies for most major museums. The catalogue illustrates furniture fittings, including those used on American-made pieces from about 1720 to 1840, "house hardware" (locks, latches, bolts and knobs), brass and glass chandeliers and wall sconces, door knockers and hooks of all kinds, ashtrays, bookends, table lamps, porch lamps, fireplace hardware and doorstops.

The Blacksmith Shop, Box 15, Mt. Holly, VT 05758. Telephone (802) 259 2452
Brochure, $1 U.S. and overseas. MC, V.
Hand-forged shovels, forks, broom tongs, log holders and a grill for fireplace cooking. Hooks and hangers for tools, pots and anything else.

Broadway Industries, 601 West 103rd Street, Kansas City, MO 64114. Telephone 800 255 6365
120-page color catalogue, $5 U.S. and overseas. MC, V.
Hardware and bathroom fixtures in mainly traditional styles, but with some Lucite as well. There are Victorian faucets and several flowered basins with lavatories, bidets and light plates to match.

A. E. S. Firebacks, 27 Hewitt Road, Mystic, CT 06355.
Leaflet, self-addressed stamped envelope.
Firebacks were put at the back of the fireplaces to protect them and to reflect heat outward. A. E. S. Firebacks produces three fetching cast-iron firebacks inspired by the "simplicity of design and craftsmanship of Colonial America."

**P. E. Guerin, 23 Jane Street, New York, NY 10014.
Telephone (212) 243 5270**
54-page catalogue, $5; overseas $7.
Importers and manufacturers of sumptuous hardware since
1857, they are, as they say, "style and quality leaders in
decorative brass and bronze." They have never willfully
discarded a pattern since they were founded, so now have
over fifty thousand styles on their books, any one of which
can be had on special order. They will also reproduce antique pieces from customer's samples or create new ones to
customer's designs.

**Horton Brasses, P.O. Box 120C, Nooks Hill Road,
Cromwell, CT 06416. Telephone (203) 635 4400**
42-page catalogue, $2.
This is another family firm that makes reproduction brass
fittings for antiques. The catalogue has the various products
divided into styles; first Hepplewhite pulls and escutcheons,
then Queen Anne, then Chippendale, and later on comes
Victorian hardware. There is also a small selection of
hinges, latches, lock parts, bed-bolt covers and casters.

**Steve Kayne, 17 Harmon Place, Smithtown, NY 11788.
Telephone (516) 724 3669**
*Cast-brass and bronze brochure, $1; overseas $3; 2 forged-
iron brochures, $2; overseas $6.*
Hand-forged pokers, shovels, brushes and rakes for the fireplace; bolts and hinges for doors and cabinets; and cast-brass
and bronze latches for cabinets and old iceboxes "cannot be
compared with thin steel stampings selling at nearly the
same price," says Steve Kayne.

**Knobs and Knockers, 36–40 York Way,
London N1, England. Telephone (01) 278 8925**
Catalogue, free; air mail $2. V.
A small but very varied collection of door knockers, door and
cabinet handles (these in brass, iron, ceramics and glass),
hinges, locks, bell pushes, mailboxes, coat hooks and house
numbers are shown in this catalogue. The export manager
says that "our fine range of English period door furniture
seems to appeal tremendously to our overseas customers,"
but I would have thought that the most useful designs for
Americans would be the very handsome, simple modern ones
which are so hard to find in America and which are well
represented at Knobs and Knockers.

**Newton Millham—Blacksmith, 672 Drift Road,
Westport, MA 02790. Telephone (617) 636 5437**
Brochure, $1.
A neat and instructive brochure has photographs of the
interesting hand-forged reproduction early American architectural hardware and household ironware. Besides latch
and shutter hardware, there are lovely spatulas, and meat
roasters for the kitchen, and a crane with potholders for the
fireplace.

**The Renovators Supply, 743 Northfield Road,
Millers Falls, MA 01349. Telephone (413) 659 3163**
40-page color catalogue, $2 U.S. and overseas. MC, V.
Donna and Claude Jeanloz started selling hardware for
restoring old houses in 1978, when they had trouble getting
the supplies they needed to restore their own farmhouse.
They now sell brass hardware, porcelain knobs, wooden
medicine cabinets, and pull-chain toilets to restorers but also
to people who don't want modern fixtures. As writer Stephan Wilkinson, who recommends the firm says, "If you're
sick and tired of the pot metal parts and imitation-brass
junk you get at the local hardware store, this is the place. It

38

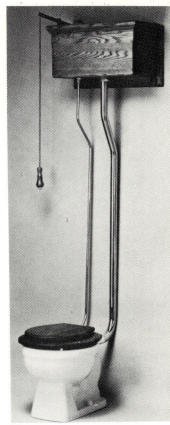
39

38 *The Renovators Supply* Wall-mounted bath caddy holds soap,
tumbler, and six toothbrushes. About $28.15.

39 *The Renovators Supply* Pull-chain toilet includes lacquered
brass pipes and wooden seat. About $639.

40

41

isn't cheap, but it's a lot cheaper than you'd pay for similar pieces in New York City decorator supply houses." The Jeanlozes say their prices are lower because over half of their stuff is made for them.

Saunna Soppi-Shop, Mannerheimintie 22–24, 00100 Helsinki 10, Finland.
Price list, free. AE, MC, V.
None of the Finnish sauna supply shops has as complete a selection as the tiny, marvelously overcrowded sauna shop which describes itself, not inaccurately, as "a unique, comfy shop full to the brim of pretty Finnish things in wood and linen." You don't have to own a sauna to like the lovely pine and juniper racks, pegs, door handles, shelves, dippers, and stools, most of which can be used in other rooms. There are also natural linen sauna sets of towels and togas, which are rough to start with but soften with use. Prices are low, but the price list is unillustrated.

Sherle Wagner, 60 East 57th Street, New York, NY 10022. Telephone (212) 758 3300
Large color catalogue, $5; overseas $24.
"Until recently," says a Sherle Wagner press release, "gold faucets were merely shaped like swans or cherubs, or snail shells; marble tubs were set off by crystal chandeliers and handcarved Louis XVI *chaises percées*. . . . Now Sherle Wagner uses marble as an art form for the bathroom with shell-shaped washbasins hand-carved in onyx with bath faucets of malachite and gold, or other real jewels, like amethyst, tiger eye, rose quartz, rock crystal and lapis lazuli." In an astounding catalogue you'll see the gold-plated towel bars and rings, paper holders, soap dishes (mostly shaped like shells), reeded and bamboo benches, knobs, pulls, hardware and medicine cabinets, often coordinated so that everything in the bathroom matches.

Household Objects and Gifts

Amazing Grace Elephant Company, 348–349 Ocean Center, Kowloon, Hong Kong. Telephone 3 699 357
Catalogue, planned, free. All credit cards accepted.
This rather grand gift shop sells an assortment of Asian handicrafts, antiques, jewelry and clothing. American owner Robert L. Green says he is planning to publish a catalogue. I very much hope he does.

Arlene's, 2640 Northaven, Suite 104, Dallas, TX 75229. Telephone (214) 484 5582
Catalogue, free; overseas $2. AE, MC, V.
Here's a catalogue which soberly calls itself "Arlene's Fine Cutlery and Grooming Aids." In fact, lovers of thingamijigs will enjoy it for its gadgets to solve life's minor problems. Anti-dog-shedding blades, splinter-removing tweezers, portable locks for hotel doors, European back scrubbers and cool and warm massagers.

Bachmaier and Klemmer, P.O. Box 220, D-8240 Berchtesgaden, West Germany
Color leaflet, $1.
This German cuckoo-clock factory has a tremendous selection of clocks on the premises, and for mail order produces a neat brochure and price list in English. Six traditional wooden clocks decorated with birds and leaves come in all

40 *Saunna Soppi-Shop* Birch dippers, thermometers, and pails for the sauna at about $4 to $15.

41 *Sherle Wagner* Hand-painted water lily basin, dark blue background with greens, pink water lilies, $463. Matching wallpaper, towels, door knobs, tumbler, and other accessories are also available.

sorts of sizes, and in nut brown or painted. Prices, including surface postage and insurance to any part of the world, are about a third lower than similar clocks I have seen on sale in the United States.

Billiards Old Telephones, 21710 Regnarot Road, Cupertino, CA 95014. Telephone (408) 252 2104
Brochure, $1 U.S. and overseas.
Billiards sells old telephones and is very eager to buy old telephones too. If you have an old phone you want to refurbish, identify your model from catalogue illustrations and order the parts here. Billiards can and does correspond in French and Spanish.

Colonial Brass Company, 88 Vine Street, Middleboro, MA 02246. Telephone (617) 947 1098
Brochure, 40 cents.
Cast metal sundials (bronze is best) for northern latitudes, although others can be made to order. About thirty horizontal and vertical sundials to choose from with the usual, sundial sayings: "I count none but the sunny hours," "Grow old along with me/The best is yet to be," or your own motto to order.

Robert Compton, Star Route, Box 6, Bristol, VT 05443. Telephone (802) 453 3778
Leaflet, $2; overseas $3.
Robert Compton is a potter who, working alone, makes fountains and aquariums in clay. His decorative aquariums come in floor or hanging models, equipped with under-gravel filter, airline hose and pump, and hidden lighting.

Coppershop, 48 Neal Street, London WC2H 9PA, England. Telephone (01) 836 2984
20-page catalogue, $5; air mail $8.
A marvelous shop for copper lovers: pots, pans, jelly molds, and eighteen old fashioned kettles, *of course;* but also punch bowls, rose bowls, bed warmers, motor horns and more, all British-made.

The Crate and Barrel, 195 Northfield Road, Northfield, IL 60093. Telephone (312) 446 2100
36-page color catalogue, $2. MC, V.
The group of stores produces a beautiful catalogue of imported things and a few crafts for the house. Much can be found in other similar catalogues, but there are also rarities. I recommend the catalogue to anyone who likes modern design.

Crispin Jones, P.O. Box 83, Monticello, IA 52310. Telephone (319) 465 5862
Brochure, free U.S. and overseas.
Drawings illustrate a delightful and unusual group of British imports: Cuckoobird tea cosies and aprons (see separate entry); Welsh character dolls and love spoons; Scottish herb sachets and soaps; Norfolk lavender soaps and bubble bath.

Cuckoobirds, Peckham Bush, Tonbridge, Kent TN12 5NH England. Telephone Maidstone 812 368
Leaflet, $1.
Cuckoobird used to make "useful presents" for children. Now this small family still makes Victorian-girl pajama cases, Beatrix Potter wash mits and growing charts, but has also started making charming fabric things for the rest of the house. Aprons, oven gloves, sachets and tea cosies are all decorated with sweet little country scenes and Victorian people. Prices are low.

42

43

44

42 *Cuckoobirds* Parlor range of tea cozy, oven gloves, potholders, jar covers, and labels for homemade preserves. Priced about $2.50 to $20.

43 *Cuckoobirds* Sachets, potpourris, and scented paper. About $2 to $14.

44 *Cuckoobirds* Lavender dolls, $1.50 each.

**Cumberland General Store, Route 3,
Crossville, TN 38555. Telephone (615) 484 8481**
250-page catalogue, $3.75; overseas $4.50. MC, V.
An amazing catalogue of old-fashioned "goods in endless
variety for man and beast" and back-to-the-land living. Do
get this catalogue if you've thought fondly of the stuff you
thought wasn't being made any more. Perhaps the most
useful are the tools, kitchen gear and farm supplies, which
include hard-to-find things like nut crackers that can deal
with black walnuts, glass rolling pins to fill with ice for
really fine pastry, and much more—all hand-powered, of
course. But the range is huge and includes larger things—
porch swings, wood-burning stoves and horse carriages, and
smaller things such as earthenware mixing bowls and reproduction cast-iron banks.

**Den Permanente, Vesterport, Vesterbrogade 8,
DK-1620 Copenhagen, Denmark.
Telephone (01) 12 44 88**
*Irregular catalogues. Specific prices on request. AE, DC,
MC, V.*
Everything shown and sold at "The Permanent Exhibition
of Danish Arts and Crafts" has been chosen by an indepen-
dent selection committee to represent the best in Danish
applied arts, made both industrially and by craftsmen. The
result is a stunning array of top-quality modern pots and
pans, glass, cutlery, ice buckets, salad bowls, etc. Some of
them are widely exported and familiar to people who like
modern design: Dansk, Kastrup-Holmegaard glass, Kaj Bo-
jesen wooden bowls and toys. Others, such as the "Cylinda"
line (a superb range in stainless steel; see the ice buckets,
designed with some sort of collaboration from Professor
Arne Jacobson) I have only seen in one New York shop.
Prices seem to be roughly one third lower than in America,
so whether you save any money depends on postage and
duty. A better reason for writing to Den Permanente is to
get beautiful things not available locally.

**Eximous, 10 West Halkin Street,
London SW1X 8JL, England. Telephone (01) 235 7222**
38-page color brochure, $1; air mail $2. AE, DC, MC, V.
Eximous—"excellent, distinguished and eminent." This fancy store claims to have supplied virtually every member of
the English royal family. The Eximous theme is caring for
the individual, and apart from that, monogramming. They'll
monogram your umbrella, your sponge bag, your boot bag,
your tie case, your tennis racquet case, your polished pewter
hair brush, your table mat, your visitors book, your hip flask
and even your sarong. They'll also sell you acrylic luggage
labels with your name and address stamped in gold. Minimum order $100.

**Gargoyles, 512 South Third Street,
Philadelphia, PA 19147. Telephone (215) 629 1700**
Color catalogue, $5. AE.
Gargoyles says they specialize in atmosphere, and have created the interiors of many restaurants and hotels. They have
an imposing array of pub mirrors, architectural gargoyles,
wrought-iron benches and stained-glass windows—both authentic and reproduction. They mainly deal with professionals, but an energetic homeowner should be able to find some
unexpected goodies here.

**The Gazebo, 660 Madison Avenue,
New York, NY 10021. Telephone (212) 832 7077**
20-page color catalogue, $4.50; overseas $6. Polaroids $5.
The Gazebo sells patchwork quilts (old and new), antique
wicker, hooked and rag rugs—old designs in pretty new color

combinations beautifully set off by lots of white. The Gazebo also has splendid silk flower arrangements, made to your
own specifications; and sweet hand-painted, soft-sculpture
Christmas ornaments. Not like any other store.

**The General Trading Company, 144 Sloane Street,
Sloane Square, London SW1, England.
Telephone (01) 730 0411**
Christmas brochure, free. AE, DC, MC, V.
The General Trading Company is housed in four discreetly
converted Victorian residences and looks more like an elegant private home than a shop. They rather extravagantly
call themselves "London's most fascinating store"—but you
might well agree. Certainly their brochure is full of beautiful and decorative things for the home. Lots of glass and
porcelain, and a small, impeccable collection of reproduction
and antique furniture.

**Halcyon Days, 14 Brook Street,
London W1Y 1AA, England**
Color leaflet, free. October.
Halcyon Days has revived the eighteenth-century art of
enameling on copper. In 1753 at Battersea, London, trinkets
and curiosities—snuffboxes, scent bottles, bonbonnieres—began to be produced and decorated with scenes and sentimental messages. Similar workshops were set up in Bilston,
Staffordshire, and although the craft only lasted for a hundred years, "Battersea" enamels, as they are now called, are
prized collectors' pieces. These fetching new Bilston and
Battersea boxes are similar to the originals in design and
coloring. For $45 each there are tiny boxes with flower or
rose bouquets; eighteenth-century landscapes or messages,
such as "Token of Friendship" or "Forget Me Not." For
$60 and up there are many round 2¼-inch and egg-shaped
boxes with the same sort of designs, plus birds and animals
and commemorative scenes.

**Hammacher Schlemmer, 147 East 57th Street,
New York, NY 10022. Telephone (212) 937 8181**
Catalogue, free.
Started 130 years ago, this well-known specialty store makes
a point of selling the latest expensive gadgets and inventions
for people who have everything. They also have a large
selection of perfectly sensible though generally higher-priced
items for the home and kitchen.

In the back pages of the catalogue you will find a very
good selection of kitchen appliances at the same prices
charged by other stores, and an array of gourmet foods,
eccentrically priced, some slightly cheaper than others listed
in this book, others at close to twice the price of their
competitors.

**Hayfields Studios, East Deering Road,
Deering, NH 03244. Telephone (603) 529 2442**
Color leaflet, 50 cents; overseas $2.
George and Ruth Wolf make things for the house with
painted decorations copied from old originals—the art was
brought to the West from the Orient by the East India
Company in the 1600s and years later became popular in
New England. The Wolfs make lamps with bases in the
shape of sap buckets, planters, candle sconces in metal and
painted with stylized flower designs.

**Hoffritz for Cutlery, 515 West 24th Street,
New York, NY 10011. Telephone (212) 924 7300**
48-page color catalogue, $1; overseas $1.50. AE, DC, MC, V.
This chain of retail stores publishes a well-organized and
beautifully photographed catalogue of cutlery and gifts.

Strong and handsome knives, shears, scissors, peelers and crackers of every description are laid out in tempting rows. You are bound to find something you've been looking for. Here's what you'll find, and plenty of choice within each category: bar sets and accessories, kitchen cutlery (which covers a lot), servers, gadgets and tableware, weather instruments, optical equipment, personal care (mustache scissors, beard brushes and automatic massagers), manicure implements and sets, tool sets, hunting and pocket knives, and gardening tools.

**Home Organizers, 1259 E1 Camino Real,
Menlo Park, CA 94025. Telephone (415) 326 6997**
Brochure, free U.S. and overseas. MC, V.
Where aids to organization are concerned, I'm insatiable. I wish this brochure had even more foldaway desks, shelf organizers, cosmetics caddies, racks, hooks, hangers, files and portfolios than it does, but it is still very helpful.

**Richard Kihl, 164 Regents Park Road,
London NW1, England. Telephone (01) 586 3838**
8-page catalogue, $2.40.
Richard Kihl sells *only* antique and modern wine accessories. Catalogued are the modern ones—champagne openers, drip stoppers, silver-plated funnels, silver wine labels, wineometers and decanting cradles. Antiques and anything not on the list, can be found to order.

**Manhattan Ad-Hoc Housewares, 842 Lexington Avenue,
New York, NY 10021. Telephone (212) 752 5488**
Catalogue planned, $1. AE, MC, V.
"High Tech" things for the house. Goods are chosen because they "work well," and you won't find much here that looks self-consciously "designed." If you live in an area where everything comes in Harvest Yellow and Avocado Green—you'll love the Ad-Hoc supplies for kitchen, office and linen closet. They have the tough Rubbermaid Commercial trash-cans in white, gray or red; their whisk broom is an "orchestra" whisk, their watering can a "radiator filler," their trolley is a factory trolley, their flashlights are made for policemen, and their cookware is of the kind used by professional chefs.

**Maximum, 42 South Avenue, Natick, MA 01760.
Telephone (617) 785 0113**
Color brochure, free U.S. and overseas. AE, MC, V.
Weather stations that enable you to check on temperature, wind speed and wind chill. These quality instruments are in brass mounted on mahogany and cost between about $160 and $700.

**Placewares, 351 Congress Street, Boston, MA 02210.
Telephone (617) 451 2074**
Leaflets, free. AE, MC, V.
Placewares sells "places to put things"—desks, desk tops, and bases, file cabinets, shelves, seating. Everything is in straightforward shapes, clear colors, and "High Tech" styles. If you've ever wondered why typing tables and folding tables are made in such nasty colors, you'll swoon at the sight of the Placewares leaflets. Three are published a year, but each one is devoted to one thing (such as hardware, workspaces or shelving).

**Puzzleplex, Stubbs Walden, Doncaster,
South Yorkshire, England**
Leaflet, $1.
Peter Stocken makes elegant three-dimensional puzzles out of fine and rare woods. The waxed wood puzzles are un-

45

46

47

48

45 *Halcyon Days* Commemorative enameled boxes at prices generally between $45 and $60.

46 *Richard Kihl* Old wine-decanting cradle in wood and brass with Georgian decanter and one of six port glasses. Similar wine accessories are available or can be found.

47 *Manhattan Ad-Hoc Housewares* Buffalo Greenband restaurant china, also available in plain white. Dinner plates, about $5 each; soup, about $4.75; salad, about $5.

48 *Manhattan Ad-Hoc Housewares* Complete bar set-up in stainless steel, pieces can be bought separately. Priced from $1.50 for the swizzle spoon to about $19 for the catheter basket used as a caddy.

49

50

51

49 *Svenskt Tenn* "Tulip" tray in four colors, designed by Joseph Frank. About $15.

50 *Bryant Steel Works* "Ideal Atlantic," one of the first stoves produced by the Portland Foundry. This richly embellished kitchen stove is occasionally available. Restored cast-iron kitchen stoves cost from $800 to $3000.

51 *Conran's* Conran's has a variety of good, basic, cooking pots, utensils, and preserving jars for the kitchen (see Furniture section).

painted and, according to the brochure, have been bought by millionaires, cabinet ministers and royalty as objets d'art. Prices go from just over $30 for round puzzles with a motif such as an eagle or a fish in the middle, to about $150 for a beautiful dragon. Special commissions can be undertaken.

Reinhart Design Center, 5225 North Greene Street, Philadelphia, PA 19144
Leaflet, $1 U.S. and overseas; air mail $3. MC, V.
This firm manufactures Closetmaster, a kit of shelves and hangers planned to better organize and double the use of closet space. Instead of the usual shoulder-level single hanging bar, the Closetmaster, for instance, has three bars. One for full-length clothes, two (to be hung one above the other) for shirts, skirts and suits. Rheinhart claims that the prefitted components can be installed in thirty minutes.

Surplus Center, 82209, 1000 West O Street, Lincoln, NE 68501. Telephone (402) 435 4366
Burdex Security catalogue, 60 cents; overseas $1; overseas air mail $4.
Surplus catalogue, free. MC, V.
An instructive "security" catalogue has burglar and fire alarms, and devices from aerosol tear-gas spray cans, to closed-circuit television systems. The surplus catalogue has both new and surplus parts.

Svenskt Tenn AB, Strandvagen 5A, S-114 51 Stockholm, Sweden. Telephone 08 63 52 10
Leaflet, $1; air mail $2. AE, DC, MC, V.
Svenskt Tenn, an exclusive home-furnishing store in Stockholm, sells beautiful decorative objects by mail. The style is not the usual Scandinavian extreme simplicity, but while distinctly modern shows the influence of eighteenth-century English design and the Far East. Another great influence has been Professor Joseph Frank, a member of the Bauhaus group in Austria, who designed furniture, lamps, textiles, and interiors for Svenskt Tenn. Bowls, vases, ashtrays, lamps, etc., are shown on the leaflets published twice a year. Recommended by Alva Myrdal.

Pentangle, Salisbury Lane, Over Wallop, Hampshire, England. Telephone 0264 788 33
Brochure, $1; air mail $3.
Perplexing puzzles for adults and persistent children are made by this firm, which will provide solutions on doctor's prescription. Puzzles include a glass marble to be removed from a cage, a silken cord to be removed from metal loops, and many wooden shapes to be constructed. Several of the puzzles have been chosen by the English Design Centre, and they are all coffeetable-worthy. Prices are low.

Telephones Unlimited, Box 1147, San Diego, CA 92112. Telephone (714) 235 8088
Brochure, $1 U.S. and overseas (refundable).
Telephones from "Versailles Rococco Ivory" to the latest multiline moderns and voicecasters. Also jacks, cords and many useful gadgets such as kits to refurbish old phones, bells with pleasant tones, loud extension bells, automatic dialers and much more.

Rowland Ward of Knightsbridge, 25B Lowndes Street, London SW1X 9JF, England. Telephone (01) 235 4844
Color catalogue, free. Prices in $. V.
Rowland Ward's theme for over a century has been natural history, and they are popular with the hunting and shooting set. The various objects in their annual Christmas catalogue usually have an animal or bird decoration. Among the most

popular things with American customers are the exclusive silk headscarves decorated with tigers, pheasants, butterflies or fish and glasses hand-engraved with fishing scenes, game birds or big game. Other gifts in the catalogue are bird-decorated coffee cups, little enamel boxes, and pretty Herend china birds and rabbits, Limoges boxes, and stone rhinoceroses.

Wynn Engineering Company, 8800 Hammerly, #509, Houston, TX 77080. Telephone (713) 464 8170
Brochure, $2 U.S. and overseas.
Machines for people who want to eavesdrop and machines to foil eavesdroppers.

Kitchen

Bryant Steel Works, Thorndike, ME 04986. Telephone (207) 568 3663
Leaflet, free; overseas $1.
For more than twenty-five years before she started selling them, Bea Bryant had been picking up old cast-iron wood stoves and sticking them in her barn with her collection of old cars and farm implements. Now, as people turn back to wood stoves and newly appreciate nineteenth-century style, she has come into her own. There is a Bryant Stove Museum, and a Bryant store in which are sold the old cookstoves, bedroom stoves and parlor heaters that were used in the nineteenth and early twentieth century. Five of Bea Bryant's children help with the restoration of the stoves, from dainty "four o'clocks" which were lit only at tea time to seven-foot-tall Montgomery Ward hotel cookstoves. The stoves may not be a typical mail-order purchase, but customers include people in Panama and the proverbial Texan who asked for the most expensive stove in the place and then brought five for Christmas presents.

The Chef's Catalogue, 725 County Line Road, Deerfield, IL 60015. Telephone (312) 480 9400
24-page color catalogue, $1. AE, MC. V.
The Chef's Catalogue sells "professional restaurant equipment for the home chef." Not all the stock is actually professional equipment, but it is very "High Tech"—basic undecorated and durable: NASA-developed storage containers, Calaphon cookware, stainless-steel wine buckets. Also good small appliances by Cuisinart, Krups and the Simac ice cream and pasta makers.

The China Closet, 6807 Wisconsin Avenue, Chevy Chase, MD 20815. Telephone (301) 656 0203
Color catalogue, free. AE, MC, V.
Modern flowery china that I haven't seen around too much, and all the better appliances and cookware, such as Calaphon and Le Creuset, for the kitchen.

Countryside General Store, 103 North Monroe Street, Waterloo, WI 53594
64-page brochure, $1; overseas $1.50. MC, V.
A small catalogue of supplies for homesteading is offered by farmer/publisher Jerome Belanger. He mostly sells equipment that he has used himself, and had a hard time finding—including many books and supplies for raising small animals. And equipment for dealing with food such as dehydrators, manual can sealers, bottle cappers, and wooden dough mixers.

E. Dehillerin, 18–20 Rue Coquilliere, 75001 Paris, France. Telephone 1 236 53 13
12-page catalogue, free. In French.
The world's most famous kitchen shop is in Paris, naturally enough, and sells by mail to America, *but* although they understand written English, they can only reply in French. They also advise customers to get together with friends and family for orders because only orders for merchandise weighing over 44 pounds are accepted (and go sea freight).

The catalogue, which is strictly for serious cooks, shows a workmanlike assortment of copper cooking pots and pans in all shapes and sizes: basic, nongimmicky utensils. Prices are not in the catalogue, and are only given upon application.

Figi's Collection for Cooking, Marshfield, WI 54449. Telephone (715) 387 1771.
60-page color catalogue, free. AE, MC, V.
Good kitchenware such as Leyson pots and Simac electric pasta and ice-cream makers, together with many smaller things—waffle irons, clay pots, butter molds and icing stencils.

Fiveson Food Equipment, 324 South Union Street, Traverse City, MI 49684. Telephone (800) 632 7342
Brochure, free U.S. and overseas; air mail $3. AE, MC, V.
Mickey Fiveson is a dealer of restaurant supplies such as walk-in coolers, dough rollers, pizza ovens, stainless-steel refrigerators and twenty-quart mixers. He does also, however, have Corning Pyrex tableware, restaurant glasses, and flatware at what he says are discount prices (I haven't checked).

Lehman Hardware and Appliances, Box 41, Kidron, OH 44636. Telephone (216) 857 5441
80-page nonelectric catalogue, $2; stove catalogue, $1.
Over four hundred nonelectric appliances and gadgets are stocked by this supplier to America's largest Amish and Swiss Mennonite community. Here you can find alcohol-run irons, kerosene refrigerators and freezers, copper-wash boilers, gas engine/wringer/washers and many smaller things for the nonelectric life. Lehman says that they get orders from mission fields in many foreign countries.

The Maid of Scandinavia Company, 3244 Raleigh Avenue, Minneapolis, MN 55416. Telephone (612) 927 7996
240-page color catalogue, $1.
A big catalogue of such fantastic supplies for making spectacular cakes, pies, tarts and cookies, candies and chocolates that it's enough to coax one into the art of cake decorating and candymaking. Besides molds, icings, edible and inedible decorations illustrating every hobby and interest, there are books to tell you how to proceed, aids to correct possible disasters, and festive novelties such as sugar babies, chocolate coins, decorated sugar, candy pebbles, crystallized violets and edible glitter. Plenty of party supplies and plates, napkins, invitations, favors too.

New England Cheesemaking Supply Company, P.O. Box 85, Main Street, Ashfield, MA 01330. Telephone (413) 628 3808
16-page brochure, free; overseas $1. MC, V.
Would-be cheesemakers will find everything needed to make butter, yogurt, buttermilk, cheddar, Gouda, ricotta, feta, Camembert, even blue cheese at New England Supply Company. There are also advice, instruction books and an inspirational newsletter.

**The Sausage Maker, 177 Military Road,
Buffalo, NY 14207.Telephone (716) 876 5521**
64-page catalogue, free; overseas air mail $2.
An ex-kielbasa maker of Polish descent has written the only
book in THE WORLD written by a sausage maker, *Great
Sausage Recipes and Meat Curing* by Rytek Kutus. The
book has smoking and fish-preserving recipes too, including
instructions on how to make your own caviar. From an
immaculate warehouse he sells through a helpful and informative catalogue almost everything you need to make sausages, including sausage stuffers, casing, preservatives and
spices.

**The Silo, Upland Road, New Milford, CT 06776.
Telephone (203) 355 0300**
24-page color catalogue, $1. AE, MC. V.
A few of the usual better brands of pots and equipment for
the kitchen: Calaphon, Krups, etc. But also many well-
designed smaller things: crafts and a smattering of luxury
foods from small firms such as the Silver Palate and the
Camille Bakery (spiced nuts, jams, sweet sesame bread-
sticks).

**Tsang and Ma, P.O. Box 294, Belmont, CA 94002.
Telephone (415) 595 2270**
*10-page brochure, free; overseas 2 International Reply
Coupons. MC, V.*
Chinese vegetable seeds; regional spices mixed by David
Tsang—and everything you need to cook and eat your produce: woks and steamers, rice bowls and soup spoons, scoop-
ers and skimmers, and plain or lacquered and inlaid chop-
sticks.

**Williams Sonoma, P.O. Box 3792,
San Francisco, CA 94119. Telephone (415) 652 1555**
50-page color catalogue, $1. AE, MC, V.
This group of shops "serving serious cooks since 1956"
publishes what seems to be everyone's favorite kitchen catalogue. Owner Chuck Williams hunts up good-looking novel
things and unusual small appliances for the kitchens of
dedicated cooks, and presents them beautifully. Everything—
from French wicker cheese trays through Belgian waffle
irons and Austrian soda syphons—manages to look highly
desirable. A few extravagant edibles are also sold, such as
cold-pressed olive oil, toasted almond oil, raspberry flavored
vinegar, and aged vanilla extract.

DISCOUNT
Please see discount information in the How to Buy section.

**Bondy Export Corp., 40 Canal Street,
New York, NY 10002. Telephone (212) 925 7785**
*Send model number and self-addressed envelope (overseas,
International Reply Coupon) for price information by mail
only. MC, V.*
Bondy has a good selection of small appliances and is efficient at giving prices by mail. I bought a typewriter and a
Sony Walkman from them by mail, and they delivered both
very promptly. Although Bondy says that they specialize in
220 appliances and will ship anything overseas, they will
only send small appliances (weighing under 50 pounds the
United Parcel limit) within the United States. Established
1950.

**Focus Electronics, 4523 Thirteenth Avenue,
Brooklyn, NY 11219. Telephone (212) 871 7600**
Will give specific prices by mail, U.S. and overseas. MC, V.
Focus sells electronic, photography equipment, watches and
large and small kitchen appliances. This is one of the few
places that have a good stock of all the small kitchen appliances; they also have Faberware pots and pans on which I
found a 25-percent discount. I ordered a Sony Walkman
from them which took over three weeks to arrive, partly
because they hold personal (noncertified) checks for two
weeks. But I have found Focus is efficient about quoting
prices by mail, and prices are very good. Established 1970.

**International Solgo, 77 West 23rd Street,
New York, NY 10010. Telephone (212) 675 3555**
Price quotes by telephone. AE, DC, MC, V.
Solgo has a very wide range of small appliances for the
home, including clocks, luggage carts, desk fans, etc. They
have many of the nationally advertised small kitchen appliances, and brands such as Faberware, Corning, etc. I have
found them better at quoting prices over the telephone than
by mail. I bought a Cuisinart and a vacuum cleaner here
and was satisfied with the prices and the service. Established
1933.

**The Underground, 311½ South Eleventh Street,
Tacoma, WA 98402. Telephone (206) 383 2041**
16-page brochure, 75 cents; $1 overseas.
Don't miss this firm. It gives 15- to 20-percent discounts on
the best kitchen machines (the ones that most discount stores
don't stock). Champion, Oster, Sanyo juicers, Millright
Electric Stone flour mill, White Mountain dough kneaders
and ice-cream makers. When I checked, their Kitchen Aid
mixers were $70 and $98 below the prices for the same
machines at nondiscount firms; their Kenwood Chef was $30
below the "special" price at Chef's Catalogue and $80 below
the regular price. Aladdin lamps, heaters, Jet power tools,
also at a discount, and nondiscounted weaving and spinning
supplies are sold. The mimeographed brochure has good
descriptive copy and clearly laid out list and discount prices,
with discount given. Established 1980.

**Zabar's, 2245 Broadway, New York, NY 10024.
Telephone (212) 787 2000**
*Specific prices given by telephone. Occasional catalogues.
AE, DC, MC, V.*
New York's famous food store is so popular that, as one of
the owner's has said, "People come from all over, wait in
line for an hour and get knocked around. You get black and
blue when you come in here." They sell hundreds of American and exotic foods, but by mail they just sell their excellent coffees (minimum order 5 pounds). *New York Times*
food writer, Mimi Sheraton, tasted a whole lot of decaffeinated coffee beans on sale in New York, and gave Zabar's
espresso top marks. They also sell kitchenwares and small
kitchen appliances at a discount. This is a really useful
source because it has the sophisticated appliances that are
hard to find at a discount: Melior and espresso coffeemakers;
Braun, Krups and Simac appliances; Leyse, Doufou and
Polaris cooking pots. BUT, although they do mail order,
Zabar's isn't really geared to it. They don't seem to answer
letters, and tend to sound distraught when you telephone.
They are, however, worth trying for any of the exotic small
appliances you can't get at a discount elsewhere. Established
1939.

Lace, Linen and Embroidery

Casa Bonet, Puigdorfila 3, Palma de Mallorca, Spain. Telephone 222117
Brochure of handkerchief monogram styles, free.
Catalogue of embroidered tablecloth and napkin sets in Spanish, free.
A famous linen shop with a museumlike display of fine old lace and embroidery. One of Casa Bonet's most popular items has been customer signatures hand-embroidered on the corner of handkerchiefs instead of a monogram or an initial. Both fine white and multicolored Marjorcan embroidery is sold here. Specific prices given on pro forma invoice.

Het Kantenhuis, Kalverstraat 124, Amsterdam, Holland. Telephone 248 618
AE, DC, V.
Het Kantenhuis imports the very best handmade lace and embroidery from all over the world, so they have a marvelous selection. Antique Venetian, Swiss Embroidery, Brussels (Princess) lace and all sorts of other laces and embroideries are attached to anything you might hope to find belaced and embroidered; collars, cuffs, bun cozies, guest towels, bridge sets, tablecloths, table runners, mantillas and bridal veils. No price list, but they answer specific questions very efficiently.

Jesurum, Ponte Canonica 4310, 1–30122 Venice, Italy. Telephone (041) 706 177
Venetian lace, probably the most expensive lace of all, is sold by this famous old shop, and made in its own lacemaking school. Prices are high, Jesurum says that their tablecloths and placemats made with precious antique lace are extremely expensive, and with modern handmade lace are rather expensive. With machine-made lace, a napkin and placemat together cost about $19, so you can guess that when they say "expensive," they mean it. Tablecloths in batiste, organdy or linen start at $185, queen-size mixed-linen sheets with embroidery, $175 and up; six-piece machine-embroidered bath sets, $175 and up. Write to Jesurum and tell them what you are interested in, the size and price range you would like, and they will send you their "best offer" with a photograph of the item.

J. Jolles Studios, Fassziehergasse 5 Vienna VII, Austria. Telephone 222 936 329
20-page catalogue of gros-point handbags, $1; air mail $3.50.
20-page catalogue of small petit-point articles, $1; air mail $3.50.
Two 40-page catalogues of petit-point evening bags, $1 each; air mail $3.50. AE, DC, MC, V.
The world's most productive needlepoint producers, the Jolles Studios, won a Grand Prix at the Brussels World Fair. They design, make up and sell an enormous number of petit-point and gros-point purses and some tapestries at their Vienna shop, and for mail order they have four good catalogues.

Maria Loix, Avenue de la Basilique 380-Bte 28, B-1080 Brussels, Belgium. Telephone 426 25 33
List, free; photographs, $1. AE, V.

Maison F. Rubbrecht, 23 Grand Place, Brussels B-1000, Belgium.
Catalogue, $1; air mail $3. Prices on specific request. All international credit cards accepted.
Belgium is not only thought to produce the finest linen in the world, but is also renowned for comparatively inexpensive lace.

52

53

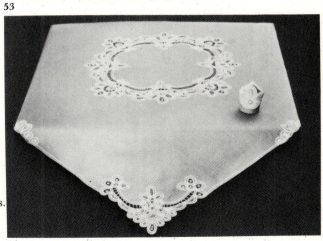

54

52 *Het Kantenhuis* White, cream or pastel linen guest towel with Battenberg lace, priced about $6.

53 *Het Kantenhuis* White, cream or pastel linen bun cozy with Battenberg lace, priced about $10.

54 *Het Kantenhuis* White or cream linen tablecloth and four napkins with Battenberg lace. About $40. *Photographs by Studio Hartland.*

Both these top shops are very well known to American tourists for their "serious" prices and "perfect" service. They stock a vast assortment of handmade lace—Duchess, Flanders, Princess, Venetian, etc.—but by far the most popular and least expensive is Battenberg, which is machine-made lacy tapes sewn by hand into the final lace shape. Prices seem to be roughly equal at both shops. Maria Loix now sells only by mail, with prices on request.

**Ed. Sturzenegger AG, Postrasse 17,
St. Gallen, Switzerland. Telephone (071) 22 78 95**
Brochure, free.
This one-hundred-year-old firm publishes a small brochure illustrating their Swiss style hand-guided machine-embroidered white cotton, muslin or Terylene curtains and their Terylene tablecloths. At the moment a 36 by 36-inch tablecloth costs about $40.

**Wilco Trading Company, 301 Wellington House,
3A Wyndham Street, G.P.O. 2225, Hong Kong.
Telephone 5 2308 72**
56-page catalogue, $1; air mail $2.50.
Wilco is the successor to China Art Embroidery Company and like them has a wider selection of embroidery and lace, with lower prices than anyone else. It has been recommended to me by a reader who says she had very satisfactory dealings with China Art, and now also with Wilco.

Light Fixtures

**Authentic Designs, 330 East 75th Street,
New York, NY 10021. Telephone (212) 535 9590**
64-page catalogue, $3; overseas $5.
Careful recreations and adaptations of Early American light fixtures are made here. Each fixture is made by one man and to a large extent made by hand, the brass arms are individually cut, bent and shaped by same methods that were used two centuries ago, and the wood is turned by hand. The lights are for electric bulbs but can also be ordered for use with candles. Most sconces cost between $60 and $80, most chandeliers between $200 and $400.

**E. Bakalowits Sohne, P.O. Box 162, Halirschgasse 17,
1171 Vienna, Austria. Telephone 45 56 36**
Photographs and prices, free. AE, DC, MC.
Austria is a leading producer of fine hand-cut crystal, and this firm makes splendiferous modern chandeliers in what they say is A-1 quality, produced only in Austria.

All sizes of lights are made: little metal and crystal candlesticks, small wall or table lights, and small to huge ceiling lights. The designs range from fairly classic and unobtrusive compact shapes to dramatic sunbursts of glittering crystal.

**Brasslight, 90 Main Street, Nyack, NY 10960.
Telephone (914) 352 0567**
Brochure, 50 cents; overseas $1.
Gregory Yanetti started by repairing old fixtures, but now makes his own turn-of-the-century style brass table lamps. Designs are straightforward—more for desk than boudoir.

**Burdoch Silk Lampshade Company, 3701 Orion Drive,
La Mesa, CA 92041. Telephone (714) 465 7291**
Color leaflet, $2 U.S. and overseas; overseas air mail $3.
"Capture the romance of an age gone by with our embroi-

dered, handsewn fabric shades." These flower-embroidered, fringed lamp shades look *very* Victorian front parlour. Prices $120 and up.

**Ducci, Lungarno Corsini, 24/r, 50123, Florence, Italy.
Telephone 055 21 4550**
10-page color catalogue, free. Prices in $. AE, DC, MC, V.
Ducci makes strikingly different table lamps with gold and silver leaf bases and reproductions from Roman and Italian masterpieces on the handmade shades. The lamps cost about $100 each including postage, shades alone cost about $45 including postage.

**Elie Epstein, P.O. Box 328, Haifa 31999, Israel.
Telephone 04 87164**
Color leaflet, $1.
Lampshades for hanging lights in unglazed clay inspired by the shape of ancient clay drums. Recommended by Dorothy George, a reader.

**Heritage Brass Artisans, Reed Road, P.O. Box 295,
Pennington, NJ 08534. Telephone (609) 737 1606**
Color brochure, $1; overseas $2. MC, V.
These solid brass reproduction oil lamps are especially appealing because the originals were workmanlike lamps made for use and not decorated. There's a "pigeon lamp" from French wine cellars, the switch tender's lamp from the American railways, the sconce from the captain's quarters on the *Independence*, and a lamp from the Orient Express, plus others. All available electrified or not. Prices $35 to $150.

**Heritage Lanterns, 70A Main Street,
Yarmouth, ME 04096. Telephone (207) 846 3911**
50-page color catalogue, $2; overseas $4. MC, V.
The widest collection of lanterns, in brass, copper and pewter, includes round globe lanterns. An interesting catalogue gives background information on the originals.

**Hans-Agne Jakobsson,
Box 82, S-285 00 Markaryd, Sweden**
23-page catalogue with some color, $1; air mail $2.
A designer, Hans-Agne Jakobsson, thought up these handsome pine lamps made in "darkest Smaland," a foresty part of Sweden. Table, wall, floor and ceiling lights have shades made from slivers of natural pine. The lamps give a specially soft, warm light so appealing that the lamps have become very popular, and not only widely exported but also widely copied. Prices start at about $15.

**King's Chandelier Company, Highway 14, P.O. Box 667,
Eden, NC 27288. Telephone (919) 623 6188**
88-page catalogue, $1.50 U.S. and overseas.
This family firm designs and assembles chandeliers from imported Czechoslovakian crystal, and uses *no* plastic parts. About fifty magnificent chandeliers and sconces in crystal, and some in brass, between $200 and $400.

**George Kovacs, 831 Madison Avenue,
New York, NY 10021. Telephone (212) 861 9500**
Brochure, $1; overseas $2. AE, MC, V.
One of the few stores in New York where really modern lamps are sold, George Kovacs started out in 1961 by importing, but has now become one of the largest manufacturers of lamps and lighting fixtures in the country. They say that lights should be "simple, inconspicuous, unpretentious and tasteful"; consequently, although the lamps are very modern-looking, they are almost always basically re-

strained arrangements of squares, cylinders and circles in black, white or shiny chrome.

Lundberg Studios, Box C, Davenport, CA 95017. Telephone (408) 423 2532
Price list and color photographs, $3; overseas $4. AE, MC, V.
Striking reproductions of the Tiffany and Steuben turn-of-the-century iridescent lamps and lampshades. Lundberg says that the lamps are virtually indistinguishable from the prohibitively priced originals, and that the shades transmit a beautifully warm light without showing the light bulb. Similar decanters, vases, stemware, perfume bottles, are also made.

Newstamp Lighting, 227 Bay Road, N. Easton, MA 02356. Telephone (617) 238 7071
28-page catalogue, $2 U.S. and overseas; overseas air mail $4.
Brass, copper and black finish Colonial lanterns and also later more formal urban ones, such as coach lanterns. Prices are lower here.

St. Louis Antique Lighting, P.O. Box 8146, St. Louis, MO 63156. Telephone (314) 535 2770
Catalogue, $3; overseas $5.
Solid polished-brass ceiling lights and sconces with glass shades. Designs are fairly restrained Victorian ones.

Richard Scofield, Period Lighting Fixtures, 1 W. Main Street, Chester, CT 06412. Telephone (203) 526 3690
Catalogue, $2; overseas $2.50. MC, V.
Early American light fixtures are hand made here with the old tools—no two are exactly alike. Outdoor lanterns are all copper, indoor chandeliers and sconces are hand-rubbed pewter, naturally aged tin or glazed Fresco dry colors. Wiring is completely hidden.

Victorian Reproductions, 1601 Park Avenue South, Minneapolis, MN 55404. Telephone (612) 338 3636
Furniture catalogue, $5; overseas $10.
Lighting catalogue, $5; overseas $10.
An amazingly elaborate collection of reproduction Victorian lamps; table, wall, and hanging unpainted and etched glass shades; fixtures replete with prisms and cherubs. Glass lampshades of all sorts are also sold.

Paints and Wallpaper

Bradbury and Bradbury Wallpapers, Box 155, Benica, CA 94510. Telephone (707) 746 1900
Brochure, $1 U.S. and overseas.
Wallpaper samples, $1 per packet.
Bradbury and Bradbury is America's smallest wallpaper company—and proud of it. They make exceptional hand-printed wallpapers in the lovely, stylized flower designs of William Morris and other 1880s designers. Colors have been 'museum researched' to recreate the rich glow of Victorian interiors.

S. Wolf's Sons, 771 Ninth Avenue, New York, NY 10019–6393. Telephone (212) 245 7777
50-page catalogue, $2; overseas $4. Color cards, mural brochures, free.
This famous paint store was started four years after the Civil War ended and is still in the same family. Stephen Wolf, the current owner, is a walking encyclopedia of paint

55

56

55 *Lundberg Studios* Iridescent glass shades, reproducing turn-of-the-century Tiffanys and Steubens, cost about $60 to $200. Paperweights, perfume bottles, and vases cost about $65 to $300.

56 *Richard Scofield* Handmade reproduction of Early American chandelier with wood-turned center. About $498.

information and collects ephemera to do with paints and wallpapers in his spare time. The store stocks absolutely everything needed to paint a house and refinish its parts: the major brands, unusual paints such as "clean" bright paints with no gray in them—mainly used by the television studios—and the Day-glos that glow under ultraviolet light. Also all the tools for graining and mottling, and gold leaf and glazing liquids, etc. The store will match paint colors, and can send wallpaper samples if you are extremely specific as to what you want. A terrific source, that can help with a lot of do-it-yourself problems.

DISCOUNT
Please see discount information in the How to Buy section.

Franklin and Lennon Paint Co., 537 West 125th Street, New York, NY 10027. Telephone (212) 864 2460
U.S. and overseas write or telephone for specific prices.
After trying several so-called discount paint firms, I was delighted to find Franklin and Lennon, the only ones to quote hefty discounts on well-known paints ($4.45 off each gallon of Benjamin Moore Wall Satin). They stock most advertised house paints, sign supplies and building materials. Established 1934.

Pintchik, 478 Bergen Street, Brooklyn, NY 11217. Telephone (212) 783 3333
Specific prices given by mail or telephone.
Pintchik sells leading paint brands: Benjamin Moore, Pittsburgh, Pratt and Lambert, etc.; they sell wallpaper by Schumacher, including wallpaper designs by Laura Ashley, Mary McFadden, Marimekko, Diane von Furstenburg, and will order any wallpaper if you give pattern name and number. Brand-name linoleum, carpeting and Levolor blinds are also sold. I checked the paint prices and found discounts of pesky 6 and 8 percent. I hope wallpaper discounts are bigger. Established 1916.

Pewter

Charles et Philippe Boucaud, 25 Rue du Bac, 75007 Paris, France. Telephone (1) 261 24 07
Brochure, free. In French.
Philippe Boucaud starts his catalogue: "Dear customer, dear customer, each year it seems to me a daring adventure or worse a gamble to sell antiquity by mail!" Nevertheless this reputable firm annually produces a small catalogue of genuine antique, not reproduction, French pewter. Strictly for the serious collector as prices are between $200 and $1500.

Colonial Casting Company, 443 South Colony Street, Meriden, CT 06450. Telephone (203) 235 5189
Leaflet, 50 cents.
After making molds for other manufacturers for many years, Colonial Casting Company decided to make some for themselves and use them. They now make a small collection of cast-pewter reproductions: stark and strong Early American plates, scalloped "Old English" Colonial plates, early-eighteenth-century goblets, Early American tavern mugs, and spoons cast from the original. A 3-inch-high rum cup costs $18; candlesticks start at $40 a pair, and plates at $12.

Pewter Crafters of Cape Cod, 927 Route 6A, Yarmouth Port, MA 02675. Telephone (617) 362 3407
16-page catalogue, $1 U.S. and overseas. MC, V.
Handmade pewter in very simple Colonial and early Federal styles, and also in modern designs that include pendants and Christmas tree ornaments.

Pilgrim Pewterers, Sudbury Road, Stow, MA 01775. Telephone (617) 568 8338
Leaflet, $1 U.S. and overseas (refundable).
Lydia Holmes casts lovely pewter spoons and buttons in antique Colonial molds. She started when her grandfather gave her a mold that had been in the family for at least five generations. Spoons cost $6 to $12 each, and the buttons just over $1 each.

Selangor Pewter Company, Mail Order Department, 321 Jalan Tuanku Abdul Rahman, P.O. Box 15, Kuala Lumpur, Malaysia. Telephone 631 633
14-page brochure, free. Prices in $. AE, DC, MC, V.
Apparently Malaysia is known for its pewter. Selangor is a large old family firm employing over three hundred pewtersmiths in two factories. But unlike some firms, they use new machinery and methods to make lead-free pewter in modernish styles. One line, the Royal Collection, has a new highly polished finish, which looks and feels like sterling silver, according to Selangor, but doesn't tarnish.

Rugs and Carpets

Fernandez Angulo S.A., Calle de Toledo 4, Madrid 12, Spain. Telephone 266 52 46
30-page color catalogue and wool samples, $2; air mail $3. Wall hangings brochure, free. Prices in $.
These brilliant baroque bedspreads and carpets from Spain have been copied all over the world, usually in strong blues and greens or reds and orange. Fernandez Angulo makes them in several patterns and any combination of a hundred colors (although service, which is slow anyway, becomes even slower if you don't choose the standard color combinations). Twin sizes start at $100. This firm was recommended to me by a friend and both of us have satisfactorily bought rugs. The only hitch is that although the catalogue is in English, English is not spoken (or written), so if you need to ask about anything special, you'll need a translator.

Carpet House, 152 Ocean Terminal, Kowloon, Hong Kong
Color leaflet, free. Prices in $.
Carpet House makes pure-wool carpets, chrome-dyed and chemically washed. Sixteen designs in color are shown on their leaflet in Floral, French Aubusson, Peking or solid-color embossed design, or to special order. Background color can be beige, maroon, blue, gold or green. Sizes are 3' by 5', 4' by 9', 8' by 10', 9' by 12', 10' by 14', 12' by 15'.

Casa Quintao, 30 Rua Ivens, Lisbon 1200, Portugal. Telephone 36 58 37
Color catalogue, free.
This well-known hundred-year-old firm makes traditional Portuguese Arraiolos needlepoint rugs. The cross-stitch rugs originated in the early seventeenth century with Persian-inspired designs later modified by national and folk art. Rugs in the catalogue are mainly in beiges and browns, but you can have your own colors or even your own designs made up. United States decorators, Hollywood film stars and

Clare Booth Luce have. Prices somewhat over $20 per square foot for petite point and $12 for gros point, with custom orders costing about $15 a square foot more.

Floorcloths, P.O. Box 812, Severna Park, MD 21146. Telephone (301) 544 0880
Brochure, $2, U.S. and overseas.
Carpets and rugs were too expensive for most people in the eighteenth century, so instead they used painted-canvas floor cloths. Now a group of artists has started a firm to produce floor cloths again.

The designs are simple, often geometric, eighteenth-century Op Art. You can either choose your own colors from an assortment of nineteen pleasant colors, or have your own mixed, for $50 extra. The designers can also adapt patterns you have in your house, adapt your own ideas, or take designs from historical sources you choose.

Folklore-Olga Fisch, P.O. Box 64, Quito, Ecuador. Telephone 231 767
Rug brochure in color, $4. Prices in $.
Handicrafts brochure, $4. Prices in $.
Folklore hand-knotted rugs are designed for Folklore by Mrs. Olga Fisch and cost about $39 per square foot (with roughly $30–$40 extra per rug for handling and air-freight charges). They come in several sizes from 4 by 6 feet to 12 by 14 feet. Most designs can be made to order in special sizes and colors, and color samples can be matched ("to perfection," they say).

The most distinctive and original carpets are inspired by old textiles and cave paintings and are in subtle dark browns, reds and cream. But there are also more conventional rugs: "Georgia," a very beautiful colonial carpet with pale blue, gray and brown flowers on white; or "Caceria" with a pattern of people, plants and animals based on Colonial embroideries. This is a terrific place for unusual rugs.

Charles W. Jacobsen, 401 South Salina Street, Syracuse, NY 13201. Telephone (315) 422 7832
Catalogue, free.
Charles Jacobsen, author of an extremely useful book, *Checkpoints on How to Buy Oriental Rugs,* has been shipping Oriental rugs on approval for thirty years and says he has never had a customer write in with a single complaint. This firm sends descriptive lists of new Oriental rugs and used rugs, semi-antique and antique—definitions of all these terms are carefully given—in fact, the catalogue is worth getting if you're thinking of buying an Oriental rug without knowing much about them, for these definitions alone. After looking at the catalogue, you fill out a form describing the kind of rug you want, size, price range, background color and type of pattern (floral, geometric, all over). Jacobsen then sends you (with a hand viewer if you have no projector) color Kodachromes of specific rugs you have asked for, plus others in sizes you are interested in. And with the Kodachromes comes a complete article and history of the different types of weaves. Finally, Jacobsen hopes you will ask them to send selections on approval. They pay the shipping costs both ways and add: "If by any chance you did not buy from a shipment, we would not feel bad. Our table of experience tells us that our shipping charges are a small item."

Monarch Trading Company of New Zealand, Pier 39, Honolulu, HI 96817. Telephone (800) 367 6002 or (808) 523 5608
16-page color catalogue, $1 U.S. and overseas.
Luxuriously thick rugs of New Zealand sheepskin in various

57

58

59

57 *Selangor Pewter Company* A new collection of highly polished pewter that looks like silver. Goblets, about $23 to $38. No U.S.A. duty is charged on many popular tourist items from Malaysia at present.

58 *Fernandez Angulo* Brilliant-colored bedspreads and floor rugs in traditional Spanish designs. Bedspreads, $90 to $280; rugs, $25 to $380.

59 *Floorcloths* Painted floorcloths were used in America from the early eighteenth to the late nineteenth century. Hand-painted canvas floor cloths in standard designs cost $15 per square foot. Special designs and colors can be made to order.

60

61

62

60 *Folklore-Olga Fisch* "Cuernos" hand-knotted rug in cream and brown (or any color to order) several sizes, $39 per square foot.

61 *Folklore-Olga Fisch* "Curiquinge" hand-knotted rug in red, brown, pale blue, and pale yellow on beige background (or any color to order), 4′ × 6′ to any size, $39 per square foot.

62 *National Welfare Organization* Needlepoint rugs, about $166 per square meter (1.2 square yards).

shapes and sizes. Prices are high, but the quality looks high too. Also blankets, rugs, jewelry from New Zealand. Suggested by Carol Campion, a reader.

National Welfare Organization, Handicrafts Department, 6 Ipatias Street, Athens 117, Greece. Telephone 322 2718
22-page color rug catalogue, free.
Color cushion and bag leaflet, free.
The National Welfare Organization has encouraged and promoted carpetmaking by peasants as a means of increasing family income. Instead of trying to compete with Oriental carpets, they have developed unusual and beautiful Greek designs, knotted, woven and embroidered. Based on folk art and Hellenic motifs, styles are simple and graceful, leaning toward small, repeated pictures of stylized flowers, birds and geometric patterns. Prices start at $117 per square meter (1 square meter = 1.2 square yards), and needlepoint cushions with similar designs cost about $22.

The Sheepskin Rug Shop, Mail Order Department, P.O. Box 12–175, Penrose, Aukland, New Zealand
6-page brochure, free.
New Zealand is, of course, known for its sheep, and the manager of this shop chauvinistically says that the sheepskins he has seen on sale in America are poorer quality and two and a half to three times the price. Rugs made out of one or two lamb or sheep skins can be bought dyed in any of fifteen colors. All are washable.

Sotainvalidien Veljesliiton Naisjarjesto r.y.n., Ryijpalvelu, Kasarmikatu 34, 00130 Helsinki 13, Finland
Color catalogue in Finnish, $3; air mail $5.
Rya-rug kits and the same rugs made-up are sold by this firm in rather wild and beautiful designs that are more like abstract paintings than the traditional rug patterns; more colors and busier patterns here than in most Ryas.

Suomen Kasityon Ystavat, Meilahti 7, 00250 Helsinki, Finland. Telephone 418 530
Color brochure, $5; air mail $6. Prices in $.
Rya rugs, the shaggy Finnish carpets, in large, blurry, abstract designs and magnificent colors. The rugs here are finely and subtly colored, but humbler versions can be bought at the Scandinavian furniture stores at much lower prices. A do-it-yourself kit here costs about $312 for a 4′ by 5′ rug (the same thing made-up costs $1087, and there is a waiting time of three months).

Tai Ping Carpet Salon, Harbour City-Phase 1 Berwick 003, Canton Road, Kowloon, Hong Kong. Telephone 366 7086
Color catalogue, $4.
Excellent, informative catalogue showing the kinds of custom-tailored carpets that Tai Ping has made for firms all over the world, including the Columbia Broadcasting System, Ford and General Motors and Grauman's Chinese Theatre in Hollywood. The carpets, manufactured in a large modern factory in Taipo, are made by hand from a blend of New Zealand and Scottish wools in any shape—any design—any size, so this is a marvelous place for anyone having trouble finding what they want. The catalogues show lots of "contemporary," "periodic," "Chinese" and "Moroccan" designs, but as each carpet is made up to order, there is always a waiting time. Prices for standard designs vary from about $8 to $11 a square foot, with 15 percent extra for custom colors.

**Tropicrafts, Turkey Lane, Roseau,
Dominica, West Indies**
Leaflet, free.
Tropicrafts makes traditional grass mats in many designs
and sizes which are not expensive and can be sent by mail.

**Zarapes de San Miguel, Carrada de la Calzada Aurora
No. 1, San Miguel de Allende, Guanajuato, Mexico**
Cataloue, $1. Prices in $. MC, V.
This firm makes handwoven rugs and wall hangings which
have won a gold medal—the first prize for design of goods
for export given by the Mexican Institute of Foreign Trade.
Owner Thomas L. Alvarez also says that his customers tell
him that the United States Customs says theirs is some of
the best merchandise crossing the border, which makes him
very proud. He sent me a thick woven rug which is certainly
of excellent quality. Rugs have names like Violetas, Pescados
("Fish"), Navajos, Turista, Moderno and Figuritas Mexi-
canas ("rugs with Old Mexican figures"). All the rugs are
small enough to go by mail, which saves trouble with air
freight or whatever, and prices go from $34 for a 2' by 4'
(including fringe) to $359 for a 6' by 4'.

DO-IT-YOURSELF RUGS

**Jackson's Rug Craft, Croft Mill, Hebden Bridge,
Yorkshire HX7 8AP, England**
Rug-kits color catalogue with samples, free; air mail $1.
Church kneelers brochure, free; air mail $1.
Kits to make Rya, Oriental, traditional or solid-color pure-
wool rugs are illustrated in color in the rug catalogue, and
so are very inexpensive kits to make rugs from "thrums."
Thrums are end pieces of yarn in mixed colors left over
from weaving manufactured carpets.

DISCOUNT
Please see discount information in the How to Buy section.

Several shops in the Discount Furniture section sell carpets
and rugs. James Roy will order and sell any brand-name
carpet at a discount.

Tiles

**American Delft Blue, 787 Oella Avenue,
Ellictott City, MD 21043. Telephone (301) 465 4297**
Brochure, $2 U.S. and overseas. AE, MC, V.
Pierre Van Rossum, scion of a family that has been making
Delftware in Holland since 1821, immigrated to the United
States in 1963. Here, he restarted the family business and
now makes hand-painted, tin-glazed earthenware tiles, plates
and bowls. Decorations are the blue and white flower and
Dutch scenes that have been used in America since Colonial
times. Bible scenes can be painted to order. There is a $100
minimum.

**Country Floors, 300 East 61st Street,
New York, NY 10021. Telephone (212) 758 7414**
20-page color catalogue, $5 U.S. and overseas.
A brilliantly colored catalogue shows a gorgeous and varied
collection of American and imported tiles. As the owner
says, tiles don't represent the most ideal mail-order business,
but in most parts of the United States there is no other way.
Customers who can't get to the shop buy a catalogue, then a

sample or two, and finally send in a complete order. You
can also get hand-painted tile nameplates made to order, and
buy large sculptured terra-cotta pots embellished with Greek
figures.

**Elon, 150 East 58th Street, New York, NY 10022.
Telephone (212) 759 6996**
Color brochure, $1 U.S. and overseas.
A beautifully designed leaflet displays the handmade Mexican tiles in modern and traditional designs that Elon has
been importing for ten years. There are simple designs,
patterns with flowers or fruit, and some really good solid
colors. Basins and bath accessories are also sold; samples are
available.

**Terra Designs, 211 Jockey Hollow Road,
Bernardsville, NJ 07924. Telephone (201) 766 3577**
Leaflet, $1; overseas $2.
Potter Anna Salibello makes hand-cut, hand-carved, hand-
painted and hand-glazed tiles, inspired by eighteenth- and
nineteenth-century folk art motifs of birds, animals and
plants.

17
HOUSES

**The Barn People, Box 4, South Woodstock, VT 05071.
Telephone (802) 457 3943**
Portfolio with current inventory, $10 U.S. and overseas.
The portfolio I have seen has lots of interesting background information and details of four post and beam barns currently for sale. In this batch, prices are under $15,000 for barn reassembled on your foundations. Very tempting.

**Strout Realty, Plaza Towers, Springfield, MO 65804.
Telephone (417) 887 0100**
Catalogue, free U.S. and overseas.

**United Farm Agency, 612 West 47th Street,
Kansas City, MO 64112. Telephone (800) 821 2599**
Catalogue, free.
Yes, you can buy a house and land by mail, although not with a credit card. These two giants yearly distribute a million catalogues of possible rural retreats mainly to urban dreamers. Properties around the country go from North Carolina "riverfront fixer-upper" for under $2000, to Missouri cattle ranch historical mansion with third-floor ballroom for over $800,000.

JEWELRY

1 *David Anderson* Bracelet, about $85; pin, about $32; pendant, about $52. In sterling silver, designed by Bjørn Sigurd Østern.

2 *David Anderson* "Saga" jewelry, a few of the pieces copied from Viking jewelry, in sterling silver. Bracelet, about $44; large ring, about $22; ring, about $12; cuff links, about $24.

3 *The Craft Shop at Molly's Pond* Devonian Period Ammonite. A solid sterling silver shell on 24" chain, about $45.

4 *The Craft Shop at Molly's Pond* Earrings in sterling silver or gold. Lost-wax castings of 400,000,000-year-old (Devonian period) fossils. The originals are about $15 to $18 in silver.

Interesting and inexpensive jewelry can also be found in the Crafts and the Museums sections.

David Anderson A/S, Karl Johansgt, Oslo 1, Norway. Telephone 41 69 55
16-page color brochure, free.
Norway's leading jewelers export widely, and are probably best known for modern enamel jewelry which they do better than anyone else. Gilt butterfly pins with brilliantly colored ribbed wings, leaf necklaces, heart bracelets, and clover pins in glowing enamel and gilded silver are among the less expensive jewels. For people who want less colorful jewelry, there is modern sterling silver, and a Saga collection of replicas of Viking jewelry. Enameled spoons and thimbles also available.

Asprey and Company, 165–169 New Bond Street, London W1Y 0AR, England
24-page color catalogue, enquire. September. Prices in $.
Asprey's won gold medals at all the famous nineteenth-century exhibitions, and have been "by appointment" to every reigning sovereign since Queen Victoria—but their grand reputation goes back to the eighteenth century when William Asprey started a silver and leatherworking firm. His descendants have been making dressing cases, fine writing paper, jewelry and silverware for top people ever since.

James Avery, Craftsman, P.O. Box 1367, Kerville, TX 78028. Telephone (800) 531 7196
16-page color catalogue, free; overseas $1. AE, MC, V.
New designs in sterling silver and fourteen-carat-gold jewelry, mainly without stones. Many small pieces such as charms, pendants, and rings that in silver are not expensive.

Bijou House, 140 Kero Road, P.O. Box 333, Carlstad, NJ 07072–0333
24-page color brochure, 50 cents U.S. and overseas. AE, DC, MC, V.
Inexpensive costume jewelry: Lucite beads and bangles, majorca pearls and cloisonné pendants.

Cairncross, 18 St. John Street, Perth, Scotland. Telephone 0738 24367
Brochure, free. AE, V.
Cairncross makes pins and rings with Scottish freshwater pearls that have formed naturally inside mussels. Apparently Scottish pearls are smaller than oyster pearls, have a softer bloom and vary in color from pale gray to pink. The small and delicate pins are mostly in the shape of flowers and plants. Prices start at $140 for two pearls set in a nine-carat-gold wild "blaeberry" sprig and go up to $700 for pearls in a branch of heather. Ask about exact sizes—they're not given in the brochure.

The Craft Shop at Molly's Pond, U.S. 2, East Cabot, VT 05647
12-page brochure, $1; air mail $1.50. MC, V.
Luella Schroeder designs and makes sterling-silver jewelry by hand. The pieces, which are in small editions, are made by a variety of techniques: some are forged, others are cast, and others are cut, hammered and soldered. Patterns are often based on wild plants in Vermont: there are pins in the shapes of three different kinds of fern, medallions decorated with wild flowers, and earrings in the shapes of balsam-fir tips and wood knots. There are also tie tacks modeled after starfish and leaping trout, and cuff links based on fossils. Prices for sterling silver go from $10 to $35 and some of the pieces can be made in gold to order.

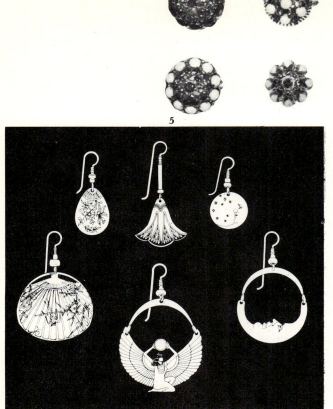

5

6

Diamonds by Rennie Ellen, 15 West 47th Street, Room 401, New York, NY 10036.
Telephone (212) 246 3930
Diamond brochure, $1.
Cubic zirconia brochure, $1.
Rennie Ellen, who has a reputation for being one of the most honest diamond dealers on 47th Street, is also one of the few women dealers. She sells, by appointment, in her office, or by mail. I am told by a friend in the jewelry business that New York dealer prices are likely to be considerably lower than those at jewelry stores around the country. Send for the jewelry brochure or write to her saying what you want and how much you want to spend, and she will advise you.

Rennie Ellen also sells cubic zirconia, a compound developed by the Swiss in 1975 as an aid for laser-beam research. The compound cuts and polishes like a diamond, and looks so much like a diamond that it has caused trouble by fooling professional jewelers. However, it is also quite popularly and honestly used in costume jewelry.

Mignon Faget, 710 Dublin Street,
New Orleans, LA 70118. Telephone (504) 865 7361
Leaflet, free U.S. and overseas. AE, MC, V.
An ex-art student designs silver and gold jewelry modeled realistically after sea creatures. There are sterling-silver sea urchin rings, sand-dollar cuff links, baby-snail earrings and pendants of moon snail, cockleshell, and clamshell on suede ties or silver chains. Hand-rolled leather belts have heavy silver buckles in the shapes of shells or crab bellies. Prices in the vicinity of $100 for sterling silver.

Frank and Company, P.O. Box 58428, Taipei, Taiwan
28-page color catalogue, $2. Prices in $.
A good selection of jade and coral jewelry set in fourteen-carat-gold or gold-plated brass at low prices. There are simple jade bangles and cuff links, decorative wedding rings set with semiprecious stones, plenty of pendants, rings and earrings for under $20 and also heavy, twisted bead necklaces.

♛ **Garrard and Company, 112 Regent Street,**
London W1A 2JJ, England
33-page color catalogue, $10. October.
Garrard (by appointment to the Queen, goldsmiths and crown jewelers—need I say more?) sends its catalogues to a selected list of important business people in America, but say that they have no mail-order service as at the moment their American customers buy when they come to London. They would, however, be happy to mail catalogues and goods to anyone else.

The gift catalogue shows very expensive modern and antique silver and jewelry. The lowest price I could find was $65 for a pair of cuff links.

Norman Greene Designs, P.O. Box 8451,
Emeryville, CA 94608. Telephone (415) 652 7464
Scientific instruments brochure, $2; overseas $3. Puzzle ring leaflet, free; overseas $1.
Norman Greene makes small pewter reproduction astrolabes, ancestor of the quadrant. Astrolabes were used for surveying, time-keeping, charting the stars and casting horoscopes. These astrolabes can be used as pendants. Norman Greene also makes six puzzle rings in sterling silver or gold.

5 *Rama Jewelry* Variations on the Thai "Princess" ring which traditionally has nine different stones, but can be made in any combination to order. Available in 12- or 14-karat gold, mostly at $100 to $120 each, but also up to $400, depending on the stones.

6 *Razzle Dazzle* Earrings handmade in gold vermeil or sterling silver, foundry-cast brass or silver plate, with pre–Columbia beads. Priced about $11 to $17 a pair.

**Hong Kong Jade Centre, 20-B Carnarvon Road,
Kowloon, Hong Kong. Telephone 664 678**
Brochure, free; air mail $1. Prices in $.
A big shop selling fourteen-carat-gold jewelry set with jade, diamonds, star sapphires, emeralds, pearls and semiprecious stones. Designs are uninspired and tend to be souveniry, but it should certainly be possible for most people to wrinkle out something they like, as styles vary and some are respectably plain. Prices are low, specially for jade—jade cuff links cost $150—and opal, moonstone or garnet rings are $85, aquamarine or onyx rings $75, all set in gold.

**Mappin and Webb, 170 Regent Street,
London W1R 6JH, England**
32-page gift catalogue, free.
Sterling-silver brochure, free.
Mappin plate brochure, free.
Mappin and Webb, silversmiths to the Queen, say that they have many customers in America. No antique jewelry or silver; instead glass, leather, dressing-table sets and stainless-steel flatware.

**Nacar S.A., 5 Avenida Jaime 111,
Palma de Mallorca, Spain. Telephone (971) 215 848**
Price list, free. Prices in $.
This large gift shop is an excellent place to buy Majorica artificial pearls by mail and, indeed, already has over a thousand foreign mail-order customers. Their list gives prices for single- and double-strand necklaces, bracelets and earrings.

**One Is Silver, R.F.D. 1, Box 10, Greene, RI 02827.
Telephone (401) 397 9660**
Brochure, $1 (refundable); overseas $2. MC, V.
Nicely made animal jewelry, designed and made by craftsman Jim Yesberger. Dragon pendants, cat cuff links, and snake rings. Everything in sterling silver or gold; rings cost under $100, everything else over.

**Rama Jewelry, 987 Silom Road, Bangkok, Thailand.
Telephone 234 7521**
Color leaflet, free. Prices in $.
Rama Jewelry has been manufacturing and exporting jewelry for the last twenty years, and in 1970 expanded into a new seven-story building of their own. They make all sorts of jewelry, including reproductions of traditional Thai jewels, but by far the most popular with tourists is the Princess Ring. A big domed ring studded with multicolored stones, the design is hundreds of years old and is supposed to bring the wearer good luck. Mr. Prapanth, the store manager, says that now when "the world of fancy fashion has taken place," the ring's design is often changed and customers can choose their own stones, sticking to one color if they like. The rings are set in fourteen-carat-gold, and traditionally have nine stones in hierarchical order—diamond, ruby, emerald, topaz, garnet, sapphire, moonstone, zircon, cat's-eye. They cost only $40 and up each, and air-mail postage for up to three rings is $6.

**Razzle Dazzle, 310 E. Paces Ferry Road,
Atlanta, GA 30305. Telephone (404) 233 6940**
Brochure, $2; overseas $3. MC, V.
New, pretty and inexpensive enamelled jewelry.

**T. Seng and Son Jewelry, 511/9–10 Petchaburi Road,
Bangkok 4, Thailand**
Color crafts leaflet, free. Jewelry brochure, free. Prices in $.
Glittering Western jewelry in fourteen- and eighteen-carat gold, with genuine stones. Many rings set with small garnets, opals, rubies, etc., for around $50, Princess Rings around $65, and silver charms for under $5. Recommended by Ane Denmark, who says she has had very satisfactory dealings with T. Seng.

**Shetland Silvercraft, Soundside, Weisdale,
Shetland, Scotland. Telephone 0595 72 275**
Leaflet, 25 cents; air mail 50 cents. MC, V.
A small workshop produces very attractive silver jewelry based on traditional local designs, many of which have been influenced by Shetland's long association with Norway. There are about thirty pieces, mostly brooches, earrings and cuff links, but there are also a few bracelets, small spoons and napkin rings. Most of the prices are between $15 and $50. Shetland Silvercraft can also make anything you want in gold, silver or other metals, and set it with precious stones. Sketches and estimates are free.

**Tiffany and Company, 727 Fifth Avenue,
New York, NY 10022. Telephone (212) 755 8000**
Catalogue, $3; overseas $5. AE, DC, MC, V.
Christmas card and stationery booklet, free. September to December.
Silver flatware brochure, free.
Tiffany was established in 1853 by Charles Lewis Tiffany, the father of the art nouveau designer Louis Comfort Tiffany, and is one of the world's symbols of luxury. For years Tiffany was run by autocratic Walter Hoving who believed not in giving the public what it wants (because it doesn't know what it wants) but in giving (or rather selling) the public good design. Tiffany refused to frame Bay of Pigs calendars in Lucite for President Kennedy; whether or not they approved of the Bay of Pigs, they certainly didn't approve of Lucite (Kennedy came back and asked for silver). They rejected a large order for $50,000 worth of diamond rings for a pro football team because Tiffany doesn't think that gentlemen should wear diamond rings.

Well, Tiffany's taste isn't perfect—whose is? but it's not that bad. The catalogue shows, besides very expensive modern jewelry, modern silver, unusual china and glass, clocks, pens and stationery.

**A. Van Moppes and Zoon, Albert Cuypstraat 2–6,
1072 CT Amsterdam, Holland**
Brochure, free; air mail $5 (refundable). Prices in $. AE, DC, MC, V.
Holland and Belgium are the world's diamond-cutting centers. This large and reputable diamond factory in Amsterdam is open to visitors, and thousands of tourists go through the plant every year. Van Moppes and Zoon imports diamonds directly from South Africa, then two hundred employees are involved in the sawing, shaping and polishing. Some diamonds are sold loose, others are made into jewelry, and for that, Van Moppes uses only top-quality diamonds: "blue/white and flawless" is the official grading. They say that their jewelry prices are 30 percent lower than American prices, but I haven't been able to check, as each piece is individual and settings vary, so I leave checking to anyone who considers buying. The brochure comes with a useful leaflet giving general information on cut and quality of diamonds. Prices for rings illustrated, $125 to $7000; earrings, $190 to $3000. If you want anything not shown, professional drawings will be sent and you can have pieces made to order.

19
MUSEUMS

Albright-Knox Art Gallery, The Shop,
1285 Elmwood Avenue, Buffalo, NY 14222.
Telephone (716) 882 8700
Brochure, free; overseas $1.25. MC, V.
This gallery of modern art sells posters, books and decorative toys and objects.

Publications Unit, Birmingham Museum of Art Gallery,
Chamberlain Square, Birmingham B33 DH, England
Color brochure, $1.
The Birmingham Museum has several things for sale that reproduce or use its holdings in nineteenth-century English art. Writing accessories, such as binders and clipboards, are covered with William Morris papers, an address book has Jonathan Heale animal woodcuts, and pocket address books illustrated by other turn of the century artists. A small but interesting collection.

British Museum Publications, 46 Bloomsbury Street,
London WC1B 3QQ. Telephone (01) 323 1234
12-page brochure of replicas and jewelry, various lists of books, prints, cards, free.
The British Museum was one of the first to produce replicas from its fabulous collections, and only a few of their most famous pieces have been on sale in the United States. Among their most striking offerings are the replicas of ivory plaques and boxes, as well as copies of Assyrian bas reliefs, Benin bronze and the like. The collection of seals and pendants is also represented with some stunning pieces, some very inexpensive (an intricate Viking snake brooch for under $5); some very dear. The Museum also has very thorough, though unillustrated, lists of its postcards and publications.

Brooklyn Museum Gallery Shop, Eastern Parkway,
Brooklyn, NY 11238. Telephone (212) 638 5000
Color brochure, 50 cents. (September to December only).
The Brooklyn Museum has a shop that is a delightful change from most museum stores, as it always has a lively and amusing collection of crafts from around the world, mostly inexpensive ones. Unfortunately, the brochure only shows a little, but it is likely to have novelties such as paper masks, scented sandalwood fans, and Russian nesting dolls.

The Cathedral Shop, Church of St. John the Divine,
1047 Amsterdam Avenue, New York, NY 10025.
Telephone (212) 222 7200
Price list, 75 cents; overseas $1. AE, MC, V.
The Cathedral's handsome shop offers a range of books, art, as well as toys with a religious theme and a section on biblical herbs (with a book on how to grow them). There are also gifts linked to the cathedral itself, including a chocolate version of the building, surely a first in Church history, and an interesting selection illustrating the Christian commitment to ecology.

Discovery Corner, Lawrence Hall of Science,
University of California, Berkeley, CA 94720.
Telephone (415) 642 1016
Catalogue, free; overseas $1. MC, V.
If your child is scientifically inclined, or you wish he or she were, send for this catalogue, which has lots of exciting-looking books of experiments and projects and explanations. Also microscopes, magnifying glasses, compasses, weather stations, games, puzzles.

1 *Albright-Knox Art Gallery* "Animal Stackers," brightly colored silk-screened animal acrobats, 4″ to 7″ tall each, can be displayed in many different positions. Two teams of six animals, each team about $35.

The Folger Shakespeare Library,
201 East Capitol Street, S.E., Washington, DC 20003.
Telephone (202) 544 4600
Catalogue, 50 cents. AE, MC, V.
The Folger Shakespeare Library is a nonprofit organization
that has a theater group, a consort that performs Renaissance music, and a research library that specializes in
Shakespeare, the Elizabethan age, and the Renaissance.
Each October, the organization produces a gift catalogue and
profits go to support the library. Gifts in the catalogue
include stained glass, needle point kits, jigsaw puzzles and
books with a Shakespearian, Elizabethan or Renaissance
theme. An excellent place for presents for the theatrical.

The Freer Gallery of Art, Smithsonian Institution,
12th Street at Jefferson Drive, S.W.,
Washington, DC 20560. Telephone (202) 357 1432
12-page catalogue, $1 U.S. and overseas; overseas air mail $2.
The Freer is best known for its treasures of Oriental art,
richest in Chinese and Japanese, but also strong in Islamic
and Indian art. The Freer cards and writing papers are
particularly delicate and pleasing; and there are also beautiful needlepoint kits, desk accessories and jewelry, at lower
prices, than things from the larger museums.

The Gift Collection, Lincoln Center for the Performing
Arts, 140 West 65th Street, New York, NY 10023.
Telephone (516) 997 6411
Catalogue, free. (None in January or August). AE, MC, V.
Presents for people interested in the performing arts—especially music. Mozart lovers can proclaim that interest with
bright red T-shirts, aprons, totes, ties, scarves, diaries, umbrellas and briefcases, and even bibs all printed with Mozart
music. There are also music boxes, framed opera posters,
binoculars, records and books.

The Hansen Planetarium, 15 South Street,
Salt Lake City, UT 84111. Telephone (801) 535 7317
Kitt Peak Observatory catalogue, 48 pages, $1. Brochures,
free.
The perfect source for astronomers or stargazers, a list of
stunning posters, postcards and slides of the heavens. Lovely
photographs, in color and black-and-white of stars, planets,
nebulae, galaxies and clusters. Very reasonably priced, these
make lovely presents not just for amateur astronomers but
for anyone interested in the beauties of nature, known and
unknown.

The Huntington Library, 1151 Oxford Road,
San Marino, CA 91108. Telephone (213) 792 6141 x 253
24-page black-and-white catalogue, 50 cents; overseas $1;
overseas air mail $2.50.
California's famous library publishes a series of prints, posters, broadsides and cards that should delight both biblio-
philes and gardeners, since the library's garden inspires
many of the printed materials. Of special interest are the
library's inexpensive reprints of their most famous children's
books. The library also has some striking regional material,
and a collection of historical broadsides, all very reasonably
priced, as is everything in this handsome listing.

The Jewish Museum Shop, 1109 Fifth Avenue,
New York, NY 10028. Telephone (212) 860 1866
Catalogue, $1; overseas $1.75; overseas air mail $2.50.
New York's Jewish Museum offers a catalogue that offers
some gifts which, as the ad campaign goes, you don't have to
be Jewish to enjoy. A number of the loveliest items are, of
course, of particular interest to Jews and intimately linked

2

3

2 *Discovery Corner* Prehistoric dinosaurs by Tatsuya Kodaka,
ready to assemble in die-cut laminated wood. About $6 to $8 each.

3 *The Huntington Library* 10″ × 14″ reproduction of "Provence
Rose" from *Les Roses* by Pierre Joseph Redouté, Paris, 1817–1824.
Priced about $3.

4

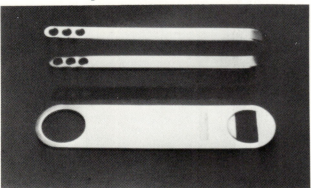

5

6

4 *The Met by Mail* An operatic shower curtain designed by Edward Gorey (you, the bather, stand center stage and sing). Black and white on clear vinyl, liners available. About $27.

5 *The Museum of Modern Art* Stainless steel ice tongs designed by Arne Jacobsen and produced in Denmark, about $8.50. Stainless steel bottle opener, designed by Henry Altchek and represented in the Museum's Design Collection, about $6.

6 *The Museum of Modern Art* Stainless steel oven-proof serving tray, about $40; stainless steel strainer for the tray (good for fish), $25; serving board, $35; oven-proof stainless steel serving bowls, two for about $45. All represented in the Museum's Design Collection.

to Jewish ritual. There are seder plates, passover tiles, a lovely porcelain menorah adapted from a nineteenth-century Polish lamp in the museum's collection as well as amulets, mezuzahs, etc.

International Museum of Photography at George Eastman House, 900 East Avenue, Rochester, NY 14607. Telephone (716) 271 3361

Catalogues, free U.S. and overseas. MC, V.
This distinguished museum has the most thorough list of books on photography that I know, both the current and older in-print titles. Very specialized books are listed as well as magazines from abroad, slide sets, microfiche and a number of very attractive (and inexpensive) posters. Finally, the Museum publishes photographic portfolios in limited editions of 100 to 200 copies, which run in the hundreds of dollars.

Library of Congress, Central Services Division, Box C, Washington, DC 20540

Catalogue, free U.S. and overseas. (No catalogue June to August).
The most important library in the country has some of the nicest cards available. But their gift catalogue shows a wider range, including some marvelous "Master Photographs," prints made from the fantastic collection, and featuring photographs by Walker Evans and others. There are also much less expensive reproductions of photos as well as some of the collection's rare maps.

The Met by Mail, (The Metropolitan Opera of New York), 1865 Broadway, New York, NY 10023. Telephone (212) 582 6713

40-page color catalogue, free; overseas $1; overseas air mail $3.50.
Opera lovers should enjoy the Met's catalogue: records, posters, opera glasses—even Met mugs, all carry through the operatic theme. Some T-shirts decorated by Edward Gorey (whose mugs are also available) and Pavarottiana galore (even a bent-nail pendant; apparently a classic operatic good luck charm).

The Metropolitan Museum of Art, Box 255, Gracie Station, New York, NY 10028. Telephone (212) 879 5500

116-page color catalogue and books and prints catalogue, $1 U.S. and overseas.
America's best-known museum produces the Neiman Marcus of museum catalogues; more lavish every year, and featuring an ever more elegant selection. The decorative household objects are mainly reproduced from, or inspired by, its own collections, and a few are only available here. From delicate hand-blown Early American flasks for under $30 to Asian statues for close to $3000, there is silver, porcelain, glass, jewelry galore, and always lovely calendars, address books and diaries, and wrapping paper. A smaller Books and Prints brochure has books, a few reproductions and posters.

The Minneapolis Institute of Arts, 2400 Third Avenue South, Minneapolis, MN 55404. Telephone (612) 870 3046

166-page color catalogue, free. MC, V.
A selective but original and valuable catalogue, offering gifts not to be found elsewhere. The current list includes some striking reproductions of Russian icons, hand-blown glass, a porcelain nativity set and bronze candelabra, bookends, etc.

Musee du Louvre,
Editions de la Reunion des Musees Nationaux,
10 Rue de L'abbaye Paris, 75006, France
General gift catalogue, 24 color pages, plus specialized cata-
logues of museum reproductions, jewels, slides, prints, post-
ers, religious art, slides, bronze reproductions and postcards,
$1 or 1 International Reply Coupon for air mail.
The most exciting new entry in the museum catalogue field
is the Louvre. For years the French have been reluctant to
sell by mail but they have now started with impressive
Gallic thoroughness and their catalogues are a delight. The
general gift catalogue includes jewels, silver reproduction,
lovely traditional French ceramics and copies of ornaments
or porcelain objects. Stunning reproductions of Roman and
other ancient glass objects, of old playing cards, etc. Prices
tend to be high but not at all unreasonable for objects of
such beauty and originality. Clearly a "must" catalogue.

The other catalogues can also be recommended highly.
The jewelry selection is markedly different from what is
offered in United States museums, more daring, more original in its selection. The sculpture reproductions from the
Louvre collections are far more extensive than the Metropolitan's offerings. Even the postcard catalogue is completely
illustrated, with over five hundred cards from all the leading
French museums, not just the Louvre. Finally the list of
religious art reproductions includes some of the masterpieces
of French art, a selection, one would think, of interest to
churches and institutions as well as individuals.

Museum of the City of New York Shop,
Fifth Avenue at 103rd Street, New York, NY 10029.
Telephone (212) 534 1672
16-page black-and-white catalogue, $1 U.S. and overseas;
overseas air mail $3. AE, MC, V.
This Museum of New York's history is best known for its
exhibits of the City in the late nineteenth-century, and for
its collection of toys from that period. The current catalogue
is a good source of old-fashioned toys: stuffed animals galore,
replicas of old dolls, some dollhouse kits and cast-iron toys
that I haven't seen anywhere else. Books on these interests
are also sold as are, of course, a few on New York history.

Museum of Fine Arts, Box 1044, Boston, MA 02120.
Telephone (617) 427 1111
34-page color catalogue, $1 for two years; overseas $2. AE,
MC, V.
The Boston Museum sells many reproductions from its own
collection, and apart from the imposing Paul Revere silver
plate coffee and tea sets, most things are decorative yet not
too expensive: table mats, aprons, Shaker boxes, wastepaper
baskets and playing cards, are sold with jewelry, needlepoint
kits, and jigsaw puzzles. Cards, a calendar, and wrapping
paper are produced for Christmas every year.

The Museum of Modern Art, 11 West 53rd Street,
New York, NY 10019. Telephone (212) 956 7264
32-page color catalogue, $1. AE, MC, V.
New York's pioneer museum of art and design used to be
known for its colorful cards and its distinguished art books,
which it still sells, but the nature of its listings has changed
dramatically. It is now a major source for well-designed
objects for work and the house, many reproductions from its
own collection. From pens, scissors and lamps to Breuer
chairs and the famous Aalto tea cart, glassware from Finland, jewelry, children's toys, even tools round out the selections.

7

8

7 *The Museum of Modern Art* Portable AM/FM radio designed
by Marco Zanuso and Richard Sapper and produced in Italy.
Represented in the Museum's Design Collection. About $150.

8 *The Museum of Modern Art* Postal marker stamps designed by
Bruno Munari and produced in Italy, five for $25.

9

10

Museums of Great Britain Gift Selection, North Eastern Road, Thorne, Near Doncaster, DN8 4AS, United Kingdom
16-page color catalogue, free; air mail $2.50. MC, V.
This private firm works closely with many British museums and offers an appealing catalogue listing gifts from several of them. Prices are about those of American museums, but of course, the chances are you'll find something none of your friends have seen, such as the Victoria and Albert's fashion diary or some lovely reproduction plates for well under $10. Antique toys and lovely old playing cards, gorgeous tea towels and other English specialties. A listing filled with original and attractive gifts.

The National Gallery, Publications Department, Trafalgar Square, London WC2N 5DN, England. Telephone (01) 839 3321
32-page color brochure, $1.15.
A good brochure of small reproductions with a separate price list. The National Gallery is intelligently pessimistic about rising prices and advises customers to ask for a new price list if the brochure has been around for more than six months.

The actual reproductions are of 138 famous and favorite European masterpieces from Fra Angelico's *The Rape of Helen by Paris* to Monet's *Pond with Water Lilies*, both about ten square inches and both $2. Postcards also available.

The National Trust for Historic Preservation, 1600 H Street, N.W., Washington, DC 20006. Telephone (202) 673 4200
Color catalogue, 50 cents; Canada 75 cents; overseas $1; overseas air mail $2. MC, V.
The fact that wherever you live, you can enjoy the work of the National Trust, should be an incentive to buy through this catalogue. Many objects shown are not exclusive to the National Trust, but they do usually have connections with history or architecture. There are paper model kits of National Trust properties; attractive jardinieres made in Chesterwood, a National Trust property; reproductions of an Old New Hampshire blanket, and a rag rug. Blue pineapple china and Correira Art glass has been made especially for the Trust; and there are Christmas tree decorations, writing paper and a few books on crafts, doll-house building, and architecture.

The Shop in the Garden, The New York Botanical Gardens, Bronx, NY 10458. Telephone (212) 220 8705
Color catalogue, free U.S. and overseas. MC, V.
A few natural cone fir wreaths and table centerpieces are exclusive to the Botanical Garden. Most of the other nice flowery things in this catalogue have been well chosen from the products of other manufacturers. Soaps, herb pillows, herb baths, lavender sachets are flower covered, and so are cushions, place mats, cannisters, dishcloths, tote bags and greeting cards.

Oceanic Society Gifts, Stamford Marine Center, Magee Avenue, Stamford, CT 06902. Telephone (203) 327 9786
Color brochure, free U.S. and overseas.
A series of marine gifts, some just for sailors such as waterproof and rubber coated binoculars, others, such as stuffed toys, whale and dolphin sculptures, and old-fashioned rotating globes, are of more general interest.

9 *The Shop in the Garden* A full-color family tree chart in Pennsylvania Dutch design. Lets you trace your family through six generations. Two for about $7.

10 *Old Sturbridge Village* A bunch of New England dried flowers native to Massachusetts. About $28.

Museum Gift Shop, Old Sturbridge Village, Sturbridge, MA 01566. Telephone (617) 347 9843
Catalogue, free; overseas $1; overseas air mail $2. AE, MC, V.
"A living museum of family, work and community life in early-nineteenth-century rural New England. Among the pleasant, simple and historically accurate crafts sold at Old Sturbridge Village, many have been reproduced from pieces in their own collection, and some have been actually made at the Village. Here you'll find such things as a cheese basket, a hogscraper candle holder, a handmade broomcorn hearth brush, a farmer's work shirt, a butter churn. Also salt glaze and red pottery, tin sconces and lanterns, blown and pressed glass, pewter, trivets, theorem paintings, simple toys and furniture. Sturbridge Village is also supplying miniature collectors with carefully made copies of the eighteenth-century furniture on display at the village. For accomplished woodworkers, there are measured drawings, with bills of materials and construction notes so that you can make your own reproduction furniture.

The Pierpont Morgan Library, 29 East 36th Street, New York, NY 10016. Telephone (212) 685 0008
Leaflet, free.
As could be expected from New York's famous collection of rare books, the Morgan list is filled with exceptionally handsome cards, posters and books. From a Maurice Sendak poster for a mere $2.50 to a calligraphy set for $12.50, here are reasonable gifts for those who love the printed (or written) word. The Morgan's own publications are listed as well as a welcome choice of cards, etc., at lowered prices.

The Rijksmuseum Foundation,
Department of Reproductions, Hobbemastraat 21,
Amsterdam 1071 XZ, Holland
Price list, free.
The Rijksmuseum is one of the world's great museums known for its holdings of Holland's incredibly artistic heritage. Unfortunately the price list only lists the names of pictures reproduced, so it's as well they are all famous. Reproductions, posters, postcards and publications are all sold.

The Smithsonian Institution, Mail Order Division, Box 199, Washington DC 20560
Catalogue three times a year, color, 60 pages, $1 U.S. and overseas. AE, MC, V.
Representing all thirteen of its museums, the Smithsonian catalogue is a very mixed bag, strongest in Americana, where a range of furniture, china and even clocks are reproduced, many from the museums' collections. Embroidery, a particularly handsome carpet bag and reproductions of musical instruments are all featured. Toys, Christmas tree ornaments and model airplanes are also part of this grabbag. If the Metropolitan is closer to Neiman Marcus, this list invokes the spirit of L. L. Bean. Little to suggest that some of the museums deal in high art, but the perfect place to buy your model train or a reproduction hearth broom.

South Seaport Museum, Museum Shops,
203 Front Street, New York, NY 10038.
Telephone (212) 766 9020
Catalogue, free U.S. and overseas. MC, V.
The South Street Seaport Museum, an entity restoring and revitalizing Manhattan's nineteenth-century port, is now putting out a catalogue of beautifully designed gifts with a maritime theme. For children there are irresistible painted

11

12

11 *Old Sturbridge Village* Pressed glass reproduced from museum pieces: 1830 plate, about $18; decanter, about $38; tumblers about $6.

12 *Old Sturbridge Village* Linen for the kitchen, with a design taken from the Sheaf of Wheat plate. Apron, about $12.50; tea towel, about $3.75; oven glove, about $3.75; potholder, about $3.50.

13

13 *Textile Museum* In the background, richly colored prints of rare textiles, $25 each. A wastepaper basket with a Chinese pillar rug design, about $12. Left, on cotton, "America Salutes France," an eighteenth-century design commemorating France's support of America during the Revolutionary War, $15. In front, pillows made from kilim fragments, about $65 to $100 each.

wooden bathtub boats and nesting sailors, felt fish puzzles and whale clothes-hangers. For adults, a brass porthole mirror, Delft ashtrays with ship decorations and prints, cards, aprons, and T-shirts all with sailing ship designs. A few picture books about sailing too.

The Tate Gallery Publications Department, Millbank, London SWLP 4RG, England. Telephone (01) 834 5651
Color catalogue, sea mail $2.50; air mail $5.
The Tate's catalogue of its color prints is a model for other museums. Each reproduction is shown in color, whether a print or a poster. Here are the famous Museum's most famous paintings, from Turner and Stubbs to Klee and Kandinksy. The poster selection is exceptionally attractive. Prices are very reasonable, largely from $5 to $10.

Textile Museum, 2320 S Street N.W., Washington, DC 20008. Telephone (202) 667 0442
Catalogue, 50 cents. MC, V.
A small collection of wearable gifts: silk ties in designs from the museum collection; cloisonné and enamel beads and amulets from China for jewelry or macrame; Victorian pouches, made from turn-of-the-century sari ribbon embroidered in China, and silk Disco handbags with gold and silk embroidery, dragons, birds and fish, $15. Also books about Oriental carpets, weaving, and embroidery with special emphasis on patterns and techniques.

Winterthur Museum and Gardens, Winterthur, Delaware 19735. Telephone (302) 656 8591 X 355
8-page color brochure, free; overseas $1. MC, V.
Henry Francis du Pont's Museum of American decorative arts has recently started reproducing and adapting objects from its own collection. Some unusual and appealing things, in folk art and in more refined designs.

Instruments

Sam Ash Music Stores, 124 Fulton Avenue, Hempstead, NY 11550. Telephone (800) 645 3518; New York State (212) 347 7757
Paul J. Ash says "We are presently one of the largest mail-order houses in the music industry; selling musical instruments, electronic keyboard instruments sound gear, instrument amplifiers, and recording equipment to players all over the world.

"Our mail-order department boasts six full-time salespersons who take calls, answer letters and Telex Communications. In addition, we have typists, billing clerks, order pickers and shippers. One thing we do not have is a catalogue.

"We have found that we can serve our customers very well by discussing their needs on our toll-free line and following up with mailing pertinent price and tear sheets."

Carvine Equipment, 1155 Industrial Avenue, Escondido, CA 92025. Telephone (800) 854 2235; (714) 747 1710
64-page color catalogue, free U.S. and abroad.
Carvine manufactures, and sells only by mail, reasonably priced sound reinforcement equipment. Electric guitars and parts, speaker systems and sound systems—they are all here, and you get to try them for ten days.

M. G. Contreras, Mayor 80, Madrid 13, Spain. Telephone 248 5926
Price list in Spanish, free. AE, DC, MC, V.
This workshop makes guitars and mandolins of various kinds and at various prices. As I write, the least expensive concert quality classicial guitars cost about $920 and the most expensive classical guitars cost about $1740, made in special Brazilian palisander wood. Although prices start well below, M. G. Contreras feels that it isn't worth sending instruments costing less because the air freight (which they always use with foreign customers) is expensive. Although there is a brief price list, this firm prefers that you write to them (in English if you like) telling them exactly what you are after, and they will answer (in Spanish) giving you the appropriate information.

Giardinelli, Band Instrument Company, 151 West 46th Street, New York, NY 10036. Telephone (212) 575 5959
Custom mouthpiece brochure, free U.S. and abroad. AE, MC, V.
Giardinelli makes custom mouthpieces for trumpets, trombones, tubas, French horns, and cornets. They also have a large selection of top brand brass and woodwind instruments, which they sell at about 30 percent off list price. Recommended to me by a professional musician.

Guitar's Friend, Route 1, Box 200, Sandpoint, ID 83864. Telephone (208) 263 7640
16-page catalogue, free U.S. and abroad. MC, V.
Laurence Ostrow and a group of dedicated people sell brand-name string instruments, together with very well reviewed locally made ones. Local handmade instruments include a guitar based on the well-known Martin OM, several mandolins and some dulcimers.

Frank Hubbard, 144 Moody Street, Box 13, Waltham, MA 02154. Telephone (617) 894 3238
Catalogue, $1 U.S. and abroad.
Most famous and admired of the harpsichord kit makers,

recommended by David Burrows, a reader, who says "Impressive! *Very* good reproductions of specific harpsichords, spinets, and even a pipe organ."

Hughes Company, 4419 West Colfax, Denver, CO 80204. Telephone (303) 572 3753
Catalogue, free U.S. and abroad. MC, V.
Hughes specializes in kits that allow you to make dulcimers, guitars, Irish harps, balalaikas and similar instruments at home. Hughes was the first to manufacture such kits and the large assortment is popularly priced; dulcimer kits start as low as $20, with the finished instrument costing $37. Only the simplest tools are needed to assemble the instruments, and Hughes calculates that time needed ranges from four to five hours for a small dulcimer to forty to fifty hours for a guitar.

Koch Recorder, Haverhill, NH 03765. Telephone (603) 989 5620
Leaflet, free U.S. and abroad.
William Koch was the first American to make recorders up to the standards of European craftsmen, and since his death in 1970 his son has carried on after him. Koch recorders are held in high esteem; still, they continue to be the least expensive of the fine recorders you can get in America.

Lindberg, Sonnenstrasse 15, D800 Munich 2, Germany. Telephone (089) 558601
48-page color brochure in German, $1.
"Das Paradies der Musikfreunde" puts out a jolly catalogue full of laughing groups playing away on pianos and accordions (thirty Hohner models at prices from $260 to $2850). "Organettas," "pianets," over thirty kinds of guitars—Western Spanish, electric ("Wandervogel," the least expensive, costs $36)—two electric Hawaiian guitars, six banjos, a ukelele, zithers, saxophones, clarinets, trumpets and horns, drums, violins and even a lyre. Lindberg says that Americans buy a lot of folk-music instruments by mail, especially concert zithers, Hackbretter recorders, harmonicas, violins, also German sheet music. Unfortunately the catalogue is in German.

Morley Harpsichord, Pianoforte and Harp Galleries, 4 Belmont Hill, Lewisham, London SE13 5BD, England
Complete catalogue, $2; air mail $6. AE, DC, V.
Morley's specializes in both new and second-hand pianos, harps and early keyboard instruments and antiques. Americans, apparently, are most interested in classical early keyboard instruments, as well as some of the antique and restored pieces. Morley lists early-nineteenth-century pianos, old lutes, spinets and a double-manual harpsichord. The well-illustrated and extremely helpful catalogue has photos of spinets, virginals, clavichords and the simpler, modern pianos. These include a large number of British makes as well as the increasingly widespread Japanese and other models.

1 *Morley Harpsichord* Clarsach, the small (34″ high) portable Celtic harp which has been revived as an accompaniment for now-popular Irish folk songs and ballads. The harp is finished in the traditional dark green with gilt decorations; carrying case and videotaped playing instructions are available. Priced about $1500, delivered to the customer's nearest port in the United States.

2 *Wayne Moskow* Handmade red clay Doumbec, $55. Considered by Wayne Moscow to be the finest folk drum made.

Wayne Moskow, Musical Instruments of the World, 3095X Kerner Boulevard, San Rafael, CA 94901. Telephone (415) 453 7560
34-page catalogue, $1; abroad $1.50. MC, V.
A fascinating catalogue of unusual ethnic instruments from around the world: clay ocarinas, coconut afuches, abalone shell kalimbas, gourd khamakas, bean coco flutes for snake charming and lots more, mostly inexpensive. Wayne Moskow also repairs "almost anything."

John Nicholson, Old Forge Workshops, Sparrows Green, Walhurst, Sussex, England. Telephone 089 288 3715
Catalogue, 35 cents or 3 International Reply Coupons.
John Nicholson builds organs and other instruments, most of which are sold directly to American customers, many of them university music departments and other specialized music groups. All his instruments, including the organs can be shipped to the United States: Nicholson also offers a range of much less expensive instruments, mostly replicas of early music instruments, such as psalteries of various sorts, rebecs, pibgorns and panpipes.

Paxman Musical Instruments, 116 Long Acre, London WC2E 9PA, England. Telephone (01) 240 3642
Price list, $2.50 air mail.
Paxman is a maker of French horns and accessories, which they export all over the world. They are the only British manufacturer of these instruments and one of the few left in the world who still build horns to order. Their horns are made in different alloys, at different prices, and cover the classic range of single and double horns, besides many types of descant-horn.

The Renaissance Gilde, P.O. Box 5, Cambridge, WI 53523. Telephone (608) 423 4125
Brochure, free U.S. and abroad.
This unique enterprise was established to provide "good, playable, authentic lutes and other historic stringed instruments" for performers of early music. Basing their endeavor on meticulous research and, judging from the photographs, extraordinary workmanship, they make various kinds of lutes in three qualities. All instruments are sent out on approval, and a trade-in allowance on your old lute is possible.

Rhythm Band, P.O. Box 126, Fort Worth, TX 76101. Telephone (817) 335 2561
34-page color catalogue, free U.S. and abroad. MC, V.
Rhythm Band is the country's largest manufacturer of elementary musical instruments and has a thorough catalogue, which it mails to schools, but which is also available to individuals. While many of its listings, such as the rhythm bands, are of interest only to schools, or to very large families, there are a great many instruments which parents or children may wish to send away for.

Robinson's Harp Shop, Mount Laguna, CA 92048
Leaflet, free.
Here you can get plans to make harps or finished and assembled harps—Irish, Paraguayan or miniconcert.

Robert S. Taylor, 8710 Garfield Street, Bethesda, MD 20817. Telephone (301) 530 4480
Brochure, free.
Taylor is the American importer of the harpsichords, spinets and clavichords made in Germany by Kurt Sperrhake. This is a one-man operation, the instruments being on display in Taylor's home and sold directly to customers. As a result, his prices are lower than those charged for any similar, famous make harpsichords if you are buying in the United States.

Waltons Musical Instrument Galleries, 2–5 North Frederick Street, Dublin 1, Ireland. Telephone 747 805
Catalogue free; air mail $5. Most major credit cards accepted.
Waltons makes and sells Irish harps and also sells most

3

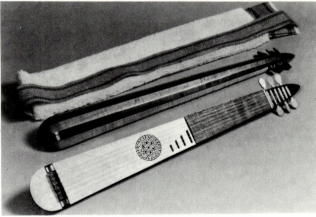

4

5

3 *Wayne Moskow* Bousouki, made in Italy. About $400, including case and postage.

4 *Wayne Moskow* Bar made of teak wood fitted with skin, 10″ to 18″ diameter. About $25 to $35.

5 *The Renaissance Gilde* The "Coryn" designed by William Daum who wanted an instrument light enough to take hiking, biking, and traveling by plane. He says it has a superb sound, somewhere between a guitar and a lute but softer so that it doesn't disturb other people. Most guitar and lute music can be used. With a furlike fabric carrying case, the Coryn costs about $275.

6

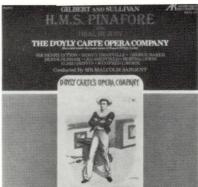

7

8

6 *Early Music Stands* Solid cherry wood music furniture, oiled and hand-rubbed. The stand (carry case available), about $178; the performer's bench is especially comfortable and has removable legs and a carry case, about $168; the musician's table, for keeping music and instruments within easy reach, disassembles, about $122.55. The recorder rack holds recorders, flutes, and oboes, about $26.50.

7 *Caedmon/Arabesque* The D'Oyly Carte Opera Company performing *H.M.S. Pinafore* and *Trial by Jury*. Record or cassette, $15.96.

8 *Caedmon/Arabesque* Anthony Quayle reading "The Voyage of the Dawn Trader" from *The Chronicles of Narnia* by C. S. Lewis. Record or cassette, $8.98.

other musical instruments, sheet music and records related to Ireland.

The Williams Workshop, 1229 Olancha Drive, Los Angeles, CA 90065. Telephone (213) 254 2115
Brochure, $1.
Inexpensive harpsichords, good for beginners, available ready made or as kits.

DISCOUNT
Please see discount information in the How to Buy section.

Elderly Instruments, 541 East Grand River, P.O. Box 1795C, East Lansing, MI 48823. Telephone (517) 332 4331
Three catalogues: instruments, books and music, records, all free in the U.S.; abroad $2.
Extremely engaging catalogues, of the pulp paper and lots of helpful information variety. Hard-to-find stuff from small manufacturers, high-quality stuff from large manufacturers at 10 to 50 percent off list price, they say. The folk instrument catalogue gives useful background information on the manufacturers and models. Don't miss this firm if you are interested in folk, bluegrass, blues, jazz or ethnic music. Established 1972.

Freeport Music, 144 Wolf Hill Road, Melville, NY 11747. Telephone (516) 549 4108
24-page catalogue, $1 U.S. and abroad. MC, V.
"From a piano to a piccolo, from a clarinet to a PA system—if it makes a musical sound, chances are we have it or can get it for you at a discount of 20 percent to 60 percent," says Lon T. Palmer, president. The oldest mail-order music house in the U.S., specializes in "name-brand musical merchandise sold at a large discount by mail." The catalogue I saw had mainly instruments for rock groups, amplifiers and disco light controls. Established 1921.

Silver Horland, 170 West 48th Street, New York, NY 10036. Telephone (212) 869 3870
No catalogue. AE, MC, V.
Silver Horland sells musical instruments and accessories (but no percussion or keyboard instruments) new, used and vintage. The policy is to give a 30-percent discount. Although they have no catalogue, they answer specific requests and keep a wanted file for hard to find things. Established 1929.

Music Stands

B. W. M. Benn, 4424 Judson Lane, Minneapolis, MN 55435. Telephone (612) 922 2280
8-page leaflet, 50 cents U.S. and abroad.
Mr. Benn, his wife and some outside help have been making harpsichords for eighteen years, turning out some five to ten instruments a year, built from scratch in their own shop. More recently, they have started making elegant walnut music stands with inlaid decoration.

Early Music Stands, P.O. Box 277, Palo Alto, CA 94302. Telephone (415) 328 5044
30-page brochure, $1 U.S. and abroad (refundable). MC, V.
Lovely hand-rubbed solid cherrywood music stands with candle cups; especially comfortable folding stools; handy instrument stands. This well-liked firm makes good-looking chamber music furniture and accessories for professional and amateur musicians around the world.

Open-Reel Tapes

Barclay-Crocker, 11 Broadway, New York, NY 10004. Telephone (212) 952 0068
40-page catalogue, $1; abroad $2.
What with cartridges and cassettes, one doesn't hear so much about the old open-reel tapes these days. Nevertheless, excellent tapes are still being made and have an enthusiastic following among music lovers who appreciate the high quality and low prices. Prices are about one third under "audiophile" discs and cassettes of the same quality. Barclay-Crocker is the leader in the field, and their carefully made tapes of classical music are derived from master tapes from the better record companies.

The Reel Society, P.O. Box 55099-C, Valencia, CA 91355. Telephone (805) 257 4150
44-page catalogue, $1; abroad $2; airmail $3.
A varied selection of open-reel tapes that includes film scores, popular music and sound tracks and original cast albums, as well as classical.

Printed Music

Blackwell's Music Shop, 38 Holywell Street, Oxford OX1 3SW, England. Telephone (0865) 4911
Catalogues: General Music Books, free; Organ Music, free; Piano Music, free; Records, free. MC, V.
A division of Blackwell Bookshop, Blackwell's Music Shop thinks and hopes that this is the largest shop in the world devoted to books on music and printed music. They stock English, European and American music.

I am told that although American records are less expensive than any others, foreign records cost less if bought directly from abroad. Blackwell's sells records by all the major English companies, and the complete Erato range from France.

William Elkin Music Services, Station Road, Industrial Estate, Salhouse, Norwich NR13 6NY, England. Telephone (0603) 721 302
William Elkin Music Services supplies (promptly, they say) sheet music and books on music from all publishers in the United Kingdom and Europe. No catalogue; write and tell them what you want.

Free Library of Philadelphia, Logan Square, Philadelphia, PA 19103. Telephone (215) 686 5313
Information, free U.S. and abroad. 956-page catalogue, $75.
A scholarly catalogue of the Edwin A. Fleishner Collection of Orchestral Music, one of the largest and most important catalogues in the world, costs $75. However, the Philadelphia free library lends out orchestral music from its collection to organizations around the world—"recognized symphony orchestras, universities and colleges, conservatories of music and to outstanding organizations interested in the furtherance of music." Write to the library for lending fees and details.

G. Schirmer, 40 West 62nd Street, Attention Order Department, New York, NY 10023. Telephone (212) 784 8520 x 52
Schirmer's is the country's best-known music store and sells sheet music by mail "if it is in stock." But they have no catalogue, so you have to know what you want.

Records and Tapes

In buying records by mail, you can find many interesting and unusual records not handled by the majority of record stores.

The Schwann catalogue is a great help in buying records and tapes by mail. It contains a selective but very extensive list of all kinds of records and tapes sold through U.S record stores (although it excludes records sold only by mail). Single copies are sold through record stores such as Record Hunter (below). An annual subscription to fourteen catalogues costs $25 within the U.S., $35 in Canada and $40 elsewhere and may be obtained from ABC Schwann Record and Tape Guides, P.O. Box 2131, Radnor, PA 19089.

For classical music lovers, a few small American firms are still producing imaginative records, but European firms, and especially English ones, now seem to be willing to spend more money and to produce records more innovative than those generally produced here. You can find out about English records through "New Records," sold by the English shops.

American Music Warehouse, P.O. Box 3400, Nashville, TN 37219
48-page catalogue, free U.S. and abroad. MC, V.
Two hundred and fifty thousand records and almost as many tapes, of American popular music. They'll order any record not in stock if you give them artist, title, record company name and number.

James Asman, 23a New Row, St. Martin's Lane, London WC2 4LA, England
James Asman sells new, used and out-of-print records and especially traditional jazz by mail and is accustomed to supplying new discs that overseas readers have seen reviewed or advertised. No catalogue, write and tell them what you want.

Big Band 80's Record Library, 9288 Kinglet Drive, Los Angeles, CA 90069. Telephone (213) 858 1980
46-page catalogue, $1; abroad $3. MC, V.
All the big bands, mainly on record but some on tapes too.

Ditta Francesco Bongiovanni, Via Rizzoli 28/E Bologna, Italy. Telephone (051) 225 722
Brochure, "a few International Reply Coupons."
This family firm produces records of operatic arias recorded live, and also famous opera records of the past for collectors.

Caedmon/Arabesque, 1995 Broadway, New York, NY 10023. Telephone (800) 223 0420
Catalogue, free. MC, V. (Teakfield in Europe, Trutone, South Africa)
Caedmon produces excellent spoken word records and cassettes—The Shakespeare Recording Society, Dylan Thomas reading Yeats, Ogden Nash reading Ogden Nash, J. R. R. Tolkien reading *The Lord of the Rings* and all sorts of nice children's books being read by actors and actresses. Recently the firm has started producing medium-priced historical records mainly from the British EMI catalogue, for collectors. All sorts of interesting historical material from the thirties.

Chesterfield Music Shops, 12 Warren Street, New York, NY 10007. Telephone (212) 964 3380
Price lists, free. MC, V.
Chesterfield is one of a number of firms specializing in record sales by mail. It is one of the largest and oldest in the

9

10

field and will send you its price lists several times a year, once you send them your name. They have a number of exclusive, imported items and sell records in all fields of music and the spoken word.

Colon Records, 33 Orientales 955/57,
1236 Buenos Aires, Argentina. Telephone 922 5323
Price list, free; air mail $1.50.
New and used unusual records for collectors.

Country Sales, P.O. Box 191, Floyd, VA 24091.
Telephone (703) 745 2001
Brochure, 50 cents (stamps O.K.); abroad $1.
David Freeman started County Records in the sixties by making records from twenties recordings featuring mountain fiddle music, and country string bands (the beginnings of modern bluegrass and grass roots music). The firm still produces excellent records, and also sells bluegrass, old-time and fiddle music by mail.

James H. Crawley, 246 Church Street,
London N9 9HQ, England. Telephone (01) 807 7760
List Vocal Art, one issue, $2 (annual subscription, $5).
Tape list, $1.
James Crawley buys and sells rare vocal 78-rpm records, mostly ones that look and sound absolutely new. They also have some rare recordings transcribed onto 12-inch long-players for about $11 each, and will transcribe others at customers' requests. Crawley also now has set cassettes of musical comedy, music hall, operatic rarities, unpublished tracks, orchestral music and spoken word costing about $5 per tape. Also tapes made to order.

Dobells Jazz Record Shop, 77 Charing Cross Road,
London WC2, England
Bimonthly bulletin of obscure records, $2.50 for six.
"New Records," all U.K. records issued each month, $4 per year.
This shop specializes in hard-to-find jazz, folk and blues records. These include a great many rare discs which, the store warns, are in very limited supply and should be ordered quickly.

Down Home Music, 10341 San Pablo Avenue,
El Cerrito, CA 94530. Telephone (415) 525 1494
Catalogue, $2; overseas $3. AE, MC, V.
Down Home says they have the largest and best selection of folk, traditional and ethnic music in California (including vintage rock and roll, blue grass, old-timey, country music, Western and much more). They also carry prestigious imported records of "authentic ethnic music, beautifully recorded and extensively annotated": German Bahrenreitter, Phillips UNESCO, Sonet, Le Chant du Monde, and all the Ocora.

Folkways, Records, 43 West 61st Street,
New York, NY 10023. Telephone (212) 586 7260
Records, New Releases, and Records for Children. Price lists, free U.S. and abroad.
A marvelous assortment of out-of-the-way recordings is produced by Folkways: history and documentaries, old jazz reissues, lots of ethnic, and a very superior series of folk songs and stories for children.

House of Oldies, 35 Carmine Street,
New York, NY 10014
82-page price list, $2 U.S. and abroad. MC.
"World Headquarters for out-of-print 45s," says the price list of the "oldest oldie shop" in New York. The store

9 *Chesterfield Music Shops* Mozart, "Sonatas for Violin and Piano."

10 *Country Sales* "Nashville, the Early String Bands," two volumes, each about $5.75.

specializes in rock-'n'-roll oldies, LPs and 45s, with over a
million titles in stock, five thousand of which are listed in
the closely packed price list. The store also stocks rhythm
and blues, 1950s pop and sound tracks. If you've outgrown
your collection, the House of Oldies will consider buying

**Indian House, P.O. Box 472, Taos, NM 87571.
Telephone (505) 776 2953**
Leaflet, free, U.S. and abroad.
An anthropologist and his Indian wife make first-rate hi-
fidelity recordings of North American Indian music. The
Isaacs recommend their records for Indian study programs at
all levels. They say that children can easily learn the social
dances and especially enjoy the strong rhythms. At more
advanced levels, the songs contain information about Indian
history.

**In Sync Laboratories, 2211 Broadway,
New York, NY 10024. Telephone (212) 873 6769**
Price list, free U.S. and abroad.
Prerecorded cassette tapes are known for their inconsistent
quality and rarely satisfy very demanding music lovers. In
Sync has pioneered a series of superior cassettes. The cassettes are recorded on the new German BASF Professional
II tape, directly from master tapes at the real speed (not
high speed). All quite different from the usual inferior recording procedures, and the payoff is very good definition
and range, and almost no background noise.

**Library of Congress, Motion Picture,
Recorded Broadcasting, and
Sound Section, Washington, DC 20540**
Price lists, free.
During the Depression years, John and Alan Lomax and
their associates went through the United States recording
our folk music and folk tales in much the same way that
photographers from the Farm Security Administration recorded the visual aspects of American rural life. The result
is one of the monuments of American history, a unique
attempt to capture a vital aspect of life that came just in
time and left us all a heritage that might otherwise have
been lost. Though the Lomaxes' efforts are known to many
who have a serious interest in folk music, relatively few
people know that many of these original records are still
available from the Library of Congress and that they have
been supplemented by several other programs, including a
major one of recording the music of the American Indian. The
Library's brochure lists the contents of each LP: there are
Afro-American spirituals, blues and game songs, work songs
and calls, as well as a marvelous record of religious songs
and actual church services. White work songs include songs
of anthracite miners, railroad songs, songs of Michigan lum-
berjacks, sea songs and chanties, cowboy songs and cattle
calls from Texas, Mormon songs and folk music from Wisconsin. There are also several records from Latin America:
folk music from Venezuela, Mexico, Puerto Rico and Afro-
Bahia (Brazil).
   The Library also has an extensive catalogue of spoken
recordings, based for the most part on its famous poetry
readings.

**Lyrichord Discs, 141 Perry Street, New York, NY 10014.
Telephone (212) 929 8234**
Price lists, free U.S. and overseas.
Two leaflets, one for classical music, and one for ethnic
music from around the world, mainly nonEuropean (Afri-
can, Eastern, South American, etc.).

11

11 *Library of Congress* "Songs of Love, Courtship and Marriage,"
one of fifteen records of American folk music, about $8 each.

12

13

14

Maildisc and Company, 280 Central Park Road, London E6 3AD, England. Telephone (01) 472 8969
Gramophone record and cassette price list: Classical, $6.50; Pop and Jazz, $4.
Specialists in selling records by mail, Maildisc sends out the general British "New Records" leaflet, with its own price lists.

Monitor Recordings, 156 Fifth Avenue, New York, NY 10010. Telephone (212) 989 2323
Brochure, free.
Popular music from around the world on records and tapes. Folk music, yes, but also "Yves Montand and His Songs of Paris," "Fiesta Mexicana," "Russian Cabaret," and the like.

Musical Heritage Society, 14 Park Road, Tinton Falls, NJ 07724. Telephone (201) 544 8440
192-page catalogue, $2; overseas $4. MC, V.
A marvelous source for lovers of serious music. If you register with the Musical Heritage Society, you get a monthly record review and can buy as many as you like of their three thousand recordings on record and tape, at very low prices. Recommended by several people including Dr. Michael Humphreys of Rocky Mountain Audio who says the recordings are great.

Parnassus Records, P.O. Box 493, Woodstock, NY 12498. Telephone (914) 246 3332
Price list, free U.S. and abroad.
Used classical records. Will search for wanted classical LPs and 45s.

Ralph Records, 444 Grove Street, San Francisco, CA 94102. Telephone (415) 431 7480
Leaflet, free U.S. and abroad.
Small company producing and selling underground music.

Recommended Records, 583 Wandsworth Road, London SW8, England
25-page brochure, 1 International Reply Coupon.
This small cooperative was started by Chris Cutler (of Henry Cow) and Nick Hobbs, to bring the United Kingdom the records of unknown but good musicians. They say, "Our integrity is all we have to offer; if you find your tastes in harmony with ours, please take a chance on the stranger names." They sell unusual old and new rock. The brochure is handwritten and personal.

Rose's Collectors Records, 300 Chelsea Road, Louisville, KY 40207. Telephone (502) 896 6233
Price list, free U.S.; abroad $2. MC, V.
Records for collectors that are not in record stores: old country western, big bands, old radio shows, old personalities, old soundtracks.

Roundup Records, P.O. Box 147, East Cambridge, MA 02141
64-page catalogue, $1 U.S. and abroad; overseas air mail $3. MC, V.
Outstanding collection of about 350 small labels, not in most record stores: bluegrass, folk music, jazz, rock, reggae, and some comedy. Good prices and service.

Peter Russell's Hot Record Store, 58 New George Street, Plymouth, PL1 1PJ, England. Telephone 0752 669511
Price list, free. MC, V.
Jazz and blues records, including "the REALLY good older jazz LPs, not now carried by many stores," also jazz books and magazines. Peter Russell will also order any major or minor in-catalogue English label.

12 *Roundup Records* Tom Varner Quartet. The first record of "an exceptionally talented young jazzman" who plays French horn. About $8.50.

13 *Roundup Records* "Dread Beat an' Blood," Linton Kwesi Johnson. About $6.50.

14 *Roundup Records* "Riders in the Sky," Cowboy Jubilee. About $6.50.

Saydisc Specialised Recordings, The Barton,
Inglestone Common, Badminton,
Gloucestershire GL9 1BX, England.
Telephone Wickwar 266
Price list, free; air mail 3 International Reply Coupons.
Saydisc is a small record company specializing in esoteric
fields neglected by the larger firms. They have no distributor
in America and therefore sell a great deal by mail. Americans are most interested in the "ragtime reissues as well as
the recordings of musical automata, English bell change
ringing and English dialect issues." Saydisc's records include
selections from old Wurlitzers, mechanical organs and hon-
ky-tonk nickelodeons.

Smithsonian Recordings, 955 L'Enfant Plaza, Suite 2100,
Washington, DC 20560. Telephone (202) 287 3350
24-page brochure, free U.S. and overseas. MC, V.
The Smithsonian Museum is doing splendid work, producing recordings of all-American music. Specially interesting is
the six LP set of classic jazz "Smithsonian Collection of
Classic Jazz," an anthology taken from the archives of sev-
enteen record companies, and sampling five decades of recorded jazz. There are other early jazz recordings, popular
old rags, nineteenth-century songs and a new series of original Broadway cast albums.

Systematic Record Distribution,
Berkeley Industrial Court Space #1, 729 Heinz Avenue,
Berkeley, CA 94710
Price list, free; overseas $1.
Punk, new-wave and electrorock records, American and im-
ported; good list; constantly updated selection.

Thomas J. Valentino, 151 West 46th Street,
New York, NY 10036. Telephone (212) 246 4675
Price lists, free U.S. and overseas.
"From a cat's meow to a lion's roar—from a pistol shot to a
world war" is not only this firm's motto but a description of
its product, long-playing and 78-rpm records that provide
sound effects and other special recordings. Valentino's index
is, as a result, an extraordinary document, from pigs squealing
to seals barking, coyotes howling or crowds shouting.

DISCOUNT
Please see discount information in the How to Buy section.

The Record Hunter, Mail Order Department,
507 Fifth Avenue, New York, NY 10017.
Telephone (212) 697 8970
Catalogue, free U.S. and overseas. Schwann catalogue, $1.75;
abroad $4. AE, DC, MC, V.
The Record Hunter sells records, tapes and cassettes at
discount prices, and has a worldwide mail-order service.
They do produce free catalogues which consist of manufacturers' advertisements and special offers, so the chances of
what you want being in the catalogue are slim. Better write
to their mail-order department but, as always, try to be
specific, otherwise you will just get the appropriate page
of the Schwann standard reference catalogue.

Records International, P.O. Box 1140, Goleta, CA 93116.
Telephone (805) 687 0327
14-page price list, free U.S. and overseas.
Records and unusual and little-known classical music are
imported by this firm, which also supplies overseas customers with American records. All prices 20 percent off list
price (correspondence in French, Spanish, Swedish and Portuguese).

15

16

15 *Saydisc Specialised Recordings* "The Gay Nineties," disc musical boxes and pianola selections from stage shows and popular
music of the 1890s. Record or cassette, about $10.

16 *Saydisc Specialised Recordings* "Invitation to North America,"
ex-members of the South Devon group, Staverton Bridge, sing folk
songs about the "supposed wonders of emigration and other English
involvement in North America over the past 400 years." Record or
cassette, about $10.

PERFUME, COSMETICS AND MEDICINES

1

2

1 *J. Floris* English bath oils, about $11; talcum powder, about $5; and soap in Victorian-style packages, scented with lavender, wild hyacinth, or moss rose, about $8.

2 *Penhaglion's* "Victorian Posy," an eau de toilette, made for the Garden Exhibition held at the Victoria and Albert Museum in 1979. About $18.

ENGLAND

The Body Shop, 1 Crane Street, Chichester, West Sussex PO19 1LH, England
Price list, $1.
Anita Roddick's first Body Shop was opened next to a funeral parlor, an event which did not amuse the funeral director. He sent cross letters through his lawyer trying to get her to change the name. She didn't, and her back-to-nature and fill-your-own-bottle cosmetics were so popular that her one shop has become a chain of twenty-five. The idea behind the shops is to sell products made from natural ingredients, with minimal packaging because it "messes up the environment." If that sounds selfless, the cosmetics sound pleasantly self-indulgent—pure almond oil, elderflower eye cream, strawberry body shampoo and orange spice hair shampoo, along with concentrated perfume oils, Elizabethan washballs, and Tudor potpourri.

Cathay of Bournemouth, Cleveland Road, Bournemouth BH1 4QG, England. Telephone 37178
Catalogue, $2; air mail $3.
Cathay's ("Herbalists of the highest repute and integrity") is the largest dealer in herbs in England and offers a fascinating contrast with its counterparts in the United States. While in America herbal remedies are part of rural folklore or buried within the subcultures of hippie experimentation or Puerto Rican botanicas, Cathay's catalogue exudes scientific respectability. A spotless factory, packaging equal to posh Bond Street shops, a wide range of natural cosmetics side by side with Tiger Headache pills, Emerald Jade (diuretic) tablets and a little old-fashioned booklet on *Male and Female Sexual Difficulties and how to SAFELY Overcome Them.* Here we find that Black Pearls or Yellow Emperor drops were useful for some of the classic masculine complaints, with ginseng appearing discreetly, as it does in my local drugstore.

Culpepper, Hadstock Road, Linton, Cambridge, England. Telephone 223 891196
Price list, free; air mail $1.
Culpepper is a serious herbalist. All products sold have the approval of the Herb Society and their honeys are from unpolluted areas, and their teas are unsprayed with chemical insecticide. This is a delightful and plentiful list of cosmetics, foods and herbal remedies. Amongst the stephanotis bath crystals, and milk of lilies cream, there are herbs and spices for cooking, nutmeg jelly and banana chutney for eating, and all-natural mustards for health food buffs. Also unexpected and pretty extras such as crystallized seeds for decorating desserts, herbal pillows, potpourri ingredients, reproduction apothecary jars, and do-it-yourself pressed-flower greeting card kits. Wonderful place for presents.

J. Floris, 89 Jermyn Street, London SW1Y 6JH, England. Telephone 01 930 2885
Brochure, free; air mail $1. AE, DC, MC, V.
Floris, which claims to have been perfumers to the Court of St. James since 1730, was started by Juan Famenias Floris, who sailed to England from Majorca, and has remained in the family ever since. The shop, which until a few years ago was the only place that sold the perfumes, is the original shop, although it has been extended and adorned with mahogany fittings brought from the Great Exhibition of 1851. The perfumes are especially nice because they are flower perfumes which catch the smells of the original English flowers beautifully without spoiling and cheapening them, as so often happens with flower scents. Perfumes include Eng-

lish violet, gardenia, honeysuckle, jasmine, lily of the valley, rose and stephanotis, and they come in colognes, powders, bath oils and soap, and red rose even comes in a mouthwash. In other scents there are potpourris, pomanders, vaporizers and candies. For men there are shaving creams and lotions, shampoos, brilliantine in lime, verbena, new-mown hay and other rustic smells.

Norfolk Lavender, Caley Mill, Heacham, Kings Lynn, Norfolk, England. Telephone (0485) 70384
Leaflet, free.
A family lavender farm, established in 1932, is open to visitors who come to watch the harvest and eat in the cottage tea room. Pure oil, perfume, soap, bath cubes and sachets are made only from their own lavender. Americans should buy from Tottenham Court, (below) in California.

☛ Penhaglion's, 41 Wellington Street, Covent Garden, London WC2, England. Telephone 01 836 2150
Catalogue, $3. AE, DC, MC, V.
This distinguished perfumer, established in 1870 and now official manufacturer of toilet requisites to H.R.H. the Duke of Edinburgh, publishes an enticing catalogue. For gentlemen there are toilet waters, shampoos, shaving soaps, and after-shave lotions in Hammam or Blenheim bouquet. For the ladies, skin balm, bath oil and shampoo in Bluebell or Victorian posy. There are scented handkerchiefs for both, and scented candles for the house. Antique bottles for perfume available on request.

Taylor of London, Perfumery Shop, 166 Sloane Street, London S.W. 1, England. Telephone (01) 235 4653
Leaflet, free; air mail $1. AE, MC, V.
Taylor of London says they have been making status scents for royalty and the cream of English and Continental society for the past ninety years. Gardenia, lily of the valley, carnation and lilac are hand-distilled and made into soaps, bath essences, dusting powder, cologne and perfume, and during the summer, delivered in a horse-drawn brougham to customers in London's West End. Taylor also makes sachets to perfume drawers and potpourris of flowers to be emptied into bowls to perfume rooms for several months. But most popular of all are their Crown Staffordshire and Wedgwood pomanders filled with an Elizabethan essence, guaranteed to last for fifty years.

FRANCE

It is well worth buying French cosmetics and perfume from France. You can save $10 to $30 on an ounce of perfume, even after paying postage and duty. Besides which, most French perfumes sold in America are made in America and do not have the benefit of superior French alcohol. Another good buy are the very statusy Rigaud perfumed candles and refills, which cost almost twice as much in the United States as they do in Paris.

J. W. Chunn Perfumes, 43 Rue Richer, 75009 Paris, France
Price list for perfume, Lancome and Orlane cosmetics and Rigaud candles, free. When price lists are not correct, will quote prices in response to specific enquiries for perfume and designer scarves and ties.

Freddy, 10 Rue Auber, 75009 Paris, France
Will quote prices on request, including mailing for specific perfume and Rigaud candles.

3

4

3 *Penhaglion's* "Hammam Bouquet," an eau de toilette, bath oil, and soap, also available in shampoo, after-shave, and scented candles.

4 *Taylor of London* English flower fragrances in sachets, box of three, about $4.50; foaming bath seeds, about $1; potpourri, $4 to $12, depending on amount; bone-china pomander, about $10.

Michel Swiss, 16 Rue de la Paix, 75002 Paris II, France. Telephone 261 6111
Will quote prices of perfume and Orlane cosmetics. AE.

UNITED STATES

Ella Bache, 8 West 36th Street, New York, NY 10018. Telephone (212) 753 2175

Ella Bache, 8 Rue de la Paix, 75002 Paris, France
Leaflet, free.
Creams, lotions and face masks, also cold and hot wax for hair removal. Canadians and Americans can buy from New York, everyone else from Paris.

Boyds, Chemists, 655 Madison Avenue, New York, NY 10021. Telephone (212) 838 6558
Price list, free. AE, CB, DC, MC, V.
Boyd's sells their own cosmetics and less-advertised brands from Denmark, Italy and France. Also extras such as make-up brushes and genuine swans-down powder puffs.

Capriland's Herb Farm, Silver Street, Coventry, CT 06238. Telephone (203) 742 7244
Price list, self-addressed stamped envelope.
Capriland's, which provides everything for the herb gardener—including luncheon programs to which guests are begged to wear gardening clothes and flat heels—also sells supplies from its own gardens to make fragrances. Lavender, lemon verbena, frankincense, myrrh, etc., for sachets; rose petal and orris root for potpourri; Zanzibar cloves and spice mixture for pomanders.

Caswell-Massey Co., 575 Lexington Avenue, New York, NY 10022. Telephone (212) 620 0900
90-page catalogue, $1; overseas air mail $2. AE, CB, DC, MC, V.
George Washington, Captain Kidd and Edgar Allan Poe are among Caswell-Massey's former customers, and the present owners of this historic apothecary shop are determined not to lower the tone or allow elegant things to die. In their hands, Oral Hygiene Aids and Medicine Chest Necessities become essential accessories of a gracious life. After a look at the Caswell-Massey catalogue you don't just grab the toothpaste any more, you select Email Diamant from France, Pasta del Capitano from Italy or Aronal from Switzerland, and you apply it with an imported black-boar-bristle bone-handle toothbrush; you pick your teeth with Le Negri goose-quill toothpicks from France, and stick your dentures in with Eucryl plate fixative from England. If the bad-breath ads have been getting to you, you foam away your worries with Caswell-Massey's foaming mouthwash made from aromatic oils. You shave with a straight razor sharpened on a horsehide strap imported from Scotland, dab your cuts with an English styptic pencil (it won't crumble like an American one), comb your hair with a handmade natural-horn comb (never mind the charming way it warps), brush your hair with an English hardwood brush and smooth it down with Chandrika Brahmi Hair Oil from India.

In addition to an astonishing variety of unguents and instruments for pampering, preserving and perfuming yourself, you'll find quite a few things here that you'll have trouble finding anywhere else, among them: mustache wax, lavender smelling salts, chamois nail buffers, cosmetic vinegar, and snuff.

Come to Your Senses, 321 Cedar Avenue South, Minneapolis, MN 55454. Telephone (800) 328 4593
46-page brochure, $2 U.S. and abroad. MC, V.
A group of therapists and counselors sell through a retail store and by mail massage tables, massage equipment, oils, vibrators, and body paints. They also sell hot tubs and saunas and, although these are not listed in the catalogue, will answer questions about them.

Haussman's Pharmacy, 534–536 Girard Avenue, Philadelphia, PA 19123. Telephone (215) 627 2143
Price list, free; abroad 50 cents.
One of Philadelphia's oldest pharmacies says it has specialized for over a century in filling difficult and unusual prescriptions, and makes a point of foreign shipments and a staff that can speak and translate six languages. The brochure lists an impressively long list of medicinal herbs and spices, essential oils, pure herb extracts, and Chinese compounded-herb specialties. Write or call for specific information on their homeopathic remedies. Unusual drug and chemical specialties (such as beeswax and rosin) are stocked so this is a place to remember when your own pharmacy proves deficient.

Homebody, 8521 Melrose Avenue, Los Angeles, CA 90069
Price list, $1.
Lotions, creams, soaps, natural oils (such as jojoba, eucalyptus, and rosemary) mostly with touches of plants and flowers. Several lotions can be scented to order. Also unusual things such as Chinese violet powder and Japanese massage wands.

Hove Parfumeur, 723 Toulouse Street, New Orleans, LA 70130
16-page brochure, free U.S. and overseas. DC, MC, V.
A seductive brochure, illustrated with flowers, cherubs and 1890s ladies clutching fans, lists over fifty perfumes made in an old Spanish house in New Orleans—the closest thing to Paris, anyway. The business was started in the 1930s by Mrs. Alvin Hovey-King and has been owned and run by the women of the family ever since, meanwhile gathering a faithful clientele, many of whom have bought here for thirty years. If that, and the fact that the perfume, at $17 the ounce, is about a quarter of the price of French perfume, doesn't persuade you to buy American, maybe the "petite samplers" will. For $10 you can try any four floral perfumes or any four New Orleans blends, or any three men's colognes. Besides the many perfumes, you can buy bath and body oils, candle oils, sachets, solid perfumes, and oils for making rose jars, sachets and potpourris at home.

Pure Planet Products, 1025 N. 48th Street, Phoenix, AZ 85008. Telephone (602) 267 1000
Price list, 25 cents; overseas $1.
"High-quality products, at lowest possible prices . . . All food products contain 100% natural ingredients. None contain refined sugar, refined flour products, or synthetics." Herbal capsules, Dr. Bronner foods, ginseng roots, herbal cigarettes, bee pollen, biodegradeable dishwashing liquid, herbal toothpaste and wooden combs. There are discounts if you buy in bulk (five gallons of lemongrass lotus shampoo, anyone?).

The Soap Box, Crabtree and Evelyn, Box 167, Woodstock, CT 06281
Color comestibles catalogue, $2 (refundable).
Color cosmetics catalogue $2 (refundable).
A mere ten, or so, years ago, Crabtree and Evelyn was

established to produce naturally based toiletries and traditional foods. They very cleverly concentrated on beautiful, mock-antique packaging and hired well-known English photographer Tessa Traeger to do their catalogue photographs. The result is an exquisite catalogue and utterly tempting products that make perfect presents. The toiletries include foaming bath gels; soaps in fruit shapes and "brown Windsor" popular in the Victorian era; Hungary water, the earliest perfume and most popular for four hundred years (with lemon, orange and mint); French shampoos (sage for oily hair and thyme for dry); potpourris and pomanders with decorated jars; perfumed candles and drawer paper, and herbal sachets and pillows.

Tottenham Court, 12206½ Ventura Boulevard, Studio City, CA 91604. Telephone (213) 761 6560
40-page brochure, $2 (refundable); abroad $3. MC, V.
A charming shop in Studio City puts out a chatty catalogue of their soaps and room perfumes illustrated with old photographs and engravings. Some of the goodies (by Crabtree and Evelyn, Floris, Mary Chess and Rigaud) can be found elsewhere; but others, (such as Woods of Windsor) I haven't otherwise noticed. Special to this shop are scented heating-pad covers, lace-trimmed message pillows, bouquet-topped Victorian boxes, lace and satin baskets; and made-to-order commemorative glass paintings—all made by local women. Also delicious sounding liqueur-laced preserves from a small farm in California.

Tuli-Latus Perfumes, 146–36 13th Avenue, P.O. Box 422, Whitestone, NY 11357. Telephone (212) 746 9337
Price list, 50 cents; abroad $1. MC, V.
Milton Benz copies expensive French perfumes, comes "as close as is humanly possible," he claims, and sells them for a third or less of the price. *You* may think he is just a copy cat. *He* says his business theory is the "cornerstone of the capitalist system." Also the law is quite clear: It is perfectly legal to copy another product as long as you do not confuse or deceive anyone into thinking the copy is the original. So buy yourself a hand-blown scent bottle from Peter Tysoe (crafts), a perfume funnel from Boyd (above), and look forward to a lifetime of Mr. Benz's version of Joy by Patou, at $22 an ounce instead of $84 (from France) or $115 (from Fifth Avenue).

The Xandria Collection, P.O. Box 31039, San Francisco, CA 94131. Telephone (415) 863 2266
34-page brochure, $3 (refundable).
List of Raffaelli films, free. MC, V.
An earnest catalogue of sex aids with evaluative comments; photographic books, instruction manuals; and Raffaelli films "synonymous with excellence in erotica." Everything arrives under plain wrapping, and customers' names are not sold or traded.

DISCOUNT
Please see discount information in the How to Buy section.

Not much use for the sudden attack of sore throat or flu, but a tremendous boon to people taking medicine regularly, are the discount pharmacies. They will fill prescriptions for brand-name medicines, exactly as your doctor prescribes. If you are willing to take, and your doctor will prescribe, generic medicine (when available), you can save even more money here or at your local drug store. Generic medicines

5

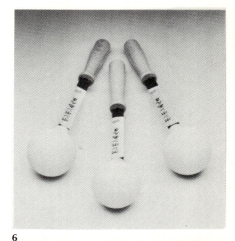

6

7

5 *Homebody* Chinese violet dusting powder and puff, about $15.

6 *Homebody* Japanese massage wands, used in pairs to break up tension areas in the body. About $15.

7 *Homebody* Candlestands with fans give a shaded light.

are medicines on which the patent has expired, so that other manufacturers can make them. The competition keeps prices down even though the FDA has officially stated that "there is no significant difference in quality between brand- and generic-name drugs."

Getz Pharmacy, 916 Walnut Street, Kansas City, MO 64199

32-page catalogue, free. MC, V.

Getz publishes a nice clear catalogue which lists many prescription drugs, well-known nonprescription drugs, vitamins and deodorants, toothpastes, etc. They will open an account for you, and say that they deliver five to eight days after receiving your order. I compared prices with my local discount drug store, and found that on toiletries there was no significant difference. Seven of the medicines were 20 to 35 percent cheaper at Getz; one was, oddly, $2.12 more expensive. If you are taking medicine regularly, do compare for yourself. Getz was established in 1958.

Pharmaceutical Services, 127 West Markey Road, Belton, MO 64012. Telephone (816) 331 0700

Price list, free.

Excellent discount prices on prescription medicines, similar to or even a few pennies lower than Getz's. Also nonprescription medicines, plus a long list of typical drugstore stock. Established 1968.

Western National Products, Department B, 511 Mission Street, P.O. Box 284, South Pasadena, CA 91030. Telephone (213) 441 3447

Brochure, free. MC, V.

Vitamins and minerals such as kelp, iron, and jojoba oil at prices which Western Reserve says, and I have found, are a third or more below equivalent goods from other sources. Established 1971.

22

PETS, LIVESTOCK AND SUPPLIES

Birds

Bird n' Hand, New Ipswich, NH 03071.
Telephone (603) 878 1000
Leaflet, free. AE, DC, MC, V.
A convincing leaflet describes posh, gourmet birdseeds that birds love (no more rejects under the bird seeder). You can order "automatic resupply."

Val Clear, 1001 Martin Drive, Anderson, IN 46012.
Telephone (317) 642 0795
Price list, free. MC, V.
Exotic cage birds, mostly bred by Val Clear himself, from humble red-ear waxbills to classy yellow-collared macaws. Also wild caught soft bills.

Duncraft, 33 Fisherville Road, Penacook, NH 03303.
Telephone (603) 224 0200
24-page brochure, 25 cents; overseas $1. MC, V.
Plastic and metal bird feeders are made and sold here. There are twenty-four models, besides post and hanging feeders, some for seeds and some for suet or bread, as well as feeders to clip onto window sills and one to stick to the wall by suction. Binoculars, bird books and wild-bird seed are also on sale.

GQF Manufacturing Company, 2343 Louisville Road, P.O. Box 1552, Savannah, GA 31498
24-page catalogue, 25 cents U.S. and overseas.
Equipment and information for quail breeders.

Cats

Felix The Katnip Tree Company, 416 Smith Street, Seattle, WA 98109. Telephone (206) 282 0195
Brochure, free; overseas $1.
This useful brochure gives cat-care advice and lists standard things such as portable cages, nail clippers, harness leashes and a come-and-go door.

1 *Val Clear* The colorful Australian zebra finch, half the size of a canary, has a scarlet beak, orange cheeks, red legs, polka-dotted sides, and a striped breast. "His 'song' sounds like a cross between a toy New-Year's horn and a squeaky barnyard pump." He sings while performing a courting dance. Val Clear says the zebra finch is rivaling budgies and canaries in popularity. One mated pair costs about $49.95 (plus air freight to your nearest airport).

Dogs

Du-Say's, P.O. Box 1036, Picayune, MS 39466.
Telephone (601) 798 9263
32-page catalogue, 25 cents; overseas $1. AE, MC, V.
This astonishing catalogue shows a complete line of useful accessories for dogs and cats: leashes, car beds, brushes and clippers, medicines, "no mate tablets," and a special spoon for giving medicine. There are lots of helpful little solutions to any dog problem. However, the catalogue also shows goods for people who have gone far along the road toward turning their dog into a baby substitute: doggie pajamas come with a pompommed nightcap; "Our Puppy's Baby Book" comes in pink or blue; and the Pet High Chair enables doggie to join you at meals. And for people who want to dress up their dog there are collars with bow ties, and a collection of doggie hats and sunglasses, "Ivy League" hat to "Calypso," trimmed with colorful fruit.

2

Fish

Aqua Engineers, 335 Mill Street, Ortonville, MI 48462. Telephone (313) 627 2877
24-page catalogue, 50 cents U.S. and overseas. MC, V.
Fish and supplies for home aquarium owners, basics and "fun" aquarium ornaments such as shipwrecks and octopus aerators.

Daleco Master Breeder Products, 4611 Weatherside Run, Fort Wayne, IN 46804. Telephone (716) 836 6704
40-page Aquarists Supply manual, $4; overseas $5; overseas air mail $9.
Live food cultures, equipment and supplies for advanced aquarists and commercial breeders. The catalogue lists a great deal of sophisticated and professional equipment, with information on the products, and advice on dealing with problems. Invaluble source for beginners and experts alike. The prices I checked were 10 to 25 percent below Aqua Engineers.

General

Petco Animal Supplies, 8693 La Mesa Boulevard, P.O. Box 1076, La Mesa, CA 92041. Telephone (714) 469 2111
100-page catalogue, free U.S. and overseas. MC, V.
Very good source of useful basic supplies for most animals, including birds and aquariums.

Stromberg's Chicks and Pets Unlimited, Pine River, MN 56474
48-page pet catalogue, $1; overseas $2. MC, V.
This firm, whose catalogue is full of encouraging maxims such as "Pets Provide Much Pleasure and Pride!" "Have Fun—Variety Is the Spice of Life!" and "Encourage Hobbies Early in Life to Make a Happier Future," breeds fowl (a million chicks a year) and sells pets. The catalogue shows lots of aristocratic-looking chickens, some that lay extra-large eggs, some that are delicious to eat, and others whose great appeal is that they will be admired by friends and neighbors—there is an impressive choice of breeds. Exotic ducks, geese and turkeys are also illustrated.

As for pets, Stromberg's says that "a youngster with hobbies and pets is happy and rarely a delinquent." To keep him happy and rarely delinquent there are flying squirrels, wallabies and cackler midget honkers, not to mention the chow-chow dogs, Himalayan cats, mynahs (better talkers than most parrots), Mexican burros and skunk kittens. The catalogue is conveniently full of photographs of these superior pets with the prices underneath; cages, houses, baskets and even caskets are listed, and so are all the books and other little things you need. In fact, I'm sure that by the time you've finished looking through this persuasive catalogue, you'll be availing yourself of the Special Birthday Gift Service and sending someone a black bear cub with your card.

Supplies

C. H. Dana Company, Hyde Park, VT 05655. Telephone (802) 888 2912.
104-page catalogue, free.
Anyone who raises livestock, particularly cattle, will find just about everything for the barn, pasture or show ring,

2 *Robert Compton* (see House section) Hanging ceramic aquarium, with hidden lighting. Prices from $140 for a 1-gallon aquarium to $450 for a 7-gallon aquarium.

ranging from portable steel corrals to brass balls for the horns of show cattle.

PBS Livestock Drugs, 2800 Leemont Avenue, N.W., P.O. Box 9101, Canton, OH 44711.
Telephone (800) 321 0235
56-page catalogue, free.
Drugs, including prescription drugs. PBS sells veterinary supplies: drugs, including prescription drugs, and small instruments for the care of dairy and beef cattle, swine and sheep. Recommended by Orville Schell.

Wholesale Veterinary Supply, P.O. Box 2256, Rockford, IL 61131.
Telephone (800) 435 6440 or (815) 877 0209
80-page large animal catalogue, free; overseas $1.
80-page small animal and horse catalogue, free; overseas $1.
MC, V.
Wholesale veterinary catalogue has a somewhat more varied stock than PBS; in addition to drugs, Wholesale sells antibiotic feed additives and all sorts of other supplies such as grooming aids for show animals.

23

PHOTOGRAPHIC EQUIPMENT

The Lab, Box 15100, St. Louis, MO 63110.
Telephone (314) 371 0059
Brochure, free; overseas airmail $2. MC, V.
Lab sells and processes color film and prints photographs in four different qualities, including "exhibition" standard. Also mounts and frames photographs in sizes up to 20″ by 24″ for customers all over the world.

Modernage Photographic Services,
1150 Sixth Avenue, New York, NY 10017.
Telephone (212) 661 9190
Price list, free. MC, V.
An excellent but expensive film-developing service for professionals and for amateurs who want their photographs to look more professional (photographic exhibitions printed by Modernage are often shown at the Metropolitan Museum and the Museum of Modern Art in New York, as well as other museums throughout the country). Besides routine developing and printing, almost anything can be done to special order. When you get your contact sheet, you can decide which photographs you would like enlarged, and then, by marking the contact with symbols, show where you would like the print to be darkened to lightened and where you would like it cut.

Modernage can also file negatives for out-of-town customers and then send them out when wanted for publicity or publishing.

Photo Weber b/Bahnhof, Pilatusstr. 1,
CH 6002 Lucerne, Swtizerland.
Telephone 041 23 35 35
Price list, $21. Or send model number for price.
This very reputable Swiss firm publishes an enormous listing of photographic equipment in the fall. I have not checked, but assume that prices are not lower than New York discount prices. However, this may be a useful address for people looking for something special. They also sell watches, but these are not listed.

Zone VI Studios, Newfane, VT 05345
30-page catalogue, free U.S. and overseas. AE, MC, V.
A very interesting small firm run by photographers, sells carefully chosen equipment for perfectionists. They sell tested supplies by others (Schneider lenses and an English rotary trimmer, for instance) or make their own, when they think they can do it better. A persuasive catalogue describes the virtues of their own papers, chemicals, archival washers, cold light heads, tripods, etc.

DISCOUNT
See discount information in the How to Buy section.

HONG KONG

Note: I have done quite a bit of price comparing, and I have found that Hong Kong and United States discount prices for photographic equipment, audio equipment, etc., are fairly similar. If anything, American prices tend to be lower.

T. M. Chan and Company, P.O. Box 33881,
Sheung Wan Post Office, Hong Kong.
Telephone 450 875
106-page catalogue, free.
Color fine jewelry brochure, free.
A complete stock of photographic and film equipment, plus

1 *Zone VI Studios* This field camera, designed and made for Zone VI, is of cherry wood with brass fittings, and folds into a self-protecting package. A ground glass fitted with an image-brightening Fresnel lens is included. About $575.

binoculars, cassette radio/recorders, calculators, Seiko and Rolex watches.

Far East Company, P.O. Box 97335 TST, Kowloon, Hong Kong. Telephone 3 666 647
82-page catalogue, free; air mail $1.50.
Photographic and film equipment, stereo equipment (especially the new compacts) radios, TV, video and calculators and Seiko watches.

Albert White and Company, K.P.O. Box K-202, KCPO, Kowloon, Hong Kong. Telephone 3 673 18
46-page brochure, $1; air mail $1.50.
Photographic equipment, stereo equipment, Seiko watches.

UNITED STATES

Camera Discount Center, 89A Worth Street, New York, NY 10013.
Telephone (212) 226 1014 or (800) 221 3496
Catalogue, $1.89. Write or telephone with a model number for a price.
Specialists in photographic equipment and accessories and dark room accessories, Camera Discount Center stocks the most popular brands as well as less common ones. Established 1972.

47th Street Camera, Mail Order, 36 East 19th Street, New York, NY 10003.
Telephone (800) 221 5858 or (212) 260 4410
112-page catalogue, $2. Write with model number for price. AE, MC, V.
47th Street Camera is the outstanding discount store for photographic equipment including darkroom accessories, also electronics, video, and computers. They are outstanding because of their wide range of top brands, their consistently low prices, and their efficient service. I buy here, my friends buy here, and if you make the mistake of wandering into their jam packed retail store, you'll think the whole world buys here. It may be that you can find a bigger stock, or better price, or faster service elsewhere, but I certainly haven't found the three combined as well anywhere else. If you write and ask them for a price quote, they'll scribble the answer on your letter or postcard, and cut out your address—as you write it—and stick it on their envelope. Established 1972.

Garden Camera, 135 West 29th Street, New York, NY 10001.
Telephone (800) 223 0595 or (212) 868 1420
Occasional catalogues, free U.S. and overseas. Write or telephone (Sunday through Friday 9:00 A.M. to 6:00 P.M.) with a model number for a price. AE, MC, V.
Garden Camera sells photographic equipment, electronic equipment, calculators and video equipment. They sell: Canon, Nikon, Olympus, Pentax, Konica, Rollei, Vivitar, Sun Pak Sony, Pearlcorder, Panasonic, Hewlett Packard, Texas Instruments, Kodak, Mamiya, Hasselblad, Bronica, Yashika, Elmo, Sankyo and more. Established 1969.

Focus Electronics and Foto Electric Supply also sell photographic equipment.

2

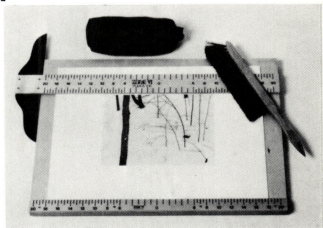

3

2 *Zone VI Studios* Designed and made for Zone VI, these tripods are made of clear mountain ash in a natural finish. They can be set up using thumb and finger pressure only; the heavy-duty feet can be used in sand, mud, or snow; and the legs can be spread out flat to put the camera as low as ground level. Priced about $165 and $195.

3 *Zone VI Studios* Designed and made for Zone VI, this dry-mount jig is made of laminated birch with oversize markings. A print 6″ to 21″ wide, by any height, can be precisely positioned and tacked in thirty seconds. It comes with a foxtail brush for dusting the print back and mount face, and a weight bag to hold in place. About $45.

Bookbinding

J. F. Newman and Son, The Sign of the Book, Belvedere Court, Dublin 1, Ireland. Telephone (01) 743 548
Price list, free.
This very reputable firm does work that ranges from simple cloth bindings on small books at just over $20 to full calf or Niger goatskin binding on large books for over $200. Repairs, preservation, gold tooling and other services are available.

China and Glass

Pattern Finders (Discontinued China and Stemware), P.O. Box 206, Port Jefferson Station, NY 11776. Telephone (516) 928 5158
Stacy Davidson, who used to work in the china department at Macy's, will help you find missing pieces of china and glass, from discontinued patterns. She charges $10 to look, and negotiates the price for you on what she finds. Send her a photo copy if possible, if not a drawing, and a description of the piece you want matched.

Engraving

Elgin Engraving Company, 940 Edwards Avenue, Dundee, IL 60118
16-page brochure, free; overseas $1. MC, V.
Elgin Engraving Company will engrave your name or initials on "the world's most unusual gift," an ordinary-size pin which arrives in a blue pouch, for $2. More usefully, they will engrave door plates, door knockers, combs, coathangers, shoe horns, bookmarks, screwdrivers, luggage tags, and plaques for almost anything you are likely to lose or want to identify, such as cameras, golf bags, umbrellas, scissors, hats and glass cases. Most prices are below $5.

Mapmaking

Anthony Fyffe, 30 Chantry, Madeira Road, Bournemouth, Dorset, England
Information, free.
Anthony Fyffe makes "How to Find Us" maps both for businesses and for private homes. Two hundred copies of a 7-by-10-inch functional but not beautiful "social" map cost a minimum of $200 plus postage. The customer sends the name and address of the place to be pinpointed, and a map of the area, which can be a local map or a rough sketch. The rough sketch is sufficient because Mr. Fyffe has official maps of the United States on a 1:24,000 scale.

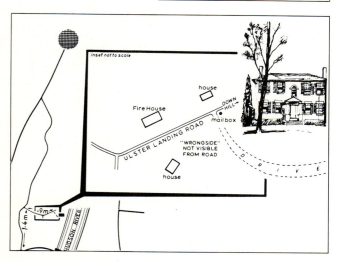

1 *Anthony Fyffe* "How to Find Us" maps for businesses and private homes can be made to order in quantities of 200 and up.

Needlepoint Mounting

Modern Needlepoint Mounting Company, 11 West 32nd Street, New York, NY 10001
Leaflet, free.
The leaflet gives details of this firm's needlepoint mounting

service. They will mount customer's work onto almost anything, common requests being for handbags, tennis-racquet covers, telephone-book covers. Prices on request.

Portraits

Facemakers, 140 Fifth Street, Savanna, IL 61074. Telephone (815) 273 3944
Paintings catalogue, $5 U.S. and overseas.
Facemakers present "The Great Art of the Past" at prices starting at $500. They'll paint you a picture in the style of Titian, Rembrandt or any other famous artist, they'll copy one of the Old Master paintings with any little changes or improvements you can think of. They'll even put you in the picture, paint you as your own ancestor, or do your portrait as a General (no less) of the Civil War, a coquette from the court of Louis XIV, a Colonial couple or any other historical character.

Shoe Repair

Ken Kap, 5155 Rio Vista Avenue, Tampa, FL 33614. Telephone (813) 886 7573
Leaflet, free U.S. and overseas. MC, V.
Ken Kap resoles all brands and types of athletic shoes, tennis, jogging, basketball, boating, etc., and guarantees their workmanship and materials for the life of the shoe.

Silhouettes

Silhouette Studio, 52 Woodhouse Avenue, Wallingford, CT 06492
No catalogue.
Natalie Garvin is one of the few scissor artists, or silhouette cutters, left in the country—she thinks there are about thirty professionals now. The young don't seem to be taking it up, she says, and the older ones are dying off. She hopes, however, that an increase in the popularity of silhouettes will cause more people to take up the art. For $8 postpaid, she will cut your likeness and mount it on a plain white card; you must send a *clear* side-view snapshot.

2

3

4

2 *Facemakers* "The Birth of Our Flag" by Henry Peters Gay, a copy with changes requested by the client. Oil paintings in any style to order start at $500 (frame not included).

3 *Facemakers* The client as Queen Elizabeth I in the style of Holbein. Portraits to order in any historical style start at $500.

4 *Silhouette Studio* Silhouettes cut by Natalie Garvin. About $8.50 each.

American Printing House for the Blind, P.O. Box 6085, Louisville, KY 40206. Telephone (502) 895 2405
Catalogue for: talking-book publications (records and cassettes), music publications (large-print and braille music); large-type publications; vacuum form publications; educational and other aids; all free.
A nonprofit agency, chartered in 1858, the American Printing House is by far the largest publishing house for the blind and visually impaired in the world. They publish records, cassettes, books and magazines in braille and textbooks and educational aids for all ages.

Better Sleep, New Providence, NJ 07974. Telephone (201) 464 2200
16-page catalogue, 25 cents; sea mail $1; air mail $2.
A firm that is devoted to furthering the comfort of insomniacs and "bedpressers" (as lazy boys were called in Dr. Johnson's day) with inflatable pillows for most parts of the anatomy. For relaxing in the bath, there are seven different bath pillows and a "soaker's Delite"—a rubber cap that fits over the overflow valve so you can get a nice deep bath. And if, when you've staggered out of the bath, you want to fall asleep again in a chair or the car, you'll find a good assortment of little pillows to help you do that.

Duk Kwong Optical Company, 27 Cameron Road, Tsimshatsui, Kowloon, Hong Kong
Leaflet, free.
If you have your own prescription, you can buy glasses by mail from this firm. They send a picture page illustrating forty-two shapes that you can have made up with clear or tinted glass or plastic lenses. The shapes are a good, up-to-date assortment, and Dr. John Pong, the manager, says that folding glasses, metal frames and lorgnettes are the most popular with his American customers. As I write, safety glasses cost $10, plastic $16, and frames from $10 to $25 for metal. Hard and soft contact lenses can be copied from your own.

On the Rise, 2282 Four Oaks Grange Road, Eugene, OR 97405. Telephone (503) 687 0119
Brochure, $1; overseas air mail $2. MC, V.
A few easy-to-put-on and comfortable clothes for handicapped children and adults, designed by two mothers of handicapped children. Brochure is illustrated with line drawings.

Royal Association for Disability and Rehabilitation, 25 Mortimer Street, London W1N 8A3, England. Telephone (01) 637 5400
Publications list, free.
RADAR, a voluntary organization for all physically disabled people that is particularly active in access, mobility and housing, has a list of publications which it sells. Publications include travel guides to England and various European countries, and booklets of advice for the physically disabled and their families.

Royal National Institute for the Blind, 224 Great Portland Street, London W1N 6AA, England
Catalogue of apparatus and games for the blind, free.
The Royal National Institute for the Blind has a big export mail-order service with a special export price list. Prices tend to be lower than in America, and although many goods are the same in both countries, many are not. Perhaps predictably, England does not have as many kitchen gadgets but has many more games: card games, a solitaire board

with instructions in Braille, a bridge scorer, jigsaw puzzles which can also be used by partially sighted children. Also more mathematical aids, writing equipment and devices for speaking to the deaf-blind.

SFB Products, Box 385, Wayne, PA 19087.
Telephone (215) 687 3731
56-page catalogue, free U.S. and overseas.
Aids for the visually impaired and the blind that include touch-and-sniff books and games for children, magnifying glasses, playing cards, aud-o-balls and bathroom scales.

Universal Suppliers, P.O. Box 4803, Hong Kong.
Telephone 5 224 768
Assorted catalogues, free; air mail $3.20.
Universal Suppliers makes prescription glasses from American optical lenses made by A. O. Company of America with simple modern frames made in France, Spain and West Germany. Prices, which include frames and air-mail postage, are mainly between $30 and $50, except for certain 14-carat gold-plated frames by Rodenstock of West Germany, which are around $70. Hard contact lenses are also made for $30 per pair. Once you have been properly fitted in your own country for contact lenses and are used to wearing them, if you need replacement lenses, send a full prescription, which should include the fit as well as the graduation, to Universal Suppliers.

Wuensch, 33 Halsted Street, East Orange, NJ 07018.
Telephone (201) 674 2600
30-page catalogue, free. MC, V.
More aids for insomniacs. Norman Dine, whom *Time* magazine called "the dean of beducation," claims to have solved over a million sleep problems over the past thirty years, but besides pillows and noise drowners for better sleep, the catalogue lists all sorts of gadgets for people who spend waking hours in bed: trays with pockets for books, bags to keep things that tuck into the mattress, stands to enable you to read while lying down. Italian carved headboards, round king-size beds, push-button beds and exercise machines of all sorts are for sale.

J. Barbour and Son, Simonside, South Shields, Tyne and Wear, NE34 9PD, England. Telephone (0632) 552 251
Catalogue of waterproof and protective clothing for fishing, shooting and country wear, free. September.
Barbour thornproof, waterproof clothing is well known and highly thought of; if you don't know it, you'll find out about it from reading the press quotes in the catalogue. The catalogue illustrates a large selection of jackets, pants, coats, hats, boots, mitts and socks. Prices for jackets and coats are between $40 and $100.

Cabela's, 812 13th Avenue, Sidney, NE 69162. Telephone (308) 254 5505
66-page catalogue, free; overseas, inquire. MC, V.
An all-around sports catalogue basically aimed at the hunter, and heavy on clothing, guns and hunting gear. Of general interest are outdoor gifts, at reasonable prices, and sleeping bags, parkas and boots at low prices. Spring catalogue emphasizes fishing equipment.

Greaves Sports, 23 Gordon Street, Glasgow G1 3PW, Scotland. Telephone 041 222 4531
Manufacturers' brochures for clothes and equipment for bowls, camping, climbing, crickets, ice skating, squash, soccer, table tennis and tennis, $1.
Greaves describes itself as "a retail sports outfitting shop with a very broad coverage of the trade in general. There is virtually no sporting requisite which we cannot obtain, and we pride ourselves in the fact that we provide a good back-up service." If you tell Greaves which sports you are interested in and send them $1, they will send you (surface mail) brochures from the best English manufacturers of clothes and equipment in that field, many of which have international reputations and sell their products for much higher prices abroad.

Randall Made Knives, Box 1988, Orlando, FL 32802. Telephone (305) 855 8075
32-page brochure, $1 U.S. and overseas. MC, V.
World famous for handmade knives for hunting, fishing and fighting.

Thomas D. Robinson and Son, 321 Central Avenue, White Plains, NY 10606. Telephone (914) 948 8488
Catalogues, free. MC, V.
Robinson produces catalogues of brand-name equipment for camping, fishing and hunting, just before the seasons. Prices are said to be low.

Sports-Schuster, Rosenstrasse 5–6, 8000 Munich 2, Germany. Telephone 237 070
168-page color catalogues in German, free (surface, mail); air mail $2. April, October.
This large sports shop puts out two luscious catalogues a year crammed with famous brands of gear and clothes. An excellent place for anyone who wants to buy ski clothes by mail, because although prices are higher than in Austria, there is a terrific selection: sweaters, jackets, goggles, shaggy-fur boots and every sort of ski boot; and ski outfits for adults and children.
   The summer catalogue shows tennis clothes and parkas; and for camping and the great German pastime—hiking—pages and pages of boots, ropes, rucksacks, picks, sleeping

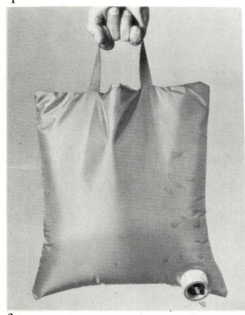

1 *Randall Made Knives* "Hunter," completely handmade knife with stainless steel blade and stag handle.

2 *Eastern Mountain Sports* "The Water Sack," for carrying water, folds up flat when not in use. About $6.

bags, tents and other necessary things. Also skin-diving gear and sailboats with motors.

Alas, the catalogue is in German. However, prices are right next to pictures and Sports-Schuster will answer letters in English *when asked* (otherwise they assume you know German).

Backpacking and Camping

Charles Flynn recommended Stephenson's backpacking equipment to me. When I got the Stephenson catalogue, I was so impressed by the informative text that I wrote and asked Jack Stephenson whether he could suggest any backpacking firms of interest that I should include in my book.

He tackled my question with enthusiasm and sent me a whole sheaf of information so helpful that I have used it "as is." All the following backpacking section (except the Stephenson entry) has been written by Jack Stephenson.

BACKPACK AND CAMP
EQUIPMENT CATALOGUES

Specialized equipment needed by self-sufficient campers is widely sold through mail-order catalogues. Suppliers range from giants like REI and EMS with chains of retail stores and catalogue sales, down to very small highly specialized shops making the very finest equipment.

We have attempted to contact all known backpack equipment companies that sell by mail-order catalogue. Some previously well-known companies have stopped catalogue sales (Holubar, Kelty, Marmot) or are out of business (Alpine Designs, Synergy, Trailtech). Some companies have changed their product lines so they mostly sell clothing for everyday wear (L. L. Bean, Bauer) so they are listed in the clothes section.

Many catalogue-sales companies produce no equipment of their own, merely acting as mail-order retailers; of these we have included only those that offer real advantages of price or product selection. We have been selective to avoid duplication and confusion, this does not mean that companies not listed are less useful or reliable.

For many years camp equipment catalogues were rather low-key and straightforward, kind of like Sears, Roebuck. Only a couple made extravagant claims. In the last seven years or so we have seen a new wave of wild, exaggerated, often false, advertising, with flashy, expensive catalogues. Most backpacking equipment has evolved from a few basic ideas repeated over and over with minor variations. Major improvements are rarely introduced, and often are slow to be accepted, especially if not heavily advertised.

I encourage you to look behind the claims: evaluate items on the basis of good engineering or scientific principles, or just skeptical logic.

For intelligent buying, more information on materials, insulation, construction methods, sleeping bag and tent designs can be found in my (Stephenson) catalogue, and in Robert Wood's book *Pleasure Packing,* published by 10 Speed Press, Box 7123, Berkeley, CA 94707.

Alpenlite, 3891 North Ventura Avenue, Ventura, CA 93001.
Telephone (800) 235 3410 or (805) 653 0431.
Catalogue, $1 U.S. and overseas. MC, V.
Makers and originators of a version of wraparound hip-carry backpacks that uses direct attachment of hip band to a forward-bent portion of the frame. This can be very comfortable for people who walk with very little hip movement relative to upper body. Similar in function to the original A-16 pack frame and later copies by Jan Sport.

Campmor, 195 West Shore Avenue, Bogota, NJ 07603.
Telephone (201) 488 1550
Catalogue, free.
A low cost, small scale version of REI. Even their catalog shows savings: economy paper, black-and-white print, very concise presentation, thirty-six years of experience shows in a good practical selection of equipment from summertime roadside type to serious winter camping. Very little equipment analysis or comparison, so get catalogues from REI, EMS and Stephenson for information, but look at Campmor's prices before you buy.

Down Home, West Fork Road, Deadwood, OR 97430.
Telephone (503) 964 3012
Catalogue, $3 U.S. and overseas; overseas air mail $4.50
Beautifully crafted, top-quality all-down sleeping bags, with some of the most advanced features, such as Vapor barrier, IR reflective insulation, dual zippers, and well-fitted hood and collar. All sewn at home, a one-family operation.

Eastern Mountain Sports (EMS), Vose Farm Road, Peterborough, NH 03458. Telephone (603) 924 9212
100-page color catalogue, free; overseas $1; overseas air mail $2.
EMS is the eastern, modern version of REI, except it's a private business with no charge for membership or catalogues, is not hampered by committee control, and has a larger chain of eighteen retail stores. Like many others, they have been expanding the line of more profitable everyday clothing.

Gregory Mountain Products,
4620 Alvarado Canyon Road 13, San Diego, CA 92120.
Telephone (714) 284 4050
Brochure, free U.S. and overseas. MC, V.
Another one-family business dedicated to excellence. Wayne and Suzy make the finest internal frame pack, with super attention to important details. They do equipment repairs and washing of down gear of all makes. Very dependable, dedicated people you'll enjoy doing business with. I know them well.

Indiana Camp Supply, Box 344, Pittsboro, IN 46167.
Telephone (317) 892 3738
Catalogue, free U.S. and overseas. MC, V.
A most complete source for medical supplies and dried foods. This business is run by a medical doctor who likes Arctic exploration. He knows the difficulty of determining what medical supplies to take, and where to get them. I suggest you review your selections with your own friendly doctor, who might round out your medical chest with prescription drugs. Other equipment is also offered, but you can find better, at lower prices, many other places.

Komito Boots, Box 2106, Estes Park, CO 80517
Catalogue, free.
Offers mountaineering boots, with hints on how to solve the difficult problem of buying boots by mail. Provides excellent boot-repair service by mail.

Peter Limmer and Sons, Rte. 16A, Intervale, NH 03845.
Telephone (603) 356 5378
Leaflets, free.
Top-quality, individually made, custom-fit mountaineering

3

4

5

3 *Eastern Mountain Sports* "Mino" deluxe 6-person holiday cook set. About $36.

4 *Eastern Mountain Sports* Clip-on light. About $3.

5 *Gregory Mountain Products* "Day Pack" is the smallest of the Gregory packs—for skiing, day hikers, bikers, and increasingly popular with students as the "ultimate indestructible book bag." Priced about $69. Gregory packs have been extremely favorably reviewed by *Backpacker* magazine: "Carrying a Gregory for the first time is like driving a Ferrari after a lifetime of grunting about in a VW bug."

boots. Very limited production. Order backlog was eight months in December 1981. They also stock identical boots, made to their specs in Germany, in sizes *they* find are most common. If you have a boot fit problem, Limmer can solve it. Often they'll fit you right away with their special stock boots, but if not, will make it to fit you. Limmer has been known for over forty years for the finest construction methods and materials. Their boots are intended for the most rugged rough mountaineering and rocky trails. For soft trails you'll find lighter lower-cost boots in your local shoe store, although they won't last as long.

Moss Tent Works, Box 309, Mt. Battie Street, Camden, ME 04843. Telephone (207) 236 8368
Catalogue, $1; overseas $2. MC, V.
In 1955 Bill Moss designed the dome-shaped pop tent. By 1962 he had designed arc top tents like covered wagons. In 1975 he and Marilyn Moss opened a shop in Camden, Maine. Since then they've produced the most advanced, beautiful curved tension structures, ranging from one-man backpack tents to large tent homes. I can't adequately describe the beauty of Bill's creations; you must see his catalogue. It is interesting to note the number of "new" tents being marketed that copy the shapes of Moss tents, a great compliment to the superiority of these esthetically pleasing and most storm resistant designs.

North Face, 1234 5th Street, Berkeley, CA 94710. Telephone (415) 548 1371
Catalogue, free. AE, MC, V.
A large manufacturer of tents and sleeping bags, North Face has survived by sticking to good quality but not exotic equipment. They were first with geodesic dome tents, just when geodesic dome houses became popular. Now many other makers are copying North Face, just when North Face and backpackers are discovering dome tents aren't well shaped for people and their gear, and are too heavy and too difficult to handle for backpacking. Like many others feeling the pinch of poor profits in backpacking gear, they have expanded into the much more profitable line of clothing, ski wear and luggage, again offering quality designs and construction.

Dave Page, Cobbler, 2101 North 34th and Madison, Seattle, WA 98103. Telephone (206) 632 8686
Price card, free.
Dave Page doesn't sell boots or have a catalogue, as such, but does provide top boot-repair service.

Recreational Equipment (REI), P.O. Box C-88125, Seattle, WA 98188. Telephone (206) 575 4480
Catalogue, free; overseas $4. MC, V.
REI is a co-op "owned" by its customers, who must be members to buy items. Membership costs $5. At the end of each year a part of net profit is returned to members as a credit for more purchases, based on the total purchased that year by that member. They have a complete catalogue of backpack equipment and clothing. The past emphasis was on low-cost equipment, but now they carry lots of expensive clothing. In the past REI was known as *the* place to buy *if* you could find something that met your needs adequately. During the last several years they expanded into many retail stores. The resulting high sales costs and losses is reflected in higher prices. Generally you can find better prices at EMS or Campmor or your local discount house. REI has been very slow to accept new ideas and products and thus has avoided some of the big problems of new fad products that didn't live up to claims. But, they

have also been slow to recognize the proven advantages of pile, foam, radiant and vapor barriers.

Although you may never find anything you'd want to buy from REI, you'll still likely find the $5 membership fee well spent to have their catalogue for product reference and comparison.

Chuck Roast, Odell Hill Road, Dept CC, Conway, NH 03818. Telephone (603) 447 5492
Color brochure free; overseas $1. MC, V.
Day packs, gaiters, rain gear, and very nice pile clothing. A growing, small business, known for low prices and top quality, with an expanding product line.

Stephenson, R.F.D. 4, Box 145, Gilford, NH 03246. Telephone (603) 293 7016
48-page color catalogue, $3; overseas $5. (Background information on choosing backpacking gear available with catalogue if you ask for it.)
Jack Stephenson (who has written this backpacking section, except for this entry; please see Backpacking introduction) is an engineer who makes tents and down sleeping bags to his own original designs. These have been very favorably reviewed in *The Next Whole Earth Catalogue.* This is what Stephenson customer Charles E. Flynn, who recommended this firm to me, says: The Warmlite tents "continue to be the lightest most wind-stable ones available. . . . The two-person model 2R tent weighs two pounds fifteen ounces including poles. . . . Model R tents use two layers of coated fabric with an insulating air gap between them, which greatly reduces condensation. . . . Warmlite triple bags . . . the bottoms are equipped with two sets of zippers which allow the use of a thin top, a thick top, or both together. The bags have integral vapor barriers, radiant-heat-reflecting interior fabrics, individual hot-cut parts, and are hand-filled with down that has a loft of 750 cubic inches per ounce . . . the result . . . is in a class by itself."

Incidentally, the Stephenson catalogue is extraordinarily informative and interesting, and if you ask for it, he will include, with the catalogue, extra background information on the design of outdoor gear.

Trail Foods Company, Box 9309, North Hollywood, CA 91609. Telephone (213) 897 4370
Catalogue, 50 cents; overseas $2. MC, V.
Large selection of dried trail foods by several makers, with discount prices for large orders. Also list some better Eureka tent and Camp Trails products.

Bicycles

The firms listed here were suggested and described to me or written up by reader Charles E. Flynn, an enthusiastic cyclist who buys by mail a good deal. He chose these sources from many, because he thinks they each provide something of real interest. As far as prices go, Charles Flynn found them similar at all these firms. For low prices, he strongly urges buying components out of season (December through February) and for discount prices, looking at the "sales" advertisements in *Bicycling* magazine *at the time you want to buy.*

Bicycle Lighting Systems, 3420 Green Tree Drive, Falls Church, VA 22041. Telephone (703) 941 0666
Leaflet, free.
A rechargeable quartz-halogen bicycle light that *really* lights

6

7

8

6 *Moss Tent Works* "Cricket," a one-person tent that is light and easy to set up. The tapered shape gives room without bulk and weight. The rain fly is attached, and the window screen is of very fine no-seam netting. Weighs 2 lb. 14 oz. Priced about $142.

7 *Moss Tent Works* "Eave," an arch-tunnel tent with twin zippers for easy access, a large rain fly for extra storage, and an optional snow fly and frost liner. Two-person tent weighs 5 lb. 4 oz. and costs about $280. A three-person and a mountain version are also available.

8 *Chuck Roast* Pile jacket gives warmth without weight and has nonrestricting fit. Light blue or gray, (matching pile trousers available) about $39.50.

9

10

9 *Emily K* Bicycle clothing in natural or natural-blend stretch fabrics, ready made or to order.

10 *Touring Cyclist Shop* A slim briefcase designed for the commuter who needs to carry papers, notebooks, music books, and other large flat objects by bike. It is easily attached and removed so it can be carried to class, office, etc. In navy blue waterproof Cordura, about $30. Also available in light-reflecting fabric for nighttime cycling.

up the road. Made with tractor lamp components, this is an effective and expensive lamp of interest to people who do a lot of cycling in the dark.

Bike Warehouse, 215 Main Street, New Middletown, OH 44442. Telephone (800) 321 2474
40-page catalogue, 50 cents; overseas $2. MC, V.
Exotic components for racing and touring bikes. Some of the prices are typical, but there are a few real bargains. They have a "guaranteed lowest price" policy which you can take advantage of if you can cite a source of price when ordering. The firm also has an emergency service for distressed touring cyclists. If you telephone with Master Card or Visa, they'll ship out parts by three o'clock the same day.

Cycle Goods Corporation, 2735 Hennepin Avenue South, Minneapolis, MN 55408. Telephone (612) 872 7600
178-page catalogue, $4 (refundable with $30 order); overseas $6. AE, MC, V.
This unusually thorough catalogue contains not only components and accessories for racing, touring, and traditional three-speed bicycles, but also offers thousands of replacement parts for most brands including Campagnolo. The components are illustrated with carefully prepared exploded diagrams, which are especially useful for complex mechanisms such as Sturmey-Archer and Shimano three-speed hubs. Good selection of tools.

Emily K. Cycling Clothing, 505 Calle Palo Colorado, Santa Barbara, CA 93105. Telephone (805) 966 5748
Catalogue, $1.
Unusually comfortable and durable cycling clothing. The comfort is the result of good design informed by cycling experience, and the durability comes from a combination of careful workmanship, top-quality fabrics and chamois, and the provision of detailed laundering instructions. The shorts are outstanding.

Palo Alto Bicycles, P.O. Box 1276, Palo Alto, CA 94302. Telephone (415) 328 7411
50-page catalogue, $1 U.S. and overseas. MC, V.
This is a catalogue that many cyclists really look forward to receiving. It offers a thoughtfully chosen selection of high-quality products from the better-established manufacturers along with a few exotic parts which, often as a result of their inclusion in this catalogue, are henceforth considered to be of long-term interest. Components of the same type, such as tires or chains, are grouped together, well photographed, and described with information that makes an informed choice possible, including weights for many items. Some inexplicably high prices.

Third Hand, 990 Park Street, Ashland, OR 97520. Telephone (503) 482 1750
Catalogue, free; overseas 1 International Reply Coupon.
Best source of hard-to-find bicycle tools. The illustrated catalogue explains the uses of the tools.

Touring Cyclist Shop, 2639 Spruce Street, P.O. Box 4009, Boulder, CO 80306. Telephone (303) 449 4067
48-page brochure, $1 (refundable) U.S. and overseas. MC, V.
Anyone planning to take a long trip by bicycle should choose the pannier bags and handlebar bags used for storage with great care. There are three brands of general interest: those produced and sold only by the Touring Cyclist Shop, and those made by Kirtland Tour Pack and Eclipse, which are available in many catalogues, including Palo Alto Bicycles.

The Kirtland bags are copies of the Touring Cyclist bags and are equipped with stamped-steel "carrier hook plates." These are adequate for around town use, however, metal fatigue sometimes destroys the stamped-steel hooks, which can bring a tour to an abrupt end. The Eclipse bags are beautifully made and have a few ingenious features, but seem needlessly complicated and expensive and have rounded bottoms which prevent the panniers from staying upright on the tent floor. The Touring Cyclist bags have flat bottoms and will stay upright zipped together to form a small suitcase. This uses less floor space and makes removing and replacing things easier. The Touring Cyclist products are thoughtfully designed and have quality materials and excellent workmanship.

DISCOUNT
Please see discount information in the How to Buy section.

Stuyvesant Bicycles, 349 West 14th Street, New York, NY 10014. Telephone (212) 254 5200
Catalogue, $2.50. Write or telephone for a specific price. MC, V.
A large general bicycle store that sells everything at 10 percent off list price, and sometimes more. Children's bikes, three speeds, ten speeds, unicycles, tandems, folding bikes and mopeds. Brands: Atala, Bianchi, Columbia, Corso, Raleigh, Ross, etc. (bicycles); Campagnola, Regina, Suntour, etc. (parts).

Boats

James Bliss & Company, Route 128, Dedham, MA 02026. Telephone (617) 329 2430
288-page annual catalogue, $2 U.S. and overseas; $5 overseas air mail. AE, MC, V.
"Everything marine" states the catalogue cover, and it is hard to imagine anything, short of the boats themselves, that is not listed in this encyclopedic volume. Bliss caters primarily to a yachting crowd, judging from the pages devoted to cruising accessories, yacht-club signals, logbooks, guest registers, and the like. But there are also full selections of more serious items: searchlights, pumps, marine paints, and hundreds of spare parts, tools, nautical hardware, etc. Illustrated in detail, the catalogue is a good guide to what is available.

Nauticalia, 121 High Street, Shepperton, Middlesex, TW17 9BL, England. Telephone 0932 244396
8-page catalogue, free.
An exjournalist manufacturers elegant brass objects: a telescope, a compass, bells, lamps, a Boatswain's Call (whistle) and signs. Everything can be engraved.

Northwest River Supplies, P.O. Box 9186, Moscow, ID 83843. Telephone (208) 882 2383
38-page color catalogue, free; overseas $1. MC, V.
A complete selection of rafts, canoes, kayaks and supplies, in a really excellent informative catalogue. Some is made here, lines from other manufacturers have been tried before being stocked.

Ship Shop, Andries de Jong BV, Muntplein 8, 1012 WR, Amsterdam, Holland. Telephone 020 24521
Leaflet, $2. In Dutch.
The Ship Shop has been selling ship's lanterns, ship's clocks,

11

11 *Touring Cyclist Shop* Shopping bag that is large enough to hold a full-size supermarket shopping bag completely loaded with groceries. A drawstring gives protection against the rain. In several colors, about $33. Also available in reflecting fabric for nighttime cycling.

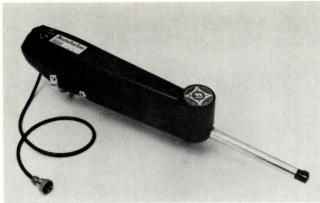

12

13

14

12 *Thomas Foulkes* Autopilot "Autohelm 1000" for tiller-steered yachts between 17′ and 35′, 12-volt, 3-watt consumption. About $250. (This costs about $390 in the United States.)

13 *Thomas Foulkes* Depth Finder "Seafarer 3." About $80.

14 *Goldberg's* The sun heats 2½ gallons of water, and a sensor gives you the water temperature. Includes an off-valve and shower-head. About $15.

bells, pennants, flags, flagpoles and a range of nautical articles since 1787. The catalogue contains a very handsome collection of lamps and lanterns, barometers, compasses, brass nameplates (in English).

**Henri Vaillancourt, Mill Street, Box 199,
Greenville, NH 03048. Telephone (603) 878 2306**
Leaflet, free.
A strictly one-man operation, Henri Vaillancourt makes Malecite birch-bark canoes by the same processes that Indians have used since time immemorial. Each one takes a month to make (but there's a long waiting list).

DISCOUNT
Please see discount information in the How to Buy section.

**Defender Industries, 255 Main Street, Box 820,
New Rochelle, NY 10801. Telephone (914) 632 3001**
168-page catalogue, $1; overseas $3.
Although several firms give discounts from "list prices," Defender has a reputation for giving the lowest prices of all the marine supply firms. According to my calculations, they do. An *excellent* source for basics for boat owners, builders, and maintainers. No frivolities here. Established 1938.

**Thomas Foulkes, Sansom Road, Leytonstone,
London E11 3HB, England. Telephone (01) 539 5084**
16-page catalogue, free; air mail $1. MC.
Reputed to have the biggest selection in London, Foulkes has been exporting for twenty years. Prices are dramatically lower than U.S. prices for some English products such as Gibbs winches.

**Goldberg's, 202 Market Street, Philadelphia, PA 19106.
Telephone (215) 627 3700**
200-page annual catalogue and six "mini-catalogues" of sale items, free; overseas $5; air mail $10. AE, MC, V.
Goldberg's has been selling boating supplies for thirty-five years and claims to be the country's largest firm in its field. They have stores in New York and Philadelphia, but much of their business is done by mail. The large, thorough catalogue is businesslike and serious—"no gadgets, just 'real' items," they wrote me. The catalogue centers on basic equipment, but does not have boat-building supplies as such. Established 1945.

**Yatchmail, 7 Cornwall Crescent,
London W11 1PH, England. Telephone (01) 727 2373**
Price list, free.
Yatchmail sells a basic range of marine equipment for cruising yachts, by top British manufacturers at discount prices (somewhat lower than Foulkes'). I asked Yatchmail what the good buys for Americans are, and Tom Crumby replied "We have had a look at the items which we have been sending to the U.S.A. recently, and the following items seem to be popular:

Autohelm Autopilots. These have been in great demand since 1980 when the first and second yachts in the OSTAR Transatlantic Race used Autohelms. There is still quite a big price difference between U.K. and U.S. prices.

Zeiss/Freiberger Sextants. Although these are made in East Germany, London is a centre of export for them, as Americans will not deal with communist countries. Zeiss sextants are very competitively priced compared with sextants on sale in the U.S.A.

Seafarer Echo Sounders. Mini Seacourse Autopilots and Seafix Radio Direction Finders. Seafarer is the largest U.K. manufacturer of Echo Sounders."

He agreed with my finding that Avon dinghies now cost much the same in the U.K. and the U.S.

Body Building

**Gem Sporting Goods, 29 West 14 Street,
New York, NY 10011. Telephone (212) 255 5830**
8-page brochure, free U.S. and overseas. AE, DC, MC, V.
Gem sells physical fitness equipment, mainly for body build-ing. This is serious stuff: dumbbells, weights to wear, head harnesses, stands for "curling" exercises, and even more otiose things. For regular keep-fitters there are a few jump-ropes, rowers, exercise bicycles, and the very hard-to-find (but popular with children) doorway bar.

Boomerangs

**Boomerang Man, 311 Park Avenue, Room 9,
Monroe, LA 71201**
Leaflet, free; overseas 3 International Reply Coupons.
Richard Harrison, the Boomerang Man, asks me not to put him in the toy section as most of his customers are adults. Certainly boomerangs have a long and dignified history. One was found in King Tutankhamen's tomb, other very old ones have been found around the world and in Arizona, Florida and New Mexico; and a clublike nonreturning boomerang was widely used as a weapon. However, Richard Harrison does not recommend boomerangs for hunting, but as a sport. His cheerful leaflet is full of tips, news about boomerang contests, and happy comments from new throwers who have had fun and won popularity around the world ("Did some throwing in Nepal and Bali. It was a rage!"). Boomerang prices start at just a few dollars, and there are books to tell you how.

Climbing

**Forrest Mountaineering, 1517 Platte Street,
Denver, CO 80202. Telephone (303) 433 6419**
24-page color catalogue, $2; overseas $3; air mail $4. AE, MC, V.
Manufacturers of climbing equipment, with a first-rate line of bivouac gear. Nothing is sold without having been tested in the field.

**The Great Pacific Iron Works, P.O. Box 150,
Ventura, CA 93001. Telephone (803) 648 3386**
54-page catalogue, $1 U.S. and overseas; overseas air mail $5. MC, V.
This firm began as Chouinard Equipment Company in 1965 and is now the manufacturer and distributor of high-quality mountaineering equipment for technical rock and ice climbing. Its catalogue is one of the handsomest I have seen, showing a sensitive appreciation of the environment and of the beauty of classical tools. The seriousness of commitment is clearly shown in the helpful text.
  This family firm has a worldwide reputation for its hard-

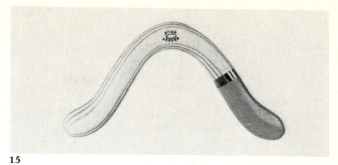

15

16

15 *Boomerang Man* "Stick around" boomerang in 5-ply birdseye maple, will hover back to the practiced thrower after transcribing one and often two circles. In five sizes, about $7 each. The wood and instructions for making your own boomerangs are also sold.

16 *Boomerang Man* "Hawes" is a popular adult-sized boomerang that is "easy to toss and safe to catch." About $7.

ware, and is experimenting with new "software" for use under extreme conditions—bags, shoes and clothes.

Mountain Safety Research, 631 South 96th Street, Seattle, WA 98108. Telephone (206) 762 0210
12-page color catalogue, free U.S. and overseas. MC, V.
Started in the sixties as an organization to test the safety of climbing equipment, MSR now manufacturers and sells a few pieces of equipment for mountaineers, backpackers and cyclists. Charles Flynn recommends their stove as the most reliable one he has seen. He cooked breakfast on his, one windy morning, for an entire camping ground, when no one else could keep their stoves alight.

Diving

M & E Marine Supply Company, Box 601, Camden, NJ 08101. Telephone (609) 858 1010
160-page diving catalogue, $2 U.S. and overseas. MC, V.
Established in 1946, this firm produces the largest catalogue there is of commercial, military and sport-diving equipment. An impressive stock of name-brand gear is listed. Be sure to ask for the *diving* catalogue as there is also a boat catalogue.

New England Divers, 131 Rantoul Street, P.O. Box 307, Beverly, MA 01915. Telephone (617) 922 6951
32-page catalogue, free U.S. and overseas. AE, MC, V.
A very good firm, New England Divers, shows some of its sports, military and commercial diving equipment in its catalogue. However, they stock the complete lines of major manufacturers, so ask them for anything special you want.

Sunland Sports, 8677 Wilshire Boulevard, Beverly Hills, CA 90211. Telephone (213) 652 4990
Custom wet suits catalogue, $2; overseas $4.
Underwater photography catalogue, $3; overseas $5. MC, V.
In two separate catalogues, this firm gives details of the made-to-order wet suits it sells, and its underwater photography equipment. The photography equipment ranges from the popular yellow Minolta Weathermatic pocket camera which is useful for photographing in the rain, to very complicated professional systems and their accessories.

Fishing

The recommendations and many of the words in this fishing section are reader Jerry Hoffnagle's, who says that some of the best fishing tackle buys are to be found not in sporting good stores, but in mail-order catalogues.

Dan Bailey, P.O. Box 1019, Livingston, MT 59047. Telephone (406) 222 1673
66-page color catalogue, free U.S. and overseas; overseas air mail $2. MC, V.
This famous store has thirty tyers making hand-tied flies for customers in the U.S., Canada and thirty-five other countries. It outfits for fly fishing only, and stocks equipment for the serious fly fishers, such as insect collecting kits, stream thermometers and books.

Bass Pro Shop, 1935 South Campbell, Springfield, MO 65807. Telephone (417) 887 1915
96-page color catalogue, $1 U.S. and overseas. MC, V.
One of the few catalogues that has a complete stock of

supplies for spinfishing and baitcasting (mainly for bass and saltwater trophy fish) rather than for fly fishing.

Hardy Brothers (Alnwick), 61 Pall Mall, London SW1, England. Telephone (01) 839 5515
22-page color catalogue, $2; air mail $6. January.
The most famous rod-makers in the world, Hardy Brothers is even more—an international status symbol according to the English *Harper's Bazaar*. They make tackle and are fanatically interested in improvement and innovation, and say that all their management people are "ardent anglers." An excellent catalogue gives full explanations of all their products, most of which are cheaper when bought directly from England. The exceptions are single rods that are too long to be mailed; shipping these costs so much that it is better to buy them from Hardy agents in your own country.

Kaufmann's Streamborn, P.O. Box 23032, Portland, OR 97223. Telephone (503) 639 6400
62-page color catalogue, $1 U.S. and overseas; overseas air mail $3. AE, MC, V.
Another source for fly fishing, Kaufmann's has heavy equipment for steel heading and salmon fishing, and interesting accessories for fly tying.

Orvis, 10 River Road, Manchester, VT 05254
Catalogue, free.
The ancestor of the mail-order fishing-tackle business in America, and still one of its best practitioners. Outdoor clothing and decorative accessories with a sporting theme have overshadowed the actual items of tackle in recent years, so that Orvis now publishes a separate fishing-tackle-only catalogue in spring. This is top-of-the-line fly fishing equipment—including saltwater—with a nod to spinning and so-called "combination" spinning-flycasting outfits for travelers. The highlights of the Orvis catalogues are really the unusual accessories with a sporting theme and outdoor clothing, notably designs from Hardy of England.

Tom C. Saville, Unit 7, Salisbury Square, Nottingham, England. Telephone 0602 784 248
128-page catalogue, $2; air mail $3. MC, V.
Specialists in trout- and salmon-fishing gear, and fly-tying materials. A nice, informative catalogue.

Thomas and Thomas, Rodmakers, P.O. Box 32, 22 Third Street, Turners Falls, MA 01376. Telephone (413) 863 9727
72-page color catalogue, $2; overseas $5.
Two ex-philosophy teachers make very fine custom bamboo rods (Ronald Reagan gave one to the Australian prime minister), but only three hundred a year, so there is sometimes a wait. They also sell other supplies, clothes for and books on, fly fishing.

Golf

Golf Day Products, 3015 Commercial Avenue, Northbrook, IL 60062. Telephone (312) 498 1400
50-page catalogue, 50 cents; overseas $2. AE, MC, V.
Parts, tools and advice for people who want to repair or refinish their golf clubs, or even put together and finish putters and drivers from unfinished parts.

DISCOUNT

Please see discount information in the How to Buy section.

**Las Vegas Discount, 4813 Paradise Road,
Las Vegas, NV 89109. Telephone (800) 634 6743**
Price list, free; overseas $4. AE, DC, MC, V.
A long list (no description or information) of discounted
major brands of golf equipment at about 30 percent off list
prices. Clubs, drivers, putters, clothes and bags for men and
women are included. Established 1975.

**Professional Golf Suppliers,
2086 North University Drive,
Pembroke Pines, FL 33024. Telephone (800) 327 9243**
Price list, free U.S. and overseas. MC, V.
Golf sets, putters, carts, shoes, balls and miscellaneous
equipment. All at discount prices. Established 1977.

**Telepro Golf Shops, 17642 Armstrong Drive,
Irvine, CA 92714. Telephone (800) 854 3687.**
16-page brochure, free U.S. and overseas. MC, V.
Telepro sells well-known brands of golf equipment at
roughly 30 percent below list price. If you know exactly
what you need, you can order directly. If you want advice,
you can get it by telephone or mail. The brochure describes
at length a small selection of clubs. Established 1973.

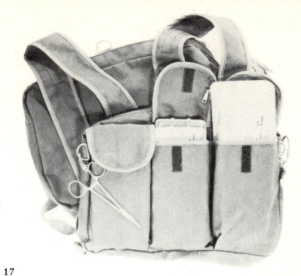

17

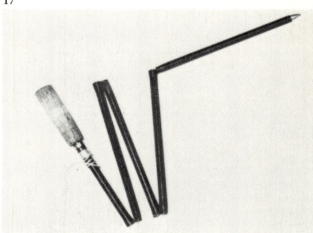

18

Hunting

**Firma Edward Kettner, Krebsgasse 5, Postfach 10 11 65,
D5000 Cologne, West Germany. Telephone 0221 59650**
Color catalogue in German, $5; air mail $12.
A reader recommended this firm, praising it for very good
service. A splendid 300-page catalogue shows an enormous
selection of guns and hunting accessories, dog-grooming supplies, bags to carry catch home, plaques to mount antlers,
bird whistles, hideouts for hunters and a great deal more
than I've ever seen in any American catalogue. There is also
an excellent clothes section showing all green loden coats,
capes, jackets, sweaters, pants, hats, shoes, boots, socks,
gloves, and even slippers for men. For women the same,
with some additional dirndls and blouses, and there are even
a few corduroy pants and loden coats for children. And
finally, this is obviously a good place to find presents for
hunters, as hunting motifs decorate just about anything for
the house: beer mugs, ashtrays, glasses, cigarette boxes,
coasters, dinner services, clocks, wall plaques, lampshades
and even wallpaper.

Ice Skating

**Rainbo Sport Shop, 4836 North Clark Street,
Chicago, IL 60640**
34-page catalogue, free; overseas $2. MC, V.
Boots, clothes, boot bags, books and even buttons ("I spin to
win," "It's great to skate") for ice skaters. Rainbo also has a
boot-repair and blade-sharpening service.

17 *Thomas and Thomas* A new angler's pack to carry fishing gear
holds more and is more comfortable than a vest (weight is distributed across shoulders instead of nape). About $34.50.

18 *Thomas and Thomas* Folstaf wading staff, folds and attaches to
vest or belt. About $25.75 to $35.75, depending on length. It also
makes a good walking stick.

Riding

Miller Harness Company, 123 East 24th Street, New York, NY 10010. Telephone (212) 673 1400
100-page catalogue, $2 U.S. and overseas. Spring. AE, DC, MC, V.
Miller is a major supplier of riding equipment: formal riding clothes, Marlborough riding boots and shoes from England, accessories, etc., and a large selection of saddles, listing a number from America and Europe. An extensive choice of such relatively technical items as protective equipment, treatment books, schooling and breaking equipment, and the like. There is a selection of Western saddlery and appropriate clothing, along with grooming and stable equipment and the materials needed by those who own horses as well as ride them.

☙ **George Parker and Sons (Saddlers), 12 Upper St. Martin's Lane, London WC2, England. Telephone (01) 836 1164**
Catalogue, $1. Fall.
Another very reputable English saddler says that the reason English saddlery is so popular in America is not only the fine quality and competitive prices but also that some of the things sold in England are not available in America.

Running

Moss Brown and Co., 1522 Wisconsin Avenue, N.W., Washington, DC 20007. Telephone (800) 424 2774 or (202) 342 1888
32-page color catalogue, free; overseas $1. AE, MC, V.
Manufacturers of clothes, underwear and shoes for running. This catalogue also has handy things, such as purses that attach to the shoes, a belt to carry water for long-distance running, a pedometer, etc.

Skiing

Akers Ski, Andover, ME 04216. Telephone (207) 392 4582
18-page catalogue, self-addressed stamped envelope. August. MC, V.
Akers specializes in cross-country ski equipment, with some ski-jumping equipment. The owner says that when he first opened twenty-two years ago, there was very little demand for touring equipment, whereas now it makes up seventy-five percent of his sales. Almost all the skis, boots, clothes and accessories have been imported from Scandinavia.

Sporthaus Witting, Maria Theresienstrasse 39, Postfach 270, A6020 Innsbruck, Austria. Telephone 29–1 44
68-page summer sports catalogue, free. In German.
68-page color ski catalogue, free. In German.
This one-hundred-year-old firm says "we are always receiving several orders from U.S.A. for different sport equipment as well as sweaters, jackets, Loden, ski-equipment and so on." The summer catalogue has a smattering of camping, climbing, tennis equipment and clothes. The winter catalogue has skis and ski clothes.

Tennis

Hills Court, 1 Tennis Way, Manchester, VT 05254. Telephone (802) 362 1200
32-page color catalogue, free. AE, MC, V.
Tennis clothes for men and women, also a little court equipment, and accessories such as sweepers, nets, scorecards. Some clothes for jogging and exercise too.

Rayco Tennis Products, 1434 University Avenue, San Diego, CA 92103. Telephone (800) 854 6692. California and outside U.S. (714) 295 4777
12-page catalogue, $1 U.S. and overseas. MC, V.
Equipment for tennis and courts, for the professional or the gadget lover; restringing equipment, ball mowers, ball pick-up and ball throwers—plus a telephone hotline with "straight answers to all your string, stringing and tennis-equipment questions."

DISCOUNT
Please see discount information in the How to Buy section.

Lombards, 1861 NE 163rd Street, North Miami Beach, FL 33162. Telephone (305) 944 1166
Leaflet, free.
Lombards, which says it is the largest pro shop in the U.S. publishes a brochure listing good brand-name tennis and squash racquets, tennis shoes, ball machines, etc. They are well used to exporting, and have a page of special information for overseas customers. I found discounts of 10 to 17 percent. Established 1944.

Professional Tennis Suppliers, 2086 North University Drive, Pembroke Pines, FL 33024. Telephone (800) 327 9243, or (305) 432 6636
Price list, free U.S. and overseas. MC, V.
A neat and tidy price list for tennis racquets, shoes and supplies, racquet-ball racquets, bags and balls, and squash racquets. I checked prices on some tennis racquets, and they were 20 to 30 percent lower than New York nondiscount prices. Established 1977.

27

STATIONERY AND OFFICE SUPPLIES

Déjà Vu, 1979 Shattuck Avenue, Berkeley, CA 94704. Telephone (415) 849 2969
18-page catalogue, $1.50 U.S. and overseas.
Actually more avant garde than déjà vu, Diana Kehlmann and Sandru Ruth gather postcards from museums and small presses. Cards by famous photographers and artists, and subjects such as fashion, rock stars, cowboys. An odd and interesting assortment that includes Christmas postcards. Unfortunately there is a $10 minimum and only a few of the cards are actually shown.

The Drawing Board, 256 Regal Row, Box 220505, Dallas, TX 75222
Catalogue, free.
The Drawing Board sells business forms and office aids. Design and quality is definitely above average, so many of the supplies will be helpful for people trying to run a home efficiently. There are cheerful memo pads, phone-message pads, even long-distance telephone call log books, also canceled-check files, storage boxes for old tax returns, etc.

Valerie Harper, West View, Compton Street, Compton Winchester, Hants SO21 2AT, England. Telephone Twyford 714 068
Price list and paper samples, $2.
Valerie Harper, an English graphic designer, makes cards, postcards and writing paper with a drawing of your house taken from a photograph. The drawings are in a pleasant style; the good-quality paper comes in five pastel shades. Prices for first printing and drawing (subsequent printings are much cheaper) about $84 for two hundred postcards; about $92 for two hundred cards with address and message inside; about $100 for two hundred sheets of printing writing paper with two hundred printed envelopes and one hundred sheets of matching plain paper.

Jesse Jones Industries, P.O. Box 5120, Department CNC, Philadelphia, PA 19141. Telephone (215) 425 6600
Color brochure, free U.S. and overseas. AE, MC, V.
To keep the desk (and house) in order, and everything findable, Jesse Jones produces matching "storage products": files for magazines and pamphlets, canceled checks, and personal records; binders for telephone directories; boxes for photographs, postcards and recipes; racks for records and tapes. A treasure trove for anyone who wants to get organized.

Littlehouse, P.O. Box 141, Lindenhurst, NY 11757. Telephone (516) 888 6982
Leaflet, free U.S. and overseas.
Rita De Lisi has a one-person mail-order business selling ingredients to make your own postcards: plain cards to be painted on; sticky backs to apply to cut-out pictures; cards and envelopes to make postcards into note cards. Lots of colors and nicely designed.

Milford Paper and Ink, 36 Milford Street, Boston, MA 02118. Telephone (617) 451 5170
Samples, $2 U.S. and overseas (refundable).
Thick creamy paper, turn-of-the-century engravings, four type styles and four subtle ink colors can be combined, as you want, to make your own writing paper or postcards. Engravings are mostly of plants or clocks and the effect is most tasteful. Seventy-five sheets and envelopes cost $48 postpaid the first time and $39 on reorders.

1 *Valerie Harper* Houses are drawn from photographs and reproduced on cards, post cards, and writing paper. Prices for drawing and first printing start at about $84 for two hundred postcards; later printings cost much less.

2

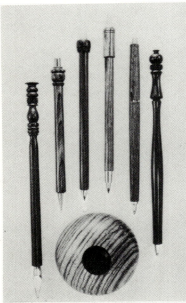

3

**Smythson's, 54 New Bond Street,
London W1Y 0DE, England. Telephone (01) 629 8558**
*Gift brochure; Proprietary list, writing-paper samples, $1.50;
air mail $4.*
The English *Harper's Bazaar* called Smythson's "an international status symbol" (along with Hardy's, sports; and John Lobb, clothes); indeed, Smythson's has a "secluded lounge" where they advise ambassadors on "protocol and stationery etiquette." They are famous for their blue writing paper, which, they say, is by far their greatest export to America, and will send samples of their poshy plain blue-and-cream stationery and their address dies. Paper can be bought plain, printed or initialed.

Smythson's also makes diaries, which are not sold by mail, since they are distributed in America. But other distinguished-looking things for the desk are sold by mail: loose-leaf morocco address books, from about $67; polished pigskin visitors' books embossed with your house name in gold, from about $148; wallets; leather desk sets; a series of record books in which to make notes in an orderly way about hobbies and special interests (garden, golf, hunting, motoring, music, theater, wine, etc.); and the most expensive of the lot—$15 for one indexed "Blondes, Brunettes, and Redheads." And, in various sizes, indexed notebooks labeled "Christmas," "Gifts," "Menus" and "Guests," or a tycoonish three-city address book—"London-Paris-New York."

**Tiffany and Company, 727 Fifth Avenue,
New York, NY 10022. Telephone (212) 755 8000**
General catalogue, $3; overseas $5.
Stationery brochure, free. AE, DC, MC, V.
A price list with samples gives details of the excellent writing papers that Tiffany die prints with addresses.

DISCOUNT
Please see discount information in the How to Buy section.

**Copen Press, 100 Berriman Street, Brooklyn, NY 11208.
Telephone (212) 235 4270**
Occasional brochures, free.
No frills printing. They are slow, and you get little choice of color and paper, but prices are very low. I've used them for pamphlets and have been satisfied.

**Frank Eastern, 625 Broadway, New York, NY 10012.
Telephone (800) 221 4914**
56-page catalogue, free.
Rather dull office furniture, but also smaller supplies such as files, paper, envelopes, staplers, typewriter cartridges, etc. I try to buy all my writing equipment here, as their prices are 15 to 40 percent below those at my local stationers.

**Quill Corporation, 100 South Schelter Road,
Lincolnshire, IL 60069. Telephone (312) 634 4800**
150-page catalogue, free.
The most popular of the discount office-supply firms, Quill sells absolutely everything: stationery, files and furniture and all equipment. Recommended by writer Stephan Wilkinson, who says ". . . I order *all* my stationery supplies, from IBM ribbon to pencils. They're very fast, and I think the prices are excellent (especially if you order in quantity)." Established 1955.

2 *Milford Paper and Ink* Writing paper is made to order from old engravings: four different type styles and four different ink colors. Prices start at about $48, postpaid.

3 *Penmakers* Desk ball-point, retractable ball-point, deluxe drafting pencil, drafting pencil, accountant's pencil, dip pen, and a single penstand. Made from rosewood and other exotic woods. Priced about $14.50 to $20 each.

Pens

Fahrney's Pens, Catalogue Department, Suite 503, 123 North Pitt Street, Alexandria, VA 22314. Telephone (703) 548 2005
Color brochure, $1. AE, MC, V.

International Pen Shop, Arthur Brown and Brothers, 2 West 46th Street, New York, NY 10036. Telephone (212) 575 5544
Color pen brochure, free. AE, DC, MC, V.
Both these stores have fully illustrated brochures showing beautifully designed pens (and calligraphy sets) by Aurora, Lamy, Montblanc, Parker, Pentel, Sheaffer, Waterman and others. Fahrney's has good sales at least once a year.

Penmakers, Route 1, Box 292A, Winters, CA 95694. Telephone (916) 795 2648
Leaflet, 50 cents; overseas $1.25.
Several good-looking pens and pencils and stands made out of exotic hardwoods and naturally finished, prices roughly $16 each. Pens use pressurized cartridges, except for a calligraphy set which has a dip pen and wooden ink stand.

Phoenix Studios, P.O. Box 2963, Fayetteville, AR 72702. Telephone (501) 442 2503
Color card, free.
Michael Bailot makes hand-turned pens (ball point and ink) and pencils with holders in matching wood such as Honduras rosewood, cocobolo, morado and ebony. No two designs are exactly the same.

DISCOUNT
Please see discount information in the How to Buy section.

It is possible to get 20- to 30-percent discount on some pens if you know the model number you want: Michael C. Fina and International Solgo have Cross, Parker and Sheaffer; LVT Appliance Hotline has Parker, Ronson, and Shaeffer, and Schiphol Airport, Holland has Mont Blanc pens at about half New York prices.

Typewriters

Tytell Typewriter Company, 116 Fulton Street, New York, NY 10038. Telephone (212) 233 5333
Tytell has typewriters that write in 145 languages; they have keyboards for doctors, dentists, botanists who need special symbols; they have keyboards for the disabled; and they have type styles of all kinds and sizes and carriage widths to thirty inches. They have no catalogue, but can adapt typewriters to suit almost any need, so write with your request—over half of the Tytell orders come by mail from abroad.

DISCOUNT
Please see discount information in the How to Buy section.

Typewriters are very suitable for buying by mail at a discount. It is easy to find a 30-percent discount on list prices, and as shipping is relatively inexpensive, it sometimes equals the sales tax that you don't pay when buying out of state. You must know exact model name to buy.

Bondy Export Corporation, 40 Canal Street, New York, NY 10002. Telephone (212) 925 7785
Write only with stamped self-addressed envelope (overseas 1 International Reply Coupon) and model name for a price.
Bondy, an appliance discount store, stocks only Smith Corona typewriters, but I found the best prices for these here. I bought a Coronamatic 2500 by mail here for $265 when the list price was $399, and they shipped immediately (I had paid with a certified check). Established 1950.

International Solgo, 77 West 23rd Street, New York, NY 10010. Telephone (800) 645 8162 or (212) 675 3555
Write or telephone with model number U.S. and overseas. AE, MC, V.
This general-appliance discount store, says that they sell most brands of manual and electric typewriters. I found 30 percent a typical typewriter discount here. Established 1933.

Pearl Brothers, 476 Smith Street, Brooklyn, NY 11231. Telephone (212) 875 3024
Write or telephone with model name for price.
Pearl Brothers specializes in typewriters and small office machines. They stock reconditioned IBMs. Established 1948.

Typex, 119 West 23rd Street, New York, NY 10011. Telephone (800) 221 9332 or (212) 243 8086
Write or telephone with model name for prices, U.S. and overseas. AE, MC, V.
Typex specializes in typewriters and other small office machines at a discount. Mr. Elizikovitz says that he stocks or can order most brands of typewriters. I bought a Smith Corona Enterprise here for $184 at a time when the list price was $263. Established 1979.

Wolf Office Equipment, 1841 Broadway, New York, NY 10023. Telephone (212) 581 9080
Leaflet, self-addressed stamped envelope. MC, V.
Wolf has sales on typewriters, including reconditioned IBMs, calculators, dictating machines, furniture and files, (including reputable Steelmaster files) and miscellaneous equipment. Be sure to check prices, as I am not sure whether the discounts are constant. Established 1938.

28
TOYS AND GAMES

John Adams Toys, Reed Road, P.O. Box 35, Pennington, NJ 08534. Telephone (609) 737 1608
30-page color catalogue, $1; overseas $2.
If you've ever wondered what happened to old-fashioned, nonmechanical toys, look here: felt mobiles for babies, balancing wooden parrots, rag dolls, fishing games, tops, bubble pipes, tiddlywinks and snakes and ladders. All redesigned with flair, by an English manufacturer.

Animal Town Game Company, P.O. Box 2002, Santa Barbara, CA 93120. Telephone (805) 962 8368
Brochure, free U.S. and Overseas.
Ken and Ann Kolsbun object to most games available which "glorify the military and war, the automobile culture, space exploration, computer technology, real estate, TV and movie celebrities" and point out that "rarely will you find games that honor Old Mother Nature, peace, artists, poets and humanitarians." The Kolsbuns' answer is about six games (and a new one added every year) with titles such as Back to the (Small, Organic, Family) Farm and Save the Whale, presented in a cheerful catalogue sprinkled with "seeds for thought and action" such as "Encourage women to invent toys and games" and "Support small business enterprises." Games cost $14 to $21 each.

Bellerophon Books, 36 Anacapa Street, Santa Barbara, CA 93101
20-page brochure, self-addressed stamped envelope; overseas 50 cents.
Fifteen complicated coloring books, "all from superbly amusing historical sources," cover subjects like the Renaissance, Chaucer, the Old and New Testaments and a medieval alphabet. The designs are small and intricate but look smashing after some judicious work with felt-tip pens, and are demanding enough for adults; in fact, a friend of mine has colored more pages of The Greeks than her ten-year-old daughter.

Big Toys, 3113 South Paine Street, Tacoma, WA 98407. Telephone (206) 572 7611
12-page catalogue, free U.S. and overseas. MC, V.
Big Toys has been supplying schools and parks with rugged, natural-looking backyard climbing equipment for eleven years. Now they are supplying families as well. The frames are made of soft wood logs, steel pipes and tires. They look good and last well, according to Big Toys.

Cherry Tree Toys, 6731 Mills Road, St. Clairsville, OH 43950. Telephone (614) 695 3348
Catalogue, $1 U.S. and overseas.
Plans to make very nicely designed pull and other small wooden toys (rocking horse and larger toys will be added). You buy your own wood, Cherry Tree has wheels, cords, knobs, etc.

Child Life Play Specialties, 55 Whitney Street, Holliston, MA 01746. Telephone (617) 429 4639
24-page catalogue, free. MC, V.
Child Life designs and manufactures a very well made collection of wooden play equipment which should keep any child amused and healthily exercised. It is mainly for outside, although one or two things such as a slide and a doorway gym are for indoor use. There are several swings for children of all ages, including babies and toddlers; slides, seesaws, rocking boats, punching bags and sandpits are available, and all sorts of climbers and jungle gyms. Also several playhouses and a tree house.

1 *Museum of the City of New York* (see Museum section) Bisque baby dolls, replicas of antique bisque dolls, reproduced from collections of Kaiser, Limbach, Goebels, and other famous doll manufacturers. Fully jointed and dressed in lace-trimmed costumes, priced about $17 to $28.50; a musical doll with moving head, about $39.95.

Childcraft Education Corporation, 20 Kilmer Road, Edison, NJ 08818. Telephone 800 631 5657
32-page color catalogue, free. AE, MC, V.
The catalogue is divided into several sections: "First Toys" for babies up to about the age of two; "Let's Pretend" has puppet theaters and disguise kits; "Housekeeping" has child-size wooden kitchen appliances, pots, pans, housecleaning sets, doll's beds; "Active Play" has various jumping and rocking inventions, as well as throwing games such as wall quoits and mini-basketball. Finally there are large "Learning Through Fun" and "Science" sections, which have counting-number and word games, and science and nature study supplies. There are plenty of toys in this catalogue I haven't seen before, and most of them look interesting.

Community Playthings, Rifton, NY 12471. Telephone (914) 658 3141
Catalogue, 50 cents.
A religious community which began in Germany after the first world war, was ordered to dissolve under Hitler, moved first to England, then Paraguay and finally the U.S. and Canada. Visitors are welcome to stay for a while and share life and work in an "open and seeking way."

The New York Branch of the Community manufactures large plain and sturdy wooden toys and equipment, including a series for the handicapped. Most customers are schools and playgroups, but if you are interested in goods that really last, you'll find here child-sized kitchen furniture, climbing sets, blocks, easels, wagons, scooters and doll furniture.

Constructive Playthings, 2008 West 103 Terrace, Leswood, Kansas City, MO 66206. Telephone (913) 642 8244
170-page catalogue, some color, $2; overseas $6. MC, V.
This big catalogue illustrates toys, games and supplies mainly for schools, but it will be extremely useful for parents because it is just about all-inclusive, and anyone who wants to simplify life can get almost everything for children of all ages here. All the things usually stocked by toy shops are here in quantity: dolls (including a boy doll with a penis), doll carriages, trains, farm sets, animals, puzzles, board games, books and records, larger equipment such as furniture, seesaws, doll houses, playhouses and puppet stages.

There is also lots of equipment for parents who want to help children with schoolwork—from the earliest games that teach recognition of numbers and letters and time through "Action-Fraction" games to sets of charts and cards of simple science experiments. An invaluable catalogue.

The Dolls House Toys, 29 The Market, Covent Garden, London WC2E 8RE, England
Catalogue, $2; air mail $4.
This is a good source of doll-house furniture for both children and adults. My daughter, who is a doll-house owner and miniature collector, comments: "The Dolls House seems to have combined the $5 accessory with the $500 Georgian doll house with everything in between. They were opened in October 1971 and have accumulated a lot of variety since then." In furniture they have over four hundred handmade pieces besides cheaper mass-produced furniture from Korea and Taiwan. In houses there are sixteen designs including "Pink Regency," "Dickens" and "Georgian Mansion."

Easy Pieces Puzzles, P.O. Box 445, Harbor Springs, MI 49740. Telephone (616) 526 5471
Brochure, free.
Handmade jigsaw puzzles for very young children, in natural oak and rich colors. Good-looking enough to be used as

2 *Museum of the City of New York* (see Museum section) A selection of basic toys from the traditional playpen of Edwardian times, nesting blocks, and animal pillows. About $7.95 to $17.95.

3 *Clothkits/Charing Cross Kits* (see Clothes section) A PVC-coated cotton tablecloth printed with favorite games such as "Snakes and Ladders," tiddlywinks, Parcheesi, checkers and chess. Tiddlywinks and dice come with the cloth, checkers are available separately. About $14.95.

4 *Cherry Tree Toys* Sells plans (about $1.50 each), wheels, and cords to make toys. Customers provide their own wood. *Photograph by Colin C. McCrae.*

5

6

decorations when not in use. There are animals, name puzzles, alphabet and animals trees and a clock. Recommended by reader Sally Silver.

The Enchanted Doll House,
Manchester Center, VT 05255. Telephone (802) 362 3030
Catalogue. Fall. Ask about price, U.S. and overseas. AE, MC, V.
The Enchanted Doll House is an 1812 Colonial house full of imported, handmade or out-of-the-ordinary toys, books and games. The specialty is, of course, superior dolls and doll houses. The dolls range from original rag dolls at $20 through realistic baby Victoria "just home from the hospital" to original bisque creations at over $400. There are four classic doll houses to choose from, two little hand-painted Vermont carrying houses sold here only and an unpainted precut kit to make a small doll house for $90. Complete supplies for doll-house builders are also available.

Family Pastimes, Rural Route 4,
Perth, Ontario, Canada K7H 3C6
Brochure, 25 cents.
In my family Happy Families always ended up *un*happily, and Monopoly ended up with someone locked in the bathroom crying. Jim and Ruth Deacove noticed how many pushy and resentful feelings most games arouse in the players. They also noticed how the competitive behavior required by games conflicts with the cooperative attitudes of kindness and helpfulness that most people try to teach their children in real life.

The result has been a collection of toys that require players to cooperate to meet challenges. Instead of Monopoly there is "Our Town" and "Community" in which players fight inflation, strikes and taxes to bring schools, co-ops, and parks to a neighborhood; in "Mountaineering" players help each other to get to the top; and of course the space games do *not* consist of conquering alien beings. One game, "Choices," created at the request of a church group, tries to teach adolescents through evaluation and discussion the need to choose instead of "just being dragged along by society." Games are similar in spirit to the Animal Town ones but design is less sophisticated and brochure more earnest. Thirty more games, many costing under $5 postage paid.

Galt Toys, 63 Whitfield Street, Guilford, CT 06437.
Telephone (203) 453 3366
Color leaflet, free.
England's leading "educational" toy manufacturer, with a store at the end of Carnaby Street, makes handsome, strong toys in wood rather than plastic, which are moderately experimental and are generally pleasing to design-conscious parents as well as to many English schools. The United States outlet publishes a leaflet which shows about fifty attractive toys for babies and young children.

Giggletree, Winterbrook Way, Meredith, NH 03253.
Telephone (603) 279 7071
Catalogue, free.

Just for Kids, Winterbrook Way, Meredith, NH 03253.
Telephone (603) 279 7031
Catalogue, free.
The Sabanecks (who own these shops) say that although Meredith shop and catalogues are new, their firm is twenty years old.
Both these colorful catalogues are intended to solve the "What on earth can I give him/her?" problem, rather than provide basic toys—and they do provide quite a few imagi-

5 *Family Pastimes* A noncompetitive answer to "Monopoly"—"Our Town," in which players cooperate in fighting inflation and trying to bring school co-ops, food co-ops, and people's parks to a neighborhood.

6 *Galt Toys* "See-Inside jigsaws": Lift out the picture and see what's inside. First puzzles for 1½- to 3-year-olds. About $12 each.

native solutions such as eleven-foot cardboard dinosaur models, teach-yourself-to-juggle kits and "Neighborhood Explorer sets," and *Mouthsounds* book and record: "How to whistle, pop, click and honk your way to social success."

**Go Fly a Kite, 1434 Third Avenue,
New York, NY 10021. Telephone (212) 472 2623**
Color brochure, $2 (refundable); overseas $4. AE, MC, V.
This small shop has the biggest collection of kites in the world and puts out a super leaflet with pictures of about thirty of them—eagles, centipedes, dragonflies, bats, fish, hawks and dragons—colorful, shiny and very decorative when out of action; in fact, if you're lazy you can just hang some of them on the wall and look at them.

**Green Tiger Press, Box 868, La Jolla, CA 92038.
Telephone (714) 238 1001**
80-page color catalogue, $3.75; overseas $5.50.
This wonderful firm started by reproducing pictures from old children's books and has now gone on to produce many beautiful things decorated with the works of the most famous children's book illustrators such as Walter Crane, Kay Nielson, Arthur Rackham et al., with a preference for "the romantic, the dreamlike and the visionary." Many cards, also stickers, calendars, bookplates, tiny mirrors, and very lovely and inexpensive reproductions and nursery friezes for decorations.

**Growing Child, 22 North Second Street, P.O. Box 620,
Lafayette, IN 47902. Telephone (317) 423 2624**
64-page catalogue, free. MC, V.
A black-and-white catalogue with no novelties or fancy gifts, just basic "learning and working tools" and books for children up to the age of six. Lots of building blocks and puzzles—the kind given in tests for shape and size recognition. The idea behind the store is to provide supplies to help disadvantaged preschool children start learning at home.

♣♣ **Hamleys, 200–202 Regent Street, London W1, England**
General catalogue, $4 (only available September to December).
Hamley's is the FAO Schwarz of England—a huge toy store selling every kind of traditional toy and most leading brands. The catalogue includes selections from each floor: games, puzzles, kits, planes, crafts, music, science, mechanical toys and sports. Usually, a page of aids to party giving, favors, magic tricks, fancy dress and snappers.

**House with the Blue Door, 23 Portland Road,
Kennebunk, ME 04043. Telephone (207) 985 3461**
Brochure, $1.
Doll-house kits—a terrific way to beat the high price of doll houses, and a memorable family project (my grown daughters still refuse to give away the house they made with their father). Here are twelve plywood kits to be put together with hammer and screwdriver. Prices $47 to $90. The houses are also available made up but unpainted, at very reasonable prices.

**Kinderparadeis Hamburg, Neuer Wall 7,
2000 Hamburg, 36 Germany.
Telephone (040) 343 931**
*256-page color catalogue, $1; air mail $2. In German.
Kathe Kruse Dolls, Steiff, Marklin catalogues on request.*

**Spielwaren Behle, Kaisertrasse 28, Frankfurt, Germany.
Telephone 0611 232 077**
256-page color catalogue, $2. In German.

7

7

8

7 *Green Tiger Press* Bookplates, cards, writing paper, and matted reproductions decorated with works by the great children's illustrators.

8 *House with the Blue Door* Plywood dollhouse kits at prices starting at about $47.

**Spielzeug-Rasch, Gerhart Hauptmann Platz 1,
2 Hamburg 1, Germany. Telephone (040) 33 79 22**
256-page color catalogue, $2. In German.
Germany produces superb toys, and these leading toy shops
are all quite used to sending them abroad (Spielzeug-Rasch
says they have over a thousand foreign customers, and answer letters in French and Spanish as well as English). I
have found Kinderparadeis in Hamburg especially respon-
sive and helpful, so they may be your best bet.

These three shops send out the same general catalogue
which shows a little from several of the best known German
manufacturers: Marklin and Fleishmann H.O. model railways; Faller and Kibri lineside buildings; Baufix and Fisher
Technik construction sets; Ravensburger box games and
Steiff stuffed animals. These used to cost about half U.S.
price, in Germany. I haven't found the same toys on sale in
the U.S. recently so haven't been able to compare prices; but
reader Roseann Muñoz tells me that she has been saving
about $13 on the Steiff animals she buys from Spielzeug-
Rasch. Anyway, there is plenty here for the adventurous.
The catalogue is in German, so you do need a translator,
though it is possible to manage with determination and a
stout heart as the prices are clear and right next to the toy
photographs.

**Learning Games, P.O. Box 820-C, New King Street,
North White Plains, NY 10603**
Leaflets, long self-addressed stamped envelope; overseas $1.
This firm sells a Cuisinaire home mathematics kit for adults
to help children with math. The kit contains the rods which
symbolize different numbers according to length and which
are widely used in schools now; and a series of activity cards
for the parent to use with the rods.

The Little Doll House, Sheffield, MA 01257
Leaflet, free U.S. and overseas.
A handmade, twelve-inch Godey-style doll costs $20. The
Little Doll House says: "Only the finest quality fabrics,
ribbons and laces dress the dolls, and are easily removed
with the tiniest snap fasteners . . . every doll is fully guaranteed for perfect craftsmanship." Lady Godey is dressed in an
1850 ante-bellum dress, bonnet and purse, with petticoat
and lace-trimmed pantalets.

**Mountain Toy Makers, Box 51, Long Lake, NY 12847.
Telephone (518) 624 6175**
Brochure, 25 cents; overseas 50 cents; air mail 75 cents.
Thirty cars and trains are made of white pine with maple or
birch hardwood where needed. If a toy gets broken, send it
back and Mountain Toys ("I am a very small business")
will be glad to fix it. Most toys cost under $5.

**Bill Muller's Toys, Box 1838, Oak Hall, VA 23416.
Telephone (804) 824 4373**
20-page catalogue, free U.S. and overseas. MC, V.
A good collection of unpainted, unvarnished wooden toys are
made by Bill Muller, the usual small toys and also a Noah's
ark, stick horses, and animal hangers for clothes and things.
Recommended by reader Carol Campion who says, "The
toys in the Bill Muller catalogue are really lovely. Everything is very well finished and made from sugar pine which
has a nice feel."

**Pollock's Toy Museum, 1 Scala Street,
London W1, England. Telephone (01) 636 3452**
Leaflet, free.
An old toy-theater maker, now well known for reproductions
of its original wares. Six different theaters are produced in
book form for about $5 including postage: Each book in-
cludes a theater printed on card with scenery, characters and
text for one play. It measures about eleven by eleven by nine
inches when set up. Additional plays adapted from fairy
tales to fit the theaters cost about $1.50. Rag-doll kits cost
$6 postage paid.

**Dick Schnacke Mountain Craft Shop,
American Ridge Road, Route 1,
New Martinsville, WV 26155**
Leaflet, free U.S. and overseas. AE, CB, DC, MC, V.
An arty gray sheet introduces the old American folk toys
made by Dick Schnacke and fellow craftsmen in Appalachia.
The toys are simple and very appealing, many of them
involving skills and patience that should keep you busy for
hours. There is a whimmy diddle to rub, a flipper dinger to
blow, a mountain bolo to swing and a buzz saw to twirl, not
to mention an old-fashioned top to spin—sixty-three toys
altogether and new ones are added each year. Practically all
of them cost less than $5.

**F.A.O. Schwarz, 745 Fifth Avenue,
New York, NY 10151. Telephone (212) 644 9400**
Color catalogue, free U.S. and overseas.
F.A.O. Schwarz claims to be one of the oldest and most
exclusive toy stores in the world, though now it is more than
a store—it's twenty-eight stores throughout America that
stock between ten and twelve thousand different toys from
all parts of the world. It hasn't lost its story-book toy-shop
quality—you just step inside the Fifth Avenue store and you
are surrounded by luxurious banks of expensive giant furry
animals, whirling mechanical toys, tinkling music boxes, and
elaborately dressed dolls. Every traditional toy for children
of all ages is here, and the catalogue has a little of everything: dolls and their clothes, doll houses, Steiff plush toys,
rocking horses, board games, bigger games such as table
tennis, children's typewriters, art supplies, battery-operated
cars, construction sets, craft kits, woodwork sets, nature and
science sets, electric trains, phonographs, walkie-talkies,
farms and forts. In short, it's the rather expensive dream of
many a covetous child and adult. Schwarz says that opera
singers playing the toy pianos and automobile magnates
working the toy cars are a common sight, and King Hussein
bought one and a half truckloads of toys here a few years ago.

**Stocking Fillas, Tennant House, Little Milton,
Oxford, OX9 7QB, England.
Telephone Great Milton 368**
Brochure, free. MC, V.
Lots of little favors and fillers for children: body tatoos
(actually transfers), tiny toys, magnets and puzzles—also a
few other good ideas such as make your own snapper kit.
Almost everything is under $3.

**Tryon Toymakers, Route 3, Box 148,
Campobello, SC 29322. Telephone (803) 457 2017**
Leaflet, 25 cents; overseas $1.
Owners Nancy and Chuck Heron make brightly painted
wooden toys and room decorations: woodpecker stilts, a
horse swing, a village that folds into a suitcase, soldier-
decorated bookends and crayon holders—a nice change from
the unpainted toys.

**Tully Toys, 4606 Warrenton Road, Vicksburg, MS 39180.
Telephone (601) 638 1724**
Leaflet, free U.S. and overseas.
An original gaggle of goggle-eyed rocking animals in un-
painted Southern hardwoods. Dinosaur, rhinoceros, chicken,

shrimp, etc., about $50 each. Good as companions after retirement from active use.

Frederick Warne and Company, 2 Park Avenue, New York, NY 10016. Telephone (212) 686 9630
Children's book price list, free.
Frederick Warne publishes the classic Beatrix Potter books, and a few books illustrated by the English turn-of-the-century illustrators Kate Greenaway and Randolph Caldecott. They also distribute pleasing "Beatrix Potter Creations," such as postcards, calendars, nursery friezes, trays and tea sets. Don't be put off by "minimum order" requirements, which are just for businesses, they say they sell single objects to private customers.

9

Charlotte Weibull, Gustav Adolfs Torg 45, S–21139, Malmo, Sweden. Telephone 040 1132 34
List of costume dolls, free. AE, DC.
Tourists make special trips to see Charlotte Weibull's well-known collection of lovely souvenir dolls in good Swedish taste—handwoven fabrics and hand-painted faces. There are dolls in the costumes of every Swedish province, dolls from Swedish fairy tales, doll bookmarks, and dolls to hang up. Some are about $23 and others are about $32.

Workshop for Learning Things, 5 Bridge Street, Watertown, MA 02172
Catalogue, $1.
Teachers and other educators work out new programs and materials to be used in schools. Mainly building components.

World Wide Games, Box 450, Delaware, OH 43015. Telephone (614) 369 9631
Color catalogue, free. MC, V.
A fascinating collection of traditional wooden games from all over the world: "fast and noisy" box hockey from modern America; devilishly difficult Hindu pyramid puzzle from ancient India; Tangram puzzles from China; and Shisima, brought back from the Meshack Imbunya family who live near Kaimosi, Kenya. After immersing myself in the catalogue, I can sympathize with the man who went to Africa and moped so much without his table cricket game that he had World Wide send him another, air freight.

10

Games of Fantasy

The Compleat Strategist, 11 East 33rd Street, New York, NY 10016. Telephone (212) 685 3880
Price list, free U.S. and overseas. AE, MC, V.
One of the few shops catering exclusively to "gamers," the Compleat Strategist stocks both the new fantasy games, such as Dungeons and Dragons, which are all the rage among adolescents and undergraduates, as well as the older wargames, which have a following among the older, richer people interested in buying miniature soldiers and in researching military history in order to stage lengthy and elaborate campaigns. Supplies books, magazines, and information—all available here.

Wargames West, 3422 Central Avenue, S.E., Albuquerque, NM. Telephone (800) 545 6258
46-page price list, $1.50; overseas $2.50. MC, V.
Eleven pages of fantasy and wargames listed (but with no details); also computer games and miniatures, paints, books, and magazines.

9 *Castlemoor* (see Clothes section) All-wool pile toys, prices starting at about $8 for the mouse.

10 *Charlotte Weibull* Handmade wedding couple, about 8″ high. Bride, about $32; groom, about $28.

29
WATCHES

**Amsterdam Airport, P.O. Box 7501,
1118 ZG Schiphol Airport, Amsterdam, Holland.
Watch shop telephone 020 17 57 00**
Specific prices on request.
Amsterdam airport shop sells Cartier, Edox, Favre Leuba, Eterna, Omega, Roamer, Mido, Rolex, Universal Geneve and Longines watches. I haven't checked watch prices, but the Amsterdam airport shop prices are generally much lower than American prices.

**Itracho Watch Company, P.O. Box 289,
CH 8027 Zurich, Switzerland. Telephone (01) 720 04 97**
63-page color catalogue, $3; air mail $5.
Itracho sells inexpensive novelty watches—some look perfectly straightforward, others are on rings, pendants and fancy bracelets; there are two pages of children's watches, and a two-hour timer. All to be valued for their pretty faces and low prices. I had an Itracho, which my watch repairman refused to mend on the grounds it would break again immediately. Most prices about $10 to $40.

DISCOUNT
Please see discount information in the How to Buy section.

Several firms in New York sell watches at a discount, but the most dramatic savings are to be had when buying Seiko watches from Hong Kong.

**T. M. Chan and Company, P.O. Box 33881,
Sheung Wan Post Office, Hong Kong.
Telephone 5 450 875**
106-page catalogue of photographic equipment, calculators and watches, free. Prices in $.
Seiko and Rolex watches. I didn't check the Rolex, but I compared Seiko prices and found that a Seiko quartz sports watch that was selling for $139 at 47th Street Camera cost only $92 including air-mail postage from T. M. Chan. A Seiko LCD quartz solar alarm calendar that was selling for $124 at 47th Street Camera cost only $88 including air-mail postage, from T.M. Chan.

**M. I. Haberman, 122 East 42nd Street,
New York, NY 10168. Telephone (212) 697 5270**
AE, CB, DC, MC, V.
This seventy-year-old firm sells jewelry and watches at a discount. Manager Irving Schulman says that they give a 25-percent discount on most watches, and stock Movado, Seiko, Bulova, Longines, Citizen and more. For a quoted price, give them a model number by mail or telephone (best time to phone Monday through Friday 10:00 A.M. or after 3:00 P.M.).

**International Solgo, 77 West 23rd Street,
New York, NY 10010.
Telephone (800) 645 8162 or (212) 675 3555**
Give model number for specific price by telephone.
International Solgo stocks Bulova, Casio, Citizen, Pulsar, Seiko, Timex and says that they give 15- to 30-percent discounts on these. They are also willing to order watches by other leading manufacturers. Established 1933.

**Jean's Silversmith, 16 West 45th Street,
New York, NY 10017. Telephone (212) 575 0723**
Send model number for specific price by mail only.
Jean's will special order watches by Cartier, Concord, Piaget and other leading manufacturers. Established 1910.

Universal Suppliers, P.O. Box 4803, General Post Office, Hong Kong. Telephone 5 224 768
Rolex and Seiko watch leaflets, free; airmail $3.20. Prices in $.
Reader Roseann Muñoz tells me that she bought from Universal Suppliers two Seiko diver's watches, which she received two weeks after ordering. At the time she was working for a watch company, so she could have bought, for instance, her lady's diver watch at the United States *wholesale* price of $120, but the Universal Supplier price was only $60. She says that Universal Suppliers are not only cheap but dependable.

APPENDIXES

Clothing Size Chart

Since clothing sizes vary according to the manufacturer, always add measurements.

Dresses, Knitwear, Lingerie

British	10	12	14	16	18	20
United States	8	10	12	14	16	18
Continental	38	40	42	44	46/48	50
Inches	32/34	34/36	36/38	38/40	40/42	42/44
Centimeters	81/88	86/91	91/96	96/102	102/107	107/112

Women's Hosiery

British and United States	8	8½	9	9½	10	10½	11
Continental		0	1	2	3	4	5	6

Men's Shirts (collar sizes)

British	14	14½	15	15½	16	16½	17	17½
United States	14	14½	15	15½	15¾	16	16½	17
Continental	36	37	38	39	40	41	42	43

Men's and Women's Shoes

British	3	3½	4	4½	5	5½	6	6½	7	7½	8	8½	9
United States	4½	5	5½	6	6½	7	7½	8	8½	9	9½	10	10½
Continental	36	—	37	—	38	—	39	—	40	—	41	—	42

*The numbers in inches and centimeters refer to the bust and hip measurements, respectively.

Imperial and Approximate Metric Equivalent Measures

	Imperial Measure	Metric Equivalent
Weight	1 ounce (oz)	28.4 grams
	1 pound (lb)	453.6 grams
Volume	1 fluid ounce (fl oz)	28.4 cubic centimeters
	1 pint (pt)	0.6 liter
	1 gallon (gal)	4.5 liters
Length	1 inch (in)	25.4 millimeters
	1 yard (yd)	0.9 meter
	1 mile	1.6 kilometers
Area	1 square yard (sq yd)	0.8 square meter
	1 square mile	2.6 square kilometers

Conversion Table*

Note: Within the United States you can get up-to-date exchange rate information from Deak-Perera, 41 East 42nd Street, New York, NY 10017. Telephone (800) 223-6484. Deak-Perera sends out free leaflets with exchange rates, and by mail sells foreign currency, checks in foreign currencies, and travelers checks. Call them for more information.

	.10	.25	.50	1.00	5.00	10.00	25.00	100.00
United States Dollars (U.S.$)	.10	.25	.50	1.00	5.00	10.00	25.00	100.00
Australia Dollar = 100 cents	.09	.23	.46	.92	4.63	9.27	23.17	92.70
Canada 1 Dollar = 100 cents	.12	.30	.60	1.21	6.07	12.15	30.37	121.50
England Pound Sterling = 100 New Pence	.05	.13	.27	.54	2.73	5.46	13.66	54.64
France Franc = 100 Centimes	.60	1.51	3.03	6.07	30.39	60.79	151.97	607.90
Austria Schilling = 100 Froschen	1.68	4.20	8.40	16.80	84.00	168.00	420.00	1680.00
Germany German Mark (D.M.) = 100 Pfennig	.23	.59	1.19	2.39	11.97	23.95	59.88	239.55
Spain Peseta = 100 Centimos	10.13	25.34	50.68	101.37	506.85	1013.70	2534.25	10137.00
Switzerland Swiss Franc (S.F.) = 100 Rappen	.19	.47	.95	1.91	9.57	19.14	47.86	191.45
Hong Kong Hong Kong Dollar (H.K.$) = 100 Cents	.10	1.47	2.94	5.88	29.41	58.82	147.05	588.23
Sweden Swedish Krona (S.K.R.) = 100 Ore	.58	1.45	2.90	5.81	29.08	58.17	145.42	581.70
Portugal Escudo (E.S.C.) = 100 Centavos	6.98	17.45	34.90	69.80	349.00	698.00	1745.00	6980.00
Denmark Danish Krone (D.K.R.) = Ore	.78	1.96	3.92	7.84	39.20	78.40	196.00	784.00
New Zealand	.12	.30	.60	1.20	6.00	12.00	30.00	120.00
Norway Norwegian Krone (N.K.R.) = 100 Ore	.60	1.50	3.00	6.00	30.02	60.05	150.12	600.50
India Indian Rupee (I.R.P.) = 100 Paise	.73	1.82	3.64	7.28	36.40	72.80	145.60	728.00
Netherlands Holland Guilder (HFL) = Cents	.26	.65	1.31	2.62	13.13	26.26	65.65	262.60
Italy Italian Lira (LIT) = 100 Centesimi	127.80	319.50	639.00	1278.00	6390.00	12780.00	31950.00	127800.00
Japan Yen = 100 Sen	24.06	60.15	120.30	240.60	1203.00	2406.00	6015.00	24060.00

Compiled by: Deak-Perera, J. F. Kennedy International Airport, New York, NY   11430 .
*Based on rates prevailing as of March 1982. Subject to change.

Additional Import Information

U.S.A.

Duty is gradually being reduced in most categories. For up-to-date information on duty, ask your nearest customs department or write or telephone the Office of Information and Publications, Bureau of Customs, Treasury Department, Washington, DC 20026, telephone (202) 566 8181. This office also gives out useful free leaflets:

Know Before You Go gives general information about what is and is not allowed into the country. It is intended for tourists, but most of the information also applies to shopping by mail. It also lists current duty rates for about eighty items and is revised whenever necessary. Telephone or write your nearest customs office or district director of customs for anything not covered.

GSP and the Traveler gives a list of developing countries (India, Mexico, Hong Kong, etc.) whose "popular tourist items" are now (1976–1985) allowed in the U.S.A. free of duty.

U.S. Customs International Mail Imports gives information useful for shopping by mail, such as how to send purchases overseas for repairs and how to protest duty, and it lists Customs International Mail branches around the country.

Importing a Car gives regulations and advice to people thinking of bringing a foreign-made car into the United States.

Trademark Information lists those foreign articles bearing "prohibited" trademarks recorded in the Treasury Department, such as certain perfumes, cameras, watches, and stereo equipment, which must not be brought into the country with the trademark on. However, it is perfectly legal to bring in the articles with their trademarks removed, and if you want to bring something in that has a registered trademark, you can do one of two things: You can ask the shop you buy the article from to remove the trademark, or you can wait until it arrives and is inspected by American customs officers. If they feel it is necessary, a form declaring that you agree to remove the trademark yourself will be sent for you to sign. After signing the form, you mail it back, and the goods will be forwarded to you in the normal way.

Paying

U.S.A.

Registered letters containing money or checks to African, Indian and South American countries.

Personal Checks. Saves a trip to the bank and can be used to pay both American and foreign shops. However, personal checks can hold an order up, as most shops wait until your check has cleared (which can take up to four weeks for overseas shops). Overseas banks will charge the recipient about $3 for converting to dollars, so if the check is for a small amount, better add $3.

Certified or Cashier's Check (Bank). Can be used (only within the United States) to speed payment. At the bank, you make out a personal check, and the bank stamps it signifying a guarantee that money will be held in your account to clear the check. Once the check has been paid, it is returned to you, just as other personal checks are, so you have proof that the money was paid out. My bank charges $2.50 for certified checks.

Money Order (Bank). Can also be used (only within the United States) to speed payment. At any bank, you buy a money order for the correct amount, write in the name of the shop, and mail it. As the money order has been paid for, the shop can cash it immediately. The duplicate you receive when buying the money order is proof that you bought it, but you do not get proof that it has been cashed. My bank charges 75 cents for a money order.

International Money Order (Bank). This is the best way of paying for overseas orders. Fill out a form at the bank, and you will be given an international money order to mail to the shop. There is no delay at the other end, and the bank will work out the exact rate of exchange for you. Costs you roughly $2.50 in bank charges.

Cable Transfer (Bank). Very speedy, takes about two working days. If you know the bank and account number of the shop you are buying from, the money can be delivered directly. Otherwise your bank chooses a bank near the shop and notifies the shop that the money is there. Costs you roughly $10.00 in bank charges.

Money Order (Post Office). To send money within the United States, you can buy a money order at the post office for any amount between $1 and $500, and send it yourself. Charges vary between 75 cents and $1.55, depending on the amount. People on rural routes can avoid a trip to the post office by having their postman buy the money order for them.

International Money Order (Post Office). To send money abroad, you can buy at the post office, an international money order made out to the shop you are dealing with. The post office mails the order in the right currency; you get a receipt. Charges vary between $1.30 and $1.80, depending on the amount.

BRITAIN AND CANADA

Personal Checks. Unpopular with and not accepted by most American firms, as they are slow to clear and the bank charges the recipient about $3 for converting to U.S. currency. Firms in other countries seem to be less fussy, although most do wait for the check to clear (up to four weeks). Add $3 for the bank charges the recipient will have to pay.

Bank Draft. The best way to pay. At any bank buy a foreign currency bank draft for the right amount in the right currency and mail it yourself. The shop can cash it immediately.

Cable/Telegraphic Transfer. Your bank puts the money straight into the shop's account (if you know the branch and account number) or into a nearby bank, and lets the shop know by cable that it is there. Speedy but pricey.

Post Office Money Order. At the post office you can buy a foreign currency money order, but this is sent by the post office, so it arrives inconveniently separated for your own letter to the shop.

AUSTRALIA

Bank Drafts. In foreign currency these can be bought at the bank, are inexpensive, and are the best way to send money abroad. For greater speed, banks can send cable transfer.

Charge and Credit Cards

One of the big recent changes in mail-order shopping is the increased use of credit cards. Cards are a fast and easy way to pay by mail and for *real* speed can be used to pay on a telephone order. (Americans can use MasterCard and Visa to pay *any* store in the world, even stores that do not accept the cards, through Western Union money order, although these are expensive.)

Cards are also an amazingly simply way of buying from abroad. If a shop accepts the card you have, you simply give the shop your card number, expiration date and signature. As long as you know, for your own sake, roughly what you are paying, you don't have to deal with precise currency conversion. You are charged at the going exchange rate on the day the shop presents the bill to the bank or office in the shop's country.

Most shops require a minimum purchase of about $10 or $20 with cards, so you can not pay for catalogues with them.

Here is a list of cards and how to apply for them. Although none of the card firms will give exact criteria for the giving out of their cards, being "credit worthy" seems to consist of having a steady job with a high enough income and having a good payment record. Credit cards are much easier to get than charge cards. As I write it is generally thought that with a steady income of $15,000 and a good payment record, you have a good chance.

AMERICAN EXPRESS

At least 280 shops listed in this book accept American Express cards. They are charge cards, not credit cards; they don't lend you money, so you must pay American Express bills as soon as they are presented to you. There is a charge of about $35 a year to card holders in the U.S., and application forms are available wherever the cards are accepted. For more information, there are toll-free numbers in most U.S. telephone books, and American Express offices in London, Calgary, Brisbane, and most capital cities.

DINER'S CLUB

At least 100 shops in this book accept Diner's Club cards. They are charge cards not credit cards, so bills must be paid promptly and in full. There is a charge to card holders of about $40 a year. Get an application form from New Applications, 10 Denver Tech Center, Englewood, CO 80110. Telephone (303) 771 9230, or their offices around the world (they are proud of having been the first card accepted in Russia).

MASTERCARD/ACCESS/BANCARD AUSTRALIA

At least 550 shops in this book accept MasterCard and its affiliates, such as Access in England and Bancard in Australia. It is a credit card which mean that MasterCard is delighted if you don't pay the bill or your entire outstanding balance, as you can then be charged interest. The card is available through many banks and throughout the world. The annual fee is about $15 to $20, depending on the bank.

VISA (BARCLAYCARD)

At least 700 shops in this book accept Visa cards. It is a credit card, so you needn't pay your whole Visa bill immediately but will then be charged interest. The card is available through many banks throughout the world, and there is a charge of about $20 per year, depending on the bank. Visa says that on currency conversion they give their card holders the interbank rate (the "wholesale" rate banks charge each other), which is lower (and better for the card holder) than the rates other cards, banks, hotels, etc., gives the public. Get more information from a bank (or Visa International Public Relations, P.O. Box 8999, San Francisco, CA 94128.)

Shipping from Abroad

MAIL

Most parcels can be delivered exactly like domestic parcels, and if there is any duty it is paid to the postman, along with a $2.50 handling charge, which the post office calls "postage due." However, there is a limit on the size and weight of a parcel that can be shipped by mail—it must not weigh more than 22 pounds, and the combined length and circumference of the parcel must not add up to more than 72 inches. This means that the length of the parcel is measured in the usual way, but the width is measured with the tape right around the parcel.

AIR FREIGHT

This is used mainly for single objects which are too large to go by mail—framed pictures, large carpets, small pieces of furniture. Cargo of any size can be sent by air freight and is charged according to weight, volume and distance, and there is a minimum charge. The goods arrive at the airport nearest your address that has customs facilities, and you are notified of the arrival. You then go with identification and the bill from the shop (for customs) to the airport during office hours and see the parcel through customs (storage is charged if you don't go within five working days). If you want to employ a broker to get the parcel through customs, the airline can give you a list of firms.

SEA FREIGHT

This is only for large items such as furniture. Some of the shops in this book will arrange to have furniture delivered to your door by an agency, others just deliver to your nearest port. If furniture is delivered to a port, the steamship company will tell you when it arrives. You can then call a trucking firm to see it through customs and deliver to your door, or you can save the flat fee of about $60 to $100 and get the furniture through customs yourself. If you do it yourself, you take the bill of lading and the bill for the furniture, both of which the shop will have sent you, and go to the steamship company to have the bill of lading stamped, then go to the customs house. Your crate will probably be opened, inspected and closed again, and you pay the duty. Then, with a certificate of clearance, you can take the goods away. If the package is too large, call someone experienced, who can tell you the exact cost of a job before they take it on; they charge by weight and distance. A few years ago I bought a couch from Spain and asked a small trucking firm to bring it over from the New Jersey docks to Manhattan. They charged by the hour, and as they were inexperienced, they kept arriving when the dock was closing, or at rush hour (and then consoling themselves with coffee breaks). I had to pay them $30 more than I would have paid a big, more professional firm. Some big trucking firms are customs brokers too and take care of everything.

Bringing Things Back with You

If you are coming back from abroad by boat, you can save on shipping by bringing goods back with you as part of your family's baggage allowance. (I have brought a sofa, an armchair, a bathtub and several smaller objects back with me this way without paying any sea-freight charges.) Have whatever you buy abroad delivered straight to the steamship company's offices at the port. They will load it; you don't even see your purchases until you arrive at the port of entry to America, where you take them through customs and make arrangements with one of the shipping companies on the docks to deliver the things to your home. If you live in the same town, delivery should not be too expensive; mine has always been under $20. But if you live farther away, you should definitely find out about delivery costs, which can be high, before you buy.

U.S.A. Customs Charges

Figures in ( ) are for goods made in Communist countries (no matter where they were bought).

Antiques: Produced prior to 100 years before the date of entry—Free (free). (Have proof of antiquity obtained from seller.)
Automobiles: Passenger—2.9% (10%)

Bags: Hand, leather—8.1% to 10% (35%)
Beads: Imitation precious and semiprecious stones—4.7% to 10% (40 to 75%)
    Ivory—9.3% (45%)
Binoculars: Prism—18.5% (60%)
    Opera and field glasses—7.9% (45%)
Books: Foreign author or foreign language—Free (free)

Cameras:
    Motion picture, over $50 each—5.8% (20%)
    Still, over $10 each—6.9% (20%)
    Cases, leather—8.1% to 10% (35%)
    Lenses—11.6% (45%)
Candy:
    Sweetened chocolate bars—5% (40%)
    Other—7% (40%)
Chess sets—9.5% (50%)
China:
    Bone—16.3% (10¢ per dozen pcs. + 75%)
    Nonbone, other than tableware—20.8% to 26% (70–75%)
China tableware, nonbone, houshold, available in 77-piece sets:
    Valued not over $56 per set—37% (75%)
    Valued over $56 per set—17.1% (75%)
Cigarette lighters:
    Pocket, valued at over 42¢ each—20.8% (110%)
    Table—11.1% (60%)

Dolls and parts—16.8% (70%)
Drawings (works of art): Done entirely by hand—Free (free)

Earthenware tableware, household, available in 77-piece sets:
    Valued not over $38 per set—22% (55%)
    Valued over $38—10.5% (55%)

Figurines: China—11.8% to 20.8% (70%)
Fur:
    Wearing apparel—8.1% to 17.1% (35–50%)
    Other manufactures of—5.5% to 15.5% (50%)
Furniture:
    Wood, chairs—8.1% (40%)
    Wood, other than chairs—4.7% (40%)

Glass tableware—14% to 48.5% (60%)
Gloves:
    Not lace or net, plain vegetable fibers, woven—25% (25%)
    Wool, over $4 per dozen—37.5¢ lb. + 18.5% (50¢ lb. + 50%)
    Fur—9.2% (50%)
    Horsehide or cowhide—15% (25%)
Golf balls—5.6% (30%)

Handkerchiefs:
    Cotton, ornamented—4¢ each + 40% (4¢ each + 40%)
    Cotton, plain—25% to 5¢ lb. + 35% (37 to 55.5%)
    Linen, machine-hemmed—9% (50%)

Jewelry, precious metal or stone:
    Silver chief value, valued not over $18 per dozen—27½% (110%)
    Other—11.3% (80%)

Leather:
    Pocketbooks, bags—8.1% to 10% (35%)
    Other items made of—3.5% to 11% (35%)

Musical instruments:
    Music boxes, wood—7.4% (40%)
    Woodwind, except bagpipes—7.2% (40%)
    Bagpipes—Free (40%)

Paintings done entirely by hand—Free (free)
Paper, items made of—8.1% (35%)
Pearls:
    Loose or temporarily strung and without clasp:
        genuine—Free (10%)
        cultured—2½% (10%)
        imitation—18.5% (60%)
    Temporarily or permanently strung (with clasp attached or separate)—11.3% to 27.5% (45–110%)
Perfume—7¢ lb. + 7.2% (40¢ lb. + 75%)
Printed matter—2% to 7.2% (25–45%)

Radios:
    Transistor—9.9% to 10.1% (35%)
    Other—6% (35%)
Records, phonograph—4.8% (30%)

Shoes, leather—2½% to 20% (10–30%)
Skis and ski equipment—7.4% to 8.6% (33.3–45%)
    Ski boots—6% to 20% (35%)
Stereo Equipment: depending on components—5.3% to 10.1% (35%)

Stones, cut but not set:
  Diamonds not over ½ carat—1% (10%)
  Diamonds over ½ carat—2% (10%)
  Other—Free to 4.4% (10–20%)
Sweaters, of wool, over $5 per lb.—37½¢ lb. + 20% (50¢ lb. + 50%)

Tableware and flatware:
  Knives, forks, flatware:
    silver—3.5¢ each E 8.1% (16¢ each + 45%)
    stainless steel—½¢ to 2¢ + 6% to 17½% (2–8¢ +45%)
  Spoons, tableware:
    silver—11.8% (65%)
    stainless steel—17% (40%)
Tape recorders—5.3% to 7.2% (35%)
Televisions—5% (35%)
Toilet preparations:
  Not containing alcohol—7.2% (75%)
  Containing alcohol—7¢ lb. + 7.2% (40¢ lb. + 75%)
Toys—16.2% (70%)

Truffles—Free (free)

Watches: on $100 watch, duty varies from $6 to $13 ($24–$52)
Wearing apparel:
  Embroidered or ornamented—21% to 42½% (45–90%)
  Not embroidered, not ornamented:
    cotton, not knit—8% to 21% (37½–45%)
    cotton, knit—21% (45%)
    linen, not knit—7½% (35%)
    manmade fiber, knit—25¢ lb. + 32½% (72%)
    manmade fiber, not knit—25¢ lb. + 27½% (76%)
    silk, knit—10% (60%)
    silk, not knit—16% (65%)
    wool, knit—37½¢ lb. + 15½% to 32% (52–78.5%)
    wool, not knit—25¢ to 37½¢ lb. + 21% (33–50¢ lb. + 45–50%)
Wood:
  Carvings—7.6% (33.3%)
  Other items made of—7.6% (33.3%)

BRITAIN

For up-to-date information on duty and VAT payable on goods from the U.S. and other countries (rates differ according to country), contact your nearest customs and excise office, or HM Customs and Excise, Kent House, Upper Ground, London SE1 9PS. Here is an approximate list of 1982 rates of duty on goods from the United States (*add 15% VAT except where noted*).

Antiques over 100 years old	free (no VAT)
Appliances (domestic)	
refrigerators and freezers	5%
washing machines	7.5%
sewing machines	6–12%
irons	11.5%
Other appliances	
radios	14%
record players	9.5%
dictating machines and other sound recorders	8.5–9.5%
typewriters	6.5%
calculators	14%
Books	free (no VAT)
Cameras	up to 13%
Chinaware	
dinner sets	up to 13.5%
statuettes	up to 11%
Clothing (other than leather and fur)	up to 18% (no VAT on children's clothes)
Cosmetics	11.2%
Film (unexposed)	8–12.8%
Jewelry	up to 9%
Linen, tablecloths, towels, etc.	up to 19%
Leather goods, including handbags	up to 9%
Leather clothes and gloves	8–13%
Perfume and Cologne	11.2% (plus excise duty)
Records (music)	7%
Silverware, household	up to 7.5%
Sporting goods	5–13.5% generally
Tapes (prerecorded with music)	7.5%
Toys and games	8.5–19% generally
Watches	7.5%

CANADA

Canada has different rates of duty, depending on the country of origin: one for "Most Favoured Nations," which includes the U.S.; lower rates for Britain and the Commonwealth and underdeveloped countries; and another rate for "general." Besides duty, most incoming goods are charged a 9% federal sales tax. Duty is being gradually lowered by just under 1% a year until 1987.

Canada has regional customs offices in Calgary, Halifax, Hamilton, London, Montreal, Quebec, Regina, Toronto, Vancouver, Windsor and Winnipeg and a marvelously helpful office that will tell you by phone or mail the exact duty for anything you are thinking of importing: Customs & Excise Information Unit, 360 Coventry Road, Ottawa, Canada K1K2C6 (613) 993 0534.

Here is a list of approximate Canadian duty on goods imported from the U.S.A. in 1982:

	Duty, %	*Federal Sales Tax, %*
Antiques (over 100 years old)	none	none
Appliances		
large (refrigerators, washing machines, etc.)	20	9
small (can openers, irons, sewing machines, etc.)	14.8	9
video equipment	12.8	9
typewriters	12.5	9
stereo equipment	9.4	9
Books	none	none
Cameras	10	9
China		
dinner sets	15	9
ornaments and figurines	14.8	9
Clothes		
cotton	22.5	none
knitted	27.1	none
silk	24.2	none
synthetic	25	none
wool	25	none
Cosmetics	15	9
Linen (sheets, tablecloths, etc.)		
over 50% cotton	22	9
over 50% synthetic	25	9
Perfume	16.3 (plus 10% excise duty)	9
Records	15	9
Tableware (knives, forks, etc.)	22.2	9
Toys and games	17.2	9
Shoes	20	none
Sporting Equipment		
golf clubs	15	9
fishing rods	14.8	9
tennis racquets	15	9
tents (synthetic fabric)	25	9

AUSTRALIA

Australian customs representatives in New York won't give me details of Australian rates of duty for publication on the grounds that there are too many rates and they change too much. To get Australian rates, contact the Bureau of Customs in the capital city of each state. You can also try the Bureau of Customs, Department of Business and Consumer Affairs, Canberra ACT. They didn't answer my letter; maybe you'll have better luck. Australian duty seems to range from none for a few things—such as art, books, cameras—to a high of 50 to 80 percent for things made of fabric, such as household linen and clothes, with quite a few things such as small appliances and toys in the 25 to 30 percent range. Federal sales tax is charged on imports, as it is on domestic goods, at rates that vary between 2.5 and 30 percent.

INDEX